VIEWS OF AMERICA

VIEWS OF AMERICA

Alan F. Westin
Columbia University

Julian H. Franklin
Columbia University

Howard R. Swearer
University of California at Los Angeles

Paul E. Sigmund
Princeton University

UNDER THE GENERAL EDITORSHIP OF ALAN F. WESTIN

HARCOURT, BRACE & WORLD, INC.
New York / Chicago / Burlingame

Preface

Anyone who compiles still another book of foreign commentaries on the United States bears the moral equivalent of the burden that American law places on each inventor who seeks to patent his discovery: to show a substantial element of originality that distinguishes this creation from similar items already in existence. After all, over a thousand books of foreign commentary on America since colonial days are listed in bibliographies and library catalogues. Three twentieth-century collections of such commentary have appeared under the same title, *As Others See Us,** and a 1965 addition, Bryant M. Wedge's *Visitors to the United States and How They See Us,* shows that publishing in this field has not faltered noticeably in the computer age.

At the same time that libraries and bookstores feature a stock of foreign observations, some American commentators have complained recently that Americans pay far too much attention to this literature. Though books and articles of foreign observers are often based on a fusion of factual misinformation and ideological hostility, Americans continually worry about changing their "image" to meet such criticism. Thus it has been suggested that we ignore intercontinental analytical missiles and concentrate instead on mature self-analysis.

There are several direct answers to these dual challenges of "What can be new?" and "Why bother?" First, measuring foreign commentaries every decade or so provides helpful insight into the changing patterns of foreign judgment about American life. Second, we maintain the "decent respect for the opinions of mankind" pledged in our Declaration of Independence when we study and respond to the serious comments made about our society and its values by foreign observers. And, even though there have been no master interpretations of American society in recent years, there are still revealing "middle-level" commentaries that help considerably to enlarge America's understanding of its own society.

Several books have offered collections of foreign commentary, concentrating either on a particular country or region or on a certain group of commentators

---

* John Graham Brooks, *As Others See Us* (1910); André Visson, *As Others See Us* (1948); Franz M. Joseph, ed., *As Others See Us* (1959).

(such as foreign visitors to the United States or foreign journalists working in this country). We feel, however, that there is still a special need for a structured collection of current views of the United States throughout the world, as expressed by diverse commentators—members of the academic community, political figures, journalists, and so forth.

We believe that international conditions since 1945 have produced three distinctive views of America—those of Europe, the Communist bloc, and the developing nations. At one end of the spectrum are the relatively open-minded views from Western Europe, at the other end the very stringent ideological controls imposed on Communist views, and, in the middle, the special ideological issue of anticolonialism that dominates the views held by most of the developing nations.

The first part, edited by Julian H. Franklin, presents the view from Western Europe. European commentary today stems from two centuries of extensive economic, political, and cultural contacts with the American Republic, some harmonious and some harshly abrasive. With Western Europe now a prosperous, proud, and restless ally of the United States, current European commentary has a special sophistication about American life—arising in no small part from the uneasy realization of European intellectuals that the economic and cultural "Americanization" of Europe is proceeding rapidly.

The second part, edited by Howard R. Swearer, presents the view from the Communist nations. Here the American image is perceived through the prism of Marxist-Leninist theory and Communist Party tactical objectives. Commentary on America is thus "official" and "political," but it is still enormously revealing, not only for insights into the Communist mind but also as a measure of how far Communist ideology has come toward the acceptance of "facts" about America in the post-Stalin and post-Khrushchev eras.

The third part, edited by Paul E. Sigmund, presents the view from the developing nations. Here we find far more restricted opinions concentrating overwhelmingly on issues such as race relations, foreign aid policies, and cold-war military tensions, which preoccupy the leaders of the Afro-Asian and Latin-American nations. European or Communist views of America are often adopted by leaders of the developing nations as the starting point for judgment about America. There are, however, many independent elements in the view of the developing nations toward the United States, and the selections in this volume show what they are.

Organization of contemporary foreign commentary about the United States into views from three camps obviously stresses the dominant, characteristic views from these areas rather than the divergent ones. It is certainly true that a collection of European views of America could run the ideological gamut from "Chinese-Communist" to "Catholic-aristocrat," and there is also a considerable spread of views among African leaders. There are even significant differences among Communist commentators. Yet we are convinced that there is a core of opinions about America held in each of these three camps, and it is this core that we have presented here.

We have also concentrated on foreign commentaries of the 1960's, because it is so important to capture the contemporary nuances of foreign judgment. For much of the world, the Kennedy-Johnson era marked a new period in post–World War II views of America, and we have tried to register that shift with our selections. In addition, we have avoided presenting straight "factual" accounts of the United States by foreign commentators, even though this has meant ignoring some of the more knowledgeable and careful foreign writers. Our focus is on the characteristic *interpretive* view of America held by each of the three camps.

We also considered whether to include an "American response" to the major criticisms leveled by the three camps. But such a response would inevitably have been apologetic, would have required a great deal of space to meet adequately the range of foreign attacks, and would have had to respond to the quite different ideological and cultural wellsprings of the three camps. In addition, given the diversity of views among Americans on so many of the issues raised by foreign critics, we would have had to decide arbitrarily who spoke for America—a Stevenson or a Goldwater, a Russell Kirk or an H. Stuart Hughes, a Jerry Lewis or a Stanley Kramer. The solution that we adopted was to present both historical and contemporary reactions of Americans to the *fact* and *nature* of foreign commentary, rather than to its substance. The fourth part, edited by Alan F. Westin, explores the ways in which Americans have reacted to foreign observers, especially recent attempts to analyze systematically the sources and meaning of foreign commentary.

We hope that this volume will offer a provocative cross-cultural experience to Peace Corps trainees, high school and college students, adult discussion groups, and general readers. We have tried to let the American nation study her image (and the feminine gender seems fair here) in three reflecting pools. And, if the final section on American responses does its job, the reader will appreciate why "reflecting pools" rather than "mirrors" is the figure of speech to adopt when considering foreign views of America.

The editors of this volume are indebted as a group to The New World Foundation of New York City for its interest in this volume and its aid in enabling the editors to begin work on the project in 1963. In addition, Julian Franklin thanks Mr. Charles E. Cohen for his editorial assistance and Miss Ene Sirvet for her help in typing the manuscript; Howard Swearer expresses his appreciation to Mr. Arnold Springer for his editorial and translating assistance and to Mrs. Deborah Oakley for her editorial help; and Alan Westin is grateful for the editorial assistance of Mr. Gordon Stevenson, Mr. George Osborne, Miss Elisabeth Hansot, and Miss Caren Goretsky.

ALAN F. WESTIN
JULIAN H. FRANKLIN
HOWARD R. SWEARER
PAUL E. SIGMUND

Contents

VIEWS OF AMERICA

I

VIEWS FROM WESTERN EUROPE

This collection of articles is a selected survey of European views of the United States as they have developed in about the last ten years. With one or two exceptions they are all reasoned interpretations of some general aspect of American life, as opposed to personal impressions or reportage of a specific event or issue. The reader should be aware, however, that personal impressions of the United States are very popular in Europe and that European reporting of American affairs is often of the highest quality, in perceptiveness as well as in coverage.

In collecting these materials an attempt has been made to represent the more important trends in European thought, with the deliberate exception of official or semiofficial Communist opinion. For although European Communist parties still have considerable power, especially in Italy and France, and although much of their output is less clichéd and inflexible than many Americans might think, Communist opinions are in the main sufficiently represented by Soviet and Chinese viewpoints included elsewhere in this volume. There is, however, a considerable and often very thoughtful body of non-Communist Marxist literature that is much more influential in Europe than in this country, and examples of it have been included.

Since European opinion is highly diversified, no particular selection should be taken as fully representative of the group or trend with which the author is identified. Within each trend, moreover, preference was given to articles that take a definite, and most often critical, stand on the matter under discussion, and that at the same time reveal a reasonable degree of information and sophistication about American affairs. This does not mean that the articles collected here are endorsed as accurate in fact or in interpretation. Indeed, in one or two cases glaring errors and rather extreme conclusions may be noted. But most of the pieces are sufficiently well considered to be taken seriously by a great many European intellectuals.

The selection of materials for each section in this part has also been affected by the choice of a general theme or issue in which Europeans have shown special interest in recent years. Comprehensiveness has thus been partly sacrificed. But it seemed that a concentration of different points of view around a central theme would reveal more of the general character of European thinking than a more scattered series on a wider variety of topics.

The central focus in the first section, on American ideology, is the changing role of the intellectual in American society. The pattern of alienation and, frequently, even expatriation of the American intellectual from his society has been counterbalanced in the postwar period by a trend toward mutual appreciation. And there has been something of a debate among European intellectuals as to whether the trend toward reconciliation is a healthy sign of American maturity or a retreat from effective social criticism at a time when such criticism is badly needed. That important tensions still remain is clearly evidenced by the sense of bitter alienation manifested among university students and young intellectuals in the past two years. Also represented in this section is a variation on the old theme of America's pragmatic temper. With the increasing Americanization of European society, the attitude of Europeans toward this aspect of American philosophy has tended to shift from mild contempt to relatively enthusiastic approbation.

From the very beginning, the characteristic of American politics that has most impressed the European observer is the relative decentralization and dispersion of political power. In former times this was often regarded as the singular good fortune of a people who had no need as yet for a powerful centralized state. But more recently the fragmentation of American political life has been criticized by Europeans as an obstacle to democratic social change in an industrial society and a hindrance to the formation of coherent foreign policy in a period of American world leadership. Around this theme, therefore, a "classical" statement of the criticism from a democratic-socialist point of view has been provided, as well as a more conservative and moderate reappraisal by a European who is primarily concerned with the ability of the United States to achieve continuity of policy. Although not connected to the central theme, an article on anti-Communism and American civil liberties has been included because it touches on an issue that has greatly troubled Europeans of many political persuasions.

In their judgment of American society, Europeans have always been alarmed by the absence of stable social communities with relatively fixed traditions. What was once the product of competitive individualism and the pioneering spirit is now associated with the pressures of mass industrialism, and this, in the European view, has very serious adverse consequences for the human personality. The disorientation of the individual in American society is, in fact, a favorite theme of French and German existentialists. Their views on this problem are represented here along with an article representing the European reaction to the related issue of American commercialism.

The performance of the American economy is a matter of urgent interest to Europeans since American prosperity is so pivotal to the world position of the West as a whole. And there is among European intellectuals considerable doubt as to whether American capitalism in its present form can maintain a high level of growth. Presented here are a social-democratic and a Marxist diagnosis. Both were prompted, at least in part, by signs of stagnation that appeared in the late fifties and early sixties. It should be pointed out, however, that Europeans have also been impressed by indications that American capitalism is becoming more stable and socially responsible, and many have been considerably influenced by the views of American writers such as those of A. A. Berle on corporate responsibility and of J. K. Galbraith on countervailing power.

In the area of foreign policy, the most pressing issues for most Europeans are the quality and potentialities of American leadership of the Western alliance. In this section an attempt has been made to sample responses ranging from nationalist doubts about the American commitment to European defense, through federalist and democratic objections to the goals and strategy of American leadership, to outright charges of American imperialism. Almost all these pieces attempt to define the basic forces and attitudes that shape our position in the world. Most of them were occasioned by the efforts of the Kennedy Administration to restate and reorient American goals. The Johnson Administration has not as yet evoked much comment on this level; European responses have been limited, thus far, to evaluations of specific situations, such as the decision to intensify our military commitment to South Vietnam and the decision to intervene with armed force in the Dominican revolution.

In reading these articles many Americans may be surprised to learn that Europeans no longer say much about the United States that is not said by Americans themselves. They will find, indeed, that European views of America are very often heavily dependent on the work of American commentators such as David Riesman, C. Wright Mills, J. K. Galbraith, and Hans J. Morgenthau. One fundamental cause of this phenomenon is the growing similarity between European and American society. In the days of De Tocqueville the contrast between the class, status, and authority-bound societies of Europe and the relatively "classless," competitive, and democratic American society inevitably produced different ways of perceiving social processes. But now that both America and Europe have become increasingly industrial, these differences of perspective have been drastically diminished. Intelligence on both sides of the Atlantic is now shaped by similar experiences.

But a second and more immediate cause is the emergence, in the postwar period, of a truly international culture, the unity of which is especially marked in Western Europe and North America. Within this region intellectuals and scholars are at the present time in almost constant motion from one country to another—teaching, lecturing, observing, and making contacts with their local counterparts. Not only is multi-

RECENT CARTOON VIEWS FROM WESTERN EUROPE

The Devil's Circle

Mussil in Frankfurter *Rundschau* (Frankfurt)

"I can't think, Harold, why the possibility of Barry Goldwater becoming President last November frightened us so much . . ."

Cummings in the *Daily Express* (London)

Abu in the *Observer* (London)

Camerini in *Paese Sera* (Rome)

"I'm muddled enough in this bog, and I've got to get out as soon as I can, to save face."

Moisan in *Le Canard Enchaîné* (Paris)

The New American Symbol:
Liberty Asphyxiating the World

Mansbridge in *Punch* (London)

"One and four are okay, two's obviously
a Commie, and I have grave doubts about
three, five, six, and seven."

Bil in *Nebelspalter* (Rorschach, Switzerland)

Proud Alabama

Il Borghese (Milan)

Difficult Sailing
(Smoke rising is money spent
on foreign aid.)

lingualism taken for granted within this intellectual élite, but significant books in foreign languages are now translated with little delay for an audience of educated laymen. European periodicals increasingly turn to American contributors for their articles about America, so that the European view of the United States is often shaped directly by Americans themselves. This does not mean, of course, that Europeans, even when they are borrowing directly, are simply transmitting American opinions, for they are often drawing on American ideas that have themselves been deeply influenced by theories originating in Europe.

It may also be noted that this internationalization of culture is even more marked among the Western Europeans themselves, especially on the continent. Hence, although the articles collected here are in fact drawn from five European countries, no special effort has been made to represent national differences in the European point of view. Such differences no doubt continue to exist and have been indicated on occasion. But they are now too slight or too subtle, at least on the level of abstraction with which we are presently concerned, to warrant special treatment.

Finally, some Americans will be surprised to learn that contemporary Europeans, unlike their forebears of the nineteenth century, are less inclined to think of American society as "the great experiment," full of promise and portent for the future. For better or for worse, America, in the middle of the twentieth century, has taken a relatively cautious attitude toward domestic social innovation and has been somewhat suspicious of revolutionary movements elsewhere in the world. And we are now regarded as conservative not only by the Communist countries and by the revolutionary leaders of the developing nations, but by the Europeans as well, who have moved further than we have in the elaboration of a welfare state. Now, as in the past, the optimism and generosity of the American people are appreciated and admired. But the question, as many Europeans pose it, is whether these traditional American virtues will become the resources of constructive leadership or the rituals and gestures of complacency.

1

American Ideology

DEMOCRATIC OPTIMISM AND PRAGMATIC PHILOSOPHY

Mino Vianello

Mino Vianello is an Italian liberal democrat who often writes on American society and culture. This article documents the emergence of a relatively new attitude in European assessments of American philosophy. Europeans have often been contemptuous of the anti-metaphysical, nonsystematic, and pragmatic temper of American philosophy, and even now there are some Europeans who would continue to deny that this kind of thinking may be called philosophy at all. Vianello, on the other hand, accepts the description but not the valuation. American philosophy, he argues, is the inevitable and proper outlook of thought in a society committed to democratic values. And he prefers this outlook to a way of philosophizing in which the goals seem too closely bound to the tradition of a closed and authority-ridden society.

. . .

In the West the principal requirements for a philosophy are that it be a *critical comprehension* of reality that tends toward a *universal vision* and yet is at the same time endowed with *rigorous logical structure.* . . .

In the course of the nineteenth century this typically Western schema was extended to embrace a third requirement, influenced and confirmed by the development of science, namely, *verifiability*. This, carried over into the domain of action, has given rise, along with the prevalence of democratic ideas, to the growth of a fourth requirement, *positive results*.

These last two requirements have rapidly become the predominant trends in the schema of Western philosophy. This is not to say that the great systems of the modern period are unable to confront the variety of problems crystallized within the other two trends. But to present them is not the same as to be

FROM "Filosofia e società in America," *Communità,* Anno 13, No. 71 (July, 1959), pp. 94–98. Translated by the editor with permission.

able to satisfy them equally, and it does not seem arbitrary to say that these last two requirements have gradually come to the forefront through the position and the weight accorded them and through the function that they actually exercise not only in the individual philosophical system but in the society as a whole as a result of the various responses they call forth. . . .

America, it is often said, does not have the grand philosophical tradition of the other countries of the West. But those who say this sort of thing do not consider its absurdity. In the first place it would be necessary to compare European philosophy of the past hundred years with American philosophy of the same period, because one cannot speak of an American philosophy prior to the middle of the last century. But then I ask, why make this comparison at all? To what can a comparison of two philosophic constellations lead if not to a sterile parochialism? That America has produced a philosophy of its own is conceded. What matters, then, is to try to understand it, above all in the premises that characterize it and constitute its driving elements.

The United States was born toward the end of the scientific revolution. A conception of the world oriented to material values was developing to the detriment of the traditional sciences of Western philosophy: metaphysics and formal logic. Faced with an attack from the two characteristic demands of the mental attitudes originating in this new scheme of values, verifiability of theories and positive results for human beings in the moral and political fields, interest in suprasensible reality tended to retreat from the soil in which live ideas are germinated. In America, a continent not burdened with traditions, an intellectual life could be initiated that was closer to the needs of the society being born. It is my firm conviction that here is to be found the kernel of the question, the deeper reason why American philosophy has taken the path we all know.

I do not know how much recognition has been given to the fact that it was in America that the physical sciences and then the social sciences were first separated from the bosom of philosophy, which in Europe was still considered "the mother of sciences." Is it not remarkable to discover that at Yale the young [Jonathan] Edwards read Newton while he was still alive, whereas at Cambridge, thirty years after Newton's death, the textbook was still Rouhault? And is it not important to repeat here that the democratic system, that is, the system that puts man in the center of political life, became a reality for the first time on the soil of the New World? There is no doubt that the emphasis given from the very beginning to the sciences (or the requirement of verifiability) and to the democratic ideal (or the requirement of positive contribution to human life) is more than sufficient reason for the genesis in America of a profoundly original intellectual universe.

In the beginning this originality appeared in a way that seemed to suggest to contemporaries a negative element of spiritual indolence and poverty. That is to say, in order for an idea to have an impact in America, it had to prove itself both useful and correspondent with the facts, so that time alone, and not academic or intellectual fashion, was its judge. It may well have been that to Europeans—accustomed to ideological conflicts, imbued with prejudices in large measure left over from a past not connected to the developments of science, and victimized by dynastic ambitions—the slow growth of a different culture on the other shore of the Atlantic may have suggested a lack of originality and creative spirit, in a word, a retrogression. This may very well have been the case, since we find that such impressions were shared, at least in part, by De Tocqueville.

. . .

"A better life" is something that cannot exist without the desire for a better life. This desire appears everywhere in human history. But it has become a reality only in America, and a reality so absorbing as to have become the sole reality. It is in relation to this reality that we must seek the requirement of philosophy in America, for it is by this [standard] that the life of individuals and institutions is measured. A society so oriented cannot tolerate anything that leads to withdrawal into self, to the search for satisfaction anywhere else than in visible goods, or to the creation of fixed social bonds. If an idea does not make a contribution in this sense [to a better life], it is worse than a waste of time; it is an obstacle, a social crime. If, on the other hand, it contributes to the betterment of life, it is energetically supported, whatever its theoretical implications.

It is not difficult to show that this position, certainly simplistic to the European eye, contains an inner contradiction. On the one hand it seems that America depends on convictions of a deeply rooted ideal character, and on the other hand that its life is focused on the pursuit of material goods with no consideration for the life of the spirit. But the error here is to take logical activity as the central characteristic, for in America the fusion of principles with the fervor of practical life takes place on the level of individual conscience without any formal systematization, least of all one imposed by an external authority, which is the case in countries with a Catholic tradition.

But neither the assertion that Protestant individualism constitutes a large part of the American tradition, nor the assertion that America, without having produced a philosophy like Hegelianism or Marxism, has been so successful that it now shows the way to the Western world, are fully sufficient to explain what motivates the American thinker. The point is that the triumph of science and democracy has deprived religion of its dogmatic aggressiveness and has transferred its interests to the moral plane. An emphasis on the theoretical aspect of philosophy could not help but revive the great questions of Western thought that, in their turn, would resuscitate religious polemics. Besides involving a departure from the trend they have followed up to now, this would threaten Americans with the risk of breaking up their political unity and, consequently, their entire way of life. A people cannot change its mental habits unless driven by the force of circumstances, and in America, today as in the past, the circumstances require *tolerance*. The demand for complete liberty of the individual in the realm of ideas is not only a Protestant tradition; it is also enforced by the environment because an ideological struggle would signify paralysis. One may believe that his own ideas of the ultimate principles of reality are alone correct, but it is inadmissible to say that the ideas of others are mistaken and should therefore be eliminated. Willingly or not, the Catholic Church itself has had to adjust to this situation. It has not thereby become a liberal institution, but it is unable to prevent the mass of its faithful in America from participating in and becoming an integral part of a society inspired by this principle. And it is also because of this situation that, for the first time in history, the Jew is fully and first of all a citizen like everybody else.

. . .

Before I go on to examine America's philosophy more directly, I would like to make it clear that the American way of life is the product of environmental circumstances, among which the following three predominate: the immensely vast and virgin territory, industrialism, and the Protestant tradition. American democracy developed in this framework and is inconceivable apart from it.

. . .

And because these elements necessarily depend upon each other, when one attempts to transplant American pragmatism elsewhere, it very quickly leads to a miscarriage. Since philosophy in America is unlike philosophy anywhere else—that is, *an instrument of life* founded on the requisites of empiricism and practicality—it is inimical to, and in a certain sense even immune from, the excesses of speculation, and is optimistic, progressive, and antitotalitarian.

. . .

[*After a survey of the history of American philosophy, Vianello concludes with a brief examination of pragmatism, which he takes to be its most mature and characteristic phase.*]

At the center of pragmatism, as is generally known, is an interest in the future: an idea is valid insofar as it functions in experience. One can even say that our third requirement [of philosophy], namely verifiability, has been subordinated to the last, a situation completely peculiar to American philosophy. This is not the place to examine the development of this theme from Peirce to James and from Mead to Dewey. It is important to emphasize, however, that this philosophy is typically American, although its roots are European. It is well known that Peirce's theory of mental attitudes was founded on the Kantian analysis of the nature of the idea, and Darwinian biologism served only to confirm Kant's point of view. But the importance of pragmatism lies not so much in its epistemological theory as in the fact that the goal it assumes is control of the environment. . . . At bottom pragmatism is closer to English utilitarianism than to German idealism, and for the motto of the former, "The best idea is that which produces the happiness of the greatest number," it substitutes, "the best action is that which produces the happiness of the greatest number." Its most complete expression on the philosophical level is found in Dewey, for whom ideas are instruments that control the adjustment of the individual to the environment, "mind" being conceived as the expression of organic behavior. And in the socioeconomic sphere its most complete expression is Veblen's masterful analysis of the institutional contradictions in American capitalist society.

In all of this, the center of attention is man in an industrial and democratic society, and the entire emphasis of this movement is essentially a mighty voice in defense of the common man.

. . .

It can thus be seen that in the last one hundred years Americans have developed systems of thought more adapted to the ends of modern society than have the Europeans, assuming, of course, that the end of society is the constant elevation of man's situation and that the meaning of culture is the knowledge of how to attain harmony between the demands of the individual and those of society.

Some say that this instrumental philosophy is not systematic, and that since it implies, in addition, a denial of God (or perhaps primarily on this account) it is not philosophy at all. But this seems to me a play on words, as if the definition of philosophy were the kind of thing about which argument is possible. . . . The issue that is real because it is founded on reality is that either one wants a democratic society, in which case speculative endeavor ought to be directed to resolving the problem of a common social life, or else one does not, in which case one can undoubtedly continue with the philosophy of the closed system and allow the academic chairs to remain in the power of the rhetoric of the absolute.

THE END OF ALIENATION

Herbert von Borch

Herbert von Borch, a German journalist and commentator with an impressive scholarly background, has in recent years devoted much of his energy to reporting American affairs and to studying American society. In his book *The Unfinished Society,* Von Borch maintains that America is finally reaching its age of sophistication and maturity and that many of its youthful characteristics, which once so charmed or horrified the European observer, are destined to be modified in this process. But he thinks the tendency is not so much the complete rejection of the American experiment as the incorporation of its impulses into more balanced and viable arrangements that could be highly instructive not only to Europe but to the world at large. In the present piece, excerpted from his book, Von Borch considers a particularly revealing indication of this change: the tendency of American intellectuals to move from an attitude of alienation and expatriation toward a qualified acceptance of their own society. (See Part IV, p. 321, for an American book review of *The Unfinished Society.*)

Intellectuals are no longer necessarily left-wing, as they so definitely were in the thirties. This observation applies to America no less than to Europe. For example, during the second Eisenhower campaign against Adlai Stevenson (who dared to bring some of the finest qualities of an intellectual mind into the political arena), the Republican Party set up a committee to attract the "eggheads." In the hundred years of its history, the party had shown little enough interest in that species of man—and now it proceeded to create a body for the express purpose of winning his allegiance.

FROM "The Reconciliation of the Intellectuals," *The Unfinished Society* (New York: Hawthorn, 1962), pp. 107–19. Reprinted by permission.

Where, then, are intellectuals at home, if not on the left? The American intellectual combated his own society for so long that he furnished anti-Americanism throughout the world with its choicest arguments. How does he react to that society today? Has something happened to him that he should deserve the attentions of the political party strategists? Has he changed?

The answer goes far beyond the ballot paper. The position of the American intellectual has changed indeed, just as the society has changed. Instead of rebellion and fruitful protest, there is assent. Instead of social estrangement and hostility, there is danger of social conformity, of intellectual orthodoxy. Independent thinkers, writers, even poets have become the exception. The rule is the socially integrated, sheltered intellectual, either openly or tacitly indebted to the status quo.

This development took place in the fifties, and it is perceptible even in the style of American writing. A closer look at the situation reveals some astonishing facts. America, it appears, is at a sophisticated stage of civilization; America is becoming conservative; ideological fires have spent themselves. At the same time we find an America in which education and taste have spread on a previously unimaginable scale, however much the discontented, the voluntary expatriates, or the confirmed heretics may still revolt against it.

Merle Curti has called the conflict between thought and action the "American paradox," a term he uses as the title of a book. He examines the very evident paradox of a society which in its origins was fed by the unity of thought and action, and yet has become so anti-intellectual. The explanation, according to Professor Curti, lies in the leveling action of the pioneers, the acquisitiveness of an industrial society, and the rigidity of the society's sects. However, the tension with which the American intellectual reacted to his country's highly developed capitalist civilization was creative for three whole decades.

Out of this tension, there arose the great, rebellious works of the twenties and thirties, including the poems of Ezra Pound and T. S. Eliot (who at that period still counted as an American), the novels of Faulkner, Dos Passos, Scott Fitzgerald, Henry Miller, Sinclair Lewis, Thomas Wolfe, Hemingway, all of which developed the theme of the writer's estrangement from the society in which he lived. Whether living or not, these writers have found no equals among their younger successors (with the exception, perhaps, of Tennessee Williams, the playwright, who not so much protests against society, but evades it, investigating the darkest corners of the human condition at society's periphery). The "American paradox" is on the way to solution, and if this means less pain, it also means less literary greatness. Society has opened its arms to the intellectuals, and only a few have sought to evade the embrace.

. . .

Of course, this relationship did not immediately develop from its opposite. George Kennan, that intellectual among diplomats, could still write recently: "I can think of few countries in the world where the artist, the writer, the composer, or the thinker is held in such general low esteem as he is here in our country." Edmund Wilson sought to depict the position of the intellectual in society in *The Wound and the Bow*. The hero, Philoctetes, is a Greek warrior compelled to live out his life in solitude because of the stench given off by his wound. Nevertheless, his friends go back to him because they need his unerring magic bow. In somewhat the same way, American society needs the intellectual *qua* expert, but does not grant him anything even approaching the status of, say, a university professor in the German social hierarchy.

With the "lost generation" (a term coined by Gertrude Stein to describe the youthful Hemingway), a group of literary expatriates of the twenties living in physical separation from America, with the "sad young men" (like Fitzgerald, Hemingway, Dos Passos, Sherwood Anderson, and E. E. Cummings), there came about a radical break with American society. The First World War had hurled this generation "into the dark jaws of violence." Rootless as they were, their war experiences were bound up with Europe; their estrangement from their own society was complete. It led in the thirties to despair about the social order, to the uncompromising doctrine of the "two nations" of America propounded by John Dos Passos in *USA*. Raging over the execution of Sacco and Vanzetti, he wrote, spurning punctuation

They have clubbed us off the streets they are stronger they are rich they hire and fire the politicians the newspaper editors the old judges the small men with reputations the college presidents the wardheelers . . . they hire the men with guns and uniforms the policecars the patrolwagons . . . they have built the electric chair and hired the executioner to throw the switch . . . all right we are two nations.

This class war between the two social nations within America no longer exists; the welfare state has made this kind of social protest pointless. To put it another way, it has subtilized the desires of the malcontents. Hence, those desires are harder to formulate. In any case, as [David] Riesman has put it, "the reasons developed by intellectuals for the benefit of previous proletariats are of course quite irrelevant." From a literary standpoint, the utopian content of socialism-communism is void.

In the latter part of the forties, directly after the end of the war, a new literary group, with independent, nonconformist views, seemed to enjoy an influence and an esteem such as their elders of the postwar generation of 1920 had enjoyed before them. But for some reason not easy to elucidate, these extremely gifted postwar novelists—Norman Mailer, James Jones, John Horne Burns, Irwin Shaw, Paul Bowles, Truman Capote, Carson McCullers—some of them rebellious, brutally realistic, culling their material from war, sex, neurosis, and sometimes even the slums, have receded both in standing and in achievement since the opening of the fifties. Norman Mailer, for instance, author of the violent war novel *The Naked and the Dead* is said by one reviewer to have "dedicated himself to comfort, alcohol, and marijuana." It is as though something essential to these writers has been lost in the present intellectual climate of America. There would seem to be a significant connection between their inadequacy and what *Time* has celebrated as the "reconciliation" of the intellectuals with America.

Though *Time* is ever prepared to approve the status quo, the facts it adduces are not in dispute. The rift between intellectuals and society has narrowed in consequence of a mutual rapprochement. *Time's* star witness for the position of American intellectuals is Professor Jacques Barzun, who teaches history at Columbia. Actually, Barzun is highly critical of that position; what matters to Mr. Luce's editors [of *Time*], however, are the statements they can quote by Barzun and other intellectuals as evidence of a reconciliation.

The intellectuals of America, Barzun says, have today "won recognition in tangible ways beyond any previous group of their peers." Grumbling is out of date. Intellectuals who still grumble, Barzun says, "forget that the true creator's role, even in its bitterest attack, is to make us understand or endure life better. Our intellectuals do neither when they entice us to more self-contempt." The reference is to something that is already past, for by the end of the Second World War, Barzun says, "it was no disgrace, no provincialism, to accept America and admire it. . . . America was quite simply *the* world power, which means the center of world awareness; it was Europe that was provincial."

Similarly one of the leading literary critics, Lionel Trilling, points out: "An avowed aloofness from national feeling is no longer the first ceremonial step into the life of thought. . . . For the first time in the history of the modern American intellectual, America is not to be conceived of as *a priori* the vulgarest and stupidest nation of the world. . . ."

The literary success barometer of recent times has shown that those authors who emphatically assent to the social situation which America has achieved also enjoy the favor of the reading public. Herman Wouk, for instance, followed up his *The Caine Mutiny*—that triumph of military discipline over subversive thought—with *Marjorie Morningstar,* the story of a girl who succumbs to temptation in the person of an unconventional writer, then surmounts her weakness and embraces middle-class respectability. The male counterpart to *Marjorie Morningstar* is Sloan Wilson's *The Man in the Gray Flannel Suit,* a literary eulogy of the new style of life in suburbia adopted by the wealthy upper-middle class. The man in the gray flannel suit finds himself in a not very unusual dilemma involving power, wealth, and prestige on the one hand, and personal happiness on the other. He chooses compromise and, of course, finds personal happiness in a socially satisfactory framework. Both young novelists, Wouk and Wilson, have become millionaires on the strength of a single book, a quite new species of literary plutocrats, thriving on a geometrical progression of successes procured in turn by book clubs, pocket-book editions, Broadway, Hollywood, and television. In his last novel, *Youngblood Hawke,* Herman Wouk even makes this personal situation of the writer the central topic of the book. One critic (in *New Republic*) calls the novel "a fictional autobiography in cash terms." A writer like Norman Mailer, haunted by the terrible images of the war in the Pacific, must perforce remain on the popular-success sidelines in this game. This does not mean that only those writers achieve success who assent to the social status quo. The exception to the rule may be even more significant in highlighting the general trend. As, for instance, *Lolita,* by Nabokov: here is dissent, but of a kind which does not touch the substance or heart of the social situation at all. Social protest in such books is comfortably obscure.

In 1952, the *Partisan Review* published a survey based on what was then the new phenomenon of intellectual conformity to society. Mailer reacted indignantly that he was "in almost total disagreement with the assumptions of this symposium." He found it by no means gratifying that important older novelists like Dos Passos, James T. Farrell, Faulkner, Steinbeck, and Hemingway should "have traveled from alienation to varying degrees of acceptance, if not outright proselytizing for the American Century," as the *Partisan Review* had observed.

Such resistance of the artist to reconciliation with society is still—apart from the Beat generation—an isolated phenomenon. For this reconciliation is already much more than mere ideological adjustment; it has led to a structural integration of the intellectual, especially of the poet and novelist, in specific institutions, and this in turn has had quite definite stylistic consequences. As the title of his book indicates, John W. Aldridge, a brilliant young professor of literature, is *In Search of Heresy*. His search has been in vain. The picture he draws is of an institutionalized, intellectual orthodoxy, reflecting a political position of conservative moderation. Aldridge pours bitter scorn on the literati and professors, the critics and their reviews, the cultural foundations and colleges, all indissolubly linked with one another, forming this new intellectual orthodoxy. Nevertheless, he accepts the process as inevitable. A vacuum has developed where previously there had been creative protest. Time, as yet, has offered no alternative to this vacuum but conformity. The values of isolation, of revolt, have disappeared. The ingenious struggle against American "materialism" is no longer possible, and so the "institutional values" have interposed themselves on their own: security, money, power, assent, order, normality.

Novels like Cozzens' *By Love Possessed* or O'Hara's *From the Terrace* reflect a conservative mood which sees failure, not progress, as the basic human condition. Published at the end of the fifties, these novels won wide acclaim; they evidence a sophisticated, somewhat weary sobering.

A development that is intimately bound up with this mood is the emergence of an American Alexandrianism, out of the union of the universities with literary criticism, with writing as such, with the literary reviews, with the great foundations which give the money. A change has taken place in the avant-garde. Instead of the rebellious avant-garde of independent writers and poets, there is an academic avant-garde, orthodox both in its relation to society and in its concepts of style. Its major contribution in the realm of style is the "New Criticism," a strictly esthetic, immanent mode of observation, which has triumphed in the universities over sociological, psychological, or naturalistic interpretations of literary works. "Studying the writer's craft"— this has been defined as being the essence of the New Criticism.

. . .

Intellectual orthodoxy has received an influential accretion in the shape of the formerly "liberal," or leftist, *Partisan Review,* which is independent of the universities, but distributes stipends from foundations such as the Rockefeller Foundation. The way the clever members of this New York literary circle have effected their reconciliation with American society makes the frustrated heresy-hunter, Professor Aldridge, particularly bitter. Here we see serious literary figures, he says, anxiously taking shelter behind the new American mother symbol of egalitarian mass culture. A critic of the *Partisan Review* circle, Leslie Fiedler, sees the history of the American novel as a chain of disguised adolescent homosexuality, emerging now in a new "maturity." But Aldridge sees in this kind of "maturity" only that orthodox values of social conformity have triumphed over the potentially disturbing values of the creative life. This, precisely, is the general tendency. "I assume the institutionalization of the intellectual in America today to be an accomplished fact," writes Aldridge (himself a professor).

Because ⟨the intellectual⟩* could no longer love Communism or the élite culture of Europe, he began to love democracy and the mass culture of America, and as anything less than total commitment was unthinkable to him, he felt obliged to love everything about America: equal rights, mass production, mass education, free enterprise, television, supermarkets, used cars, baseball games. . . .

But the position of American intellectuals is not really as hopeless as the temperamental scholar depicts it. The integration of the intellectual in society holds obvious dangers for the creative process, but it had to take place some time, if only because on the other side it takes place by quite different, totalitarian means.

So far, we have dealt with only the literary intellectuals, as the avant-garde of the creative mind in its relationship with society. But much of the conflict between thought and action, which Merle Curti has called the American paradox, may have been relatively resolved by President Kennedy's inclusion of a number of intellectuals from the great universities in government. This is different than the "brain trust" of Franklin Roosevelt. This time, the intellectuals have been integrated in the daily workings of government, with their own responsibilities. They are not mere "experts." While it is true that the questions of politics, particularly in the domestic field, are decided by the President and his inner circle, it is the intellectuals who form the "new style" which has become so characteristic of the Kennedy Administration. This is particularly apparent in the brave attempt to control political decisions, especially in foreign policy, by a cool, anticipatory planning intelligence, at least as far as the elementary forces which rule the world of power politics will permit of such an approach.

Many liberals seem to have expected more from the political elevation of their colleagues. What they forget is that the influence of the intellectuals with whom Kennedy has surrounded himself is in direct relation to their chief's freedom of action. To the extent that this presently somewhat narrow field can be broadened over the years—after Kennedy has successfully dealt with the legacy of unresolved crises that was bequeathed to him—the influence of the intellectual planners and advisers will be able to unfold. It is hardly their fault that their magic touch is not really visible. It is the fault of the circumstances, and these can change.

If there is disenchantment among the liberal intellectuals outside the government, it is not because the President is not "intellectual" enough for them. On the contrary, the obvious intelligence, the absence of the customary clichés, the unconventional mastery with which Kennedy dismisses prejudices deep-rooted in the American tradition, particularly in the tradition of the business world—all these traits appear to have won favor with intellectuals everywhere. The doubts are of another sort. Is the intellectual element in Kennedy and his entourage the result of conviction, of belief in the things of the mind, or only of the realization that the intellect is an indispensable tool of managerial technique in the government of so complex a society?

This question takes the form of a conflict between "pragmatism" and "statesmanship." Many liberal intellectuals believe the Kennedy Administration too pragmatic, or too "political," by which they mean too cautious in questions such as civil rights or the liquidation of unemployment. But such disenchantment overlooks the fact that responsible politics is always the art

* Inserted by the author.—Editor.

of the *possible*. Few intellectuals, therefore, would agree with Alfred Kazin, the literary critic, when he says: "Kennedy's shrewd awareness of what intellectuals can do . . . is irrelevant to the tragic issues and contributes nothing to their solution." David Riesman's measured words, speaking for the "liberal left," are fairer: "We wish the Administration well. . . . We are critical, but we are not alienated."

If liberals ceased to be critical they would cease to be liberals. But what is historically important is that intellectuals are now "in," inside the little circle that makes history. This may be the height of their reconciliation with American society.

THE ABSENCE OF EFFECTIVE CRITICISM

Stuart Hampshire

Stuart Hampshire is a well-known British philosopher now teaching at Princeton University. The piece below is a more or less direct comment on an article by Arthur M. Schlesinger, Jr., the American historian and adviser to the Kennedy Administration, which appeared in an "American Number" of the *New Statesman,* a British review that normally reflects the left wing of the British Labour Party. Schlesinger there maintained that the reconciliation of American intellectuals, including their assumption of political responsibility, is an essentially healthy phenomenon. And he also argued that even would-be outsiders such as Paul Goodman play a recognized role within the system. Although their critical suggestions are impractical, they serve to remind the more pragmatic intellectual élite of the ultimate social values. Hampshire replies, however, that this incorporation of the outsider clearly indicates the emasculation of his role as a social critic. The cause, he argues, is a failure to confront the material realities of life in a capitalist society and a consequent retreat into spiritual and psychological criticisms. Although not a Marxist himself, Hampshire holds that Marx's procedure of starting from the crude material realities is the surest guarantee of the critic's integrity. A similar attitude can be found among many young American radicals who have recently challenged the reconciliation of the intellectual.

As a theory of the development of modern societies, and as a means of predicting the future in politics, Marxism is dead. It has lost its claim to be believed, since many of the specific predictions which the theory entailed have proved false. But for this very reason the theory, and even more its author, have deserved respect. The theory was not entirely vague and empty

FROM "A Plea for Materialism," *New Statesman,* Vol. 65, No. 1665 (February 8, 1963), pp. 186–88. Reprinted by permission.

of content, for it could be tested in experience. This in turn has made it possible for sociologists and for historians to concentrate their research on the proved points of inadequacy. At the very least, Marxism has left, as a lasting inheritance after its death, the possibility of rational inquiry into social change.

But still the demise of Marxism as an adequate instrument of political analysis has left a yawning gap. No hypothesis of comparable range and precision has been suggested to replace it. Neo-Marxists of various persuasions in France, England, and America have tried ineffectively to tamper with the theory to accommodate the recalcitrant facts: the horrors of Stalinism, the Hungarian Revolution, the sustained growth of the capitalist economy in the United States and Western Europe, the political weakness and lack of solidarity of organized labor, the aggressive foreign policies of the Soviet Union and of China, the persistence of nationalism. But they have probably not even convinced themselves that they have some reliable key to the future, a hypothesis that enables them to plan for the future welfare of mankind; certainly they have not convinced their followers in the West that they are, or soon will be, in strategic control of events, rather than reacting to them with tactical maneuvers. A theory that is always being propped up by supplementary hypotheses, to explain away its own failures, soon becomes ridiculous.

It is, of course, possible to ask: why look for theories of social change at all? Have we not learned, from past failures, and from the deceptions of Communists and fellow-travelers, that such comprehensive theories are the opium of the intellectuals? There is a strong movement of liberal opinion among intellectuals in Britain and the U.S. which has happily drawn this conclusion from the evident failures of Marxism, and, in the name of an empiricist philosophy, called for an end of political prophecy and of the type of large-scale planning which it encourages. One may recall the many celebrations of the "end of ideology" by liberal professors in America and in England; the exasperation of leaders of the Labour Party, provoked by the dying embers of nineteenth-century theory on their left; also the jaunty pragmatists of the New Frontier who, as men of great affairs, have no patience with theorists who have not proved themselves in practice.

The weakness of this new liberalism, proudly empirical, is the weakness of any dismissal of theory, whether in politics or elsewhere: that undeclared, and therefore unexamined, assumptions will creep in to fill the vacuum. A party of the left, whether of reform or revolution, always looks to intellectuals for some working hypothesis about the determinants of social change, the points of leverage at which political action will be effective. The great nineteenth-century radicals, whom the new liberals are now pleased to quote, had expected that the social sciences and individual psychology would together provide the general truths that are needed to plan the direction of progress. But the human sciences, with the exception of economics, are still insecure, uncertain, and their findings are disputed among ideologists of different schools. The only social science which is fully established and reliable is quantitative, and deals with material realities. Without benefit of Marx, we may doubt whether this is enough.

To fill this vacuum there has been an outpouring, in the United States and on a smaller scale in Britain, of journalistic and speculative sociology, closely allied with literary criticism, which is supposed to constitute a basis for radical reform and to inspire political action from the left. Mr. Paul Goodman is a member of this new, unanchored left, suggestive, surprising, never humdrum or boring, and yet politically harmless and tangential.

The thought that guided the old left, both Fabian and Marxist, was painfully constructed on Blue Books, reports of commissions, government and local government statistics; its atmosphere was that of the public library and of the reading room of the British Museum, and its rhetoric was in percentages and mortality rates. Its core was a scholarship of social fact. It was the relentless use of this scholarship to destroy social myths which largely discriminated left from right. This tradition survives in the work of Professor Titmuss, Mr. Townsend, and others in Britain.

Those who would defend the existing social and economic order have an interest, as they well know, in lifting discussion from the crude material realities of contemporary living to a higher, more vague, and spiritual plane; the moral issues become less embarrassingly sharp and clear when the alleged social evils, being spiritual in their nature, cannot be precisely ascertained or measured; for then no inconvenient political measures are unambiguously indicated. Nothing suits the Sunday supplements, or Mr. Luce's magazines, better than a Great Debate on the Spiritual Malaise of Our Time, in which the young literary radicals are invited to lead.

Mr. Goodman humorously remarks that he is treated by the present American authorities as a jester, and is urged in Washington to keep up his cries of dissent, as some useful contribution to the social whole. He is a member of the intelligentsia, and dissent is what the authorities expect from an intelligentsia, as they expect battle plans from an admiral. There is, in America, as it appears to an English academic visitor, a self-conscious radical intelligentsia with a recognized role and license: that of the popular moralist criticizing the American way of life. This Russian word is not out of place, just because it is taken for granted that a member of the intelligentsia will be cut off from the machinery of government and that he will be properly concerned with moral ideas of the utmost generality. From the centers of power he can therefore be viewed with complacency, as someone who has a stimulating effect within universities, and as an ornament of culture in a free society. He does not threaten property.

It was exactly this diversionary role of a freely speculative and morally concerned intelligentsia which aroused Karl Marx's destructive rages. He understood very clearly why the ruling classes would always feel safe as long as radical thought was kept in these speculative, philosophical, spiritual channels; his polemic against utopian socialism, and his argument that a movement of the left must rest on a materialist philosophy if it is to be linked with effective political action, are suddenly worth recalling; surely there is a truth buried in that dead metaphysics. Reading Mr. Goodman, or the *New Left Review* in Britain, and sometimes also *Dissent* and *Commentary,* the German utopian radicalism of the 1840's seems to have come to life again, with one significant difference: that with most of the American new radicals, concepts derived from clinical psychology have replaced the concepts of Hegelian metaphysics. "Alienation" now has a pathological, and not a metaphysical, sense, but it remains as abstract a notion as before.

I wish to enter a plea for materialism, and against the conspicuous consumption of abstract ideas: any improvement in the quality of life, either in

England or the U.S., demands first an improvement in the material circumstances of life of the ill-fed, ill-housed, ill-educated, and medically unprovided poor, whether abroad or at home. We can calculate the effects of economic planning in these spheres; but we do not possess the means to operate, on the large scale of political action, on the more intimate spiritual realities; and we cannot yet calculate the costs and consequences of any such action. Perhaps every man who thinks at all must have some uncertain opinions about the determinants of happiness, and of a sense of freedom and fulfillment, and about the sources of the imagination and of the emotions. Some will have the power to express persuasively an apparent insight into the states of mind of their contemporaries, and the images, or fictions, that they use may be unforgettable, and may for a time dominate our thinking about the quality of life around us. They create a new social myth, which may very indirectly inspire political action, as Carlyle or Ruskin did. But one cannot justifiably redesign a health service, or the prevention of crime and delinquency, or foreign policy, or otherwise methodically alter men's conditions of life, with principally the evidences of good literature on one's side. And least of all now. For the small fragments of knowledge that have so far been collected about the immaterial conditions of human welfare have suggested that they are immensely complex, and buried in the intimate histories of unpredictably varying individuals: unpredictably at least within the present categories of individual psychology. Freudian sociology is still only a literary invention.

Mr. Goodman, like many American essayists, playwrights, and novelists, confidently identifies the social causes of sexual and other emotional frustrations. But there is no reason to believe that his diagnoses, taken as more than impressionistic descriptions, are valid. What medical services are available in Mississippi? How many are homeless in London, England? Perhaps the intelligentsia of the left in America is too entertaining.

2

American Politics

A "CLASSICAL" CRITICISM

Harold J. Laski

Harold J. Laski, who died in 1950, was an internationally famous British political scientist and socialist theoretician. Throughout his career Laski was a knowledgeable, sympathetic, but often highly critical student of American politics and wrote, along with smaller pieces, *The American Presidency* (1940) and *The American Democracy* (1948), both of which were highly influential. A favorite theme in Laski's writings is that the American system of separation of powers and political decentralization is becoming increasingly inadequate for the needs of modern democracy. In the present article this theme is succinctly formulated as part of an exchange between Laski and Don K. Price, an American political scientist, over the relative merits of the American Presidential and British parliamentary systems.* British political scientists today would not draw the contrast quite so sharply and would adhere to Laski's view only in a qualified form. Yet Laski's article remains particularly instructive because it so clearly and uncompromisingly reveals a doubt about American institutions that is still the starting point for a great deal of European reflection.

.　　.　　.

If I venture some remarks upon Mr. Price's picture of American tendencies, I do so, first, with the sense that few foreigners can ever understand from within the "feel" of a system that is not their own, and, second, because, as I think, the Congressional system raises vital problems with which Mr. Price has omitted to deal. He writes [in the *Public Administration Review,* Autumn, 1943]:

America is a federation that is becoming a nation; the institutional system that has helped her do so will be of interest to the whole world as it moves toward greater

---

* For a rebuttal by Price to the article below see "A Response to Mr. Laski" in the *Public Administration Review* (Autumn, 1944).

REPRINTED FROM "The Parliamentary and Presidential Systems," the *Public Administration* Review, Vol. 4, No. 4 (Autumn, 1944), pp. 347–59 by permission of the publisher.

unity. She gets her job of government done by popular control over two cooperating branches—an executive that provides unity and enterprise, a legislature that furnishes independent supervision and the restraining influence of local interests. Members of her public service are as varied in their origins and experience as the mixture of public and private institutions in her society itself; the leading members of that service come from private life and return to it freely, looking on the government as the people's agency open to their participation.

It is difficult for a foreigner not to feel that these remarkable sentences belong less fully to the literature of political science than they do to the realm of poetry. It is true that Mr. Price elsewhere lays stress on the "parochialism of the pork-barrel" and that lack of individual responsibility for the federal program in Congress which "often" overemphasizes "local interests." But he likes the "flexibility" of the Presidential system, the ability it confers "to make progress piecemeal," and the looseness of party discipline that it permits. It prevents, he surmises, the kind of opposition which is "apt to become uncompromising and irreconcilable." In modern society, "if a legislature is to keep the whole organism working in the public interest, it cannot depend on a power to hire and fire the head of it, but it must approve one action and condemn another, encourage here and reprove there, expand this agency and restrict that one." The assumptions of the parliamentary system, he thinks, would, in the United States, "handicap the legislative and executive branches alike in their efforts to work together to meet the demands of a new age."

I hope these quotations do justice to Mr. Price's point of view. I note with some surprise the thesis that the executive provides "unity and enterprise."

.   .   .

The "unity and enterprise" of which Mr. Price speaks is operative in the American system only when there is a genuine Presidential leadership, and when Congress is prepared to cooperate in its acceptance. What Mr. Price calls "independent supervision" seems to me only too often an attempt on the part of Congress to destroy the effectiveness of that leadership. . . . Indeed, I think a strong case could be made out for the view that when cooperation between the President and Congress is lacking there is, behind either the one or the other, a "sinister interest," in Bentham's sense of the term, which deprives the people of the United States of the legislation to which it is entitled. The "parochialism" to which Mr. Price refers seems to an outsider like myself to have many and more evil results than he notes. It can arrest the development of great projects, as when the hostility of Senator McKellar to Mr. Lilienthal holds up the progress of the TVA. It maintains the evil practice of "senatorial courtesy," which only too often has been no more than a polite name for enabling a particular senator to insist that the power of patronage be used to protect his hold upon the party machine in his own state. It results in a considerable wastage of public funds in the fulfillment of works projects which are not seldom indefensible in conception and inadequate in execution, and when the "independent supervision" of the executive by Congress results in investigating committees like that of Mr. Martin Dies, the abyss between the purpose Mr. Price attributes to the system and the consequences actually achieved seem to me far wider than he seems to admit.

It is easy to say lightly that the United States is "a federation that is becoming a nation"; that seems to pass over not only the degree in which American federalism is obsolete but, also, the degree in which the Presidential system intensifies that obsolescence. That emerges, I suggest, in the vastly different standards of education, factory conditions, public health, to take three examples only, in the different parts of the Union. That infant mortality in San Antonio should be worse than in any great city save Shanghai is a serious comment upon the results of the division of powers. That the level of educational opportunity in the South should be so different from what it is in the North or in the West raises issues of the first importance for a democratic society. Mr. Price emphasizes the urgency of keeping "the administration of government under the control of the people, to invigorate it for executive action in their behalf," especially in this time of crisis. But he does not inquire whether there is in fact that popular control, nor whether the Presidential system is a method of invigorating the administration. . . .

. . . It is at least open to debate, for example, whether it ought perpetually to require a grave emergency to give the American commonwealth an effectively coherent policy. It is not less open to doubt whether a party system that becomes effectively national only during election time enables the people really to know what men they are choosing and what issues they are deciding. . . .

Nor do I find it easy to be enthusiastic about Mr. Price's praise for a public service in which "the leading members . . . come from private life and return to it." I note, in the first place, that the quality of administration in the United States has, in the main, improved in the degree that the spoils system has given place to the merit system. I note, in the second place, that as soon as the head of a government department has really learned how to handle his office, he is only too likely to return to private life, so that most departments contain some permanent official upon whose advice and judgment his minister is compelled to rely. And I note, in the third place, that every member of the executive, from the President downwards, is driven, as he makes his plans, to bear in mind not merely the objective he may have in view but the fact that, just because it is his objective, the legislature will want to shape it differently lest the full credit for its achievement be accorded to the executive, and not to the legislative, branch of the government.

.   .   .

Nor is it entirely fair to leave out of account in any discussion of the Presidential system the quite special influence it offers to pressure groups by reason of the separation of powers. . . . Lobbying in Whitehall is not, of course, any more unknown than lobbying in Washington. But there is, I think, the significant difference between the two places that, in the one, the responsibility for the result is direct and unmistakable, while in the other it is so thinned out by dispersion that it is often beyond the reach of the elector's insight. . . .

It is, further, significant enough that Mr. Price makes no serious comment on the rule requiring local residence for congressmen and senators. It is a rule that has had vast influence, almost wholly evil, on American public life. For, in the first place, it excludes from politics a large number of citizens, except in an indirect way; and, in the second, it makes the congressman or senator balance the alternatives between, for example, a small law practice in a backwoods township and the interest and excitement of life in Washington. The result is twofold: it makes him a perpetual candidate living by the favors he can secure for his district or his state; and, in most instances, it compels him to build or use a machine in his support, lest he be ousted by some ambitious rival. And to this must be added that the very fact that so large a number of people to whom politics is a natural métier are excluded from it multiplies the number of pressure groups through which they may hope to win alternative influence. And the rule of local residence gives by its nature a secret source of power to the great economic interests of America. The Du Ponts in Delaware and the Anaconda Copper Corporation in Montana are only classical examples of this kind. And where there arises this relationship, there is almost bound to arise also intermediate machines to collect "brokerage," as it were, on the service they can render the politicians or the corporations. . . .

These annotations have, I hope, established the thesis that the problems involved in any comparison between the parliamentary and the Presidential systems are far more complicated than Mr. Price is willing to concede. I should not for one moment claim that one system is better than the other, still less that the parliamentary system is more suited to the genius of the American people than the Presidential. A system of government is very like a pair of shoes; it grows to the use of the feet to which it is fitted. But it is well to remember of governments what is true, also, of footwear—that the shoes must be suited to the journey it is proposed to take. It ought, I think, to occur to Mr. Price that if Lord Baldwin did not examine whether the British system of nineteenth-century institutions could be improved, he himself failed to examine whether improvement was possible in the American system of eighteenth-century institutions.

· · ·

A CURRENT REAPPRAISAL

Herbert von Borch

Herbert von Borch, who is introduced on page 11, here presents another aspect of what he regards as the American process of maturation: the tension between the traditional pattern of decentralization and the need of a world power for coherent leadership. Von Borch is more sympathetic than Laski in his appraisal of the inherited pattern because he is more concerned with the guarantees of pluralism than with the obstacles to social change. But he argues that the gradual emergence of a "power élite"—a phenomenon which he associates primarily with the making of foreign policy—is an inevitable and desirable counterweight to decentralization in a period of American world leadership. (See Part IV, p. 321, for an American book review of *The Unfinished Society*.)

The United States government is curiously permeable in structure. It was born of the deepest distrust of the phenomenon of power. At its birth, it was in no position to act powerfully, and certainly not on a global scale, as history now obliges it to act. It is almost a mystery how the United States, without substantially altering the Constitution it adopted in the eighteenth century, has been able to play its part as the leader of a global coalition of anti-Communist states; how this great experiment in government, this politico-legal creation of the Founding Fathers, who dreaded equally the concentration of power at the top and the influence of radical majorities, has been able to survive under the conditions of the twentieth century.

The Founding Fathers established a federal government as the loose framework for what has come to be called the democratic process. The nation which was destined to spread across a continent flanked by two oceans had to be rendered capable of governing itself after the overthrow of British rule. But in their hostility to power, the settlers were also concerned with obstructing government as such, with splitting and neutralizing the exercise of power, by means of a multiplicity of safeguards. The government was set up as a permeable structure, as a transparent organism through which the energies of society would be able to flow freely and unimpeded. Thus, there came into being, as a result of the revolutionary Declaration of Independence, the system of checks and balances which has no parallel in anything that in Europe is called a government.

. . .

The bare outline of the governmental powers which hold each other in check gives only an insufficient idea of the way in which the will of society flows through this permeable structure.

Whatever is absorbed from this flow is politics; in this way the laws, decisions, actions, planning, which together constitute the government and administration of the country, are, as it were, crystallized. That is how America is governed, if this may be called government. But this "democratic process" has, perhaps, a boundary, beyond which lies the real kernel of government action. The exclusion of undivided power from the state has had the unlooked-for consequence that American society has become the most power-conscious, indeed the most avidly power-seeking society in the world. Power oscillates in the immense apparatus that extends from coast to coast, and every ambitious man has always been tempted, in the absence of an hereditary aristocracy, to grasp at that ephemeral prize. But power is seldom sought for its own sake; history shows that power as such, in the sense of dominion over others, has no particular attraction for Americans. Hence, too, power—in the widest sense, and in its multifarious aspects, from political, financial, or military power to technological, religious, or social power—does not have a restrictive effect, as it has in Europe; it does not restrict the freedom of others. It does so, of course, in the sense that free competition may give an advantage to one at the expense of another; but out of the power-saturated atmosphere of this society there also develops its constant forward striving, its dynamic inability to stand still, its restlessness.

Power is often sought for the sake of the riches it can procure; that is why

FROM "The Permeable State," *The Unfinished Society* (New York: Hawthorn, 1962), pp. 38–45, 65–76. Reprinted by permission.

corruption and not dictatorship is the greater danger where politics is conducted as a profession. But today this danger is largely confined to the party "machines," themselves on the decline, which contend for the lucrative control of the big cities.

In the last few decades certain definite power shifts have taken place, but they have not crystallized to the point where one can say that this or that group, stratum, or class dominates the state. The growth of government operations has favored a concentration of power in the executive rather than in the Congress. A military build-up is unavoidable under present international conditions. The giant corporations are becoming increasingly powerful at the expense of the smaller enterprises and farmers. The mass media of the press, the radio, and especially television have overtaken older institutions such as the universities, churches, and clubs as factors of influence. The almost uninterrupted stream of commercial advertising which inundates the daily life of the nation, equipped as it is with psychoanalytic techniques and "motivation research," constitutes a source of influence of dubious merit. And yet none of this has really changed the fundamental character of this society, a character which also determines the political element: it is a fluid, open, pluralist society, splintered into countless power centers (for instance, fifty states), into ethnic minorities (everyone belongs to some minority in relation to the whole, from the old dominant Anglo-Saxon group to the Asians and Negroes) which all contend for their status, to keep it or to gain it, into rival pressure groups, individual social forces which try to move the gigantic Leviathan in the direction of this or that set of interests.

The Founding Fathers' fear of the mass rule of the majority has not been justified by events. America has become a mosaic of minorities. Not merely minorities in the usual sense of national groups (which have preserved themselves much better in the "melting pot" than was to be expected), but also in the sense of purely individual forces, representing no one but themselves, which work at the fabric of political power: lobbyists in Washington, industrial leaders, trade-union leaders (who have not long been sitting at the table of the mighty), chairmen of Congressional committees with investigatory powers (which the late Senator McCarthy, though not unpunished, could abuse), the "veto groups" which, if they cannot make their own policies prevail, are nevertheless in a position to obstruct the policies of others (as for instance the Southern senators on the racial question)—all these are tiles in the great power mosaic. The two political parties are no exception to this rule; they too are composed in mosaic fashion, representing more or less loose coalitions of groups and not homogeneous political organisms.

American society could be as flexible and pluralistic as we have described it and still bear some resemblance to the older governmental structures of Europe were it held together by a strong professional civil service. But that too is lacking, and, despite the growing concentration of administrative power in Washington, it is doubtful that it will ever come into being. Although the spoils system—the apportionment of official posts to the victorious party of the moment—is on its way out on the administrative level simply for reasons of efficiency, at the highest echelons of the administration, including the greater part of the personnel of the government departments, the rule still holds that no one must own the government, least of all the civil servants. The American public service, including the civilian personnel of the Pentagon, comprises 2.4 million persons, only a small percentage of whom can be compared with the permanent civil service in Europe. The barrier to a strong bureaucracy in the United States partly consists in this: a post filled by appointment carries only slight prestige with the public as compared with a post won in an electoral contest. It may be an exaggeration to say that a professional civil service is regarded as "un-American," but it is certainly not a distinctively American institution, as the strictly hierarchical bureaucracy, with its traditions of high self-esteem, is characteristic of Germany.

．　　．　　．

The looseness and elasticity of the American political system acts as a shock absorber in serious conflicts. Thanks to it, the profound social upheavals of the last decades—the self-corrective action of capitalism, the taming first of capital, then of organized labor, racial integration by judicial decision— have taken place without political institutions having to be changed, without the incessant revolutions in the social sphere developing into political revolutions. The very conservative character of the system of separation of powers has not prevented change, only slowed it down and canalized it.

Strife pumps the blood through the arteries of this political organism, but what happens when strife ceases? Will the organism not become anemic? Can it remain fully competent when the will to fight slackens at every hand, when "moderation," the "middle way," becomes the watchword? Too much strife can destroy this singular form of government, but too little strife can be paralyzing too. This danger is endemic in the American system. For the past twenty years America has not had a decisive majority—Roosevelt lost it in Congress in 1938. Decisive majorities result from strife between the parties. The clearer the issues and the more passionate the debate, the greater the prospect that finally one party, for a time, will dominate the country and the centrifugal loci of power will be held together. But if the political climate becomes more temperate, as it has since the end of the last world war, if the "moderates" determine election results (there has been talk of the "revolt of the moderates" of the fifties) then party differences become more blurred than ever and neither Democrats nor Republicans can achieve a lasting, as opposed to merely a flash-in-the-pan, majority.

．　　．　　．

When Wilson lost his majority in Congress in 1918, it became clear how disastrous such a situation, however temporary, could be for foreign policy. Although a farseeing majority in the Senate had decided in favor of American accession to the League of Nations, the decision was ineffective because it lacked the necessary two-thirds vote. Internal political pressures had triumphed, and they will triumph with increasing frequency in the conduct of foreign affairs, once the Chief Executive has lost his influence over the majority in Congress.

This state of checkmate between the powers of government is a permanent threat in a permeable state. When America's political system was developed, the protective ocean lay between what was later to be the United States and the rest of the world. To have spoken then of the primacy of foreign policy would have been absurd. But the strategical revolution of the atomic and rocket age has depreciated all protective ocean frontiers. At the shortest notice, the North American continent can become the object of a surprise attack. To survive, America has had to accept the painfully Prussian concept of the primacy of foreign policy. But how does this concept square with a political order which is an ordered disorder, designed to make government as hard as possible? How can it result in anything but indecision, hesitation, drift, obscurity? That is the gravest problem confronting the United States as a world power in contest with other world powers.

Something needs to be said about the solution which America is in the process of finding for the vital problem of how to become capable of action in the sphere of foreign policy. The textbooks say nothing about it. The problem of American competence as a world power has emerged through a process known to biology as osmosis. One dictionary defines osmosis as a tendency to "percolation and intermixture of fluids separated by porous septa." The egalitarian American society is studded with the most varied élites. These élites are "fluid" in that they have no institutional demarcations. They are simply there thanks to their sociological specific weight. Some of these élites, by a process of osmosis, have coalesced into what C. Wright Mills has termed the "power élite." This power élite rules America in respect to formation of foreign policy. It has taken over the invisible helm where the decisions are made which determine the crucial issues of peace and war.

. . .

The American power élite is not a planned element of government. It is, as it were, the spontaneously generated response to the challenge of America's emergence as one of the two superpowers. (Here we see how apt is the analogy with osmosis.) But it has naturally crystallized around existing institutions. It has constituted itself, logically, at the top and is assembled around the Presidency. But the way it has done so is very different from the way such problems have been resolved in the past in Europe. Here, we do not find an authoritarian or totalitarian head of state creating his tools from a strong bureaucracy or a powerful party apparatus. The American power élite is not the tool of the President who is chosen by plebiscitary process; rather, the reverse may be the case.

. . .

The concept of a power élite was coined by C. Wright Mills in his book of that title, published in 1956; since then it has passed almost uncontested into the working language of political sociology. Other social scientists had, of course, recognized the situation of fact, but Mills subjected it to systematic investigation. Since he violates a great many democratic taboos, he is not exactly a standard authority in civics. But he was recognized in university circles and taught at Columbia University in New York until his death early in 1962. His central thesis is as follows:

There is no longer, on the one hand, an economy, and, on the other hand, a political order containing a military establishment unimportant to politics and to money-making. There is a political economy linked, in a thousand ways, with military institutions and decisions. . . . If there is government intervention in the corporate economy, so is there corporate intervention in the governmental process. In the structural sense, this triangle of power is the source of the interlocking directorate that is most important for the historical structure of the present.

The high military, the heads of the great corporations, the politicians at the seat of government have coalesced because they have discovered that their interests coincide structurally. This is no conspiracy; the power élite has become the point of intersection for developments in the three fields of government, industry, and defense, and that is precisely why it is not a "ruling class" in the Marxist sense. (The rather irrational aversion of business to President Kennedy is evidence of this point.)

Even in the central directorate there remains something of the loose coalition that is characteristic of American life. The three élites have united, but they are not identical. Their interests agree, but this agreement is primarily a common front, against an external danger, brought about by the primacy of foreign policy. The system, so it has been maintained, required a foe; in this point it may in the future prove vulnerable. It came into being by a very American, that is, a very dynamic, process. The élites poured into the vacuum which the traditional democratic methods of handling foreign policy decisions had been unable to fill.

The emergence of a power élite had no connection with the tendencies of either of the political parties. The process began under a Democratic President, was strengthened under a Republican President and confirmed by the new Democratic President. The presence of a power élite is the real reason for President Kennedy's appointment of so many Republicans to the highest posts in his Administration. The parties can take over from one another, as they did in 1952, and the incumbents of the highest executive posts change accordingly. But what is more important is that they all come from the same circles. The problem of America's competence in the field of foreign policy has been partially resolved in mid-century because the leading industrial managers have profited from the increased powers of the state. These industrialists, who are neither professional politicians nor professional civil servants, but political outsiders, fill many of the key posts in the government.

One condition for the emergence of the power élite was the expansion of government power; a second condition was the concentration of economic power in the hands of a few hundred companies closely linked with the government through defense contracts arising out of a defense budget of some $50 billion. A third condition is the state of permanent mobilization in which the two superpowers find themselves as a result of the cold war and the destructive new weapons technology. Important foreign policy decisions are no longer taken without consultation with the military. The hierarchy of some five hundred giant concerns, headed by industrial managers and the government hierarchy, headed by industrialists temporarily turned political leaders— these have crystallized as an action cell around the elected President, the only "democratic" figure in this élite. That is the strong framework of power which makes America competent to act, however chaotic may be the situation on the middle levels of decision, where pressure groups, parties, commissions, and committees, as well as hundreds of technical agencies, jostle for position. Mills contemptuously calls these middle levels the semi-organized congestion; but it is hard to see how the endlessly variegated American society could govern itself freely in any other way, at least where the issue is not peace or war.

The top decisions in Washington are taken by a group of some fifty men, comprising the President, the Vice-President, the Cabinet members, the directors of the principal technical agencies, the Chiefs of Staff, the head of the Central Intelligence Agency, and members of the White House staff. Only a few of these are professionals in government, party politicians, or officials; most of them come from other fields, and many—many more, at any rate, than in any European state—from the world of finance and business. Even though Kennedy has filled many important posts from the economic sector of the power élite, it is quite evident that he does so because he values the administrative abilities of these men, not because he wants to have them as advocates of the business world in the executive. (His attitude to the steel industry has made this abundantly clear.) Kennedy is applying a new principle in selecting members of the power élite for service in Washington: the men he chooses must not be defenders of the social status quo, but liberal pragmatists of the New Frontier. (There is hardly a speech in which Kennedy does not refer to the great "unfinished business" before the country.)

Perhaps the most influential members of the power élite are the legal consultants to the investment bankers, or the investment bankers themselves, who have the best knowledge of the key personnel in the economy and an overall view of the industrial potential. They are key figures in the interlocking of the political, industrial, and military hierarchies. Men like McCloy, Clay, Allen Dulles, Dillon, Dewey, Brownell, and Acheson belong to this group, as did the late John Foster Dulles. The rule is interchangeability. Generals like Clay or MacArthur become company presidents. Company presidents like the late Charles Wilson, McElroy, or McNamara become Defense Secretaries. Bankers like Aldrich and Whitney become ambassadors. A banker and repeated Cabinet member like Lewis Strauss bears the rank of an admiral. Generals like Gruenther and Bedell Smith occupy high civilian posts.

The British concept of "the Establishment" covers a broader group, but at the top it refers to the same kind of people as those described as the "power élite." In his *The American Establishment* (1962), written somewhat—but not altogether—tongue-in-cheek, Richard Rovere names McCloy as the former, Dean Rusk (now Secretary of State, previously of the Rockefeller Foundation) as the present "real chairman of the Establishment." McCloy's curriculum vitae reads, indeed, like an inventory of the key positions of the power élite. Rovere enumerates them: "Chairman of the Board of the Chase Manhattan Bank; once a partner in Cadwalader, Wickersham & Taft, and also in Cravath, de Gersdorff, Swaine & Wood . . . as well as, of course, Milbank, Tweed, Hope, Hadley & McCloy; former United States High Commissioner in Germany; former President of the World Bank; liberal Republican; Chairman of the Ford Foundation and the Council of Foreign Relations; Episcopalian." He was also Special Adviser on Disarmament to President Kennedy.

The members of the power élite have much in common socially: a rather conservative style of life, the same universities or military academies, and the same clubs. Often they are allied thanks to the almost dynastic marriage policy practiced by some of the old and wealthy families. Hardly any of them owe their posts to election.

Considering the power of the unions in American life, one may well ask why their leaders have not joined the ranks of the power élite as, in fact, they have not. They remain on that middle level where interests are the issue, not decisions affecting the nation. The nonpolitical tradition of the American unions explains a good deal; however, their exclusion from the inner power circle need not, and probably will not, be final.

America is far from being frozen in fixed institutions. Even the power élite, born of the unaccustomed primacy of foreign policy, is not the last word. Its composition can alter. America's problem in this century is to act competently without becoming torpid in the sphere of decision, politically paralyzed by the precarious balance of terror. The power élite at the top is likely to be a permanent structure, to the extent that anything in history is permanent. But its composition, its thinking, its attitude to the world and particularly to the rivalry with the other superpower, these points have not been finally determined. New forms of osmosis are conceivable. Under President Kennedy, for the first time, intellectuals from the universities are able to penetrate the power élite as members of the White House staff. The partition between this élite and American society remains permeable.

THE THREAT OF INSTITUTIONALIZED ANTI-COMMUNISM TO CIVIL LIBERTIES

Richard Drinnon

Richard Drinnon is a young American scholar who contributed this piece to an influential liberal British review while he was a Fellow in American Studies at the University of Leeds. His view that institutionalized anti-Communism continues to pose a very serious threat to civil liberties in the United States is an unusually clear statement of a very characteristic doubt about American democracy on the part of Europeans. The British especially, have tended to look upon McCarthyism and its aftermath as an indication of serious immaturity and weakness in American democracy, and there is a large body of opinion that sees the problem in much the same light as Drinnon does.

.   .   .

Like the weather or economics, current American civil freedoms would seem to be mixed. Take, for instance, the "Disappearance of Subversive Hams" from Washington, D. C. One's elation is checked on reading further that these are Polish hams which are disappearing from the capital's grocery stores, thanks to the alertness of the Committee to Warn of the Arrival of Communist Merchandise on the Local Business Scene, organizations of which have been established in all fifty states within the past few months. The campaign against the hams, Czech baskets, and Yugoslav chess sets has gained the support not

FROM "Keeping U.S. Reds at Bay," by Richard Drinnon. *The Twentieth Century,* Vol. 171, No. 1017 (Spring, 1963), pp. 61–70. Reprinted by permission.

only of the John Birch Society but also of Rotarians and other civic groups, parent-teacher associations, veterans' organizations. How much this has cut the Russian export of caviar I have no way of knowing, but it is a fact that the City Council of Billings, Montana, recently passed an ordinance which imposes a $1,000 license fee on firms that sell such products and requires them to display a sign announcing "licensed to sell Communist products." On the other hand, H. Stuart Hughes, not a Communist, but an avowed Socialist, atheist, and peace partisan, ran into none of this supermarket intolerance in his Massachusetts senatorial campaign against Teddy Kennedy. "Nobody called us Communists," he reports; "the charge would have been too absurd." (A good historian, Mr. Hughes must have momentarily forgotten that anti-Communism battens on absurdity.) And freedom apparently blossomed into a hundred flowers when Paul Goodman, the creative pacifist-anarchist, was urged in Washington "by one who has access, to continue my 'indispensable role of dissent.'" Yet at about the same moment a liberal Quaker named Trevor Thomas was being grilled over in the new Senate Office Building by McCarthy's old Internal Security Subcommittee. Thomas is the manager of a unique free forum of the air—listener-supported radio stations KPFA in Berkeley, KPFK in Los Angeles, and WBAI in New York—which presents opinions ranging from the extreme right to the extreme left. He was obviously summoned to this secret interrogation because he and his staff had taken too seriously their "indispensable role of dissent."

Now what do these swirling currents mean? Is that which is undeniably flowing against present expressions of dissent merely the backwash of McCarthyism? It is, firmly answer some American historians: following wars and other social upheavals, "crests of hysteria" temporarily sweep away precious rights but soon subside once the storm blows over. In a discerning study of the Salem trials, Marion L. Starkey observed that witch hunting always follows "in the wake of stress and social disorganization." A quick glance at the record seems to bear this out. There were waves of anxiety and repression in the 1790's following the American and French Revolutions, in the 1860's following the Civil War, in the 1880's following the so-called Haymarket Riot, in the late teens following the First World War, and most recently following the Second World War. But this interpretation is so general as to be almost useless. I have difficulty thinking of a period in which there has not been stress and social dislocation in the United States. Moreover, every war—for example, those of 1812, 1846, and 1898—did not produce the expected wave in its wake, nor were all the waves—for example, that of the late 1880's—preceded by wars. In truth, this notion of waves of "collective madness" or of "spasms of terror," as Bruce Catton has called them, is hardly more helpful for understanding the ups and downs of civil freedoms than the older notion of financial "panics" was to economists for understanding the business cycle. In both instances you are tempted to fall back in despair on sunspots as an explanation.

A more mechanical metaphor is imperative for any analysis of the *process* of suppressing dissent. Reflecting on individual waves leads ultimately to seasickness, if anywhere; considering the long range changes in the locus of the attack on civil freedoms leads to the insight that the decisive shift has been from the vigilante level to the bureaucratic level. Perhaps we might think of the governmental apparatus of executive agencies, secret police bureaus, and legislative committees as a tank which has moved up and down over the uneven terrain of recent history but with net advances on the community and the individual. Metaphors aside, the point may be stated simply: hates have been organized and made official.

Shortly after the turn of this century, for instances, unofficial definitions of Them included anarchists, syndicalists (Wobblies), socialists, Catholic and Jewish immigrants, Negroes, and other minority ethnic groups. These hatreds were often put into action on a local level: a Jew was lynched in Georgia; a Wobbly was shot in Utah; a Negro was burned alive in Pennsylvania; a socialist was tarred and feathered in Oklahoma; an anarchist was clubbed in New York. But by 1917 some of these hatreds had been bureaucratized. Then they were by definition no longer illegal or extra-legal, nor were their expressions usually physically violent, nor such hit-and-miss affairs—anarchists, socialists, Wobblies, and pacifists all over the country were jailed for opposing the war and some of those who were aliens were later deported. Over the years, especially in the 1930's and following, the relatively orderly administrative hearing, legislative investigation, or court trial tended to replace the action of mobs. Statutes accumulated which defined persons with dangerous opinions and/or associations—for example, the Anarchist Exclusion Act of 1903, the Smith Act of 1940, the McCarran Act of 1950, and the Communist Control Act of 1954, which sets forth fourteen criteria for identifying Them. Not least, executive departments, bureaus, and agencies were assembled and frequently retooled for implementation of these and other statutes, relevant executive orders, court decisions.

In a few words: the America of Huck Finn's feuding Grangerfords and Shepherdsons has become the America of Mr. J. Edgar Hoover locked in ceaseless organizational conflict with the Masters of Deceit. "A steady road," remarked Max Weber, "leads from modification of the blood feud, sacerdotally, or by means of arbitration, to the present position of the policeman as the 'representative of God on earth.' "

But the America of the man with a gun has also become the America of the army with a missile. The divine representative has two faces: turned inward toward the country, it is indeed the face of a policeman, but turned outward it is the face of a soldier. One sees enemies threatening internal overthrow; the other sees enemies threatening external annihilation. One represents the movement toward a police state; the other the drift toward a garrison state. . . .

Twin specialists of violence in a hostile world, the soldier and the policeman join in their definition of reality. "There exists a world Communist movement which, in its origins, its development, and its present practices," reads the McCarran Act, "is a worldwide revolutionary movement whose purpose it is, by treachery, deceit, infiltration into other groups (governmental and otherwise), espionage, sabotage, terrorism, and any other means deemed necessary, to establish a Communist totalitarian dictatorship in the countries throughout the world through the medium of a worldwide Communist organization." And it follows that the individual is either with Us or with Them.

.   .   .

Unfortunately no one has yet written the definitive study of How to Make Enemies and Find Them Useful. For instance, murderers bent on suicide find the state's executioner useful; the executioner has an obvious economic and professional interest in the murderer; societies apparently have a stake in both, for the executioner acts out, in a sanctioned way, lusts to destroy, and at the same time the murderer goes to his grave burdened with the guilts of the many who have secretly shared his aggressive urges. To return to the thread here; armies exist to combat foreign armies; national police exist to combat domestic enemies. In a sense, external and internal enemies are the unsung heroes of the rise of the centralized national state. If war is—or has been—the state's health, internal intimidation of real and alleged subversives has been its tonic. No one could deny the present fateful dependence on enemies. Anti-Communism is good business for everyone from Southern California rocket workers to midwestern chemical firms, and on down to the retailers of "Snooper" electronic listening devices and "Be a Spy" correspondence courses. Without enemies, there would be economic chaos. They are important too in providing the two major political parties with something to campaign on. For the individual politician, anti-Communism has been an avenue to political preferment. There are some signs, I must add, that it is losing a bit of its importance or at least is taking new forms. Nixon's most recent defeat is a case in point; for his opponent, a liberal Democrat, refused to take a back seat to Nixon or anyone else in his efforts to exorcise demons from California. When everyone has become a professional anti-Communist, what happens to the profession? Perhaps we are due to witness the rise of more sophisticated anti-Communists of a kind heralded by *The Manchurian Candidate*. Nevertheless, all but a few individuals and groups still rely on some form of anti-Communism for psychological and social sustenance. Even the increasing number of those who have become cynical, bored, or indifferent about it as an issue, hardly challenge its validity or fail to draw a measure of security from the pooled insecurities it represents. It gives some structure to a world broken in half between the United States and Russia, capitalists and Communists, free men and slaves.

·   ·   ·

The symbiotic relationship of the Federal Bureau of Investigation and the Communist Party is also well known. Mr. J. Edgar Hoover's virtually unopposed requests for ever-increased appropriations depend in part on the existence of Communists. . . . If we are to believe the testimony of one of his ex-employees, Mr. Hoover has over a thousand agents in the Communist Party; if the Party numbers five or six thousand, one out of every six Communists is an FBI agent. By all odds, the Federal Bureau of Investigation is the most revolutionary agency in the government. One is reminded a little of Louis Napoleon's secret police, who participated fully in every single action against his regime. One is reminded more of the expansion of the Russian and German secret services in the mid-1930's when, as Hannah Arendt puts it, "no opponents were left to spy on."

It would be misleading and an exaggeration of the evidence to think of a reign of terror. It would not be misleading to think of a reign of anxiety which is by no means only the "backwash of McCarthyism." The security system which was on trial in Oppenheimer's hearings remains relatively unchanged, even though another such case is not likely in the near future. The Smith Act and subsequent acts and court decisions remain very much in effect. While the atmosphere seems to have lightened, the machinery in fact grinds on. The last Congress passed a bill empowering the Post Office Department to act as a censor of "Communist political propaganda" from abroad, thus adding for the first time to the laws of the United States a mail-screening provision and making it less likely that its citizens will be sufficiently well informed about events in Eastern Europe and Asia. Key figures associated with the Women's Strike for Peace movement were recently grilled by the House Un-American Activities Committee. Staff and sponsors of the listener-supported radio stations I mentioned at the beginning of this essay were recently called before the Senate Internal Security subcommittee. Following the Supreme Court decision (June 5, 1961) which upheld the McCarran Act, Attorney General Robert Kennedy has been attempting to enforce its registration provisions. Communists must register with the government or receive a five-year prison term or a $10,000 fine or both for each day they fail to register. As Mr. Justice Black noted in his dissent, "for a delay of thirty days in filing [the] required reports, a fine of $300,000 and imprisonment for 150 years could be imposed by a trial judge." For their failure to register, Mr. Benjamin J. Davis and Mr. Gus Hall, both of whom have already served five years in prison under the conspiracy section of the Smith Act, stand under an indictment which could bring them thirty more years and a $60,000 fine each.

Yet, while institutionalized and popular anxiety moves ahead, intellectual life in America shows some signs of returning to reality. This could not have been delayed indefinitely. Gross anti-Communism so distorts reality that anyone who would think must move through or around it. The hate-love relationship between America and Russia has been carried to such insane lengths, for instance, that the former almost literally fails to recognize the existence of China and leaves this not inconsiderable country out of some schemes for a negotiated settlement. The image of a world broken in half hardly helps one understand that the Russians and Chinese are not in complete agreement on all the issues facing Communism, that Polish Communism is not Albanian Communism, or that Khrushchev's Communism is not exactly like Stalin's— the fact that Stalin shot rebellious Communist writers, whereas Khrushchev has taken to locking them up in insane asylums is an index of change, if not of the kind of liberalization some Soviet apologists claim. If a few Communist intellectuals, like Pasternak and Tarsis,* could courageously assert their independence, all the more reason has there been for American intellectuals, so much more safely placed, to return to their proper callings of criticism of the pretensions and hypocrisies of power.

.   .   .

---

* Valeriy Tarsis is a Russian novelist who was committeed to an insane asylum in 1962 for the publication in England of *The Tale of the Bluebottle,* a sharp indictment of Soviet Communism, presented in the form of science fiction. *Ward 7,* published in 1965, recounts his experiences in the Moscow asylum.—Editor.

3

American Society

THE COMMERCIAL CULTURE
Francis Williams

Francis Williams is a British author who has written extensively on
the British Labour Party and on British institutions generally. A
former Ministry of Information official and newspaper editor, he
has spent much time in the United States and has often commented on its problems. In the present piece he develops a relatively
traditional theme from a somewhat new perspective. The commercialism of American life is frequently cited by European conserva-
tives to indict not only American but industrial society in general.
But Williams, who is sympathetic to socialism, is more concerned
lest the current "Americanization of Europe" through the introduction of American commercialism corrupt the communal and cultural roots that sustain European impulses toward a more humane
form of industrial society. And this would perhaps be Williams'
answer to Drew Middleton's charge (see his book review of *The
American Invasion* in Part IV, pp. 318–20) that his criticisms of
modern industrial society are too often "Tory" in tone.

In American society the need to buy takes precedence over almost all other
emotions—even that of sex, much as Americans dwell on this in their literature. At once romantic and pathetic, the urge to buy and buy again is at the
heart of the American dream. To buy and to waste.

In this society, so recently yet so tremendously removed from the struggles
of the pioneers and the anxieties and hardships of the new immigrants, conspicuous expenditure would appear to represent an essential release of the
national spirit and conspicuous waste in eating, buying, and living a compulsive rejection of the frugalities of the past.

Only so, surely, to take one example, can the huge, and to a European
taste, physically nauseating prodigality of the meals served in American
popular restaurants be explained. No one can actually wish to eat all those

FROM *The American Invasion* (London: Blond, 1962), pp. 63–67. Reprinted by permission of Anthony Blond, Ltd. and Crown Publishers, Inc.

immense steaks, those vast chops, those enormous piles of tasteless jumbo prawns, those salads garnished with so strident a mixture of sauces that the palate falters. Indeed, in many popular restaurants the managements make evident their awareness that no one can actually consume all that custom demands shall be put on their plates. They offer you a greaseproof paper bag to take the leavings home in for your dog—if you happen to have a dog. (In the better establishments these bags are embellished with pictures of the sort of dog you would be likely to meet at a dog toggery on Fifth Avenue.)

To serve such helpings, to offer deliberately more than the most gluttonous can want, to insist on waste as part of the social garnishing of a meal, this one suspects is a necessary ritualistic gesture, like the vast meals served in the desert by Arab hosts or the blow-out of a poor man celebrating a lucky day at the races.

Only in their provision of cutlery do the Americans reveal the subconscious hold on them of ancestral memories of a more frugal past. That a people so unnecessarily lavish in all else—and with so many electric dishwashers—should, except in the most expensive restaurants and sophisticated households, regard one knife as adequate for all the requirements of civilized eating is incomprehensible except on the thesis of an ancestral memory bogged down in frugal recollections of how hard cutlery was to come by in a frontier camp. In the same way the inability of a people otherwise so technically adroit to master the simple rules for making tea can only, surely, be explained on the basis of a psychological blockage in the Bostonian memory.

To buy largely and extravagantly has become a necessary expression of American personality; to have what one wants now when one wants it, hardly less so. But what one wants must be wanted by other people also. It must have a symbolic and a group value as well as a personal and practical one. It is necessary to be able to buy now to show that one is rich—as a child or a millionaire is rich, without thought of the future. But also to show that one belongs.

It is on this passionate conviction of so many Americans—not all of course, but enough, more than enough—that to buy is to grow in personality, that the whole vast edifice of American merchandising and selling is founded. Whatever else American civilization may mean—and of course it means many other things, including many that are fine and generous and uplifting to the human spirit—it means that all who participate in it must face the constant command to buy more and more. If we opt for an Anglicized version of the American way of life we must opt for this also.

In the service of that command the American advertising industry spends on behalf of national advertisers something over $4 billion a year (roughly £ 1.4 billion, or about one and a half times as much as the total annual public bill for all education, including university education, in the United Kingdom). Moreover, in addition to national advertising the American consumer is daily subjected, to an extent far beyond that known elsewhere, to a constant outpouring of local advertising by merchandising firms of all kinds. Many local newspapers receive 60 percent or more of their total advertising revenue from such sources and are as a result able to function on daily circulations, sometimes of ten thousand copies or less, which would be derisory in Britain.

And all the time the pleading, commanding voices swell in an ever larger chorus from local radio and television stations, on billboards and circulars.

When all the channels of American national and local advertising are taken into account at least $10,000 a minute is spent every hour of the twenty-four, every day of the week, every week of the year, persuading Americans to buy. It may well be more.

By night and by day the air is full of voices. For radio, which goes on practically nonstop throughout the twenty-four hours, is still important in American advertising because of the number of car radios and of housewives who listen as they do their daily chores. These voices are full of a passion, a raucousness, a treacly sentimentality, a glad-hand buttonholing mateyness, a vulgarity, and a mendacity almost impossible to believe.

There is nothing they do not try to sell, these wheedling, bellowing, crooning voices of a civilization which, if they were all one had to judge by, would seem to have lost all sense of honesty or respect for human dignity: toilet tissues, diapers, loans, new cars, second-hand cars, furniture, steaks, washing powder, cat food, banking services, dentures ("You pay as you chew"), hi-fi records, religion, soft toys, soft drinks, cremation ("Call on B. your *friendly* mortician today, folks, and find that peace of mind you're looking for"), refrigerators, deep freezers, frying pans, toasters, cold cures, lamb chops, deodorants ("When it's winter outside remember it's summer under your armpits"), hair-do's, corn cures, insurance, breakfast foods, shorts, suspenders, personalized tie tacks, potato chips, towels for him, towels for her, cut-price grocery, hardware, gasoline, drapes, silverware, houses, canned goods, beer—on and on, day in day out, night in night out, shouted, whispered, sung, acted; punctuated by drum beats, bugle blasts, ticker tapes, children singing, children crying, women cajoling, men laughing; by whispers of love, of desire, of hope, of longing, of despair: an endless, gluttonous outpouring of synthetic emotion winging its way for ever and ever across the plains and mountains, the cities and towns, the freeways and homesteads of this immense country.

But do not mock. The political and commercial pressures for commercial radio in Britain are mounting daily. For forty years British listeners have been content with public service regional broadcasting. Even when the decision on commercial television was taken, there was no serious suggestion that the principle should be extended to sound radio. It is scarcely accidental that it is only now as the pressures to Americanize British buying habits increase with every fresh inroad of American capital and American sales techniques that a campaign for local commercial radio stations should have been launched, backed by powerful advertising and newspaper interest including some, like Thomson newspapers, with trans-Atlantic experience.

In the daytime and halfway through the night the television screens take up the American story with an even more frenetic and expensive gusto. No question of natural breaks here, every man and woman's shoulder is to the wheel. The singers, the quiz masters, the comedians, the stars and starlets, even the newscasters and the commentators on world affairs, must pause in their activities to tell you confidently what their sponsor has to sell. ("And now, folks, turning aside from Berlin for one moment—but we'll be taking another look at how things are with the latest stop press flash before this program ends—let me pass on to you some news that's really worth knowing, news that means money in all your pockets. . . .") History, tragedy, music, humor, ballet, political reporting, all are impressed in the service of a common master—all must be dedicated to the all-pervasive religion of the soft or the hard sell.

. . .

THE CONFORMING INDIVIDUALIST

Jean-Paul Sartre

Jean-Paul Sartre, the internationally famous French author, is a leading exponent of the existentialist philosophy of personal responsibility. This article is one of several essays in which he recounts the impressions of a visit to the United States toward the end of the Second World War. It may be viewed as a modern restatement of the contrast, traditional in European thought, between the European ideal of personal uniqueness, rooted in a concrete communal existence, and the anarchic character of American individualism, which is but the converse aspect of a collective pressure to conform. Sartre argues that there is an absence of true community in America, which works against the achievement of authentic personality.

. . . .

[The] forces of conformism in America are mild and persuasive. You have only to walk about in the streets, enter a shop, or turn on a radio to meet them and feel their effect upon you, like a warm breath.

In America—at least the America with which I'm familiar—you are never alone in the street. The walls talk to you. To left and right of you there are advertisement boardings, illuminated signs, and immense display windows which contain only a big placard with a photographic montage or some statistics. You see a distressed-looking woman offering her lips to an American soldier or an airplane bombing a town and, under the picture, the words, "Bibles, not bombs." The nation walks about with you, giving you advice and orders. But it does so in an undertone and is careful to explain its admonition in minute detail. There is not a single command, whether in a cosmetic advertisement ("Today, more than ever, it is your duty to be beautiful. Take care of your face for his return. Buy X . . . Cream") or in a piece of war bond propaganda, which is not accompanied by a brief comment or explanatory picture.

Yesterday I lunched at a restaurant in Fontana, an artificial town built about a great dam in Tennessee. Along the busy highway leading to the dam is a big boarding with a parable, in cartoon form, on the subject of teamwork.

FROM "Individualism and Conformism in the United States," *Literary and Philosophical Essays* (New York: Criterion, 1955), pp. 98–106. Reprinted by permission.

Two donkeys tied to each other are trying to reach two haystacks which are a certain distance apart. Each donkey is tugging on the halter in an opposite direction. They half strangle each other. But finally they understand. They come together and start working on the first haystack. When they have eaten it, we see them biting together into the second one.

Obviously the commentary has been deliberately avoided. The passer-by must draw the conclusion himself. There is no pressure put on him. On the contrary, the cartoon is an appeal to his intelligence. He is obliged to interpret and understand it; he is not bludgeoned with it as with the loud Nazi propaganda posters. It remains in halftone. It requires his cooperation in order to be deciphered. Once he has understood, it is as though he himself has conceived the idea. He is more than half convinced.

Loudspeakers have been installed in factories everywhere. They are meant to combat the worker's isolation in the presence of matter. At first, when you go through the immense navy yard near Baltimore, you find the human dispersion, that great solitude of the worker, with which we are familiar in Europe. All day long, masked men, bending over steel plates, manipulate their oxyhydrogen blowpipes. But as soon as they put on their helmets they can hear music. And even the music is a kind of guidance that stealthily insinuates itself into them; even the music is a directed dream. And then the music stops, and they are given information about the war or their work.

When we were leaving Fontana, the engineer who had so kindly escorted us all about led us into a little glass-enclosed room in which a new wax disk, already prepared to record our voices, was revolving on a turntable. He explained that all the foreigners who had visited the dam had, on leaving, summed up their impressions before the microphone. Far be it from us to refuse such a kind host; those of us who spoke English said something, and the speeches were recorded. The following day they would be broadcast in the yard, the cafeteria, and in every house in town, and the workers would be pleased to learn of the excellent impression they had made upon the foreigners and would work with an even greater will.

Add to this the advice given on the radio, the letters to the newspapers, and, above all, the activities of the innumerable organizations whose aims are almost always educational, and you will see that the American citizen is quite hedged in.

But it would be a mistake to regard this as an oppressive tactic on the part of the government or the big American capitalists.

.   .   .

This educative tendency really springs from the heart of the community. Every American is educated by other Americans and educates others in turn. All through New York, in the schools and elsewhere, there are courses in Americanization.

Everything is taught: sewing, cooking, and even flirting. A school in New York gives a course for girls on how to get their boy friends to propose to them. All of this is directed at forming pure Americans rather than men. But the American makes no distinction between American reason and ordinary reason. All the advice with which his path is marked is so perfectly motivated, so penetrating, that he feels lulled by an immense solicitude that never leaves him helpless or abandoned.

I have known modern mothers who never ordered their children to do anything without first persuading them to obey. In this way they acquired a more complete and perhaps more formidable authority over their children than if they had threatened or beaten them. In the same way, the American, whose reason and freedom are called upon at every hour of the day, makes it a point of honor to do as he is asked. It is when he is acting like everyone else that he feels most reasonable and most American; it is in displaying his conformism that he feels freest.

As far as I can judge, the American nation's characteristic traits are the opposite of those which Hitler imposed upon Germany and which Maurras* wanted to impose upon France. To Hitler (or Maurras), an argument was good for Germany if it was, first of all, German. If it had the slightest whiff of universality, it was always suspect.

The peculiarity of the American, on the other hand, is the fact that he regards his thought as universal. One can discern in this a Puritan influence which I need not go into here. But above all, there is that concrete, daily presence of a flesh and blood Reason, a visible Reason. Thus, most of the people I spoke with seemed to have a naive and passionate faith in the virtues of Reason. An American said to me one evening, "After all, if international politics were in the hands of well-balanced and reasonable men, wouldn't war be abolished forever?" Some French people present said that this did not necessarily follow, and he got angry. "All right," he said in scornful indignation, "go and build cemeteries!" I, for my part, said nothing; discussion between us was impossible. I believe in the existence of evil, and he does not.

It is this Rousseau-like optimism which, where Nazi Germany is concerned, cuts him off from our point of view. In order to admit the existence of such atrocities, he would have to admit that men can be wholly bad. "Do you think there are two Germanys?" an American doctor asked me. I replied that I didn't.

"I understand," he said. "France has suffered so much that you are unable to think otherwise. It's too bad."

And then there is the machine, which also acts as a universalizing factor. There is generally only one way of using a mechanical object, namely, the one indicated in the accompanying leaflet. The American uses his mechanical corkscrew, his refrigerator, or his automobile in the same way and at the same time as all other Americans. Besides, this object is not made to order. It is meant for anyone and will obey anyone, provided he knows how to use it correctly.

Thus, when the American puts a nickel into the slot in the tram or in the underground, he feels just like everyone else. Not like an anonymous unit, but like a man who has divested himself of his individuality and raised himself to the impersonality of the Universal.

It was this complete freedom in conformism that struck me at the very beginning. There is no freer city than New York. You can do as you please there. It is public opinion that plays the role of the policeman. The few Americans I met seemed to me at first to conform through freedom, to be depersonalized through rationalism. They seemed to identify Universal Reason

---

* Charles Maurras, a French political writer and critic, who edited *L'Action française*, the newspaper of a Fascist-like nationalist organization, was sentenced in 1945 to life imprisonment for collaborating with the Germans.—Editor.

with their own particular nation, within the framework of the same creed.

But almost immediately I discovered their profound individualism. This combination of social conformism and individualism is, perhaps, what a Frenchman will have most difficulty in understanding. For us, individualism has retained the old, classical form of "the individual's struggle against society and, more particularly, against the state." There is no question of this in America. In the first place, for a long time the state was only an administrative body. In recent years it has tended to play another role, but this has not changed the American's attitude towards it. It is "their" state, the expression of "their" nation; they have both a profound respect for it and a proprietary love.

If you merely walk about in New York for a few days you cannot fail to notice the deep link between American conformism and American individuality. Seen flat on the ground from the point of length and width, New York is the most conformist city in the world. From Washington Square north, there is not a single oblique or curving street, with the exception of old Broadway. A dozen long, parallel furrows go straight from the tip of Manhattan to the Harlem River. These are the avenues which are intersected by hundreds of smaller furrows rigorously perpendicular to them.

This checkerboard is New York. The streets look so much alike that they have not been named. They have merely been given registration numbers, like soldiers.

But if you look up, everything changes. Seen in its height, New York is the triumph of individualism. The tops of the buildings defy all the rules of town planning. They have twenty-seven, fifty-five, and a hundred stories. They are gray, brown, or white, Moorish, medieval, renaissance, or modern. On lower Broadway, they press against each other, dwarfing the tiny black churches, and then, suddenly, they separate, leaving between them a gaping hole of light. Seen from Brooklyn they seem to have the nobility and solitude of bouquets of palm trees on the banks of rivers in Moroccan Susa—bouquets of skyscrapers which the eye is always trying to assemble and which are always coming undone.

Thus, at first, American individualism seemed like a third dimension. It is not incompatible with conformism, but, on the contrary, implies it. It represents, however, a new direction, both in height and depth, within conformism.

First, there is the struggle for existence, which is extremely harsh. Every individual wants to succeed, that is, to make money. But this is not to be regarded as greed or merely a taste for luxury. In the States, money is, I think, the necessary but symbolic token of success. You must succeed because it shows that you enjoy divine protection.

And you must also succeed because only then can you face the crowd as a person. Take the American newspapers. So long as you have not achieved success, you cannot expect your articles to appear in the form in which you have submitted them. They will be cut and pruned. But if you have a money-making name, then everything changes; what you write will go through without cuts. You have acquired the right to be yourself.

.   .   .

I have said enough, I hope, to give some idea of how the American is subjected, from the cradle to the grave, to an intense drive to organize and

Americanize him, of how he is first depersonalized by means of a constant appeal to his reason, civic sense, and freedom, and how, once he has been duly fitted into the national life by professional associations and educational and other edifying organizations, he suddenly regains consciousness of himself and his personal autonomy. He is then free to escape into an almost Nietzschean individualism, the kind symbolized by the skyscrapers in the bright sky of New York. In any event, it is not based on our kind of individualism, but on conformism. Personality must be won. It is a social function or the affirmation of society.

THE LONELINESS OF INDUSTRIAL SOCIETY

Dieter Oberndörfer

Dieter Oberndörfer is a German scholar whose interest in sociology and political science is informed by a philosophical commitment to religious existentialism. His present theme is the psychological cost of modern industrialism, which he thinks is best illustrated by American society, where industrialism exists in its purest and most advanced form. This problem has also been widely considered by American social commentators, on whose work Oberndörfer often draws. But, as he sees it, the present disorientation of the individual cannot be overcome unless there is a return to transcendental religious values. And he seeks this anchor not so much in traditional religious doctrine as in newer approaches to individual self-transcendence opened up by European, and especially German, existentialist philosophy.

The work which follows is a contribution to the definition of the form of modern man.

Our focus is the form of man in a society which is constantly in flux because the foundations of its industrial production are being continually altered by rationalization and technological progress. But the constant alteration of the technological basis, which modern men can no longer do without, leads to unending mass migrations such as have never been observed before. In contrast to the nomads of earlier historical epochs, the industrial nomad does not migrate in a tightly knit group based on consanguinity or nationality, but either completely alone or with a small family. He does not travel from oasis to oasis in paths prescribed by nature, but rather follows the constantly shifting winds of a technologically determined way of life. He wanders here

FROM "Einfuhrung," *Von der Einsamkeit des Menschen in der modernen amerikanischen Gesellschaft* (Freiburg im Breisgau: Rombach, 1958), pp. 1–17. Translated by the editor with permission.

and there, erratically. Millions of men are thrown into a confused whirlpool motion. The analogies which suggest themselves are the dancing dust particles in a sunbeam; the hectic traffic of a large city; the rattling, bouncing, and confusion of a stone shaken in a sieve. But we are dealing not only with a spatial [migration], but, even more, with a social migration of the greatest scope. Social position is no longer stable and determined within a social hierarchy, for the old hierarchies have been broken up and pulverized in the construction of a society molded by technology. A society of leveled masses has arisen. And it is precisely because the social "above" and "below" are so little fixed and preestablished in this society that a bitter struggle over rank and position prevails. The drive to rise higher grips all strata of the population. Social ascent or descent—in a situation where to remain at a certain level of ascent can already signify descent—identify the law of life and destiny of broad masses. Thus the law of competition penetrates all areas of human life to become the authentically ruling dynamic of human life in a mass industrial society.

The human being in an industrial society which is highly mobile both horizontally, or spatially, and vertically, or socially, is characterized above all by his capacity to adjust and his psychological adaptability. He no longer lives in the solid encasement of usage and custom associated with the firm, and, for the most part, only slowly changing pre-industrial social orders. Constantly faced with new situations and, not less important, with new individuals, he must find ever new answers to new conditions of existence. Thus does he develop that flexibility, rapidity of reactions, and capacity of adjustment which make up his essence. It should be pointed out in this connection that his capacity to adjust and to feel his way is an immediate necessity for occupational success and hence for social success as well. For in contrast to pre-industrial societies in which the predominant human type was the peasant, whose occupational success depended above all on the size and quality of his land as well as on his industry in working the soil, the majority of modern men depend, for occupational success, on the good will of other men, along with their occupational qualifications. The colleagues and the supervisors at work, with whom one has to get along and whose good will and friendship help determine occupational success, are definitive of the modern work situation. Beyond this, the traits of adaptability and psychological sensitivity to others which are attained and cultivated in this respect are spread even more widely throughout the society by the very nature of certain occupations, e.g., that of the salesman and the manager, and thus become decisive for the great mass of men.

Thus the rough-hewn and angular forms of peasant-status existence are disappearing. In their place appears a new, smoother, more polished human being who is a master of psychology and adjustment. And the danger now arises that the human being will completely lose himself in the adjustment process, that in constantly adjusting he will lose his form, that the only traits of character remaining to him will be the capacity and willingness to adjust, that a human type will dominate which is adroit in everything and knows how to find its way in any situation, an operator, a key that fits all locks, a man who loses his inwardness along with his loss of form. Inwardness, indeed, is bound to form, and without form it flows away and is dried up. Without form man becomes tensionless and flat—he becomes de-internalized.

This danger is all the more pressing because there are now wide spheres of society in which the traditional attitude of man toward religion has been lost. Where there is a confrontation of each individual soul with God, where there is personal responsibility to Him, man is not completely dissolved into society. In faith he possesses a source of strength which enables him to resist the attraction toward complete adjustment which appears in every society. But now that the power of religious faith has been abandoned, the power to resist society is disappearing, and, indeed, resistance is becoming meaningless. Instead of resisting and thereby shaping his own personality, the individual affirms adjustment and takes it as the goal of life. With this, psychiatry, psychology, education, and sociology, which are increasingly becoming the substitutes for religion, must assume the role of giving help. In these, it is believed, one finds methods and means for mastering any of life's situations. It is above all in those inevitable gloomy hours of life, which are now diagnosed as mere states of psychic sickness, that the above-mentioned sciences are expected to give counsel. Through a flood of popular scientific books, especially through that literature from which one learns psychological tricks for occupational success and psychic hygiene, a psychological awareness and sophistication is being spread throughout the whole society and is becoming a universal cultural possession. The artists at adjusting are thus becoming the dominant social types. Their ability to adjust is nearly perfect. Even in the extreme situations of life, in the inevitable situations of grief and need, they know how to protect their own psyches by manipulation and massage.

There is, of course, one respect in which adjustment goes awry. The more man needs connection with a Thou—that is, a close personal tie with his fellow men in a constantly changing and confusedly whirling society—the more he fears lonesomeness and seeks community, and the less he is able to achieve it. For the achievement of a Thou and of community, the method of manipulation fails. Indeed, it is precisely in manipulation that community and Thouness are lacking. Community and Thou-ness cannot be manipulated. They must grow up slowly and can only be achieved through personal involvement (as opposed to essentially impersonal manipulation). But they are preserved and carried sociologically by religious forces and values. Therefore, modern man, being mostly a-religious, is always alone despite his desperate efforts to flee lonesomeness, and despite his extraordinary sociability. Fear of lonesomeness and flight from it, along with the inability to overcome it, are the characteristics of his being.

The modern human type we have described is best observed in the society of the United States, for here we are looking at "the" modern society unalloyed. American society has been shaped and articulated by technology on a scale which is not to be found in any other country in the world. On the basis of the world's highest standard of living, the mass commodities produced by technology have poured forth into the society, are available to everyone, and thus are sociologically relevant for everyone. Spatial and social mobility have reached unheard-of levels. And the basis for this total technologizing of society and the unique progress of a technological industrial economy is to be found not only in favorable initial conditions—the rich supply of land, the vast expanse and market, as well as a fortunate history—but also in the tradition of the country. Industrialism and technology were decisively advanced by all of the factors. The mass migrations brought about by technology could be easily induced in a country of immigrants and adventurous pioneers. Recruitment into new occupational situations was not difficult against the background of a conception of occupation which saw in it primarily an activity for making money, that is, a "job." The movement toward a leveled, middle-class society, which is characteristic of technological society, was inevitably accepted as natural and desirable in a society oriented by the democratic ideal. The principle of competition, which is decisive for industrial society, was already present at the beginning, in that privilege of birth was absent in democratic, pre-industrial American society. Technology itself was greeted as a friend and helper in the task of settling and developing the unlimited expanses of the American continent. Without the railroad, the steamship, the cotton gin, the steam plough, the industrial mass production of axes, or the revolver, the settlement of an entire continent within a few generations would not have been possible.

Apart from this, American society is modern because the characteristically modern enlightenment style of thinking has an unbroken history there and has deeply influenced society. Despite the great prosperity of the churches and their flourishing organizational life, the belief in man and his ability to master all problems of life through rational thought has not been broken.

Religiosity has largely become an attribute of middle-class well-being and a part of the art of adjustment. In other words, where religion is "cultivated," it no longer draws its strength from a relationship to God felt to be existential and unconditioned, but becomes a part of the technique of life. That is, one has religion in order to master the problems of living with its help. Religion becomes religious technique. It becomes goal-directed and thereby loses its authentic source. On the other hand, the sciences we have mentioned, above all psychology and sociology, are increasingly assuming the dominant position. They are to make possible the desiderated adjustment.

In this respect Europe is at a level of development which is just approaching the state of affairs that America has already realized. Europe is thus in no sense becoming a colonial appendage dominated by foreign influence, but is rather completing a process of development toward a technological mass society which America has already carried out. The causes for the retardation of this development are to be sought in the traditions and the situation of Europe. The tradition of estates erected on stable, pre-industrial methods of production offers passing resistance to technology and industrialization. The tough, status-rooted frame of life must be broken up before technological society can arise. Thus, class struggle and social upheaval point to the fate of European society under the onslaught of technology. The phenomenon of class struggle is peculiarly characteristic of a society which was previously articulated on the basis of estates, for only in a society once shaped by the estate principle can a "fourth," or worker, estate develop. On the spiritual level, enlightenment self-confidence in the omnipotence of man has often been shaken, most recently in the bloody storms of the Second World War.

.   .   .

We proceed from the conviction that the cause of the failure of man in modern society, of his dissolution into pure adjustment, is to be found in the loss of transcendence. Only if we can achieve the goal of making transcendence a renewed and active life-defining force throughout the breadth of society can the demonic urge of modern society be effectively resisted. We also believe that in the German spiritual tradition positions have been worked out which could be the starting points for a new religious life and which permit the adoption of a position toward enlightenment which takes its stand on faith.

.   .   .

Here it should be emphatically stated that the author is far from agreeing with the blasts of those Pharisees whose malicious anti-Americanism can only be compared with anti-Semitism. We have tried to make it clear that the phenomena which we are describing are also to be found in Europe, although they are more easily discerned in the United States. The purpose of this work is to oppose certain dehumanizing tendencies of modern society and to sound a warning about them. In this struggle for man the fronts cut across all nations. . . .

4

The American Economy

THE NEED FOR MORE INTENSIVE PLANNING

Gunnar Myrdal

Gunnar Myrdal is the internationally known Swedish economist and student of American society whose book on race relations in the United States, *An American Dilemma* (1944), is a minor classic in its field. He has also written extensively on the American economy from a generically socialist point of view. The present piece very clearly documents the concern of European friends of the United States over signs of stagnation in the American economy that have appeared in recent years. The pace of the economy has in fact picked up considerably since this article was written. But this does not mean that Myrdal would necessarily withdraw his criticisms. In his view, a solid basis of advance depends on a commitment to economic planning and governmental intervention far more extensive than anything American opinion has been willing to accept up to now.

The American economy seems to have settled down to a sequence of recessions, short-lived and inadequate upturns, and periods of stagnation between. If there is any consistent pattern it looks as if the recoveries after the recessions tend to become ever more hesitant and to result in an ever more incomplete re-employment in proportion to the rise in output. I have seen no evidence that would render it probable that the American economy by itself—that is, as a result of the forces now at work in that economy, including present government policies—would get out of this rut.

The famous built-in stabilizers have, until now, prevented the recessions from developing into serious depressions. But such an eventuality cannot be excluded. That a depression would not be permitted to develop into anything like the Great Depression of the thirties but would call forth vigorous government action is a statement that does not satisfy me. The policies should have been applied in time to prevent such a depression. Or rather, as the whole pattern of development now established, even assuming that the recessions

FROM "Getting America Moving," *The New Republic*, Vol. 148, No. 4 (January 26, 1963), pp. 15–20. Reprinted by permission.

will remain mild, is unsatisfactory, government policies should be planned and executed in order to set the economy into an entirely new pattern of rapid, steady growth.

When we discuss developments in underdeveloped countries we are accustomed to conceiving of growth in terms of the rise in national output per head. But when, instead, we measure the rate of growth in the United States, the U.S.S.R., the countries in Western Europe and in the other industrialized regions we are usually less severe and calculate our economic growth quite simply in terms of the increase in national output. This abstention from taking the population development into the calculation of our economic progress is of particular importance in the case of the United States, where the annual population increase is around 1.7 percent, which is a fairly high rate for a rich country. If we properly deflate the average American growth rate in the way we are accustomed to do for underdeveloped countries, the figure for the United States for the last decade comes out at around 1 percent, actually a lower rate than—on a very hazardous statistical basis—we believe is about the one that poor India has realized during its two first five-year plans.

I am inclined to believe that the most important problem in the world today is how to get America out of the automatism of relative economic stagnation. A continuation of the present trend means frustration in its foreign relations as well as in its internal life, which, because of the size and weight of America and the role it has to play, is extremely dangerous. . . .

.   .   .

At present America has good reasons to urge fundamental changes in the policies of its European allies in many and diverse fields. But it has no longer the economic strength for pressing for them effectively. America has even to suppress some of its demands or present them sotto voce. This situation is almost the reverse of the one ten or fifteen years ago. . . . America is in the danger of losing out as the uncontested leader within the Western world, [a danger] which is bound to become even more pronounced if the differences in economic growth rate remain. This I regret. In any case it must be contrary to American ideals and interests.

Before I leave the international implications of the relative economic stagnation in America I must also refer to the fact that even that low rate of economic growth is dependent upon very heavy armament expenditures that swallow up half the federal expenditure budget. This is not a healthy situation for a nation that, as I am convinced, is honestly intent upon trying to reach a disarmament agreement. On an abstract level the economists can argue that a major decrease of these expenditures can easily be compensated; I have myself taken part in one of the conferences of economists holding out this prospect. But we should be aware of the real difficulties implied, if there is not a radical change in the way the American people and Congress look upon the role of government in the economy. The difficulties of an adjustment of the American economy to lower levels of armament expenditures are bigger because the growth rate is so low: in a rapidly growing economy a decrease in the armament expenditures could be taken more in stride. And we should not hide from ourselves the fact that the vested interests, working against an international agreement to decrease armaments substantially, must be much more forceful in an economy with under-utilized capacity.

UNEMPLOYMENT

The low average level of economic growth during the last ten years coincides with a particularly rapid and increasingly rapid technological development which enhances labor productivity. The result is a high and gradually rising level of unemployment. Full-time unemployment now fluctuates around a level of almost 6 percent. This figure will have to be increased by perhaps half again in order to account for the partial unemployment of those workers who are put on short-time employment or who do not bother actively to seek work as jobs are not available. In neither case is the idleness voluntary.

This situation—to which correspond idle plants and machines—is serious as it stands. Add to this that there are several changes under way that, if economic growth is not speeded up, are bound to cause a tendency to even more increased unemployment. With the coming [of] age of the big batches of children born as a reflection of the full employment during and after the war, the labor force will be growing much more rapidly in the decade ahead than in the last one. The technological progress, the revolutionary character of which is stressed by the common use of the term "automation," is accelerating and is now more and more directed upon displacing labor. So far as material products are concerned, a bigger output can be produced with an ever smaller work force. The use of computing machines also will be releasing white-collar workers and people on the lower managerial level.

Somewhat less often observed and commented upon is the tendency of the changes now under way to increase the class chasms in the American society and to stiffen the class structure. The technological progress does not release labor in a uniform way but directs labor demand more and more toward the highly skilled and highly educated. The incidence of unemployment tends increasingly to fall most heavily upon those who for social and economic reasons have less skill and education.

The population development under way gives its peculiar twist to this unfortunate situation. Back in 1950, about 2 million American youths reached 18 years of age; now the figure is 3 million and in 1965 it will be 4 million. In the next decade the age group between 25 and 45 will, on the contrary, increase very little; that between 25 and 30 will actually decrease. It is clear that with prevailing and widespread unemployment a disproportionate part of these young newcomers in the labor market will be among the permanently unemployed or live under a permanent risk of becoming unemployed, unless very much larger facilities for education and training are rapidly provided.

In a situation with such big risks of unemployment, even the trade unions are unwillingly becoming instrumental in increasing that substratum of American workers who are unemployed or have only more or less casual jobs. The process of automation is particularly speedy in sectors of the American economy where there are effective trade unions. These unions are thus forced to press for job security for their own members even when this creates incentives for the employers not to engage new workers. In a situation of growing unemployment, the unions often feel their bargaining strength weakened and find it more difficult to take a consistent and strong stand for what, from the point of view of all American workers and the nation as a whole, is the main interest—full employment. They are in danger of being reduced to protective organizations for a number of separate groups of jobholders, which, even if they are all taken together, only represent a minority, perhaps one quarter of the workers. To an outside observer it seems, when everything is taken into account, almost a miracle that big units of the American trade-union movement have seen it possible to take such a broad-minded and progressive position on national policies as they have done.

During the Great Depression, studies in many Western countries showed that a very large percentage of those unemployed were so-called unemploy-ables. Although these "unemployables" rapidly disappeared when the demand for labor revived during and after the war, we cannot in the present state of affairs have confidence that the same thing would happen now, even if we could suddenly and substantially lift the curve of economic growth. For this time, increased labor demand will be directed primarily toward skilled and educated workers, leaving a larger part of the others out. What is now needed, in addition to an upturn of the economy, is a gigantic educational and train-ing program, in the first instance put at the service of the extraordinarily big batches of young people now entering the labor force.

Meanwhile, as long as the present weak trend of economic growth is main-tained, the group of badly trained and educated workers hit by actual unem-ployment or constantly in danger of becoming unemployed, is growing and increasingly set apart from the main stream of American life. Even with increased unemployment benefits their lives are miserable. Indeed they would still be miserable even if generous proposals were acted upon—that the involuntarily unemployed should be fully, or almost fully, compensated for the lack of jobs. To be idle and to live permanently on doles is unhealthy and destructive for anybody and particularly for young people without much share in the national culture. This tenet of old-fashioned puritanism I believe to be fully borne out by recent social research. Crime, prostitution, and all sorts of shady ways of passing time will thrive, as they did in the slums during the Depression years.

Much of the rising unemployment also falls upon minority groups and implies a serious setback in the process of national integration. The largest and still most disadvantaged minority group is that of the Negroes. From about the beginning of the last war there has been a definite trend toward improved race relations in America, a development which is the more remark-able as until then there had for sixty years been no great change in the status of the Negro in America. An important cause among others of this encour-aging trend was undoubtedly the high level of labor demand that on the whole was sustained until about ten years ago.

But still Negroes are the "last hired and the first fired." Apart from a tiny upper and middle class of professional and business people, mostly thriving behind the remaining walls of prejudice, and a now considerably larger group of skilled and union-protected workers, the majority of Negroes are much poorer and have had less training and education than the average white Americans. They are, consequently, more vulnerable, particularly in the present situation when labor demand is, and must be, more and more turning toward the highly trained and educated.

But to the large number of Negro workers and workers in other dis-advantaged minority groups must be added the poor white people everywhere in America who will also be pressed down in this substratum which is excluded from the prosperity of the nation at large and the progress of the American way of life.

THE PUBLIC NEEDS

The first and obvious policy conclusion is that the government should take measures which can result in economic expansion. This means, generally speaking, that it should cause an increase in aggregate demand. I believe it to be beyond doubt that there has been a deflationary pressure upon the American economy for at least the last ten years, though with some fluctuations. An increase in aggregate demand can be induced by a great variety of possible policy measures. There is an element of sense in the argument that, as the main thing is to get the economy going at full speed, it is not of great importance what particular policy measures are chosen. The fact is that there is a very large volume of crying needs which, if they were translated into effective demand, could sustain rapid economic growth for a long time to come. This cannot be done except by government intervention on a large scale.

One category of such needs is, of course, based on the low levels of living of the fifth of the American people who are officially recognized as falling below the poverty line. Another fifth or more of the population do not share to any substantial extent in the abundance commonly assumed to characterize American society. The affluent society is largely a myth, except for a privileged upper stratum.

There is, however, so much solid truth in the appreciation of the technological revolution under way and of the capacity of the American economy to expand production rapidly in almost every field, if a higher growth rate were permitted, that a rise in the living levels of the underprivileged social strata becomes not only a desideratum from a social point of view, but almost a condition for long-term economic advance. Never in the history of America has there been a greater and more complete agreement between the ideals of economic progress and of social justice.

For the purpose of giving more purchasing power to the poorer sections in American society there are a number of redistributional policy means at disposal. The one that implies least government intervention is, of course, a radical reduction of the tax burden in the lower income brackets. Other means are assistance to organized labor in the weaker sections of the labor market, or increases of the minimum wage level. The high concentration of poverty among certain categories, such as old people, sick people, single mothers, or families with many children, is a strong reason to expand the system of social security, a field where America is still far behind the countries that are most similar to it in basic values.

In some respects the government will have to become more directly involved in providing services that are now not available, or not available on a large enough scale. Thus, as the development of technology directs demand more and more toward trained and educated labor, there is need for a much larger public investment in training and education. Particularly in the field of vocational training, America needs a new philosophy. . . . Such training, as is the case with education in general, should not be left to lead to dead ends but should be instrumental in making it possible for young people to move sidewise to other occupations and upwards to higher responsibilities. In the dynamic phase that America has now entered, this is necessary in order that training shall not be wasted.

At the same time there is an urgent need also for a retraining of older workers in order to prevent the emergence of a group of second-class workers who are permanently unemployed or only casually employed. It should be added that only in an expanding economy is there a real chance of successful efforts at rehabilitating laid-off labor or labor in the danger zone. In a situation of widespread unemployment, the retrained will have difficulties in finding jobs and will slump back in their previous status.

In filling these needs it will be necessary to invest much larger resources in schools and hospitals. But there are many other public investments which are now reasonably neglected. There is no excuse for a rich country to tolerate huge slums in the big cities and lesser ones in the smaller cities at the same time that it allows a large part of its manpower and other productive resources to go to waste.

It is fairly generally recognized by those who have studied the problem that there is a serious and irrational bias against public consumption and investment in America. It is a result of the combination of high-pressure salesmanship for private consumption and traditional suspicion against increasing public budgets. It cannot correspond to what people would really prefer, if they could as readily follow their impulses to buy the means of collective consumption as they can buy private consumers' goods, and if the former were equally well advertised. In the cities, where so much long-term investment is needed to make them really effective as containers of human life and efficient work, this becomes the more serious as now almost the whole population increase goes to swell the number of city dwellers and, in particular, of the big metropolitan districts.

The bearing of my argument so far is that, even if tax cuts can be useful to give a spurt to the economy, sustained economic growth together with many other obvious social objectives will require very substantial increases in public expenditures. . . . The role of the government in the American economy will have to be a rapidly and considerably growing one, particularly as an investor in public facilities and a provider of public services. . . . This growth of the public sector will necessitate ever more careful long-range planning.

BALANCING THE BUDGET

As the primary means for increasing aggregate demand must be decreased taxation and increased public expenditures, the public budget will not be "balanced" in the American sense of this term. At least at the start of an expansionist policy this is clear. Whether it holds good also in later years, when a higher rate of growth and fuller employment have been reached and thus the basis of taxation broadened, is more uncertain. It will depend partly upon the speed by which the government succeeds in increasing public expenditure along the lines suggested, which it must try to do if it wants the rapid growth rate to be sustained.

But the question is not very interesting. The concept of a "balanced budget" in which taxation pays for all public expenditures independently of the character and incidence of taxation and expenditures is an entirely irrational construct, which is nowadays given significance only in American popular and political discussion. What really matters is a "balanced economy," which in different settings—dependent among other things on the size and type of public expenditures and of taxes—may require an "overbalanced," a "balanced," or an "underbalanced" budget. That such a large number of American voters and responsible politicians think in terms of "balancing" the budget is, however, in itself an important fact which decidedly increases the difficulties of rational economic planning and of getting the American economy to expand rapidly and steadily.

A real risk, however, is that a higher growth rate will overstimulate investments, generally or in certain fields, so that the result is an inflationary development, which under certain conditions may come so fast that sooner or later it will have to be broken by causing a recession. This is contrary to the goal of public policy which must be economic growth that is both rapid and steady. To accomplish this objective will require not only careful planning but also the availability of flexible means for controlling the volume of investment. As monetary controls are clumsy and largely ineffective and, as, in particular, the long-term rate of interest in a rapidly expanding economy should be kept low and steady, I would seek policy means in the fiscal sphere, such as taxes adjustable on short notice on energy, on new investment in particular fields, and on consumption. Allowances for capital depreciation as well as for the costs of advertising should also be adjustable. Even if, ideally, such adjustments should be made automatic, reacting to changes in certain indices, their use for stabilizing economic growth would require very much improved long-range planning.

About the risks for inflation I would like to make two general points. First, we now know from recent experiences in many countries that there is no close relation between the rate of economic growth and the rate of inflation. Prices may rise while the economy is lagging, and they may keep steady though it is pushing ahead. Second, in the present stage of American economic development the social effects of a low rate of progress are so grave, particularly in the lower strata, that honesty demands that I should frankly confess that I am prepared to take a moderate rise in prices, if that should be a condition for economic growth.

But I want at once to revert to my first point and assert that I believe the higher utilization of capacity following more rapid growth will tend to lower costs so substantially that inflation is not a condition for economic progress, particularly if the government is prepared to extend its controls over investments and, perhaps, over prices. In regard to price control, I sometimes ask myself whether the American government, which for decades has fought monopoly with such courage and even vehemence by means of legislation and court action and yet failed to prevent a continuous concentration of market power, should not be prepared to tone down its rather fruitless fight against monopoly, but instead ask for a share in controlling administered prices, which are so decisive for the general trend of prices.

In regard to the exchange difficulties, it is clear that the fear of losing gold has been a powerful reason for the unwillingness of the American government to venture on an expansionist policy aimed at getting the American economy going at full speed. On this question I have to declare myself a radical heretic. If the American economy were set on the road to rapid and steady growth, this would by itself change anticipations and make Americans less interested in seeking investment outlets abroad and at the same time induce foreigners to invest more in American securities in order to share in American economic progress. American policy has run into a vicious circle where its anxiety about gold losses induces it to be satisfied with the relative economic stagnation that itself is the main reason for the lack of confidence in the dollar.

.   .   .

LONG-RANGE PLANNING

Among the things that have apparently not changed in America and specifically in Washington is the nearsightedness of politicians and experts; I complained about this twenty years ago in *An American Dilemma*. There is an astonishing number of competent people who can offhand give a detailed and comprehensive analysis of how all important economic indices have recently been moving and how they are likely to move in the months ahead. Everybody is excited about what is going to happen next, who is in and who is out, and who is behind whom. In regard to economic development, an altogether undue interest is attached to when the next recession or the next upturn is going to occur, a matter of very little significance to this country or to the world. I will confess that not even as a shareholder do I take much interest in this sort of pastime.

In regard to the long-range development there is a corresponding lack of interest. Long-range planning is almost altogether neglected. This is true even at the universities. Not only the President and the Congress, but also leaders in business are left without that image of what the future holds in store which is needed for rational action, particularly when it implies long-term investment or other decisions which have consequences far ahead. The negligence at the American universities [in regard to] the long-range prospects and the concentration on short-range issues and also on, by any standards, less important theoretical problems is probably responsible for the conspicuous failure of my distinguished and numerous colleagues to disseminate a reasonable degree of economic understanding to the American people, in spite of the fact that America has a larger college attendance than any other Western country. The superstitions about the balanced budget and the role of gold in the monetary system are cases in point.

What [are] needed are forecasts of what on different assumptions will happen to the American economy in five-, ten-, and twenty-years' time. . . . The economic forecasts should be worked out for alternative rates of growth and for different directions of policy. They will spell out what is possible, what is alternatively necessary to do in order to reach and maintain a postulated growth rate, and what it will imply in terms of employment and the movement of people, educational efforts, investment, and everything else.

Supervision of a type of programing should be a primary function of the President's Council of Economic Advisors. From the point of view of labor utilization in particular, the Department of Labor, the Department of Health, Education, and Welfare, and the new department for urban problems, which the President has proposed but [has] not as yet got the Congress to accept, all will have a primary interest in this type of forecasting and programing, and from their particular angles many other government agencies would also have it. I see no reason why it should not be a concern of many of the distinguished American universities.

I am wondering why the obvious need of this type of econometric exercise has been so relatively neglected in America and more generally why there has been such a shyness to discuss in a more concrete way long-term trends of the economy and the alternative policy choices that are possible. Is it because to the ignorant and prejudiced it has a Russian and Communist smell? But it is rapidly becoming a regular part of government and business planning in all West European countries. Or is it because it is felt that it invites government meddling with the economy? Such a position is out of step with the needs of the time. For, as I have been attempting to show, there is no hope otherwise of getting America to become again a country with a progressive economy, and of saving America from serious damage to its power in foreign relations and to the internal unity of the nation. Giving the government a greater role in the economy without utilizing the superb intellectual resources which America possesses and now disperses on tasks of much less importance is part of the waste in this country of abundance. Only by painting on the wall in definite and concrete figures the opportunities for a change in policies can America be made to wake up to its old ambitions and the new necessities.

THE CONTRADICTIONS OF AMERICAN CAPITALISM
Robert Keller

Robert Keller is a young American intellectual who contributed this article to an international journal published in Great Britain and devoted to the creation of a "democracy of content." His critique of American capitalism is one of the more sophisticated available statements of a non-Communist Marxist point of view that is quite influential among European intellectuals. Keller argues that the present problems of the American economy reflect basic contradictions in the capitalist system, which cannot therefore be removed by Keynesian techniques of fiscal intervention on the part of the state. Hence, unlike Gunnar Myrdal, he concludes that the United States is probably doomed to a long period of economic stagnation that will gradually build up to a major economic and political crisis.

In a series of essays on the American political past published in 1948 [*The American Political Tradition*], Richard Hofstadter gives a trenchant description of the moods prevalent in the United States during the late forties. "The two world wars, unstable booms, and abysmal depression of our time have profoundly shaken national confidence in the future," observes Hofstadter. "During the boom of the twenties it was commonly taken for granted that the happy days could run on into an indefinite future; today there are few who do not assume just as surely the coming of another severe economic slump."

The passage of a decade has not removed a general fear of war and social instability in the United States. If anything, insecurity and lack of "national confidence in the future" have become more prevasive with the "nuclear age," the "missile age" and the "cold war." But a severe economic slump comparable to the Great Depression of the thirties still has not appeared during the long postwar period, and it might be argued that on one score—notably, the condition and future of the American economy—public insecurity has abated a good deal since the forties. In fact, a mindless euphoria toward economic problems has been cultivated by almost every agency for shaping public opinion. The American people are repeatedly assured that, in the words of General Eisenhower, "one such fear—the fear of a paralyzing depression—can be safely laid away." Millions of Americans have been persuaded to believe that the postwar years mark the ascent of a "new capitalism" in the United States, a system that holds the promise of indefinite advances in output, consumption, and well-being. This view is held not only by a large section of the public, but by the great *bulk* of American economists. In both cases, the economy is conceived to be an impersonal gadget—a "new," "shiny," "booming," or "zooming" machine with "built-in stabilizers," "a flexible interest rate," and a "fast government pick-up" that invidiously recalls the advertising literature on the perennially "new" American motor car. At worst, we need only tinker with the thing, now and then, and the machine will run better than ever.

. . .

The first signs that the American economy was something more than a motor car steered by a benign state-power began to appear in the third postwar decline: the crisis of 1957–58. This crisis, like earlier ones, was not wholly unexpected. The economic horizon had been darkening for close on a year, and warnings of a decline had been posted for months in advance of its occurrence by the more sophisticated business press. The crisis "officially" began in August, 1957, with a decline in sales, followed in the next month by a fall in the Federal Reserve Board's index of industrial production, and in subsequent months by declining inventories and employment, until by June, 1958, unemployment reached a postwar peak of 5.5 million. This certainly took everyone by surprise. The depth of the crisis, however, was by no means its sole claim to distinction. The most important features of the crisis began to appear with a recovery in the late summer of 1958. For the first time since the end of the Second World War, a rapid, albeit partial, upswing in output left behind a large number of unemployed industrial workers, a substantial

FROM "The American Economy," *Contemporary Issues,* Vol. 10, No. 38 (November–December, 1959), pp. 28–60. Reprinted by permission of Contemporary Press, P.O. Box 2357, Church Street Station, New York, New York 10008.

residue of unused plant capacity, stagnation in investment after a decline in capital outlays of nearly 22 percent, and a price structure that not only failed to bend before the crisis, but even advanced during some of its worst phases.

Although recovery has been carried still further during 1959, the components of the economy have advanced very unevenly. Output, consumption, and even employment have surged up to, and in some cases surpassed, pre-crisis levels. While overall unemployment figures have been reduced, chronic unemployment has not disappeared from some of the most important industrial regions of the United States; investment, particularly in new plants, has been weak and faltering; and automation threatens to make serious inroads into jobs. A good deal of the time that the economists ordinarily allot to an upsurge before the next crisis seems to have passed away without removing lingering features of the earlier crisis. Should these features disappear in coming months, there is good reason to doubt that they will be absent for any great length of time.

The point is that the third postwar crisis is certainly not just a passing downturn marring a general economic advance, as most economists would have the public believe. The crisis has confronted the United States with long-range contradictory forces and tendencies of a downward nature. It matters little whether these tendencies assume a sharp form now or some years later. The 1957–58 crisis has shown that they are at work in the American economy and has brought them from beneath the surface of postwar economic appearances to a foremost place in the realities of the times. In short, the crisis is a portent of general stagnation, if not an overall decline, in the coming years. To evaluate this new trend requires that the forces converging toward stagnation and decline be placed in sharp relief against the superficiality and euphoria evident in postwar economic literature.

.   .   .

[The] laws of capitalist development are internally contradictory: the very conditions that promote the expansion of capitalist industry and output drive large numbers of proletarians out of industry and thereby inhibit the expansion of the market. Increasing productivity yields unemployment and relative overproduction. This self-limiting character of capitalist development was first brought to light by Marx and Engels.

.   .   .

For Marx this law is the "absolute general law of capitalist accumulation" —the law which is the general conclusion of the attempt to concretize capitalist development analysed in Volume I of *Capital*. Productivity, continually increased by competition and the process of capital accumulation, tends to reduce more and more of the population to an "industrial reserve army"— to an unemployed [stratum]—for which there is no longer any room in the economy. As this process becomes a dominant feature of the economy, it yields the increasing misery of the working class as a whole. The law, to be sure, does not operate without modifications. "Like all other laws it is modified in its workings by many circumstances"—circumstances, and indeed a context, which Marx obviously could not foresee nearly a century ago. Nonetheless the compulsion in capitalist accumulation to increase the output of commodities with less and less labor, thereby tending to create a growing stratum of chronically unemployed workers and contracting the market relative to production, is one of the touchstones of economic analysis.

To what extent are the circumstances which modified the working of this law inherent features of the American economy, presumably making for a "new" or "progressive capitalism," and to what extent are these circumstances uniquely conjunctural events of a limited and external nature? How have they operated thus far and what is their weight in arresting the broad trends described by Marx? The answers to these questions are clearly of vital importance in judging the future of the American economy.

.　　.　　.

Until the twenties, the American economy advanced on the strength of positive factors created by the prewar epoch of a broad capitalist upswing— notably, new industries whose expansion compensated for the exhaustion of older ones, and a general accumulation process that created more jobs than it reduced by growing productivity. Within a decade, all factors making for economic growth were exhausted. By 1925, the auto and electrical industries had advanced as far as the postwar institutional standard of living permitted. With growing productivity moving against a lagging market, the economy plunged into a decade of chronic crisis.

The boom of 1946–48 advanced primarily on the strength of wartime savings. These savings were induced not merely by increased income, but above all by shortages caused by a long war. The expenditures which created the boom covered a wide spectrum of economic output, ranging from consumers' to producers' durables, from residential to plant construction. By 1949, the effect of these varied expenditures as prime movers of economic expansion was exhausted. It is noteworthy that, with the exception of construction, never again in the ten years that followed were expenditures of this kind able to vitalize the economy for any great length of time without artificial supports like high government outlays or precariously loose credit.

The Korean War boom advanced primarily on high federal expenditures. As we shall see elsewhere, there are good reasons for believing that this source too has been exhausted as a means of long-range growth. Finally, the last boom—the boom of 1955–56—rode essentially on installment credit and capital accumulation. By comparison with earlier sources of economic upswing, these factors proved to be the least stable of all. If anything, the investment boom of 1956 has finally brought to the surface all the problems of an accumulation process that led the American economy into the Great Depression of the thirties.

Today, these problems can be described with brutal concreteness. On the one side, an estimated 700,000 to 850,000 new workers enter the American economy annually. This figure is net. It takes into account the normal outflow due to age, retirement, and death. On the other side, productivity per man-hour worked in nonagricultural industries has been increasing during 1947–56 at an annual rate of 3.3 percent, and in agriculture at 6 percent. In terms of 1958 output, an increase in productivity of 3 percent in 1959 would mean the loss of 500,000 jobs in manufacturing industries alone. If this rate of productivity were extended to the economy as a whole, 2 million jobs would completely disappear.

The upsurge of postwar productivity naturally invites some sort of comparison with the "prosperity decade" of the twenties; and despite the comfortable view that the two periods are dissimilar in many ways, they have in common an accumulation process and a degree of overcapacity that may well override their differences. Gabriel Kolko, whose economic vignettes in the liberal weeklies are often more pointed than most professional "studies" of the economy, warns that the employment of production workers in 1948–58 [fell] at a faster rate than in 1919–29. During 1919–29, manufacturing output increased 40 percent, and employment dropped 2 percent. From 1948–58, however, output increased 35 percent—but employment of production workers declined 6 percent. This problem has been in the making for a much longer time than is ordinarily supposed. Official data show a steady rise in chronic unemployment as a percentage of the labor force over the past decade. In the upswing of 1952–53, about 3 percent of the labor force was unemployed; by 1955–57, 4 percent of the labor force was unemployed. The upswing of 1958–59 is expected to raise this rate to 5 percent at the very least, and the number of chronically unemployed may fluctuate around 4 million. This, of course, assumes that economic conditions will get no worse than they are.

But are they likely to remain as they are? In the absence of state intervention, the prospect that the economy will surge much beyond the last postwar peaks is very doubtful. Many key industries that underlay earlier postwar booms are believed to have advanced as far as they can go. Their peaks were reached years ago and have not been surpassed since. The "recessionary trends of today are only the latest results of a much longer-term and more profound drift," notes a study by the Conference on Economic Progress.

"Our economy needs to grow about 4.5 percent a year in real terms to use our growing resources fully. This rate of growth was actually exceeded on the average during the six-year period after World War II. But during 1953–57, the average annual growth rate in real terms slowed down to 2.7 percent. In 1957, we advanced only 2.1 percent.

In heavy industry, recent increases in productivity have removed all hope that large numbers of unemployed created by the 1957–58 crisis will be rehired. The auto industry supports this pessimistic conclusion with very dramatic illustrations. As early as the spring of 1957, for example, the Chrysler Corporation could produce the same number of cars with 110,000 workers that it made in 1955 with 130,000 workers. Over 18 percent of the corporation's labor force had become redundant in two short years. A *Time* magazine survey of re-employment in the late summer of 1958 shows how much the crisis added to the number of unemployed resulting from the earlier rises in productivity.

Ford says that it will roll into full production with 106,000 workers, down from last year's 140,000. While General Motors was mum on its payroll, the United Auto Workers estimated that G.M. will swing into full production of the 59's with 300,000 to 325,000 hourly rated workers versus an average of 392,000 in the last three years. Chrysler will begin 59,000 versus last year's 100,000.

For the economy as a whole, output increased sharply late in 1958, but employment lagged far behind. A New York *Times* survey of sixteen big industrial cities showed that "some of the country's major mass production centers are haunted by the prospect of permanent pools of jobless workers as a carry-over from the recession." In December,

. . . Only 30 percent of the decline in non-farm employment had been recovered since the low point last April. This was so even though the gross national product —the sum of all goods and services—was virtually back to its pre-recession high. . . . The number of people with jobs . . . was 3,200,000 short of the pre-recession high a year and a half earlier. (January 25, 1959)

.   .   .

For years, Keynesian economists have taught American schoolboys that, during rising economic conditions, consumption tends to increase less than income, i.e., people do not spend their entire income for consumption (their "propensity to consume" declines) as the economy begins to approximate full employment. To avert a crisis, say the Keynesians, there must be an increased rate of real investment. In short, the "propensity to invest" must advance to a point where it closes the gap created by a declining "propensity to consume."

Part of the truth, however, seems to lie in the dialectic of the accumulation process itself. The self-expansion of capital slowly creates the conditions for its contraction by diminishing the amount of labor required for production. At a certain point, this diminution becomes the prevailing effect of accumulation. Far from merely filling a gap between consumption and income, the tendency of investment since the First World War has been to create gaps between the industrial labor force and employment—finally, between the output of commodities and the standard of living. The movement toward greater unemployment has been interrupted rather than eliminated by wars, spurts of industrial expansion created by and following the wars, huge government outlays of funds, and wide swings of consumer credit. Yet with each step taken to avert unemployment, the situation grows tighter and tighter.

.   .   .

[Keller now evaluates the effects of monopoly and oligopoly on the economic growth.]

Monopoly arises from competition itself. The struggle for survival between atomized, competing capitalists tends to yield fewer and more centralized enterprises. As early as the 1860's, Marx observed that the original "splitting-up of the total capitals into many individual capitals" at the inception of bourgeois society "is counteracted by their attraction. . . . The laws of this centralization of capitals, or of the attraction of capital by capital, cannot be developed here. A brief hint at a few facts must suffice. The battle of competition is fought by cheapening of commodities. The cheapness of commodities depends, ceteris paribus, on the productiveness of labor, and this again on the scale of production. Therefore, the larger capitals beat the smaller. . . ."

What needs only to be added to complete Marx's train of thought is that after the centralization of capital reaches a point where a large measure of control over industry is possible, competition by means of cheapening the price of commodities steadily gives way to administered prices. Owing to the enormous size of one or two corporations and the high percentage of output they control in any given branch of industry, the earlier interplay of supply and demand in the "free market" is supplanted by fixed prices maintained by a grip on supply. This is precisely what began to happen toward the late 1890's in many areas of the American economy.

. . .

By degrees a situation arose which stood at variance to traditional conceptions of the old "free trade" days. Administered prices, high productivity, and reductions in the break-even point of costs yielded economic stagnation and chronic unemployment on the one side, and fairly good profits for the more centralized industries on the other. In autos, for example, with "the exception of Ford and Studebaker, the record for the Depression decade was exceptionally good." General Motors earned 36 percent on its invested capital between 1927 and 1937, an average which this giant concern seldom exceeded after the Second World War. Steel, although burdened by very inefficient methods and forms of business organization, nonetheless did fairly well. By 1937 the industry as a whole reached a rate of return just about equal to what it had acquired in 1928, a boom year during the twenties. Machinery, electrical equipment, and agricultural implements had rates of profit on net worth that were as good in 1936 and 1937 as those in the twenties. Productivity continued to rise. In autos, the index of labor needs per unit decreased from 74.1 in 1930 to 67.8 [in 1937], or about 8.5 percent. Those very same years, however, saw unemployment at 15 percent of the civilian labor force.

The forces making for this kind of stagnation [were] not arrested by the Second World War. The war and its aftermath [saw] far greater industrial centralization, a firmer grip on the price structure, and serious overcapacity.

. . .

Whether sharply rising productivity eventually gives rise to mass unemployment may seem debatable. It is possible to envisage a point where so much more can be produced with so few workers that unemployment will grow even if prices fall. Recent advances in automation suggest that rising productivity has become a source of crisis in its own right. However, with the centralization of industry and with monopoly-administered prices, rising productivity now acts directly to produce more unemployment. Since higher productivity and monopoly arise from the bowels of the capitalist economy, it becomes rather meaningless to give priority to one over the other. What distinguishes the past few decades from the last century is the coalescence of both into the crucial economic syndrome of our times.

The interplay of rising productivity and monopoly has two aspects. From the standpoint of an upswing, rising productivity and capital accumulation result in overcapacity. Profits and investment tend to increase at a faster rate than mass income, partly because productivity (as recent studies by the National Bureau [of Economic Research] indicate) makes its greatest gains during upswings, partly because administered prices tend to slow up the rate of increase in mass consumption. Wages lag far behind profits and investment....

From the standpoint of a downswing, the depression during the thirties shows that the centralized industries dominate the decline. These enterprises now manipulate prices, costs, and output in a completely negative way. Once a certain plateau is reached after the lowest depths of a crisis, stagnation proves to be profitable and even supplies these corporate elements with a measure of economic security that they could have scarcely known during the twenties and earlier periods. The crisis removes fears of reckless growth, overcapacity, and sudden upsurges by competitors riding on the possibilities opened by a boom. The mid-thirties saw a degree of industrial control, domestic and international cartelization, in short, a festering "stability" amidst widespread destitution, that had never been witnessed before. . . .

Can the federal government counteract these tendencies and promote further economic development?

This question has become the key one of our day. The real gross national product of the United States must increase at a sufficient rate to absorb the net increase in the labor force without any decline in the standard of living. Liberal economists estimate this growth to be at an annual rate of 4.5 to 5 percent. More conservative estimates, based on historical performance, assert that the growth should be about 3.6 percent. This would probably not yield "full employment," but it would be regarded as "satisfactory." Be that as it may, since 1929 it has become plain that American capitalism, without state intervention, could average neither a 4.5 nor a 3.6 percent rate of increase in the real gross national product. Any overall rate of increase has been rendered possible in recent decades by high levels of government expenditures. It has thus seemed that since these expenditures prevented a chronic crisis, the federal government need only continue to spend more to prevent crises in the future. As one leading fiscal advisor suggests, if the gross national product increases at an annual rate of 5 percent and federal expenditures remain at 18 percent of the gross national product, it will be possible to increase the federal budget by $5 billion a year without raising taxes. The $5 billion a year would act as a sort of fiscal prophylaxis against crises.

The impact of federal expenditures on the economy, however, has varied much too greatly to be resolved into a simple formula. Very sharp declines in federal spending, of course, would make for an economic crisis. This occurred in 1953–54. To remove the present plateau of federal expenditures would obviously plunge the United States into a disastrous crisis within a few weeks. On the other hand, only sharp increases in outlays make for an economic boom. These increases were initiated in 1942 and 1951, each lasting for only a few years. It cannot be emphasized too strongly that the postwar upsurge of the American economy depended primarily on these two great impulses. What is interesting about the current period is that new impulses making for a boom are as difficult to conceive as a return to Hoover's "balanced budget" notions of 1930.

. . .

Sharp increases in federal expenditures cannot continue indefinitely. At the very least they would soon yield a national debt whose servicing charges would exceed the expenditures of all other government purchases combined, not to mention a staggering redundancy of military goods and eventually a paralyzing tax level. This "alternative" obviously belongs to sophomoric economics. An episodic impulse, in turn, would create the problem of absorbing the output created by the impulse once it were removed. At present levels of industrial output, not only would the impulse have to be stronger, but the problem of overcapacity it would yield would easily be greater than the economic stagnation it might overcome. The problem of federal expenditures has thus entered into a strange twilight zone where the emphasis is placed not on massive but moderate increases in spending, on selective outlays during a downswing followed by cuts during an upswing. Whatever debate has grown up around the spending issue, of late, centers on "how much," "when," and "where."

In this twilight zone, the economists tend to make very questionable assumptions. The most important of these assumptions is that a few billions of dollars "stragetically placed" can make the difference between a crisis and a boom. The economy is conceived to be sufficiently dynamic to require a catalyst in the form of increases in federal expenditures to keep things going. The error lies in a gross misplacement of general conceptions. If a crisis arises in a period of general upswing, it is probably due to dislocations which a few billions here and there may help to remove. The problem will not be over-capacity or growing chronic unemployment, but rather excessive inventory accumulation and credit dislocations. Such crises were known in the past, and they can probably be remedied by selective federal expenditures should they occur in the future. But if the gas has been turned off and the economic pot is not boiling, a lighted match will not replace the gas. A few billions here and there can only slow up a generally downward movement; it cannot change the movement itself or remove the basic forces at work.

.   .   .

At a time when so much is being written about a "new capitalism" that lends itself to close regulation and control, it may be well to emphasize that none of the basic contradictory tendencies within the "older" capitalism have been removed. Stagnation and contraction in capitalism are generated precisely by the self-expansion of capital. The very growth of capital creates the conditions for its decline. While state support may yield many significant economic gains for a time, the expansion it generates finally serves to heighten the contradictions within the system. The effects of state support are then increasingly paralyzed by all the traditional problems of capitalist expansion. Short-run gains are eventually paid for by long-run disasters.

.   .   .

But . . . the whole movement downward is slow. What faces the United States is not an acute crisis, but the closing of a perspective. Government expenditures are still high enough to keep a crisis from turning into a wild downward spiral like 1929–33—although such a spiral could occur if the government acted too late at its onset. There are strong reasons for believing, however, that these expenditures cannot prevent a period of overall decline. And this may be enough, with the tremors of the nuclear and missile age, to change the present mood of social and political indifference into a deep disquiet. With a growing awareness of the irrationalities that are slowly paralyzing the present economic system, the American people may well be foremost in turning the vast resources of their continent and industry into an economy based on human needs.

5

American Foreign Policy

THE LIMITED AMERICAN COMMITMENT TO EUROPEAN DEFENSE

Pierre M. Gallois

The French journal in which this article appeared is the organ of diplomats, statesmen, and military leaders who generally assume a conservative and nationalist position on questions of foreign policy. Its author, General Pierre M. Gallois, a military adviser to President de Gaulle, attempts to show that European countries can no longer rely on American guarantees to deter the Russians from aggression. In his opinion, the only effective guarantee is unequivocal American commitment to massive retaliation of the sort that existed in the Dulles era. But the trend in recent American defense policies he thinks, points to a desire on our part to have a "choice" of responses where European interests are concerned. Thus Gallois seems to imply his approval of De Gaulle's idea of independent national nuclear forces.

The new team which directs the White House has been profoundly affected by the evolution of armament technology.

The doctrine of President Kennedy was gradually shaped by studies of foreign policy which, whether conducted at Harvard or at Santa Monica (RAND Corporation), were carried out in the light of the scientific and technological progress of recent years. And the outcome was to be a complete overturning of the conceptions of men like General Marshall or John Foster Dulles, and thus the reversal of a foreign policy on which so many peoples had based their security.

In 1958, the United States was still tied by treaties of assistance to some forty-four countries containing 350 million people. Four years earlier, Secretary of State John Foster Dulles had explicitly formulated the unconditional nature of this commitment and the scope of the guarantees provided when

FROM "La Nouvelle Politique extérieure des Etats-Unis et la sécurité de l'Europe," *Revue de Défense Nationale,* 19ᵉ Année (April, 1963), pp. 566–93. Translated by the editor with permission.

he specified that in local situations, that is to say outside American territory, there could be no question of confronting the armed masses of the adversary with classic weapons, and that aggression had to be discouraged by the threat of "massive retaliation." But for the last two years the new American Administration has been saying exactly the opposite.

Why? What has occurred to rule out, in this fashion, the policy of total guarantee so generously accorded, for so many years, to all the allies of the United States? What reasons have moved American leaders to abandon an attitude which corresponded both to the power and the mission of America?

It is the vast revolution in science and armament technology which has reversed everything.

No doubt, at the time Mr. Dulles left the scene, America had lost the atomic monopoly, and the main advantage which she possessed at the time of the signing of the North Atlantic Treaty no longer existed nine years later. But if the sharing of the atomic monopoly ended inequality in the matter of the explosive itself, it still left America with the power of striking the U.S.S.R. without being herself within the range of the Soviets, who were at that time incapable of delivering serious blows against the territory of the United States. In the three years from 1959 to 1962, in the course of those forty months which seem to have been decisive for the next two or three decades, a relation of forces which was thought to be enduring became questionable.

Four new events, three of which result from technological facts, were at the origin of this strategic and political revolution. . . .

The first of these four events is the development and spread of missiles with nuclear warheads.

Now the United States suddenly found itself in the same strategic position as all the European countries that have so long been the theatre of major conflicts. Since the existence of ballistic missiles, one can say that there is hardly any difference between the six and seven minutes that are needed for a rocket launched from the U.S.S.R. to reach a target situated in Western Europe and the thirty or thirty-five minutes that it would take for another of these Soviet rockets to complete a trajectory ending in California or Texas.

.   .   .

Previously, to participate in a world war and to play a decisive role in it meant no more, at worst, than the loss of an expeditionary force. Today, the risk that must be taken is to be wiped off the map in a few hours.

.   .   .

[*Gallois here takes up the development of low-yield, tactical atomic weapons which, he argues, vastly increases the danger that local, limited wars will escalate into full-scale atomic conflicts.*]

The second fact, that is the spread of low caliber atomic weapons, combines with the first fact, that is the vulnerability of the United States to Soviet ballistic missiles to rule out any conflict that, begun outside the United States, could lead to the destruction of American territory—and of Soviet territory—whenever the stakes in that conflict, important as they may be (as, for example, Western Europe) are nonetheless not commensurate with the scale of this disaster.

The point, then, is to make this sort of thing impossible. Withdrawal of the "rungs" of the atomic ladder leading to an exchange of strikes between the United States and the Soviet Union becomes an urgent measure. Thus, two years ago Henry Kissinger had already proposed that in Western Europe tactical atomic weapons be grouped under a single command and placed to the "rear" so that their use would depend on a "deliberate decision" and not on the necessities of combat.

Subsequently, the American administration wished to go much further and, if possible, to withdraw these weapons from the soil of Western Europe which would then be protected only by purely conventional forces.

Everyone knows that these views are devoid of any military basis and that such arrangements would seal the fate of Europe.

Yet it should be pointed out that many Europeans, understanding little of their own security imperatives, are subscribing to the White House's new conceptions. Through its ministers and through the press, Washington, like the U.S.S.R. itself at the time of the Stockholm appeal, is exploiting the revulsion inspired by nuclear weapons to give certain Europeans, who are particularly naive on this matter, a glowing picture of the benefits of a purely conventional defense. Thus, Western Europe is gradually losing the advantage which it used to have of being assimilated to American territory itself, that is, to a zone of the world for the protection of which the supreme risk would avowedly be taken.

This is why President Kennedy himself could say that, concerning the defense of Europe, he no longer wished to be confronted with the alternative of capitulation or general war but wanted a "choice" of means, including, naturally, capitulation. It is the word "choice" that cannot be accepted by Europeans who are aware of the laws of the nuclear age.

If the territory of the United States were gravely menaced, the government in Washington would not "choose"; it would strike, and with all the means in its power.

From the moment the President of the United States declares to Premier Khrushchev that in matters of Western European security, and more particularly of the security of each of the countries of Western Europe taken separately, he wishes to be free to choose his mode of conduct, the security of Europe is deeply compromised.

That is, the American guarantee has become conditional instead of unconditional as formerly, and in consequence it is dubious under certain circumstances.

. . .

The submarine and the Polaris type ballistic missile constitute the third of the technical factors in this strategic revolution.

As long as weapons of atomic reprisal on both sides took the form of ballistic missiles on their launching platforms or buried in their concrete silos, it was still possible to plan an aggression that would be more or less rational. Knowing the emplacement of these missiles, the assailant could envisage destroying them before they were launched against him.

. . .

During the period when "counterforce" strategy could be realized, it was even possible to guarantee a friendly country, or a group of allied states, since the guaranteeing power could hope to annihilate the missiles or bombers of the adversary before their explosive heads were launched against his territory.

It is thus that the submarine with "Polaris" missiles . . . has taken the last appearance of rationality from thermonuclear war.

If the United States has at its disposal a fleet of missile submarines which today and for some years to come are nearly indestructible, at least simultaneously, it is reasonable to think that the Soviets are working in the same direction and will likewise have a submarine fleet as invulnerable to American antisubmarine weapons as American submarines are to Soviet antisubmarine weapons.

It follows that neither of these two countries can continue a counterforce strategy with respect to the other, and that each must accept peaceful coexistence with its principal adversary or else envisage national suicide.

· · ·

And this is the final bankruptcy of the systems of collective defense on which the Western world still essentially depends.

· · ·

Two years ago, at Washington's insistence, the Supreme Commander of the Allied Forces in Europe began to speak of a "pause." The "pause" was another aspect of the policy of circumspection adopted by the United States with respect to the defense of Europe. Not only was there no longer any question of a massive atomic response against any aggressor threatening, in one manner or another, any NATO territory, but the point now was to add a supplementary restraint above and beyond the idea of a response "adapted" to the threat. The idea was to renounce the use of nuclear weapons until after a period of reflection which, it was hoped, would have a salutary effect on the aggressor. In essence, Moscow was assured that the West would not reply atomically to an attack by Soviet forces. If the West did finally resort to the new weapons, it would only be from despair, with the enemy accentuating his pressure because the delay accorded did not dissuade him from prosecuting his design. Also it would very likely be done only after consultations among the allies, indeed, only after negotiation with the adversary himself.

Reassuring in appearance, this formula is in fact most dangerous. Under pretext of reducing the risks of premature utilization of the atom, it destroys the power to deter by assuring the opposing party that it runs practically no risk of coming to a test of strength.

Thus, gratuitously and without compensation, the "pause" envisaged by Washington accords the adversary a vast zone of maneuver within which he knows that he can appear as an aggressor without running any serious risk because his opponent prevents it. If such a "pause" had ever become a reality, who could have prevented the Soviets from attempting an "operation" on Hamburg or from forcibly occupying territories theoretically guaranteed by NATO, free to speculate on the preliminary conditions, set by the Allies themselves for the use of their atomic weapons.

· · ·

[The "contradictions" of American policy Gallois particularly concentrates on are the plan for a fleet of atomically armed submarines subject to multi-

lateral NATO control and the withdrawal of missiles from Turkey and Italy on the grounds that the weapons there were obsolescent.]

It might even be considered that if an atomic force of this sort were really "multilateral" so that several allied nations had rights with regard to its employment, it would be totally paralyzed; and being inoperative, it could not constitute a danger nor overly engage the United States. By counting on divergencies of view among a too numerous group of cooperators with obviously different interests, a force that could not be used was being established. Thus, despite the appearance of a certain decentralization of nuclear control and of concessions made to the national pride of European countries who have renounced the atom, the proposal following the Nassau agreements also furnished a solution suiting the concerns of Washington. If the projected atomic force were not politically multilateral, it was considered enough to associate the allies in "plans for atomic operations." But the corresponding force was neutralized by placing it under strict American control. Thus, there was every guarantee against the presumed dangers of American atomic commitment on the European continent. . . .

Although the motives of this offer are clear enough, the question only concerned a proposal submitted for discussion. On the other hand, the Cuba affair, and then the Bahamas meeting, have led to an actual American atomic disengagement in Turkey and Italy. To be sure, the whole thing was presented officially and in the press as a "modernization." In reality, the Turks and the Italians have exchanged a weapon of deterrence for a shadow of security. This is why: Let us take the case of Turkey. As long as there were deployed on Turkish soil some fifteen Jupiter rockets placed under dual control (American and Turkish), no potential aggressor could take the risk of invading Turkish territory (by conventional means) without fearing that these rockets would be used against him. They were, of course, under dual control and could not be fired without agreement of the government in Washington. But, since each of these Jupiter rockets is capable of demolishing an agglomeration of extended breadth, it would have been mad to speculate on their nonutilization. Who could have known but if, in the panic of defeat, the detachment of Turkish technicians would not have managed to get control of the "second key," and how could one have been sure in all cases that these rockets would not have carried out their function whether Washington consented or not? No plan of aggression against Turkish territory could have ignored the existence of these rockets, obsolete as they might have been, and it is quite evident that any attack against Turkey would have had to be preceded by the destruction of the fifteen Jupiters, a destruction made relatively easy by the fact that these rockets were set up in the open air on their launching platforms and that their emplacements were perfectly known.

But the aggressor would have had to take a double risk. The first did not consist only in violating the frontier but also in striking Turkish territory in the center of the country. The second and much graver risk would have been to take the initiative of spilling American blood and of destroying the rockets as well as American and Turkish technical personnel.

By substituting submarines with Polaris rockets for the Jupiters, Washington announces that it is modernizing its methods of reprisal and the Turkish government cannot but acquiesce. In reality, by placing its weapons of reprisal on the sea, Washington eases the task of the aggressor. He no longer has to take the initiative of first striking Turkish territory and no longer risks spilling American blood. Conversely, it is now incumbent on the American government to strike first and to strike atomically.

. . .

President Kennedy and his entourage have understood well the characteristics of the nuclear era in which they must live as well as their role as guarantor for the security of the world. They well know, however, that if the responsibility for maintaining a nuclear arsenal is not shared, they are obliged to accept the national deterrence forces of their friends and not to find ways of destroying them!

But if the Kennedy team had clearly seen the problems posed by the security of Europe in the nuclear epoch and in the face of an adversary heavily provided with massive weapons of destruction, they would not have inaugurated his term by demanding the increase of forces armed solely in a conventional fashion.

One knows the theme: unlike his predecessor, President Kennedy does not wish to be confronted in Western Europe with the famous dilemma; either atomic war or capitulation. He wants to have time to reflect and the capacity to choose the mode of his response. We have seen, in the preceding pages, the significance of such a policy.

. . .

The reason [for all his unsatisfactory recommendations] is simple: the leader of the Western coalition is trying to reconcile the irreconcilable. He refuses to take for his country the formidable risks now inherent in any alliance placed under the sign of the atom, but at the same time, not daring to accept the logical consequences of the new situation, he proposes substitute solutions which are ineffective, dangerous, and usually unrealizable because they are unacceptable to any country other than the United States.

If there were still time, it would be preferable to go back to the policy of the preceding Administration and return to unconditional commitments in Western Europe.

. . .

ILLUSION AND REALITY
IN AMERICAN CLAIMS TO LEADERSHIP
Editors of Le Fédéraliste

Le Fédéraliste is an Italo-French review devoted to the idea of a federalist international order and moderately neutralist on immediate questions of foreign policy. The editors are clearly sympathetic to the foreign policy of the Kennedy Administration, which they find more democratic and liberal than that of his predecessors. They are concerned, however, that the United States has continued to insist on a position of world leadership which we can no longer constructively maintain because of our relative decline in power, and they believe that responsibility for creating a peaceful world order must now be broadened and democratized. They also warn that so long as this claim to leadership persists it must appeal to nationalist biases in American opinion that tend to weaken our internal democracy.

The policy of containment consists in a commitment to use military means in any part of the world where the adversary power would expand if one were not to intervene. What is involved, then, is an extremely simplistic policy. It is based on the principle that one must use one's own power to check that of others, and as its instrument it mechanically adopts a purely military principle. It is based on the belief that all world situations can be maintained by means of the simple military principle and that one should therefore confront each country with the choice between America and Russia, and impose adherence to a military treaty. This policy at least partially succeeded, but its success depended on a peculiar conjunction of temporary circumstances. At the end of the Second World War, the United States, as Kennedy has recognized, enjoyed two impermanent monopolies: the monopoly of nuclear weapons, and the possibility of sending considerable economic aid abroad. These two elements account for the success of the containment policy. It does not involve, therefore, an active policy which envisages a line of development designed for maximum exploitation of American power and the power of her allies, but a policy which exclusively exploits the fact that the adversary power cannot move because the United States possesses the two previously mentioned monopolies. . . .

That is why the containment policy was successful only where the monopoly of atomic weapons and economic aid was important; and they were important only in Western Europe. Where situations are more fluid, where one cannot intervene militarily, where there is no economy to be reconstructed by injecting dollars, the United States is losing instead of winning. The containment policy did not succeed in maintaining America's advantage. Moreover, the policy is such that, in all situations which call for a spirit of initiative and in all the evolving and developing areas, the Soviet Union is gaining the advantage. And this state of things is greatly aggravated because America's two monopoly positions are rapidly vanishing. The atomic monopoly is completely finished, and that of economic aid is also in the process of disappearing (although at a proportionally slower pace). And as these two monopoly situations disappear, the containment policy reveals the full dimensions of its weakness.

. . . . .

In the course of his electoral campaign Kennedy directly attacked the containment policy. He could easily show that, in a situation where the competition between the United States and the U.S.S.R. involved, in his

FROM "Les Limites de la politique étrangère américaine," *Le Fédéraliste,* 5ᵉ Année, No. 1 (May, 1963), pp. 3–21. Translated by the editor with permission.

opinion, the survival of liberty, American policy had produced a weakening of the power of the United States and an augmentation of Russia's.

.   .   .

In effect, Kennedy has worked out a scheme of foreign policy which, at first glance, seems to be coherent. To begin with, he is aware that the two American monopolies of which we have previously spoken have come to an end. Consequently, he is conscious of the fact that America can no longer be satisfied with a static policy, but needs to pursue an active policy since nothing is accomplished automatically. It must be said that this realism enables Americans to see the situation as it is, and it is often noted that there is in Kennedy some aspect of that Churchillian spirit which consists in forcing his country to confront the reality of the situation, and not allowing it to hide its head in the sand.

Kennedy has reviewed the changing areas of the world and has examined them in the light of this general principle: nationalism and economic development are the two great forces which energize the situations of the new countries. It is obvious that one cannot bring about a democratic evolution in these countries, and thus lead them to the American side against the Russian, unless one is able to hold out the promise of satisfaction to the forces of nationalism and economic development. And in a situation of immaturity, political conflict, and primitive economic life, these two forces cannot fully develop if one demands of the new countries immediate adherence to a military pact and a final choice between America and Russia. There is a need to establish another principle of discrimination, a distinction between the democratic and the totalitarian principle. And this approach implies the complete abandonment of what has been called Dulles' "pactomania." The principle of military treaties is valid only for Western Europe and certain parts of Southeast Asia. In this perspective, neutralism becomes an element which no longer works in Russia's favor. It can work to the advantage of America insofar as she allows free play in the new countries to a balanced nationalism and to intensive economic development, which can lead to experiments of a democratic nature or tendency. It is in this sense that Kennedy has reexamined the international situation, as it affects not only Africa, India, and Latin America but also the Middle East, and for each of these problems, according to the circumstances, he has tried to lay down effective programs of economic aid and foreign policy which would permit the concretization of his new political approach.

With respect to Russia, Kennedy believes that a real détente is possible. America and Russia have a basic interest in preventing the spread of atomic bombs which would jeopardize their own security. This common interest would enable them to move from a cold-war policy to one of détente and competitive coexistence.

Kennedy, furthermore, (and this is the third element in his foreign policy) is aware that this overall approach cannot succeed unless the developed resources of the West are used conjointly. The opposing Communist bloc, which by its nature tends to be compact, cannot be overcome if the free world does not preserve its unity, and Kennedy's policy toward Western Europe and the Atlantic Pact flows directly from this necessity. On the one hand, Kennedy wishes to maintain American leadership because it is the condition of his entire foreign policy. And on the other hand, he wants this leadership to be democratic because it is only on this condition that the unity of the free world can be preserved. Unity of the West under American leadership is supposed to lead Western Europe to make a deeper commitment to the general line of Kennedy's policy. Hence his tendency to put pressure on Europe to become even more committed to a policy of aid to underdeveloped countries, to take up a position of détente even more than it has up to now, and to confine its military effort to the area of conventional weapons so as not to pose obstacles to American leadership. Within this framework American leadership is considered a necessary element on the grounds that it is only with leadership that Western unity exists, and that the only country which can provide this leadership is America.

. . .

It now remains to see whether the general approach in foreign policy established by Kennedy has succeeded in achieving the goals which the new administration has put forward. During the first year that this policy was applied, American reversals continued on all fronts. America was humiliated in Cuba when the military expedition attempted by Cuban refugees to reconquer their island met with a reverse. Similarly, the attempt at a détente with Khrushchev also failed. On all fronts where the situations were fluid, America tended to fall back more than to advance.

Nevertheless, in 1961, in his first State of the Union message, Kennedy still had the courage to maintain his line while evaluating the situation frankly.

. . .

In effect, despite reverses, despite the military expedition against Cuba, which lent a somewhat military tone to foreign policy, the general character of Kennedy's policy continued to be democratic in principle. Neutralism became a possible element in American policy. In Laos the Americans adopted a compromise solution, thus dropping the former policy of simple military presence. In general, Kennedy has succeeded in reversing the tendency of American foreign policy in style and method. American foreign policy is one which the world finds less extremist than those of France and of Germany.

This courage and this capacity to see situations as they really are and to confront them on constructive lines are particularly apparent in commercial policy. . . . Faced with a serious deficit in the American balance of payments, and a profound alteration in the relation of economic power between the United States and the six countries of the Common Market, the Kennedy Administration did not take the path of protectionism, which would have been the simplest and the easiest, but the more difficult yet more progressive path of a liberal policy.

Nevertheless, if we look from the outside at what has happened in world politics during the three years since the Kennedy Administration was installed, we are obliged to note that, despite these modifications of American foreign policy, in the competition between the United States and Russia and in the international alterations that have taken place, there has been no substantial change in the possibilities of taking initiatives. The situation that characterized the Eisenhower period and the containment policy has not been notably altered, although America is effectively pursuing the best possible policy for trying to reverse this tendency. What essentially has happened? From the standpoint of what has happened between America and Russia, with respect to Europe and the entire world, on the military as well as on the economic level, we note that on the whole Russia retains the power of initiative. One can see this above all in the case of Berlin, the real nerve center of the world situation. On the European front, and in Berlin especially—the front on which all the others depend—Russia has maintained her possibilities of initiative intact and has constrained America to accept them. The only sector in which Russia has perhaps lost out is the Congo. In Laos a compromise has been achieved (apparently on an equal basis) which satisfies both powers since a situation of neutrality has been established. But from the standpoint of the world balance of power, as it was possible to point out recently, the situation is advantageous to Russia and the Communist world. We have already spoken of the Cuban situation, and here it need only be recalled how America has in practice accepted Soviet influence in Cuba that she had never recognized before. . . . On the economic level, the American economy and the dollar have not succeeded in achieving a position of leadership around which the entire economy of the mature Western area could be organized, and which could then be directed toward the exertion of a powerful democratic influence on the newly developed countries. An additional proof of America's incapacity to organize and unify the economy of the West lies in the fact that the directives which the Americans have tried to impose on international bodies and on the political economies of diverse countries have not been followed.

Why, then, despite all of its important innovations, is the foreign policy of the Kennedy Administration failing? The answer is simple. To apply this policy it is not enough to say that "if one applies this policy in such and such a country, such and such consequences will be obtained." An effective policy requires much more. The foreign policy of a country is effective only if it produces a modification in that country capable of altering the world balance of power in such a fashion as to influence the particular balances of power within the various states in the sense that the desired political solutions will be effectively adopted within each of these states. To have envisaged favorable solutions, to have understood and studied them, is one element of a foreign policy; but the fundamental element is the existence of the power to alter the world balance in such a way that these solutions can become effective. It is precisely this power which the United States has lacked and is still lacking.

We have seen that the pillar of the Kennedy Administration's new American foreign policy was American leadership. In reality, this concept is empty and ideological, because it does not correspond to real power on the part of the United States to alter the world balance substantially or to guide the Western world effectively. The power of the United States is declining compared to that of the Soviet Union because the two monopolies, the atomic monopoly and the monopoly of foreign aid, have been finally lost. Hence America's freedom of action in relation to that of Russia's is declining instead of increasing.

In particular, America has power with respect to Russia only insofar as she is able to maintain the unity of the free Western world. Yet, even in the West, the United States is growing weaker. We are witnessing, in fact, a profound alteration of economic power within the Western world, as between America and the European countries, and especially those on the Continent. With the phenomenon of recession, America has experienced a great weakening that is manifested in the form of a balance of payments deficit. Given the burden which the American economy bears in supporting the foreign and military policies of the United States, the world supremacy of American industry and commerce is no longer sufficient to give the dollar the position of hegemony and arbitrament which characterized the economic monopoly at the end of the Second World War. On the basis of the great economic expansion of the six countries of the Common Market, signs begin to appear in Europe of a tendency toward military and political independence. Despite all the speeches and all the pressures, the power of the United States to keep the Western world united under her leadership is diminishing.

Even the policy carried out by Kennedy with respect to the third part of the world [the developing nations] which, taken abstractly, ought to have had positive results, has not succeeded, and for the same reason. For this policy to be effective it is precisely necessary that the weight of American policy should be increasing rather than diminishing. . . .

Consequently, Kennedy's policy is failing, not because it is an erroneous policy, but because America is not the area of the world in which modifications of power can come about that might alter the world balance in such a fashion as to permit the realization of solutions desired by Kennedy. In substance, if one wants to be objective, one must say that the *United States occupies a peripheral position relative to the modifications that must come about in the world balance in order to enhance the possibilities of peace, of economic expansion, and of democratic orientation in the world.*

A final point remains to be illuminated. This peripheral position of American foreign policy, along with American awareness of the world power of the United States, indicates that a democratic dynamic is not being generated in America and resides only in the will of the leadership. A country that, in the aim of promoting its own internal democracy and world democracy, feels constrained to assume leadership, to demand it, and to declare all but explicitly that it cannot renounce it, and yet one that is unable truly to enhance democratic possibilities in the world—such a country is inevitably in a situation that ultimately engenders a profoundly nationalist spirit instead of a profoundly democratic one. This is why, in substance, the real basis on which Kennedy's policy ultimately draws is a nationalism in which the democratic components flatter nationalism and the nation does not serve democracy.

In this sense, this analysis of American foreign policy coincides with the broad analysis that could be made of the evolution of the American state toward more centralized and nationalist forms by which the dynamic of democracy is lessened.

THE FAILURES OF AMERICAN CONSERVATISM IN SOUTHEAST ASIA

Ekkehart Krippendorff

Ekkehart Krippendorff, a German political scientist and commentator, is an independent leftist whose radical views have made him a controversial figure at the Free University of Berlin where he teaches. In this article he attempts to document a criticism of American foreign policy that is very widespread among Europeans of the center as well as the left—the charge that the United States has dangerously oversimplified the choice between support of the Communist bloc and adherence to the free world. Krippendorff maintains that in Southeast Asia the United States has tended to back unpopular reactionary rulers because they are militantly anti-Communist, in preference to more democratic and nationalist leaderships, which, although often neutralist in foreign policy, offer much better prospects for the establishment of viable democratic regimes. He thus concludes that the United States has consistently supported the wrong forces in Southeast Asia and for that reason has suffered an all but unbroken series of foreign policy reverses.

. . . To speak of American policy in Asia is to describe the complicated and often contradictory dispositions of American foreign policy since 1954 in the form of a host of small and often petty actions. It means reporting all sorts of attempted intrigues, some successful and others not; the common element in all of them is the fear of being overwhelmed by Chinese Communism, and a deep-seated distrust of the nationalist-neutralist, nonaristocratic élites in Southeast Asia. With a truly amazing instinct for failure, American policy in the 1950's has consistently backed the wrong horse, and has alienated the influential while promoting the incompetent. Thus it was with the lost chance of a neutralist Ho Chi Minh and the consequent absence of any alternative to the support of Ngo Dinh Diem; with the overthrow of Souvanna Phouma in favor of the incompetent and unpopular Boun Oum; with Dulles' unconcealed sympathy for the anti-Sukarno rebellion of 1958 in Sumatra; and with the toleration of Nationalist Chinese refugee forces in the interior of Burma, which almost led to a break of diplomatic relations and in any case to an ostentatious refusal to accept American foreign aid. Still other cases could be mentioned.

This remarkably frequent misinterpretation of the Asian situation, the Eisenhower Administration's constantly repeated cooperation with élites and groups whose influence can only be called problematic (to put it mildly) was nevertheless no accident. It rested, on the one hand, on Dulles' unambiguously formulated premise that "neutralism is amoral," and, on the other hand, on the circumstance that the local groups and individuals who were sympathetic to ideas like these were *not* identical with the young nationalistic élite. Ameri-

FROM "Amerikanische Politik in Asien," *Frankfurter Hefte,* No. 18 (April, 1963, pp. 229–42. Translated by the editor with permission.

can Asian policy thus became a sacrificial offering to the ideological narrowness of her leading diplomats.

This, however, is not all. It was also a sacrifice to the freewheeling and . . . extreme anti-Communist intelligence service, that is, the CIA. Let it be said in its honor that without the knowledge of the actual ambassador, invariably outside his jurisdiction and often against his better counsel, it was the CIA that inspired the Laotian rightists to overthrow the neutralist regime, that supported the Sumatra rebellion, and that in the case of Quemoy and Matsu nearly involved the United States in an atomic war through calculated provocations. We need only cite a single trustworthy and authoritative witness, Chester Bowles [in *Foreign Affairs*]:

In Asia, one U.S. ambassador assured the Prime Minister that we were not involved in an intelligence operation which, to the ambassador's chagrin, he eventually discovered was being masterminded in his own office. The Prime Minister concluded that the ambassador was either a fool or a liar.

We must finally mention a further factor in the precarious, but self-imposed, situation into which the United States has maneuvered itself in Southeast Asia: the corruption of American-supported groups through a truly scandalous administration of foreign aid. Not only have the local "élites" obtained enormous sums out of it by pressuring the Americans with the routine formula that they, as recipients, are the only bulwark against Communism, but the American companies involved have also made indescribably high profits. Money was pumped into these economies which they simply could not meaningfully absorb, the results of which was the sharpening, and indeed the creation of social hatred hitherto completely absent in this form, since little or nothing was obtained by those "on the bottom." The report of the Congressional committee for government activities in Laos, published in 1959, reads like a detective story, and it is sufficiently fair-minded and sober to state in circumspect terms:

The aid program has not contributed to preventing the spread of Communism in Laos. Rather, the Communist victory in the election of last year, which was fought with slogans like "corruption in government" and "governmental indifference," has given rise to the suspicion that the United States aid program has helped to bring about an atmosphere in which the ordinary people seriously question the value of American friendship.

.   .   .

[*After a survey of the situation in different parts of Southeast Asia, Krippendorff concludes:*]

The common element in all these cases can be termed (in a nonpolemical sense) the problem of controlling satellites. That the Soviet Union has been relatively more successful in this can hardly be doubted, even though cracks in the structure have recently appeared. One of its advantages is its ability to threaten alternatives. The Soviet Union has connections to more than one segment of the country in question or of the local Communist Party. But one tactical weakness of American policy is to operate without alternatives. In the case of Diem it rested so much on this one man and his regime that he could even venture to answer the cautious pressure of American diplomats in the winter of 1961–62 to bring about certain reforms, with a calculated anti-

American campaign ("We are not lackeys"). In Laos Boun Oum paid dearly enough for his indispensability, indeed almost to the tune of a complete catastrophe. This absence of alternatives applies to Sarit [of Thailand] and also to Chiang Kai-shek. "When will America learn that it is always a disaster for the cause of freedom and democracy to support a cynical tyrant as the 'sole alternative' to Communism?" Thus a leader of the Democratic Party of Vietnam, exiled in Paris, wrote to the New York *Times*.

The Kennedy Administration, taking over the catastrophic inheritance of its predecessor, seems unable to break out of the vicious circle. It undoubtedly wants democratic reforms, a rise in living standards, and stable social relationships. But it is not ready, even where it could exert almost unlimited power, to develop an alternative to the obsolete traditional élites, and must address its social conceptions to the very circles that could only lose by realizing them. And it is also the prisoner of a second, and even more vicious circle, the policy of "military liberation first." As long as Southeast Asia is threatened by Communism, it will continue to be dangerous to open the sluices of social evolution. Yet the primacy of quasi-military struggle with all its dictatorial and socially corrupting consequences prevents elimination of the soil on which these devastating little wars are nourished.

But the main obstacle to a rational solution of the Southeast Asia problem is the much greater fact of "China." The interest of the United States in the countries on the Chinese perimeter did not awaken into frenzied concern until China fell under Communist domination. The struggle for the last Western bastions in Southeast Asia is at bottom a struggle to maintain strong points against China. Hans J. Morgenthau, one of the shrewdest of American foreign policy experts, sees the key to the decision in Southeast Asia in the clarification of China policy. . . .

What holds the Chinese back today is not the military strength that the United States can bring to bear on Laos, Thailand, South Vietnam, or Formosa. It is rather China's general weaknesses. But in the not too distant future this should change. . . . Then the United States will be confronted with a full-scale choice between retreat and war. . . . This war, however, will be no jungle war, but a total atomic one.

Two years after Morgenthau's gloomy prophecy, the Kennedy Administration has as yet reached no decision—with the partial exception of Laos—indicating a way out of the dilemma. The Indian-Chinese border conflict in part bore out the prophecies, while still giving America a political breathing space. But the delaying of a conflict, if not immediately exploited, is not always favorable to its solution. In the long view, however, America's Asian policy is being decided in China itself.

AMERICA'S IMPERIALIST RECORD

Bernard Lavergne

Bernard Lavergne, an honorary professor at the Faculté de Droit de Paris, is a veteran French publicist and political commentator. Like many other intellectuals of the non-Communist left, he has often been extremely outraged by United States foreign policy. This piece attempts to show that international relations in the modern era have been consistently poisoned by irrational anti-Communism on the part of the Western powers. Lavergne argues that charges of Soviet imperialism are exaggerated and unfair, and in order to support this claim he tries to prove that the record of American imperialism is in some respects more ruthless and extensive than that of the Soviets. This piece was written in a mood of great bitterness.

In a letter granting permission to translate this article, Lavergne offered comments (appended at the end of this selection) on American foreign policy since 1963 which, although still critical, are somewhat more sympathetic toward the United States.

May it please Heaven that the pressure exerted by the United States on nearly all the countries of Central America and the Carribean islands, and on South America as well as on various Asian countries, does not greatly exceed the pressure which, naively or hypocritically, Westerners violently accuse the Soviets of exercising.

The Americans have always liked to camouflage their imperialism so as to appear completely pure and irreproachable. Yet no power is more imperialist than theirs, since over a long period they have systematically and brutally subjected the countries of Latin America to economic exploitation. In our time only Mexico, Brazil, and Chile dare to intervene, in the UN notably, against the *diktats* of the United States.

In all these countries the American system is the same. By buying a few local politicians or military leaders, America creates *pronunciamentos* or palace revolutions which give power to a dictator, usually a tyrant, who is completely subject to orders from Washington. This agent then authorizes a ruthless ransoming of the entire economy by giving American firms the right, and often the exclusive privilege, of carrying on commercial activity. By buying the raw materials furnished by these vast regions at low prices and selling the industrial products at high prices, the United States has kept almost all the countries of Latin America in a state of horrible poverty for more than a century. In addition, the regimes of many of the agents installed by Washington have been extremely bloody. In the Dominican Republic Trujillo shot more than twenty-thousand nationals, and in Cuba, prior to Fidel Castro's regime Batista did the same. The Alliance for Progress, which President Kennedy tried to initiate in Latin America last year, represents the price the American Treasury thinks it necessary to pay in order to keep all

FROM "L'Incroyable Aveuglement de la politique occidentale depuis 1945," *L'Année Politique et Economique*, 36ᵉ Année, No. 171 (February, 1963), pp. 1–24, and a letter to the editor, October 26, 1965. Translated by the editor with permission.

these countries under its domination for a few more years. Just to take a few revealing facts: until very recently, one could not come ashore in Puerto Rico, Cuba (until the advent of Fidel Castro), or the Dominican Republic— all countries said to be "free"—without a visa issued by American authorities alone.

What, then, are the pressures exerted by Moscow from time to time on the countries of Central Europe in comparison to the hard and pitiless regime with which the "Pax Americana," as voracious as the former "Pax Romana," has burdened these Latin-American countries, all of them Spanish or Portuguese in origins and language, for a hundred or a hundred and fifty years? The Soviet Union is far from putting the peoples' democracies of Central Europe under the tight control imposed by the United States in the southern hemisphere of America. Moscow promotes the economic prosperity of these countries as much as it can, and leaves them an internal autonomy that, despite all that is said, is generally very great.

It is sad that the American people, which includes so many good men, so many very generous men, should be governed by public authorities so harsh that they have allowed their nationals to put two-thirds of the American continent into a straight jacket, and this in the name of law and justice!

It is not only in Latin America that the United States has imposed its dominion. The same holds true for such Asian countries as South Korea, the Philippines, and South Vietnam, to say nothing of all the Pacific islands that are occupied by the American army. Can it be said that the populations of these countries are of American nationality and have called upon the American army for help? That the United States should have stationed troops in Japan, a country which had declared war on it, is completely natural; but what are American divisions doing in Korea? Why, for a year and more, has the American army been conducting open warfare against the patriots of South Vietnam? Is it in the name of the liberty of nations that the rulers of America have stationed armed forces in these places, and at the very moment when the Americans themselves were pressing the Dutch to get out of Indonesia, the English to give up their last colonial possessions, and [the French] to leave Algeria? Clearly, they would say, it was to "fight Communism," and in a spirit of self-sacrifice, that the United States went to war in Korea and South Vietnam. But what decree of Providence has commissioned the United States to place its yoke on countries where Americans do not live and that ask only to govern themselves?

American public opinion has become so distorted that it regards as meritorious what foreign peoples consider to be a crime. "We are bearing the entire burden in South Vietnam," said President Kennedy in a speech on December 17. "The United States is thus doing more than its share. We hope that Europe, for its part, will make a great effort." The American President thus sees great merit in the fact that the United States is carrying on a scandalous war in South Vietnam, for it is clearly a war of colonial conquest with no justification whatsoever.

Thus, in comparing the United States and the U.S.S.R. with respect to acts of oppression each has committed against foreign peoples, it is clear that the debit of the United States is strikingly heavier than that which can be imputed to the Soviet Union. As Westerners, we cannot help but be depressed by this, but the facts are there.

Despite all that is said, the Soviets count only on the moral and especially economic value of their regime to realize their hope that it will gradually and continually spread over the entire world. Although we in the West never cease to talk of the aggressiveness of the Soviet bloc, one seeks in vain for a single country, other than those confided to its tutelage by the Yalta agreements, where Moscow has sent or maintained troops since 1945. Stalin even evacuated his troops from Iran. And these are facts, not opinions.

Khrushchev very recently declared: "The era of domination (i.e., over a continent or the entire world) by this or that power is over."

. . .

LATER REFLECTIONS ON THE SUBJECT

[The following passage is taken from a letter to the editor written by Lavergne on October 29, 1965.]

The demonstration of 100,000 Americans against the war in Vietnam* gave us great pleasure. It was a demonstration by the good America we love and admire, confronting the dangerous, nationalistic America that relies primarily on military power.

I am glad to see that intellectual circles in the United States are not in agreement with the policy of the Pentagon and President Johnson. I am astonished that the President has not understood that the war in Vietnam, which has been waged with such cruel tactics and in which gas has been used contrary to international treaties, and that the landing of 30,000 Marines in Santo Domingo have aroused strong disapproval everywhere. Many Europeans subservient in some degree or another to governments loyal to the United States have not dared to protest publicly, but you can believe me when I say that in private these two American actions have been severely censured.

To make the United States feared for her military power rather than loved for her helpful deeds and her respect for the right of peoples to govern themselves (which is all that the Vietnamese people have asked) is a policy completely lacking in common sense.

We in Europe are also very fearful that giving Bonn atomic weapons would allow German generals to drag the United States into a war of aggression against Moscow some day, for how else could they try to restore Germany's frontiers of 1937? The German request [for atomic weapons] is superbly insolent.

We truly loved and admired Presidents Woodrow Wilson, Franklin Roosevelt, and John Kennedy, and we deplore the fact that the United States is now pursuing a policy diametrically opposed to theirs.

The talk of Russian aggression is absurd. The war that is now brewing and which could break out within a decade is a war of the underdeveloped peoples, who in ten years will have atomic bombs, against the rich countries, and against the United States above all. Like us, you have every reason to want to avert such a war, but your present government is, unthinkingly, doing everything it can to make the attack inevitable.

---

* Lavergne is referring to the peace marches held in many parts of the United States in the fall of 1965.

II

VIEWS FROM THE COMMUNIST BLOC

Any broad-gauged description of American social, economic, or political life, whether by an American or a foreigner, is likely to reveal as much about the experience, motivations, and situation of the author as it does about that facet of the American scene under analysis. Communist writings on the United States, in particular, are profoundly conditioned by ideological considerations, tensions between East and West, and the very nature of the Soviet Communist regime.

With the exception of two selections from Chinese Communist sources this section is devoted to an exposition of Soviet views of the United States. This focus does not imply that the Soviet Union is synonymous with the entire Communist world or that views expressed about the United States in the various Communist nations are uniform. Although within the Communist orbit considerable consensus on the nature of American society and foreign policy remains, differences of opinion have been expressed increasingly in recent years. Nationalism; rivalries for power and influence; differences in cultural heritage, economic development, and military might; varying relationships with the West; as well as other forces fermenting the Sino-Soviet dispute and the more general phenomenon of polycentrism within the Communist bloc, have also led to some differentiation in attitude toward the United States. Chinese statements on American foreign policy and such domestic events as the civil rights movement have been more truculent in recent years than the general tenor of Soviet declarations. On the other hand the Poles, for example, have expressed opinions about the nature of American society which are more moderate and sophisticated than those normally found in the Soviet press.

This volume's concentration on Soviet views has several justifications. The U.S.S.R. remains far and away the most powerful Communist country and the leader—albeit increasingly challenged—of the Communist world. The Soviets have also expressed themselves on a broader spectrum of issues and institutions in the United States than have other Communists, and therefore Soviet sources supply a more complete picture of American society. Finally, given the limited confines of this section, it seemed wiser to present a reasonably representative sampling of Soviet views than a potpourri of opinions from a large number of Communist nations.

All Soviet writings on the United States must be considered official, or at least semiofficial. If not directly inspired and supported by the Communist Party, a writer's work must at least be reviewed by party-dominated editorial boards and other censorship organs before it can be published; and the writer himself is acutely aware of official pronouncements and guidelines on his subject. Occasionally, a writer and an editorial board may test the bounds of orthodoxy, as in the case of Viktor Nekrasov's impressions of America included here; but the author is laboring under an awareness that he is courting official rebuke.

It is appropriate, then, to begin a consideration of Communist views of the United States with an official and definitive Soviet statement about the nature and prospects of "capitalism" such as the one included in the 1961 Program of the Soviet Communist Party. Treating capitalism with a broad brush, this programatic statement is relevant to themes occurring in all five categories of American life covered in this part. Although this statement addresses itself to capitalism as a general phenomenon, it is directly pertinent because the United States is regarded as the leading capitalist country in both power and maturity, and because Soviet authors analyze American events and institutions within the broader theoretical framework of capitalism. This official statement of doctrine provides the theoretical backdrop for the other, more specific and detailed Soviet descriptions of American life and provides a norm of orthodoxy by which they may be judged.

In his book, *Russia, the Atom, and the West,* George Kennan, one of America's foremost students of the Soviet Union and former ambassador to the U.S.S.R., has made a sobering comment about the Soviet view of the outside world that may serve as a point of departure for considering the ingredients blended into the Communist image of the United States.

In everything that can be statistically expressed—expressed, that is, in such a way as not to imply any judgment on our motivation—I believe the Soviet government to be excellently informed about us. I am sure that their information on the development of our economies, on the state of our military preparations, on our scientific progress, etc., is absolutely first-rate. But when it comes to the analysis of our motives, to the things that make our life tick as it does, I think this whole great system of intelligence gathering breaks down seriously. It breaks down because over all these forty years the Communist Party has made it impossible for the people who collect the factual information to accompany that information with really objective analysis of the nature of Western society. . . . The Soviet diplomatic representative or journalist abroad has no choice but to cast his analytical report in the terms of Marxist-Leninist ideology whether this is applicable or not in the given instance. In this way the Soviet leaders find themselves committed to a badly distorted image of the outside world.

This quotation raises two questions: How, and to what degree, are Soviet statements about the United States purely manipulatory to influence men's thinking, both in the Soviet Union and abroad? Or, to what extent are they the product of minds steeped in Marxism-Leninism and experiences substantially different from our own?

On the assumption that whatever promotes the interests of the Soviet Union is useful and legitimate because Communism is *ipso facto* on the side of "progressive" historical forces, Soviet leaders quite candidly state that the manipulation of information and ideas is acceptable. In a curious refutation of Marx's concern that ideas be directly grounded in scientific social research, Soviet Communists tend to treat information and ideology as a distinct sphere of human endeavor. Communication of all kinds is looked upon as an important means of waging a conflict with the "forces of reaction." To use a current Soviet cliché "There can be no ideological coexistence." Moreover, this belief in the inevitable conflict of ideas is reinforced, and the acceptability of manipulation is rationalized, by the proposition that Western and Soviet ideas and concepts are inherently antithetical because they spring from radically different and antagonistic social settings. Hence, neutral, balanced, and objective analysis of social phenomena of one another's country is impossible. There cannot be a genuinely nonpartisan social science. As an eminent Soviet legal scholar, M. S. Strogovich in *Theory of State and Law,* has put it:

. . . Communist partisanship guarantees the most profound, objective, and well-rounded conception of reality, including the political and juridical superstructure of a class society. The interests of the working class coincide with the objective course of historical development. The proletariat represents a consistently revolutionary class, and seeking a revolutionary transformation of society, it is interested in objective, that is, true, knowledge. This is why genuine truth and Communist partisanship coincide.

Soviet leaders, moreover, project their own attitudes about the management of information on the non-Communist world. Premier Khrushchev commented in the following manner on the subject of ideological conflict and Western reporting before the Party Central Committee on June 21, 1963:

I recently recounted an interesting conversation that I had with the British publisher Thompson, who visited Moscow as a tourist. Publisher Thompson has probably never studied Marxism-Leninism, but he has a strong class instinct. . . . He asked me: "Would you allow me to sell my papers in Moscow?" I replied: "This is a very complicated question. It needs thought." "What if I appoint the editor of *Izvestia,* Adzhubei, as the editor of one of these papers?" he asked. "Then that would be a different matter," I replied. "I can promise you that if you appoint Adzhubei or another editor of one of our papers as editor of your paper, then it will be sold everywhere in the Soviet Union." To this he responded: "No, this would not be advantageous to me."
Here you see a capitalist's approach to the issue. In this case, it is not material interest that assumes priority for him, but a purely ideological and class interest.

Thus, only naive people and incorrigible simpletons can believe all the ravings about creative freedom in the capitalist countries. Only some of our simpletons, regarding themselves as very clever, do not understand, or do not want to understand, the class essence in ideological matters. . . . And some people say that freedom of the press exists in Britain and America. Let them meet Hearst or Thompson and ask them to publish an article in their newspapers. From what angle will they consider this article? Perhaps from the point of view of literary form? They could spit on form! They would consider it from the viewpoint of policy and the interests of their class and evaluate it as to whom it could serve and to what it is directed. The main thing for them is the ideological question. . . .

The tendentious nature of most Soviet writings can be seen not only in their tenor and style but also in the selection of themes that play up less favorable aspects of American life. The brighter features of American society tend to be glossed over or ignored altogether. Soviet educators write about the greater number of engineers graduated in the Soviet Union, but they do not present figures on the total number of college students in the two countries, which would reveal the extensiveness of higher education in the United States. Much is said about the American mass culture of comic books, television westerns, and vulgar paperbacks; but there is little reference to the number of symphony orchestras, theater groups, or other cultural events which might convey the impression of important and widespread cultural endeavor.

American fiction published in Russian is also carefully selected. The following is a reading list recommended in 1963 by the Moscow City Library to its readers and characterized as a record of "the most important literary products of the United States published after World War II": Ray Bradbury, *Fahrenheit 451;* Lloyd L. Brown, *Iron City;* Robert Brown, *Matter of Price;* Erskine Caldwell, *Gulf Coast Stories* and *Tales and Stories;* Jay Deiss, *A Washington Story;* Martha Dodd, *The Searching Light;* William Faulkner, *Seven Stories;* Ernest Hemingway, "Get a Seeing-Eye" and *The Old Man and the Sea;* Langston Hughes, "Trouble with the Angels"; Felix Jackson, *So Help Me God;* John O. Killens, *Youngblood;* Sinclair Lewis, *Kingsblood Royal;* Albert Maltz, *A Long Day in a Short Life;* Dexter Masters, *The Accident;* William Saroyan, *Adventures of Wesley Jackson;* Alexander P. Saxton, *The Great Midland;* John Steinbeck, *The Pearl;* Robert Sylvester, *The Second Oldest Profession;* John Weaver, *Another Such Victory;* Mitchell Wilson, *My Brother, My Enemy; Dave Mallory;* and *Live with Lightning.*

Because the centralized and monolithic nature of the Soviet regime facilitates tight control over communications, information about the United States may be varied from time to time to coincide with the changing foreign policies of the leadership or to suit domestic needs. During the "spirit of Camp David" era in 1959, and again in the spring and summer of 1963 when Soviet-American tensions had cooled somewhat, there was a definite decline in vituperative statements about the United States. Not only the status of American-Soviet relations, but sensitive Soviet domestic problems are frequently mirrored in writings on the U.S. Much is printed about the low standard of living, the poverty, and the insecurity of the American working class, in part to give the Russian worker the impression that he is comparatively well off. When the Soviet leadership became concerned about the development of abstract art and experiments in literature, articles devoted to decadent bourgeois art began to appear in an effort to discredit these innovations by Soviet authors and artists.

Soviet appraisals of the United States are also highly colored by the Soviet Marxist-Leninist Weltanschauung. The reader may find that a number of the selections below do not present accounts of American life in a manner that corresponds with his own perceptions and experiences. Minor events and institutions are blown up to major significance. The American Communist Party and its front organizations, for example, are treated as a major force in American political and economic life, and statements by its leaders are taken as having significant influence in the United States. The key factor in analyzing any part of American life is deemed the nature and functioning of the "capitalist" economy. Religion, the arts, politics, and all social phenomena are assumed to be molded ultimately by the dynamics of capitalism. For a Soviet Marxist, the working classes are by definition "progressive" and are becoming better organized and politically conscious, but they are misled by opportunistic leaders who have sold out to the monopolists. In sum, the Soviet image of the United States is seen from this Marxist–Leninist viewpoint in proportions unfamiliar to most Americans.

Because politics and government are considered derivatives of, and secondary to, economic and class considerations, and because Western democratic politics are beyond the personal experience of Soviet scholars, they have tended to gloss over the American political scene and American political commentaries. Only since the late 1950's have Soviet scholars begun any detailed examination of American politics. Although books and articles on American politics have now begun to appear, they have thus far been superficial and crude in their analysis. Dr. I. D. Levin of the Soviet Institute of State and Law, perhaps the foremost Soviet specialist on non-Communist governments, has stated in his book, *The Contemporary Bourgeois Science and State Law,* that Western political science has turned its attention from more formal legal studies to investigations of the sources and exercise of political power and the application of sociological concepts to the study of the state in order "to apply, together with the old, also the new and more flexible methods, to resort to a more improved masking of the class character of the contemporary bourgeois state." Soviet authors identify the major trends of American politics as the growing intervention of the state into the economy and the society, the decline of "bourgeois legality," and an increase in the power of the bureaucracy at the expense of legislative institutions, local government, and federalism. All these tendencies are interpreted as the "deepening crisis of the bourgeois state." The selection by Yakovlev, who attempts to make use of the work of American political scientists and political commentators to prove the lack of popular restraint over the United States government, is representative of the new school of Soviet political criticism.

Are the sources of information on the outside world available to the Soviet leadership hopelessly warped by the attitudes of and constraints placed upon Soviet diplomatic personnel and journalists? Are the reports they read merely more detailed versions of the articles published in *Izvestia* and *Pravda* by TASS correspondents in the West? There is some evidence that they are not. It has been reported, for instance, that a publication called "Red TASS," a secret, uncensored, and unslanted coverage of the foreign press, is prepared by the Central Committee staff and submitted to the top leaders. On occasion, top Soviet leaders have demonstrated surprisingly detailed knowledge about some aspect of the United States. When Khrushchev visited the United States in 1959, he greeted the members of the Senate Foreign Relations Committee with, "I always follow your speeches with attention and know many of you from them." Even if Soviet leaders read unadulterated American materials, however, we still do not know whether they evaluate them in a more pragmatic and nonideological manner in private than they do in public.

The question also arises whether Soviet descriptions of the United States correspond with the views of the Soviet citizenry; or, to put it another way, have Soviet writings affected the attitudes of the citizenry about the United States? In the absence of public opinion polls and psychologically unencumbered access to Soviet citizens, no definitive answer is possible. However, most American visitors have commented on the extreme curiosity about the United States among Soviet citizens. In a sense, restrictions on the circulation of American publications in the U.S.S.R. and the stereotyped fare on the United States that is served the population may be self-defeating by whetting the public appetite for more information.

Russian-speaking Americans who have spent time in the Soviet Union report that few Russians accept the official picture of the United States *in toto*. The degree of acceptance or rejection varies greatly from one segment of the population to another. Many of the intellectuals who are familiar with the West through travel or access to Western publications appear to discount much of the official picture of the United States. A portion of the younger generation has shown a propensity to romanticize the United States and covet American phonograph records, clothes, and publications. Concern voiced by the party leadership during late 1962 and 1963 over the infiltration of Western ideas among Soviet writers and artists, and the creative intelligentsia generally, also attests to some degree of divergence between official views on the United States and the attitudes of the people.

Nevertheless, even those Soviet citizens who may be skeptical of the standard view of the United States are influenced by it to some extent.

For example, assertions about economic instability, the lack of economic security for the average American citizen, and the inherent superiority of a planned economy appear to be largely accepted.

The population may harbor some doubts about the validity of the standard version of American life because it is often internally inconsistent. The image of the United States is not as monolithic and uniformly black and white as the Party Program might indicate.

Some contradictions arise from using the theme of competition with the United States to enlist feelings of national pride and competitiveness as major psychological stimuli for greater production efforts. Everywhere in the Soviet Union are posters and graphs proclaiming and measuring the decreasing gap between the American and Soviet economies. The phrase "overtake and surpass the United States" is well worn. This competition, however, inevitably raises a question: if things are so bad in the United States, why is the Soviet Union trying to overtake it?

The official picture of the United States is also blurred because the Soviet leadership has realized that Soviet scientists, managers, and teachers can learn much from their counterparts in the United States: since the mid-1950's the government has fostered the study of American experiences and the adoption of certain American practices and products, including soft-drink vending machines, corn flakes, and potato chips.

With the easing of Russia's self-imposed isolation from the world in the mid-1950's and under instructions from the regime to learn more about the West, the last few years have witnessed a mushrooming of research on the United States by Soviet scholars. The bulk of this research is coordinated by the increasingly important Institute of World Economics and International Relations, with its active American section, of the U.S.S.R. Academy of Sciences. The Institute now has a staff of well over four hundred professionals. Members of the Institute's Staff —E. D. Vil'khovchenko, S. Menshikov, V. Rymalov, and others—wrote several of the articles reprinted here. In addition, other branches of the Academy of Sciences have been instructed in recent years to investigate bourgeoise institutions and theories more thoroughly. For example, in 1962 a sector for the study of contemporary bourgeois state and law was formed in the Institute of State and Law.

This expanding research on the United States falls into two categories: that devoted to validating and buttressing the official Marxist-Leninist view of the United States, and the more technical studies of American methods that might be applied in the Soviet Union. The bulk of the published materials and those devoted to such subjects as the political system, the social structure, and the overall operations of the American economy fall into the first category. They concentrate on describing how American capitalism is shot through with contradictions

RECENT CARTOON VIEWS FROM THE COMMUNIST BLOC

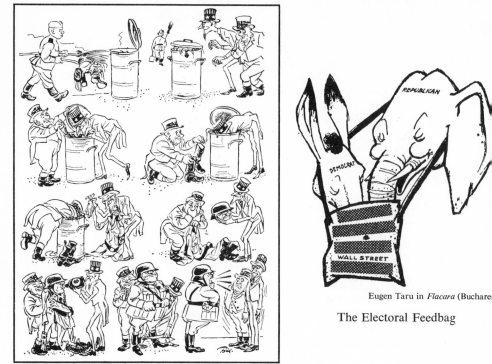

Eulenspiegel (East Berlin)

Playing with Fire

Eugen Taru in *Flacara* (Buchare

The Electoral Feedbag

Eugen Taru in *Flacara* (Bucharest)

The Alliance for Progress:
"We're gaining weight, amigo."

Ying Tao in the Peking *Review* (Pekir

Fishing

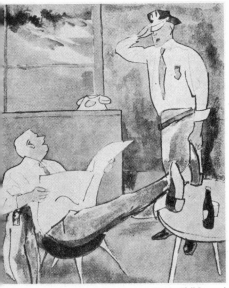

Krokodil (Moscow)

Chief, criminals have just blown up
    a Negro church!"
God will punish them."

Sandar Erdei in *Ludas Matyi* (Budapest)

"Help, help, Sergeant!"
"Sorry. Don't have time right now. We're
    looking for a suspected Communist."

(HORST SCHRADE IN EULENSPIEGEL, EAST BERLIN)

he War Against Poverty in the U.S.A.—from Roosevelt to Johnson

Guerrero in *Palante y Palante* (Havana)

and is oppressing the American people. Few subjects are left untouched: education, civil rights, race relations, American ideals, the social structure, and so forth.

The recent work of Soviet scholars demonstrates a familiarity with the relevant American sources, both primary and secondary; and some, like the Zamoshkin article, demonstrate considerable skill in handling these materials. A greater proportion of these writings is now devoted to more narrowly defined research in depth, rather than to merely rehashed clichés and broad generalizations about the evils of capitalism plagiarized from officially sanctified party doctrines as was so often the case until the mid-1950's. Although citation of the Marxist-Leninist classics, the Party Program, and leaders' speeches is still standard practice, there is less quotation-mongering than before and less slavish adherence to official texts.

Nevertheless, both because of the ideological biases of the observers and because of the dim view the regime takes toward "balanced" reporting or any compromises with "capitalism," straightforward reporting on American society should not be expected. The greater attention devoted to the writings of Western social scientists is largely for the purpose of refuting their "false theories." This point was bluntly made by V. I. Ugriumov in the introduction to his monograph *The Newest Theories of Contemporary Bourgeois Sociology* (Moscow, 1961):

The fight against these ideological diversions of the contemporary bourgeoisie occupies a serious place in our educational work in higher educational establishments. In the given circumstances, it is necessary to talk about exposing the false theories of contemporary bourgeois sociology, which receive wide distribution in capitalist countries.

M. A. Suslov, a member of the Party Presidium and a leading theoretician, lectured Soviet social scientists at the Conference of the Heads of Social Science Departments of Higher Educational Institutions in February, 1962:

However, serious shortcomings in the teaching of the social sciences and the work of scientific research in these sciences is still a weak link in this sharp ideological fight which our party and the international Communist movement is conducting against hostile ideologies. Unmasking contemporary bourgeois, reformist, and also revisionist and dogmatist conceptions is conducted haphazardly. This lowers the level of ideological-educational work.

The second category of research on the United States embraces the more specialized studies of American scientific and administrative methods and techniques. These studies are less widely distributed and appear in more specialized publications. Generally speaking, the more narrowly specialized the subject, the less distortion one finds.

More realistic information about the United States is increasing because of the number of Soviet visitors who have reported on trips to this country. Four of the selection below are based on direct observations during visits to the United States. The piece by Lev N. Mitrokhin was warmly praised by *Izvestia* and may serve to illustrate what is considered a correct model for reporting on visits abroad. By contrast, Nekrasov's account was considered a serious breach of the party line.

Encouraging more detailed investigation of the United States, however, may have its risks by permitting a greater opportunity for Soviet citizens to test the official view of the United States against reality. During the last several years the regime has shown increasing worry that some Soviet intellectuals have been imbibing Western ideas. On June 21, 1963, Khrushchev openly expressed his concern over flagging militancy toward "bourgeois ideologies":

To agree to peaceful coexistence between the Communist and bourgeois ideologies means to give the enemy the opportunity to blacken everything most dear to us, encourage slander, contribute to the corruption of the minds of the people, destroy our organizational unity, and hamper our advance in every possible way. We have struggled and shall continue to struggle irreconcilably not only against corrupt bourgeois ideology, but also against its agencies in our midst, the agencies of our class enemies. I believe that everyone understands that unceasing attention is necessary, and that those who insist on positions of peaceful coexistence in the sphere of ideology, positions alien to us, must be rebuffed.

The selections below have been chosen to present Soviet opinions on a broad spectrum of issues in the United States. They have also been deliberately selected in order to include a wide variety of Soviet sources —the Party press, literary journals, scholarly books and journals, and popular magazines.

A warning must be sounded about the use of American materials by Soviet authors. It is not unusual to find a Western writer quoted out of context or even misquoted. The quotations from Western sources in these selections have been translated from the Russian rather than taken from the original English, for our purpose is to convey the meaning and intent of the Soviet writer. For purposes of brevity footnotes in the original sources have been omitted.

The foregoing discussion about the context in which Soviet descriptions of the United States are generated by no means implies that the selections below should be rejected out of hand as "mere propaganda" of no relevance to Americans. We should be aware of what the Soviets are saying about us. Propaganda is of consequence in the world. More important, although the Soviet view of the United States may be out of focus, Soviet critiques nevertheless do normally touch on intrinsically sensitive areas in the United States. Looking at ourselves through generally unsympathetic eyes may add new understanding about our own society and our relations with the Soviet Union.

THE CRISIS OF WORLD CAPITALISM

Communist Party of the Soviet Union

The following selection from the Program of the Soviet Communist Party presents the official point of view of the Soviet leadership on the major current and future developments in the "capitalist world." The latest Party Program was adopted in October, 1961, at the Twenty-second Congress of the Communist Party of the Soviet Union.

Imperialism has entered the period of decline and collapse. An inexorable process of decay has seized capitalism from top to bottom—its economic and political system, its politics and ideology. Imperialism has forever lost its power over the bulk of mankind. The main content, main trend, and main features of the historical development of mankind are being determined by the world socialist system, by the forces fighting against imperialism, for the socialist reorganization of society.

. . .

The break-away from capitalism of more and more countries; the weakening of imperialist positions in the economic competition with socialism; the break-up of the imperialist colonial system; the intensification of imperialist contradictions with the development of state monopoly capitalism and the growth of militarism; the mounting internal instability and decay of capitalist economy evidenced by the increasing inability of capitalism to make full use of the productive forces (low rates of production growth, periodic crises, continuous undercapacity operation of production plant, and chronic unemployment); the mounting struggle between labour and capital; an acute intensification of contradictions within the world capitalist economy; an unprecedented growth of political reaction in all spheres, rejection of bourgeois freedoms and establishment of fascist and despotic regimes in a number of countries; and the profound crisis of bourgeois policy and ideology—all these are manifestations of the *general crisis of capitalism*.

In the imperialist stage *state monopoly capitalism* develops on an extensive scale. The emergence and growth of monopolies leads to the direct intervention of the state, in the interests of the financial oligarchy, in the process of capitalist reproduction. It is in the interests of the financial oligarchy that the bourgeois state institutes various types of regulation and resorts to the nationalisation of some branches of the economy. World wars, economic crises, militarism, and political upheavals have accelerated the development of monopoly capitalism into state monopoly capitalism.

The oppression of finance capital keeps growing. Giant monopolies controlling the bulk of social production dominate the life of the nation. A handful of millionaires and multimillionaires wield arbitrary power over the entire wealth of the capitalist world and make the life of entire nations mere

FROM the Program of the Communist Party of the Soviet Union, *New Times,* No. 48 (November 29, 1961).

small change in their selfish deals. The financial oligarchy is getting fabulously rich. The state has become a committee for the management of the affairs of the monopoly bourgeoisie. The bureaucratization of the economy is rising steeply. State monopoly capitalism combines the strength of the monopolies and that of the state into a single mechanism whose purpose is to enrich the monopolies, suppress the working-class movement and the national-liberation struggle, save the capitalist system, and launch aggressive wars. . . .

. . . Attempts at state regulation of the capitalist economy cannot eliminate competition and anarchy of production, cannot ensure the planned development of the economy on a nation-wide scale, because capitalist ownership and exploitation of wage-labor remain the basis of production. The bourgeois theories of "crisis-free" and "planned" capitalism have been laid in the dust by the development of contemporary capitalist economy. The dialectics of state monopoly capitalism is such that instead of shoring up the capitalist system, as the bourgeoisie expects, it aggravates the contradictions of capitalism and undermines its foundations. State monopoly capitalism is the fullest material preparation for socialism.

.   .   .

All in all, capitalism is increasingly impeding the development of the contemporary productive forces. Mankind is entering the period of a scientific and technical revolution bound up with the conquest of nuclear energy, space exploration, the development of chemistry, automation, and other major achievements of science and engineering. But the relations of production under capitalism are much too narrow for a scientific and technical revolution. Socialism alone is capable of effecting it and of applying its fruits in the interests of society.

Technical progress under the rule of monopoly capital is turning against the working class. By using new forms, the monopolies intensify the exploitation of the working class. Capitalist automation is robbing the worker of his daily bread. Unemployment is rising, the living standard is dropping. Technical progress is continuously throwing more sections of small producers overboard. Imperialism is using technical progress chiefly for military purposes. It is turning the achievements of human genius against humanity. As long as imperialism exists, mankind cannot feel secure about its future.

Modern capitalism has made the *market problem* extremely acute. Imperialism is incapable of solving it, because lag of effective demand behind growth of production is one of its objective laws. Moreover, it retards the industrial development of the underdeveloped countries. The world capitalist market is shrinking relative to the more rapidly expanding production capacity. It is partitioned by countless customs barriers and restrictive fences and split into exclusive currency and finance zones. An acute competitive struggle for markets, spheres of investment and sources of raw materials is under way in the imperialist camp. It is becoming doubly acute since the territorial sphere of capitalist domination has been greatly narrowed.

Monopoly capital has, in the final analysis, doomed bourgeois society to low rates of production growth that in some countries barely keep ahead of the growth of population. A considerable part of the production plant stands idle, while millions of unemployed wait at the factory gates. Farm production is artificially restricted, although millions are underfed in the world. People suffer want in material goods, but imperialism is squandering material resources and social labor on war preparations.

.   .   .

State monopoly capitalism stimulates militarism to an unheard-of degree. The imperialist countries maintain immense armed forces even in peacetime. Military expenditures devour an ever growing portion of the state budgets. The imperialist countries are turning into militarist, military-police states. Militarization pervades the life of bourgeois society.

While enriching some groups of the monopoly bourgeoisie, militarism leads to the exhaustion of nations, to the ruin of the peoples languishing under an excessive tax burden, mounting inflation, and a high cost of living.

.   .   .

The monopoly bourgeoisie is a useless growth on the social organism, one unneeded in production. The industries are run by hired managers, engineers, and technicians. The monopolists lead a parasitical life and with their menials consume a substantial portion of the national income created by the toil of proletarians and peasants.

Fear of revolution, the successes of the socialist countries, and the pressure of the working-class movement compel the bourgeoisie to make partial concessions with respect to wages, labor conditions, and social security. But more often than not mounting prices and inflation reduce these concessions to nought. Wages lag behind the daily material and cultural requirements of the worker and his family, which grow as society develops. Even the relatively high standard of living in the small group of capitalistically developed countries rests upon the plunder of the Asian, African, and Latin-American peoples, upon non-equivalent exchange, discrimination of female labor, brutal oppression of Negroes and immigrant workers, and also upon the intensified exploitation of the working people in those countries. The bourgeois myth of "full employment" has proved to be sheer mockery, for the working class is suffering continuously from mass unemployment and insecurity. In spite of some successes in the economic struggle, the condition of the working class in the capitalist world is, on the whole, deteriorating.

.   .   .

The uneven development of capitalism alters the balance of forces between countries and makes the contradictions between them more acute. The economic and with it the political and military centre of imperialism, has shifted from Europe to the United States. U.S. monopoly capital, gorged on war profits and the arms race, has seized the most important sources of raw materials, the markets, and the spheres of investment, has built up a unique kind of colonial empire and become the biggest *international exploiter*. Taking cover behind spurious professions of freedom and democracy, U.S. imperialism is in effect performing the function of *world gendarme,* supporting reactionary dictatorial regimes and decayed monarchies, opposing democratic, revolutionary changes, and launching aggressions against peoples fighting for independence.

The U.S. monopoly bourgeoisie is the mainstay of international reaction. It has assumed the role of "savior" of capitalism. The U.S. financial tycoons are engineering a "holy alliance" of imperialists and founding aggressive military blocs. American troops and war bases are stationed at the most important points of the capitalist world.

But the facts reveal the utter incongruity of the U.S. imperialist claims to world domination. Imperialism has proved incapable of stemming the socialist and national-liberation revolutions. The hopes which American imperialism pinned on its atomic-weapons monopoly fell through. The United States has not been able to retain its share in the economy of the capitalist world, although it is still capitalism's chief economic, financial, and military force. The United States, the strongest capitalist power, is past its zenith and has entered the stage of decline.

.   .   .

The bourgeois system came into being with the alluring slogans of liberty, equality, fraternity. But the bourgeoisie made use of these slogans merely to elbow out the feudal gentry and to assume power. Instead of equality a new gaping abyss of social and economic inequality appeared. Not fraternity but ferocious class struggle reigns in bourgeois society.

Monopoly capital is revealing its reactionary, antidemocratic substance more and more strikingly. It does not tolerate even the former bourgeois-democratic freedoms, although it proclaims them hypocritically. In the current stage of historical development it is getting harder for the bourgeoisie to propagate slogans of equality and liberty. The upswing of the international labor movement restricts the maneuvers of finance capital. Finance capital can no longer squash the revolutionary sentiments of the masses and cope with the inexorably growing revolutionary, anti-imperialist movement by means of the old slogans and by bribing the labor bureaucracy.

Having taken full possession of the principal material values, monopoly capital refuses to share political power with anyone. It has established a dictatorship, the dictatorship of the minority over the majority, the dictatorship of the capitalist monopolies over society. The ideologists of imperialism hide the dictatorship of monopoly capital behind specious slogans of freedom and democracy. They declare the imperialist powers to be countries of the "free world" and represent the ruling bourgeois circles as opponents of all dictatorship. In reality, however, freedom in the imperialist world signifies nothing but freedom to exploit the working class, the working people, not only at home, but in all other countries that fall under the iron heel of the monopolies.

The bourgeoisie gives extensive publicity to the allegedly democratic nature of its election laws, singing special praise to its multiparty system and the possibility of nominating many candidates. In reality, however, the monopolists deprive the masses of the opportunity to express their will and elect genuine champions of their interests. Being in control of such potent means as capital, the press, radio, cinema, television, and using their hench-men in the trade unions and other mass organizations, they mislead the masses and impose their own candidates upon the electorate. The different bourgeois parties are usually no more than different factions of the ruling bourgeoisie.

.   .   .

The financial oligarchy resorts to the establishment of Fascist regimes, banking on the army, police, and gendarmerie as a last refuge from the people's wrath, especially when the masses try to make use of their democratic rights, albeit curtailed, to uphold their interests, and end the all-pervading power of the monopolies. Although the vicious German and Italian Fascism has crashed, Fascist regimes still survive in some countries, and Fascism is being revived in new forms in others.

Thus, *the world imperialist system is rent by deep-rooted and acute contradictions.* The antagonism of labor and capital, the contradictions between the people and the monopolies, growing militarism, the break-up of the colonial system, the contradictions between the imperialist countries, conflicts and contradictions between the young national states and the old colonial powers, and—most important of all—the rapid growth of world socialism, are sapping and destroying imperialism, leading to its weakening and collapse.

.   .   .

1

American Ideology

FALSIFIERS OF
THE AMERICAN REVOLUTIONARY HERITAGE
Kh. F. Sabirov

In this selection, Kh. F. Sabirov analyzes the "ideological heritage" bequeathed by Jefferson, Paine, and Franklin and its current treatment—primarily falsification, he asserts—by contemporary American scholars. Although these founding fathers were representatives of the bourgeoisie (albeit, largely unwittingly), they were "progressive" for their age and many of their revolutionary-democratic ideas can still serve as ideological weapons against the forces of American reaction. However, the Communists, who not unexpectedly in the author's view lead the progressive forces, cannot fully embrace the teachings of these three enlightened thinkers because they were speaking on behalf of the bourgeoisie. Communists must carefully pick and choose only those concepts which abet the struggle against capitalism.

This work was sponsored by the Academy of Social Sciences and the Central Committee of the Soviet Communist Party. The Academy is, in effect, a graduate school of the Party devoted to research and the preparation of teaching materials in the humanities and the social sciences.

. . . The rich ideological heritage of B. Franklin, T. Jefferson, and T. Paine is becoming the object of a sharp ideological struggle in the U.S.A. On the one hand, the ideologists of American imperialism disown the revolutionary and more progressive aspects of the world outlook held by these representatives of the American Enlightenment, while on the other hand they try to elevate their weak points, which leads to the falsification of their ideological heritage in order to adapt it to the defense and justification of the rotten capitalist structure.

The true greatness of the eighteenth-century bourgeois representatives of

FROM "Amerikanskie prosvetiteli i ikh sovremennye fal'sifikatory," *Kritika sovremennoi burzhuaznoi filosofii i sotsiologii* (Moscow, 1961), pp. 204–71. Translated by the editor.

enlightened thought is that they promoted social progress, struggled against the historical remnants of feudalism in their own society, and fought for the new, higher form, which at that time was capitalism. Nowadays, when socialism shows capitalism in a bad light, the bourgeois ideologists on the one hand attempt to utilize these enlightened American thinkers in the service of reaction for the defense of the old, dying order, and on the other hand either deliberately relegate to oblivion or simply falsify the strongest, most progressive democratic and revolutionary aspects of their thought.

Such an approach to the ideological heritage of these men fundamentally contradicts the spirit and essence of their philosophy.

.   .   .

The historical limits of the age, together with the concept of idealism in the comprehension of social relationships and their bourgeois limitations, prevented B. Franklin, T. Jefferson, and T. Paine from understanding that the state was a product of the division of society into antagonistic classes and that it was created as a weapon of rule of one class over another. Instead of this, they naively and mistakenly maintained that the state, which is based on a social contract, brings happiness and prosperity to all.

These men of the Enlightenment committed a mistake in the very cornerstone of their teaching about society and the state, believing in the idealistic, metaphysical teachings about the eternal, unchanging "human nature" as the basis for understanding social relationships. They did not see man and his essence as an aggregate of definite social relationships of a concrete historical period. For them the "common man" existed outside a defined social circle, outside a definite historical period. According to this approach, all complicated social phenomena lead, in the final analysis, to the individual, to the abstract nature of man.

.   .   .

Despite their idealistic and metaphysical character, the theories of "natural law" and "social contract" of these American thinkers, under the concrete historical conditions of the eighteenth century, had great progressive significance. When we speak about the abstract nature of their teachings concerning human nature and natural rights, this does not at all mean that the content that they inserted into their theories was abstract and cut off from those concrete historical events through which they had lived. On the contrary, these theories, although in abstract form, answered those questions provided by the development of society.

.   .   .

Theories of "natural rights" and "social contract" reflected the interests and demands of the young bourgeoisie who had superseded feudalism. They were directed against the class privileges of feudal society and negated the feudal-absolutist regime and the teachings of the church concerning the divine origin of the state. Under these concrete conditions, their very attempt to explain the origins of society and the state in terms of a natural development, rather than in terms of religion, God, or metaphysical forces, was of great value.

.   .   .

B. Franklin, T. Jefferson, and T. Paine, as leading figures of their time, came forward in the support not of the bourgeois class, but of all society, and sincerely thought that the revolution, having substituted a representative form for hereditary rights, guaranteed freedom and security to each member of society, conferred equal rights on all, and led to a free, happy life for each individual.

Of course, such a conception was illusory, for the revolutions of the eighteenth-century—American as well as French—were in the interests of the bourgeoisie and led to the rule of a new exploiting class, the capitalist class. But this illusion was historically inevitable.

. . .

The revolutionary rejection of the feudal absolutist system, which recognized the right of the people to depose a government that did not ensure their natural rights, was one of the most valuable and important points which these American thinkers produced in their writings on revolution.

The ideologists of the perishing [capitalist] class cannot be happy with the revolutions and revolutionaries of past years. Reactionary philosophers, sociologists, and historians of the U.S.A. are attempting to turn the revolutionary American thinkers into harmless evolutionists. But if this was the case, what was the American Revolution? If the U.S.A. had lived through its own bourgeois revolution, then it could not have been entirely devoid of ideologists or revolutionaries. It turns out that one cannot speak about revolutionaries and the revolutionary ideology of American thinkers for the simple reason that the war of the American colonists for independence supposedly was not revolutionary. In order to satisfy this antiscientific conception, it is necessary to falsify not only the history of the War of Independence, 1776–83, but the ideological heritage of the American thinkers as well.

This falsification is needed by the imperialist reactionaries to support the false "theory" of the exceptional historical development of America and American capitalism; that is, to try and prove that the United States from the very beginning of its history did not know social explosions and social revolutions in the European sense of the word, did not know class struggle and conflict as they had taken place in Europe.

Thus H. Wish in his work *Society and Thought in Early America* (1950) denies the fact that the War of Independence was a social revolution and maintains that it did not have such social consequences as the French and Russian revolutions had, but was limited to only a few basic changes in the position of the thirteen American colonies.

An even more reactionary view of the American Revolution is expressed by H. Kohn. "The United States," he writes, "produced a social revolution entirely without a revolutionary outburst. It was carried out by the upper strata of the middle class, in which feudal aristocracy was as little known as the landless peasantry or the proletariat."

However, these very American thinkers, Franklin, Jefferson, and Paine, never doubted that the War of Independence was revolutionary.

. . .

American Marxist historians have repulsed the attempts of the falsifiers of the history of the War of Independence to deny that it was a bourgeois revolution. A member of the National Committee of the Communist Party of the U.S.A., G. Green, in his work *The Enemy Forgotten,* published in New York in 1956, disrobes one of these falsifiers, Louis Hartz, by pointing out that the American and French revolutions were bourgeois in their class content, but differed in form. The American bourgeois revolution took the form of an anticolonial revolution for the freedom and independence of the thirteen colonies. This circumstance led to the fact that it did not solve many of the problems of a bourgeois revolution. For example, the plantation-type economy based on the labor of Negro slaves was not eliminated, and this forced "the country to go through yet a second revolution in the form of a Civil War."

.   .   .

The ideologists of American imperialism, H. Kohn and R. Burlingame, have attempted to say that the American colonists supposedly did not have special causes for the War of Independence. In their presentations, the American Revolution was primarily an act of chance that resulted either from a misunderstanding between the mother country and the colonies, or was inspired by ambitious people.

.   .   .

It is obvious that the cause of the American Revolution cannot be found in the story that these American thinkers incited it; rather they themselves were formed as bourgeois revolutionaries under the influence of concrete socio-economic conditions and above all under the influence of the revolutionary struggle of the masses of the thirteen colonies. Farmers, artisans, indentured servants, the middle bourgeoisie, a part of the large bourgeoisie, all took up arms not because Paine freed their consciences from devotion to the Crown, not because the author of the Declaration of Independence and his supporters showed themselves to be adroit propagandists and politicians, but because the course of historical events and the ever growing intensification of the socioeconomic and political contradictions between England and her colonies led to revolution.

.   .   .

The American thinkers taught that the sole aim of the government was to ensure the greatest possible degree of happiness to the greatest number of people. They considered such a government to be founded on representative power. Such a government, from their point of view, stands as the general center unifying all parts of society, defends alike the interests of both poor and rich, and is a dispassionate and "objective" arbitrator in solving the disagreements among various parties and groups of the population. Such a government guarantees the "common good of all," the welfare of all the people. T. Paine repeatedly pointed out that representative rule is the very best form of state power for the republican system. . . .

The weak and mistaken aspects of the theory of representative government of the American thinkers is obvious. They did not understand that the state is a weapon of class rule, a product of irreconcilable, antagonistic class contradictions in an antagonistic society. Their misunderstanding of the class basis of state power was also expressed in their reappraisal of the form government should take. They naively and mistakenly supposed that a bourgeois-democratic republic, personified in the representative form of government, contained in itself all that was necessary to cure society, acting in the interests of both the exploiters and the exploited. T. Paine wrote that he did not defend the interests of the rich against the interests of the poor, but was "firmly convinced that the true interest of one class is the actual interest of another."

.   .   .

The American thinkers pointed out that a normally functioning democratic society demands that the people should be ensured such freedoms as freedom of the press, of conscience, of unhampered distribution of their goods. Not [even] one person, they pointed out, should be subjected to persecution and violence for his religious or political beliefs. Like their ancestors, they came forward in support of academic freedom in the U.S.A. and defended the right of each member of society to education.

T. Jefferson and T. Paine based their teaching of democracy on the principles of equality and freedom. They thought that these principles derived from eternal and unchanging human nature, but in actual fact these principles were only a declaration of formal bourgeois equality and freedom, behind which was hidden exploitation, the political disenfranchisement of the exploited, and the will of the capitalist class erected as law. The common principles of democracy about which they wrote were in essence principles of bourgeois democracy. They did not take into account that formal principles of democracy by themselves do not mean anything. And [they did not see] that the full or partial realization [of these principles] depends on the location of the economic powers of society, the class to which the instruments and means of production belong, the class in power, the relationships of class forces at any given moment, and the will of whatever class constitutes the elected representatives of the people. Even with the complete establishment of the democracy of T. Jefferson and T. Paine, society would not have exceeded the limits of a bourgeois structure. But the bourgeoisie quickly lost its revolutionary spirit, so that principles of their democracy such as self-government, universal suffrage, control of the people over their representatives, and the right of the majority remained only on paper and were never established in practice in the bourgeois states.

.   .   .

In our great epoch the transition from capitalism to socialism has given birth to new forms of democracy, one-third of humanity has established the principles of socialist democracy, and for the first time in history genuine self-government is guaranteed not in words, but in actuality. Therefore, to declare nowadays that the bourgeois form of rule is rule of the people, by the people, and for the people is to deceive the working masses, to call upon them not to go forward, but backward. But this certainly does not mean that the progressive features of these democratic thinkers have lost all significance for the working masses within the bounds of the bourgeois system. On the contrary, the struggle for the establishment of the democratic ideals of Jefferson, Paine, and Lincoln has today a democratizing effect on America and in this way furthers the struggle of the progressive forces of the U.S.A. against imperialist reaction.

.   .   .

The high priests of American imperialism, shamelessly falsifying the history of the U.S.A., are endeavoring to infuse the masses of the people with the thought that they are indebted to American capitalism for the blessings of bourgeois democracy and freedom. In reality, the American people have achieved these and other bourgeois-democratic freedoms in a stubborn struggle with the capitalist class. This struggle has not weakened and goes on to this day.

In the past few years, the United States of America has exhibited the tendency to move toward a Fascist state. This has found expression in the offensive by imperialist reaction against the democratic freedoms of the people, against the right of the workers to resist the yoke of the monopolies. [The imperialists] have strengthened the persecution of democratic organizations and the hounding of the U.S. Communist Party. Persecution of all progressive forces under the false slogan of the fight against the "Reds" has assumed great proportions in the United States of America. All of this clearly demonstrates that imperialism is antagonistic to democracy.

The American people and their progressive forces, headed by the Communist Party of the U.S.A., are once again called upon to defend their rights and their bourgeois-democratic freedoms, incorporated in the Bill of Rights adopted in 1791 after a stubborn four-year struggle by the American people led by T. Jefferson against the Federalists. The principles of bourgeois democracy, which T. Jefferson and T. Paine considered as conditions for the normal functioning of a democratic society, are being trampled upon by U.S. monopoly capital.

In America today there are actually about fifty restrictive qualifications that in fact eliminate suffrage for tens of millions of American citizens. Among these is the property qualification which Jefferson and Paine were so decisively against. . . .

In the Senate, the House of Representatives, and the government of the U.S.A. there are no representatives of the people. There sit the henchmen of the powerful monopolies and corporations who direct government business.

. . .

Control of the activities of the government is realized not by the American people, but by the National Association of Manufacturers (NAM), which embraces nearly sixteen-thousand employers. It defines and directs the policies of the U.S. government. The United States is not governed by the will of the majority of the citizens of the country as the men of the Enlightenment thought, but by the will of an insignificant minority, by the will of the bosses of the mighty trusts, cartels, and monopolies, the will of "big business."

. . .

Since the time of T. Paine, the social contrasts and conflicts of bourgeois society have immeasurably grown and deepened. The ideal of B. Franklin, T. Jefferson, and T. Paine about a society of small property owners has turned out to be utopian. But in imperialist America there are still quite a few apologists who endeavor to convince the working masses that the ideal of these American thinkers is not utopian, but lives in reality. The ideologists of imperialism write a lot about the fact that the past fifty years in the U.S.A. have produced "decentralization" of property and a softening of the character of American capitalism. The high priests of imperialism, without tiring, proclaim that imperialism is dead, that its place has been taken by "people's capitalism" or "economic humanism."

The illusion of the "decentralization" of property ownership, of the disappearance of classes in the U.S.A. or the illusion of America as a middle-class society is clearly exposed by the sociologist [C. Wright] Mills, who is not distinguished by special sympathies for Communism, in his book *The Power Elite* (1956). He writes that in 1952 corporation shares, which attract the earnings of wide strata of the people, were owned by only 6.5 million people, or less than 7 percent of all the adult population of the U.S.A., while only 1.4 percent of all industrial workers owned stock.

.   .   .

A dying class completely sheds its ideological baggage—such are the immutable laws of history. For example, the position of the ideologists and politicians of American imperialism toward the ideological heritage of their spiritual fathers, the representatives of American Enlightenment, confirms this truth. American imperialism denies all that is valuable in the democratic heritage of B. Franklin, T. Jefferson and T. Paine. Such are the relations of the America of the Rockefellers, Du Ponts, Morgans, and the magnates of American capital to the democratic heritage of the American past.

But there is another America, the America of the people, of the working class, of the toiling farmers, of the progressive intelligentsia, the America of the future genuine owners of the richest capitalist country of the world, whose wealth is created by their labor.

At the head of progressive America stands the Communist Party of the U.S.A. This America is the real inheritor and continuer of the democratic and revolutionary traditions of B. Franklin, T. Jefferson, and T. Paine. It takes for its ideological armament that which is rejected by the shameful imperialist reaction of the U.S.A.

.   .   .

A leading member of the Communist Party of the U.S.A., Eugene Dennis, as a prisoner of the "cold war" and McCarthyism, sat in prison for almost five years for his Communistic convictions. He greeted the 177th anniversary of the signing of the Declaration of Independence from jail. In a letter to his son from jail on the fifth of July, 1953, he wrote:

Reading the information and the reactionary articles, I automatically thought that if the Founding Fathers had been alive today, they would probably also have greeted the Fourth of July in jail. For if they are judged from the point of view of the present rulers of our country, Thomas Jefferson, Samuel Adams, and Tom Paine would have turned out to be among the subversive and dangerous elements, because they taught that all people were created free and equal and that they possess certain inalienable rights, among which are the right to life, liberty, and the pursuit of happiness, and that when the government becomes a hindrance for the fulfillment of these goals it must either be replaced or destroyed.

.   .   .

The ideologists of American imperialism proclaim themselves the sole and lawful inheritors of the traditions of the American people, and slanderously maintain that the Communist Party of the U.S.A. is not a national party that has grown on American soil, but that it has no connection with the traditions of the American people.

. . .

Communists are the spokesmen of the class interests of the most revolutionary and most progressive class in history, the proletariat. They are the fighters for socialism, for that social structure which once and for all time will eliminate private property as an instrument and means of production to which is tied the exploitation of man by man. From this it is clear that Communists cannot be simply inheritors and continuers of the revolutionary-democratic traditions of the past. . . .

Communists do not take anything from this heritage without a critical Marxist-Leninist analysis but defend those features, those aspects of their democratic and revolutionary heritage that have definite value today in the struggle against the menace of Fascism and the dictators of monopolistic capital, and for the preservation and broadening of bourgeois democracy in order to facilitate the struggle of the American proletariat for socialism.

. . .

Democratic, progressive America has not forgotten and will never forget its great sons, Benjamin Franklin, Thomas Jefferson, and Thomas Paine. They have gone down in the history of the U.S.A. as manly and fearless defenders of the freedom and independence of the American people and as the founders of its best democratic traditions, for the realization of which progressive and democratic America is struggling today under the difficult conditions of a dictatorship of monopolistic capital. The future belongs to this progressive side of America, and it shall be victorious!

AMERICAN MIRAGES

Lev N. Mitrokhin

The following account of the lack of spiritual feeling in American life is excerpted from an impressionistic report on the United States by a Soviet writer who twice visited this country with youth delegations in 1960 and 1961. Perhaps this piece can best be introduced by quoting from *Komsomolskaya Pravda's* glowing review of the book, *American Mirages* (January 20, 1963), which contrasts it with Viktor Nekrasov's impressions of the United States to be found in the section on American society.

L. Mitrokhin is not a professional writer. Nevertheless, his American observations are far more mature and well-grounded than, for example, the essay on the U.S.A. by the well-known writer, Viktor Nekrasov. . . . Nekrasov's essay suffered from superficiality and often from an attitude of compromise toward what the writer saw and heard in his fourteen-day visit to the U.S.A. . . . . It is surprising, to put it mildly, what Viktor Nekrasov failed to see in the U.S.A.—the crying social contradictions, the unbridled reign of militarism, the McCarthyist hysteria, attested to by even the reactionary American press itself.

But the book *American Mirages* attracts the reader both in form and in substance. It is distinguished by freshness and depth of outlook, by the author's ability to understand the complex phenomena of American reality and to give them a party appraisal. And this is precisely why it is convincing.

THE EROSION OF IDEALS

Just a short while ago the New World was completely satisfied with its thinking, moods, and ideals. However, for the last decade a serious alarm has been sounding more clearly in official America about this matter. Up until now Americans of high standing have not placed value on ideas. Dollars were considered to have the highest value—the highest goal in life was their acquisition, the greatest happiness was solid capital. Ideas, conceptions, thoughts, theories—all these were considered to be an oddity of Europeans, who with their passion for impractical "metaphysics" only manifested an inability to view life "in a businesslike manner." The traditional view of America as the "Promised Land," where human happiness flourished in abundance and was warmed by the light of the almighty dollar, was furthered by a "practical outlook upon the world" peculiar to Americans.

Americans, it seemed, had always been accustomed to the idea that their country was the richest, the most noble, and the most virtuous country in the world. For a long time the U.S.A. stood aside from the bubbling front-line cauldron, and wars there smacked of additional profits; capital invested overseas at a huge profit was listed as "philanthropy," and the enormous income derived from it was viewed as a modest compensation for a display of magnanimity. The legend of good Uncle Sam as the ubiquitous philanthropist seemed impregnable. And even though at times his manners were lacking and he obviously had no spiritual refinement, his pockets were spilling over with lollipops which he, like a Christmas Santa Claus, passed out among the multilingual barefoot crowd.

This popular picture of the prosperous businessman with the kind heart was always false. It ignored the severe crises within the country and the millions of unemployed, the tragedy of the Indians and the Negroes, and the worldwide system of robbery. For the time being, all of this seemed to be safely hidden under the pile of words about "equality," "love for one's neighbor," and "brotherhood." The stream of words grew. They were unwound on fast rotary presses: in our age there is plenty of paper.

A challenge was made by the Soviet Union.

.   .   .

In 1950 the well-known John Foster Dulles had already written in his book *War or Peace:*

FROM *Amerikanskie mirazhi* (Moscow, 1962), pp. 11–24, 165–73. Translated by the editor.

Something bad is happening to our country; otherwise we would not have found ourselves in such a position and frame of mind as we now do. The source of unrest is not of material character. . . . We lack a true and dynamic belief, and without it little else helps. Neither political figures, nor diplomats, nor the most powerful bombs can help us to compensate for our lack of faith.

"The Soviet Union," he observes, "is achieving great success" in the ideological competition, where its techniques are excelling ours in the same way that cannons excel the bow and arrow." Dulles sees the reason for this in the fact that "the Soviet Communists have worked out a program that possesses a huge magnetic attraction for all who consider themselves oppressed or deceived by the existing system, and also for some idealists who are striving to perfect the world."

During the past decade, which the American playwright Arthur Miller has picturesquely and precisely called the "decade of the expulsion of brains," complaints concerning the defects of American ideology have been made more and more persistently. The condition of the U.S.A. has been characterized by Americans themselves as a "vacuum of ideas."

American authors originally mentioned this "vacuum" in a purely pragmatic sense: American ideology is losing the battle with the teachings of Communism on an international scale. There are many acknowledgments of this type in the American press. For example, the newspaper the Washington *Post* announced: "With merely guns, dollars, and diplomacy we cannot do battle with an enemy who has all this and who is moving forward because he is armed with another more powerful weapon—ideology." The fears of the defenders of imperialism are very well founded. More and more Americans suggest that the Soviet Union is acting upon the minds of millions of peoples more successfully than the United States is.

.   .   .

But complaints have gradually come forward concerning the poverty of ideas for "internal use." The well-known American religious preacher Billy Graham says: "Despite external prosperity, America is being eaten away by a moral and spiritual cancer which will lead to the destruction of the country if we do not cure the illness in time." This statement by the prominent evangelist is printed in the book *Goals for Americans*. He further states in the book: "We have become a nation of cowards. Great courage, which at one time was characteristic of America and Americans, is seemingly abandoning us. Many of our leaders are deeply troubled over the disappearance of the desire to fight for that in which we believe."

Thus, the traditional American belief that dollars are the universal equivalent for human value is gradually being undermined. "More than anything else we are in need of a constant flow of new ideas," says President Kennedy, "—in the government, the nation, the press, and public opinion we need those who respect new ideas and the people who have them." America lacks ideals, but you can't buy them with money!

The problem of ideals has appeared in the United States as a national problem. Academic theorists and nimble journalists have been thrown into the urgent search for them. Eisenhower, when he was President, founded a special "President's Commission on National Goals" that was supposed to outline "a program of action for the 1960's." In 1960 the book *Goals for Americans* appeared, presenting the report of this committee.

One must say that even the American press reacted skeptically to the result of the committee's work. "It seemed that from such a group of authors," wrote the newspaper the New York *Times,* "one should have expected a powerful summons to battle for a more powerful and better America. . . . But the committee's report, published today, does not justify such hopes. It will scarcely be able to summon any significant wave of creative enthusiasm from amidst the people." A reading of the committee's report convinces us that this bitter confession is well founded. However, the failure of this undertaking was least of all the result of the qualifications and capabilities of the committee members—it actually was predetermined.

. . .

Ideals are not oysters: they are not swallowed whole. They cannot be decreed from above and do not become intimate merely because they are constantly flashed before one's eyes. Ideals cannot be thrust upon society if they do not flow from human experience. People must accept an ideal, believe in it, know the real paths toward its achievement, and subordinate their lives to this goal. Only then can it become "dynamic." The essence is not so much in the perfection of a formula as it is in the character of social relations in which the person is situated. In other words, the question is this: Does the given society have available real possibilities for the ideals to be translated into facts? If it does not, then all discussions about "national goals" are empty phrases.

The truth consists in the fact that contemporary imperialism, by its very essence and by its inherent laws of development, is not in any condition to advance social ideals which would be able to inspire wide sections of the population. Indeed, the main principle of the American economy, as of any other based on a private capitalist foundation, is the principle of "making money." In such a society the magnitude of surplus value is found to be that dispassionate and compulsory regulator, the action of which not one enterprise can avoid, regardless of how its proprietor forms its objectives. Under capitalism the principle "man is to man as to a wolf" is the unavoidable consequence of the objective laws of this society. Thus, the cause is not in the amorality of the individual, but in the depravity of the entire social system.

. . .

A bourgeois government cannot truthfully formulate the main objectives of its activities because they become subservient to the great monopolists. It is obliged to hide these goals, to mask internal policies with a curtain of phrases about "humanism," "interests of the people," and "democracy," and to cast illusions about the genuine motives of its activities. These illusions are still sufficiently vital among American youth. But they will inevitably come to an end because the more young men and women take an increasingly active part in the political life of the United States (and this process is characteristic of contemporary America), the more they will become convinced of the falsity of the popular sociological myths. And without fail they will arrive at a true, materialistic understanding of history.

. . .

Thus far I have not touched on one facet of culture in the United States—religion. Without this, it would be impossible to understand the spiritual life of America, the thoughts and the moods of American youth. In that country everyone speaks of God, including those who have never experienced any feeling toward the Most High. Religiosity is considered to be an inalienable attribute of the "American way of life," an indispensable characteristic of a 100 percent citizen of the United States. The fact that the phrase "In God We Trust" has almost become a national emblem testifies to the seriousness of official opinion in this regard. The phrase is even on coins and bank notes.

Religion also exerts a substantial influence upon the rising generation. Throughout the land, powerful religious organizations for boys and girls are active, and without them it would be difficult to understand the contemporary youth movement in the United States.

. . .

Recently it has become fashionable to assert that a genuine renaissance of religious fervor is taking place in the United States. Never, say many Western authors, have so many parishioners crowded into the churches; never has piety been spread so generously throughout the continent. In all this discussion there is a bit of journalistic sensationalism and publicity ballyhoo stemming from the wish to pass off that which is desired for that which actually exists. But to a certain degree, a growing religious influence is present. . . .

What are the reasons for the growth of religious sentiments?

One of them doubtlessly lies in the fact that in recent years churches and religious organizations have been significantly activated. According to data in the book *The United States Answers,* there are in America 267 different religious communities and 307,000 churches. Churches play a significant role in the educational system; 771 higher educational institutions are controlled by religious organizations. In the Catholic church alone, there are 12,850 primary and secondary schools, colleges, and universities. In 1958, 1,050 denominational books with religious themes and 12 million copies of the Bible were sold. . . .

But it is necessary to take one important thing into consideration: even though the church is so active, its activities do not serve as the primary reason for a yearning for God. The peculiarity of a religious world view is such that in a capitalistic society it is kept in the consciousness not only as a consequence of decrees from above, but mainly because in real life there are moments which prod men to search for God.

. . .

If one believes in the strength of Christian morality, then every social conflict, contradiction, and violation of the morals "given by God" only gives one the resoluteness to preach more actively religious views and to see in this his debt to society. We met many honest young men and women who were seriously troubled by the suffering of millions of simple people. They said:

We cannot indifferently sit around without doing anything. It is necessary for one to find his path toward peace and happiness among men. Christianity shows the way. If all people on this earth observed the standards of Christian morality, the world would be saved from the horrors of war and violence and pillage and moral crimes. We, of course, know that even many believers do not observe these standards. This means that our duty consists in struggling for the dissemination of these principles and for their close observance. We must be the warriors for a sincere and active Christianity which "floods the heart."

One American girl, who had lived in Japan for several years and had been active in missionary work there said: "For me, life would become senseless and would lose all its appeal if I did not believe in the strength of Christian ideas."

Religious youth organizations lean on just such sentiments to unite millions of young American men and women. It looks as if it were a closed cycle: on one side there is the very environment in which the life of American youth flows, where they are brought up with a craving for religion, thus forming a basis for broad activities of religious youth organizations; and on the other side, these organizations instill religious sentiments even more strongly into young minds, and raise in a religious spirit young people who have just entered life.

Many foreign authors emphasize that American children are completely free in their choice of a world view and that they have full opportunity independently and privately to clarify their relationship with God. . . . To speak of their "freedom" of choice of religions is senseless—everything depends upon the ideological conditions under which the beliefs of children are formed. And in America much attention is given to making a true believer out of the child, and to inculcating religious ideas in him more firmly. A well-regulated preaching apparatus binds him well and stubbornly strives to print lines from the "Holy Scriptures" upon the young mind.

From early childhood, one is shown that "a knowledge of and love for God" is more necessary than anything else in order to have a happy and fully successful life. Millions of books are printed under the guidance of the leaders for the religious training of children. Here are a few excerpts from them. What is their recommendation to parents? First, and foremost to pray themselves. "The custom of parents praying," we read in one of these textbooks, "is an integral part of the domestic atmosphere which the child subconsciously adopts and which determines his early attitude toward prayer." Further advice is constantly given to set a personal example by reading the Bible "so that the child may learn at an early age what it is all about," and to hang pictures with biblical themes in the house so that the children may ask about them, and "in this way to direct their minds toward Bible study." Parents should recommend singing religious songs to their children, who then "will direct their thoughts toward Christ." Instead of telling children the usual fairy tales, gospel stories and the Bible should be read, and so forth.

.   .   .

2

American Politics

WHO REALLY GOVERNS?

A. N. Yakovlev

The first section of A. N. Yakovlev's *The Intellectual Poverty of The Apologists of the "Cold War"* is devoted to the question: who defines foreign policy in the United States? Although the author rather crudely condemns the American governmental system as a sham, he shows an unusual familiarity with the pertinent American literature on the subject. Yakovlev is one of the few Soviet authors who recognize political science as a separate discipline—although he is bewildered by its focus and subject matter. He also reveals some detailed knowledge of American politics in a section not reproduced here, which discusses the last several Presidential campaigns. Here, in an attempt to prove that the public has little say in governmental policy, Yakovlev "tests" the various concepts about American politics held by political scientists and journalists. One of the prominent themes in essays of this genre is the fraudulent nature of the two-party system, a point colorfully made by Premier Khrushchev:

Once, in one of my addresses, I said that in the United States during elections actually two parties fight between themselves—the Republican, whose symbol is the elephant, and the Democratic, whose symbol is the donkey. During election campaigns, as the Americans say, a show is performed. . . . During these shows, [some] of the demonstrators go around with an appeal to vote for the elephant, and the others for the donkey. I can't say to which of these animals one should give preference [or] which one is more intelligent. It seems the donkey and the elephant are of equal value. But the [voters] have no other choice, for they are pressured by the capitalist press, radio, television, and advertising [February 27, 1963].

The basis of the "democratic process," on which the whole structure of political and economic life of the country is anchored, is, according to the assertion of American propagandists, the existence and political rivalry of the Republican and Democratic parties. Frequently the idea is put forth that the exchange of parties in power signifies a peculiar "vital stimulation," imparting

FROM "Kto opredeliaet vneshnoiu politiku," *Ideinaia nishcheta apologetov "kholodnoi voiny"* (Moscow, 1961), pp. 19–82. Translated by the editor.

to society a needed "dynamism" and "strength," and that Congress, as the highest legislative organ of the country, formulates the will of the people. The American bourgeois sociologists persistently drum into the heads of the voters that, by showing their preference during elections for candidates of one or the other party, they exercise "a deciding influence" on the internal and foreign policies of the government. . . .

However, the logic of facts frequently forces some American sociologists to make typical qualifications that show the total bankruptcy of the assertion of the "democracy" of the American two-party system. When authors present a concrete analysis of the practical activities of the parties, they inevitably come to the conclusion that there exists no difference between them.

For example, in the work *The United States Political System and How It Works* D. Coyle writes that "At the present time the two parties ever more resemble each other. They are sometimes called twins." American voters, he writes, feel that the Democrats and Republicans "have only different candidates," and that the parties in general are only "organizations for contesting elections and taking control of the government." The parties change policies only in words.

.   .   .

Considering the two-party system the basis of the "democratic process," the authors, at the same time, are not able to hide their concern in connection with the weakness of the party organs and their inability to define policy. The national party committees recognize that they are not empowered to define the political line, either in theory or in practice. The leaders of both parties in Congress, as well as the members of the government, act independently from the central organs of the ruling party. . . . Parties have neither staffs, nor programs, nor ideological platforms. . . .

The 1960 elections, as recognized by the American press, were a clearly defined political farce. Not having any new ideas, programs, or practical proposals that might attract American voters, the leaders of the parties offered political jabber, discussions without content, loud vaudeville acts, and theatrical performances instead of ideas. Women's hats, men's shirts, and balloons with the picture of the candidate of the Republicans, Nixon, called on the voters to vote for the "single person" who could talk "firmly" with the Soviet Union. Contemporary techniques were thrown into the pre-election battle. Short excerpts from Nixon's political declarations were recorded on tape and hooked up to a telephone net so that the voters could dial a number in order to hear Nixon's voice and learn his views on the most important political questions. But, as is known, nothing could help the candidate of the Republican Party win the Presidency.

.   .   .

Both parties are the child of one and the same class, but, at the same time, the monopolistic groupings have their "favorites," which they foster, finance, and lead to power; and they also extract benefits from the situation they have created. The struggle between the parties also expresses to some degree the antagonisms between financial combinations. And therefore the party in power, while defending the interests of the capitalist class as a whole, considers the special interests of that coalition of financial groups which led it to power.

All this makes the mutual relations of the state apparatus and the monopolistic circles pretty complicated. It would not be true to assert that a given party stands only for such and such a financial group. Both parties are in the service of the financial oligarchies of the U.S.A. as a whole. However, in recent years it has become clear that the Republican Party is enjoying the special support of the Rockefeller oil empire. Not long before the 1952 elections, the organ of the oil monopolies, *Petroleum News,* called for all oil groups to concur in an agreement. "Otherwise," it warned, "the oil industry may find itself in a position where the Eisenhower Administration might not be able to defend it." The Rockefeller oil empire urged more effort to bring the Republican Party to power in 1952 and to preserve the Republican President in 1956.

. . .

The Republican and Democratic Parties continue to occupy fairly firm positions in American political life. Many Americans still believe that by their votes they may influence policy, and that, as widely publicized, the government expresses the will of the people. But, at the same time, it is becoming clear that the gap between the point of view of the ruling political circles, the government, and the party leaders, and that of the people on many questions of domestic policy and international relations is significantly widening. . . .

Reviewing the staffing of the government after the Republican Party came to power, bourgeois propaganda was forced to recognize a massive penetration of "big business" in all the institutions of the Eisenhower Administration. The representatives of monopolies, for example, represented 82 percent of the positions in the Post Office Department, 68 percent in the Department of Defense, and 65 percent in the Department of Commerce. [*Fortune,* 1954]. Members of the government officially participated in eighty-six corporations with assets of over $20 billion. According to a count by V. Perlo, of the 272 highest posts in the state, 150 were occupied by capitalists. The remaining 122 persons were closely connected with corporations. . . .

After the Republican Party came to power, many prominent presidents of companies and banks and chairmen of trusts and corporations became the closest advisers of the President, entering the so-called power élite. Also, at the so-called bachelor meals and during golf, the President was surrounded by bigwigs of huge monopolistic combines and their henchmen. . . .

How did bourgeois propaganda explain this process? Suggesting to Americans that only the government may decide all problems of the economy, bourgeois sociologists recognized as normal and also necessary the direct participation of business people in the activities of government. Rovere, for example, wrote that businessmen are the more gifted people. They do not have experience in state administration, but they are well acquainted with economics and finances which, as they say, are much more important for the life of the country than politics. . . .

After the Eisenhower Administration came to power, the law on controls over prices was abolished, and the legal investigation of railroads and oil companies for monopolistic practices under the antitrust laws was stopped. Reform in the tax structure gave a huge gift to the monopolies and caused great losses to the wide masses of the American people.

. . .

The massive penetration of the "big business" people into governmental institutions attests to the complete bankruptcy of the assertions of the bourgeois sociologists, trying to justify this phenomenon as "in the general national interest." All the activity of the capitalists and their lieutenants, co-opted into the government, attests to the fact that under the Republican Administration the ruling monopolistic circles did not particularly mask the process of the further subordination of the state machine to the financial oligarchy. . . .

Under the Republican Administration, many generals and admirals occupied important posts in corporations and took an active part in the struggle to increase military expenditures in general and to get a large number of military orders for their companies. Generals and admirals served in the governing bodies of all corporations directly or indirectly connected with military production. The process of strengthening the ties between the militarists and the monopolists reached dangerous proportions. In 1955 alone more than two thousand military men left the army and went to the corporations. . . .

The logical consequences of the blossoming of militarism in the United States, and its component part, was the strengthening of the military organs of the state. The rapid growth of the role of the National Security Council may serve as a characteristic example. The development of an aggressive foreign policy by the United States led to a situation where the sessions of the American Congress began to have only an informational character. In the first place the National Security Council was created in 1947. Even under the Democrats, the Council decided many of the most important questions of military and foreign policy. The national-liberation struggle of the peoples of Greece, China, Indonesia, and Indochina; the annual military budget; the questions of Israel, Germany, Austria, Iran, and Korea; military blocs, NATO in particular; and many others were the subject of discussion in the National Security Council. . . .

All the posts in the National Security Council are distributed among the strongest monopolistic groups. In the first Council under Eisenhower, eight of thirteen persons had come directly from high financial circles, and three others were closely tied with them. The Rockefeller group had influence in the Council. From time to time changes were made in its composition, but they did not destroy the relationship of forces, reflecting the degree of direct participation of this and other financial groups in defining the government's policy.

. . .

Up to this time, a significant number of Americans have maintained the belief that the U.S. government can keep under control the pressures of the monopolies and their influences which cast a shadow over all of the country's affairs. The bourgeois propagandists do everything possible to preserve this illusion. But also, many bourgeois authors are not able to hide the fact that the American government is becoming less and less independent and more and more dependent on monopolistic groups. Some authors maintain that the governmental organs are put under constant pressure by certain "interest groups" through the system of lobbying. Others, more candid in their conclusions, recognize explicitly that the American government is an obedient plaything in the hands of the financial oligarchy. By the term "lobbying" in the

U.S.A. is meant a system of pressure on legislative organs and the government. This pressure is applied by monopolistic combinations, political organizations, and groups, and also by individuals soliciting some kind of privilege. Part of the operation of "lobbying" is the practice of bribing members of Congress and governmental functionaries. . . .

According to American authors, members of the U.S. Congress find themselves under the constant pressure of "interest groups," directing the activity of this organ in their own interests. "Pressure groups," is the label American propagandists usually give to lobbyists, and the emissaries of these organizations are considered in the U.S.A. to be the "third house" of Congress. The active work of "pressure groups" indicates the complete nonsense of the thesis, widely publicized in the United States, that the policy of the state is worked out in sessions of Congress. In actual fact, as D. Coyle has remarked, Congress serves only as a "market place, the goods for which are produced elsewhere, mainly in committees and corridors."

. . .

Congress and parties profit by the active influence of lobbyists and "pressure groups." However, they devote special attention to the administration of the United States which Blaisdell has called "government under pressure." He writes that to an extreme degree, "thousands of lobbyists and associations are active in Washington. . . . Today these forces are regarded as normal phenomena in the work of the government. . . ."

What means do lobbyists and "pressure groups" use to achieve these goals? Some of them search for and occupy positions from which it is easy to influence governmental decisions: the selection and promotion of people who do their bidding; the organization of special institutes (public and scientific) that render aid to governmental councils or participate in the discussion of questions; and the creation, with the help of the press, radio, television, of favorable public opinion, the necessary "political atmosphere." Under these conditions the lobbyists do not write laws, but prefer to remain behind the backs of the official representatives of the legislative and executive organs. Other lobbyists solicit official posts. In this and other cases, the deciding influence is money. . . .

Bourgeois propagandists try desperately to persuade Americans that lobbyists and "pressure groups," standing behind Congress and the government. . . . express "public opinion." This assertion is based on the fact that in the nation there are thousands of lobbying organizations which are rivals. They say that so long as the demands of one may only be realized at the expense of the others no one remains fully satisfied. Everyone, you see, receives "equal parts," which correspond to the interests of the "whole society." In this is visible the attempts of the ideologists of imperialism to conceal the active role of the monopolistic combinations and financial groups—the only real holders of power in the country—to show that the policy of the government is defined by "public opinion," expressed by the lobbyists—and not the monopolies—coming forward, according to the logic of the bourgeois sociologists, in the capacity of "petitioners" for "all other" classes, groups, and organizations.

. . .

THE ASSASSINATION OF PRESIDENT KENNEDY

Editors of Izvestia

As elsewhere, the assassination of President Kennedy on November 22, 1963, came as a shock in the Soviet Union. By and large, with the exception noted below, Soviet reporting on the events surrounding the assassination and its aftermath was straightforward and extensive, and Soviet leaders and writers paid tribute to the slain President—in sharp contrast to comments in Chinese Communist papers. Soviet coverage, however, was colored by concern over possible international consequences of this tragic event and the fact that Lee Harvey Oswald was a self-professed Marxist of sorts who had lived for a short time in the Soviet Union. Soviet commentators made every effort to place the blame on American right-wing extremists, suggesting that they sought to use the President's death as a means to force violent anti-Soviet policies. As a *Pravda* correspondent expressed it on November 25: " . . . it is possible to conclude that a long-planned provocational operation is unfolding at full speed, recalling the burning of the German Reichstag in 1933, which the German Fascists needed for a blow against Germany's progressive forces."

The selection below was printed as an *Izvestia* editorial on November 26, 1963, and can therefore be read as an official Soviet statement on the assassination.

. . . Nov. 25 was a day of national mourning in the United States of America. The American people were saying farewell to President John Fitzgerald Kennedy. The peoples and governments of many countries of the world, who have sent their high-ranking figures to Washington, were paying a tribute of respect to the memory of the outstanding U.S. statesman whose life had been so tragically cut short. First Vice-Chairman of the U.S.S.R. Council of Ministers A. I. Mikoyan is representing our country at J. F. Kennedy's funeral.

"J. F. Kennedy's death is a heavy blow to all people who cherish the cause of peace and Soviet-American cooperation." These words from the message of N. S. Khrushchev, head of the Soviet government, to the new U.S. President, Lyndon B. Johnson, reflect the opinion of the entire Soviet people. The Soviet country set a high appraisal on the broad views of the late President, who took stock of the situation realistically and strove to find a path for solving international problems through negotiations.

The Soviet government, whose general line of foreign policy is formulated on Leninist principles of the peaceful coexistence of states with different socioeconomic systems, is tirelessly fighting for an easing of international tension and the strengthening of peace. Positive changes have been seen on this complicated and difficult path in recent times. They are embodied in the Moscow

FROM "America's Hours of Grief," *Izvestia* (November 26, 1963), as translated in *The Current Digest of the Soviet Press,* published weekly at Columbia University, Vol. 15, No. 46 (December 11, 1963), p. 11. Copyright 1963 by the Joint Committee on Slavic Studies, appointed by the American Council of Learned Societies and the Social Science Research Council. Reprinted by permission.

treaty banning nuclear tests. Certain other steps in the direction of improving Soviet-American relations have been projected for the future. Although not always consistently, President Kennedy's policy proceeded from an understanding of the need for such steps. He repeatedly emphasized that a course toward solving differences through war, toward the unleashing of a thermonuclear war, would be insanity.

This sober approach toward the situation in the modern world, as well as the first timid attempts to temper the acuteness of the most complicated domestic problem in the United States—the racial problem—evoked the hatred of shameless American reaction for President Kennedy.

The madmen who are ready to gamble recklessly with the destiny of the American people, the "wild men," the Fascist racists—these are the ones who took up arms against Kennedy. Was it not they who sent the assassin's bullet into the President's head? Is it not they who are now concealing the traces of the infamous crime?

President Kennedy's death has undoubtedly exacerbated the situation in the United States. The struggle between rational-thinking Americans and the forces of shameless reaction, who are not failing to exploit what has happened, is faced with tension. It will even determine the course of the unfolding election campaign.

The peace-loving public beyond the borders of the U.S.A. wants to believe that President Kennedy's departure from life in the full flower of his strength will spur his political successors to pursue the best of his traditions in the interests of peace and for the good of all mankind. The new U.S. President is solemnly obliged to continue to carry out the cause of his predecessor. He will always find a favorable response from the Soviet people and their government to everything that will serve the relaxation of international tension.

All-out efforts for the good of this cause would be the best monument to the tragically slain President of the U.S.A., John Fitzgerald Kennedy.

THE AMERICANIZATION OF FASCISM

Georgi P. Frantsov

The Soviet press expressed great concern over the nomination in June, 1964 of Senator Barry Goldwater as the Republican candidate for President. In the following article, which appeared in *Pravda* on August 12, 1964, Academician Georgi P. Frantsov attempted to provide a Marxist explanation for "Goldwaterism" by analyzing the social and economic forces impinging on political phenomena. This article shows a greater tendency to differentiate among political groups and parties than has previously been the case. For instance, compare this article with the preceding one by Yakovlev. Frantsov, one of the Soviet Union's best-known Marxist-Leninist theoreticians, is the head of the Academy of Social Sciences of the Party Central Committee.

. . . On the eve of the Second World War it was fashionable in political circles of the West to ask: Is Fascism possible in the U.S.A.? Those engaged in the argument spoke about the "national spirit" and constantly recalled "historical traditions" but ignored the class relations in the country. At the present time as well, these people or others like them are puzzled by the question: How could it happen, for instance, that the Republican Party, which is in the opposition, is being steered toward Fascism? But the answer is clear. Where monopoly capital rules, its most aggressive and reactionary circles can prevail under certain conditions.

The aggressive and reactionary circles of monopoly capital want to become an independent leading force in the political arena. They no longer want to remain "mad" factions within the traditional parties and to base their activity on all kinds of small Fascist organizations that are on the borderline of legality. They now want either the whole political arena or at least half of it. If they succeed in getting hold of the Presidency, they will take the whole state apparatus into their hands. If not, they could exert a great influence on it as a strong opposition party. As the Tonkin crime shows, the eyes of the U.S. rulers are already turned so far to the right that they are losing their ability to see the actual situation in the world.

.　　.　　.

The nature of the present-day political crisis in the U.S.A. is of course largely determined by a most bitter struggle of the monopolies and their mad competition in the conditions of monopolistic state capitalism. In the postwar period relatively new monopolies have grown and earned enormous wealth through military orders in the U.S.A. They are now called "neomillionaires." They do not want to submit any longer to the control of the "old" monopolies, to Wall Street. They have considerable capital of their own.

They want to consolidate quickly their still unstable position, which was created with the help of ventures and speculations, and to push the old monopolies away from the government levers. Monopolistic state capitalism does not in the least ensure a fraternal division among monopolies. It is typical of it that when the struggle between the monopolies reaches a certain bitterness, it becomes political and does not remain limited to the economic and business sphere because it becomes a matter of putting one's hand on the levers of state power. Such is the nature of monopolistic state capitalism. That is why the sub-rosa factional struggle of the neomillionaires within the old bourgeois parties is rapidly developing into an interparty struggle.

But why did the neomillionaires choose this particular moment for the offensive? Why has this offensive acquired a Fascist character? To answer this question in a general form, the struggle between the monopolies not only creates a bitter political conflict in the country but also expresses to an ever greater degree a political crisis that has already matured. The offense of the neomillionaires is an integral part of this crisis.

FROM "America at the Crossroads," *Pravda* (August 12, 1964), as translated (except for the last paragraph) in *The Current Digest of the Soviet Press,* published weekly at Columbia University, Vol. 16, No. 33 (September 9, 1964), pp. 25–27. Copyright 1964 by the Joint Committee on Slavic Studies, appointed by the American Council of Learned Societies and the Social Science Research Council. Reprinted by permission.

Kennedy's attempt to resurrect, to some extent, the Roosevelt course and thereby to forestall the growing danger of an isolation of the monopolies within the country and in the international arena and to draw circles of the middle and petty bourgeoisie over to his side—this attempt ended with the gunshot in Dallas. The political shift, which had been pursued not very consistently and extremely slowly, enabled the opponents to consolidate themselves but did not consolidate or arouse its adherents to a sufficient extent. The steps that brought the government closer to the Roosevelt course were attended by qualifications, reflections, procrastinations, and over-the-shoulder glances toward the most reactionary circles of the monopolies. There was too much fear that the progressive elements would become active in the country. Everybody still remembered that this had been the result of the policy of Roosevelt, after whose death the McCarthy machine was let loose to annihilate all flights of progressive thought.

After Kennedy was removed from the political arena, the question arose: Are there forces in the U.S.A. capable of pursuing his course consistently? Many people in the U.S.A., including many capitalists, realize that life, international as well as domestic, demands a course of peaceful coexistence. Some of the "old" monopolies can afford a certain curtailment of militarism, they still have plenty of opportunity for maneuver with their capital. The neomillionaires, who have earned insane sums of money through military orders and who have grown strong in an atmosphere of adventure and speculation, are not in the least inclined to follow this course. The shot fired at Kennedy is testimony to an extreme aggravation of this struggle; it indicates that the struggle has passed beyond the framework of the political organization of contemporary American society, that it is undermining the very principles of this organization. Because the political organization of the U.S.A. naturally does not allow Presidents who are multimillionaries to be shot down in broad daylight like rabbits in the forest.

But the political organization of the U.S.A. is receiving blows not from this side alone. American newspapers carry huge headlines containing the words "black revolution." By this they mean the strong movement for the emancipation of the Negroes, which has seized the whole country. This movement already has its casualties, its martyrs, its heroes fallen in battle. This movement has already gone beyond the framework of ordinary protest meetings— it has entered the sphere of political struggle.

But so far this "black revolution" has not yet fused with the discontent of other strata of American society. However, a suppressed discontent is boiling in the American "melting pot," is building up not only among the Negro strata of society. The working class is threatened by automation, which may change the entire production process and push considerable masses of the working people outside the gates of the factories. The war economy no longer brings full employment, as in the period when the new military equipment was still being mastered. The concentration on rocket technology and on thermonuclear weapons now reduces the number of enterprises and branches of industry that are drawn into the munitions maelstrom. Another question of concern is the flow of capital to the West of the country, to the neomillionaires, and the possibility that at least some of the enterprises of the East and North may lose their former importance. . . .

The most reactionary and aggressive circles of monopoly capital decided to take advantage of this moment, while the discontent of broad strata of society has not yet taken political forms and has not yet fused with the "black revolution," in other words, while the democratic forces are still disunited. They hit upon the idea of forming a party of the "white man" and to warm up and utilize old racial prejudices that have existed in the country. American society, they believe, must have its semideprived people. There must be people predestined for unskilled work alone, and then people will value still more the illusory right to skilled labor, however little there may be. This will accent more sharply the "privileged" position of the white worker and the petty bourgeoisie. Who knows, perhaps hollow chauvinistic arrogance will help in dealing with these two segments one by one.

Here we encounter American Fascism or, to be more precise, the Americanization of Fascism, since this process is not yet completed. But its outlines are already clear. They consist of attempts to fan chauvinism in the U.S.A. with the help of reckless military ventures and to create an atmosphere in the country that will make it possible to pass all kinds of "emergency laws," to foment violence, and to earn war profits. The aggression in the Gulf of Tonkin is an index of such a course. Then there is the disgusting racist demagoguery, the attempts to set whites against blacks. There is a further offensive against workers' rights under the slogan of fighting against "the excessive powers of the trade unions." Hopes are entertained of utilizing sentiments against the trade union bureaucracy to diminish the role of the trade unions themselves. You find here also demagogic shouts against the central government and against taxes. We know that at the outset the Hitlerites tried, with the most unbridled demagoguery and all kinds of promises, to befuddle the petty-bourgeois strata and to win the allegiance of citizens who were backward in their political views.

It will not be difficult to concoct an ideology for this Americanized Fascism. The shelves of book stores and libraries are filled with lunatic-fringe rightist literature. Such literature appeared in specially big amounts in the period of the McCarthy harassment of progressive elements. At that time concern was shown for providing McCarthyism with an ideology, and the fetid ideological liquid gushed like a mighty fountain in the U.S.A., as if from a broken sewer pipe.

The millionaire Hunt, who supports Goldwater, writes essays in his leisure praising a political system that American critics have nicknamed "Fascist democracy." This, of course, is as nonsensical as, say, "hot ice." Incidentally, if in Germany, a country with old socialist traditions, Fascism used the cover of "national socialism" with amazing impudence, why is not a similar mockery of the concept of "democracy" possible in the U.S.A.? After all, we know that pirates often hoisted others' flags on their masts. . . .

These then are several aspects of the process of the Americanization of Fascism. The future will show how far this process will go. But, it is possible to say right now that the world has evolved a long way since the development of Fascism in the 1930's in Germany, Italy, and Japan. In the first place, the international situation has changed. The most important factor in the development of Fascism in the 1930's was foreign assistance, connivance, and direct support. The monopolists of a number of countries dreamed how the Hitlerites could be urged on against the Soviet Union—the country of socialism, located in a hostile capitalist encirclement. Now the situation is not the same. Many representatives of capital are afraid that the American "madmen" might drag them into a deadly war against the powerful Soviet Union, against the whole socialist camp, which is capable of giving a smashing rebuff to the aggressor.

.   .   .

3

American Society

A FIFTY-FIFTY REPORT ON AMERICA

Viktor Nekrasov

Viktor Nekrasov, a Soviet writer in his late forties who was trained as an architect, wrote an impressionistic and highly readable account of his visit to the United States during the fall of 1960 in the relatively liberal Soviet literary journal *Novy Mir*. This 25,000-word article, excerpts from which are reprinted below, was published in the fall of 1962, a period during which liberal writers appeared to be gaining ascendancy over their conservative rivals. By early 1963, however, a number of liberal writers, including Nekrasov, found themselves in official disfavor.

Nekrasov is a loyal Soviet citizen and party member; his descriptions of American life are not uncritical. Nonetheless, the account of his American trip touched off a storm of criticism, as indicated by the following quotation from the review of his article that appeared in *Izvestia* on January 20, 1963.

While he claims to have rejected a journalist's advice to follow a "fifty-fifty" ratio when describing America's contrasts, V. Nekrasov has in fact taken this stand. It would not have been so bad if he had done so in describing the factual aspects of the American way of life. The whole trouble is that V. Nekrasov follows the "fifty-fifty" rule in far more serious things, in comparing the "two worlds," the two ideologies.

What does "fifty-fifty" actually mean? If this expression is translated from Aesopian into ordinary language, we have a motto proclaiming peaceful coexistence in the field of ideology. "Fifty-fifty" is a very dangerous thing. Following it, one arrives willingly or unwillingly at equating the battle on the Volga with American canned pork, Le Corbusier's blueprints with the silhouettes of the cities of the Communist tomorrow. No, we cannot agree to this!

On June 21, 1963, then First Secretary Nikita Khrushchev also took Nekrasov personally to task before the Party Central Committee:

A tourist visiting America will see it from one aspect, forcefully shown him by people appointed for this purpose. On his return home, he will think that this was what America is like. However, it is bad enough if such a person holds mistaken views himself; it is much worse if he begins to spread his erroneous impressions and views that have been foisted upon him by a hostile ideology, as the only true concept.

We were not a delegation, we were tourists. There were twenty of us: teachers, journalists, and engineers—what is known as the Soviet intelligentsia. Each of us had paid out a considerable sum, for which we were to spend fourteen days in trains and enormous buses in the northeastern U.S.A.: New York, Washington, Chicago, Niagara, Detroit, Dearborn, Buffalo, and then New York again. The leader of our group—let us call him for the sake of simplicity Ivan Ivanovich—was a wonderful man, but he had apparently been frightened since childhood. In addition, the American Express Travel Company assigned to us as our guide a lively, poised man in a bow tie named Tadeusz Osipowicz.

. . .

I will say frankly that the Soviet tourist is not allowed to go everywhere. The South—New Orleans, Louisiana, Mississippi, the places where the Negro situation is many times more complicated than it is in the North—was not included in our itinerary. In New York, Brooklyn is strictly off limits. . . .

America is a special country. One Soviet woman writer who made a visit to America said: "What struck me most of all about America was that there was nothing striking about it." Somehow I don't believe that. In any event, a great many things struck me, although I was prepared for much that I saw, such as the skyscrapers, the vast numbers of cars, the lights of Broadway, and the Sunday papers weighing a kilogram. But these very things: the gigantic buildings, the gigantic cities, the superhighways cutting across the country and traveled by thousands of cars, the twenty-story department stores, the bacchanalia of constantly blazing advertising signs, the famous American service —in a word, all the abundance and wealth that overwhelms you immediately—make for difficulties, prevent one at first from getting to the deeper and more important things.

. . .

The things our gentle Ivan Ivanovich feared most were deviations from schedules and arrangements. He was in a constant state of irrepressible tension and anxiety, was forever counting us like chickens, and the worst thing that could happen to him was that someone would say: "I don't want to go to the National Gallery, I want to go to the Guggenheim, or maybe just take a simple stroll along Broadway." For some reason he dreaded this "simple stroll" most of all.

On our first day in New York he set up the first production conference, the first "briefing session," at the entrance to the United Nations Building after we had toured it. He asked Tadeusz Osipowicz to step aside for a moment and made a short speech about discipline, about the tasks and duties of a Soviet collective on foreign soil, about how so-and-so had been late for dinner on the very first day and had got separated from the collective so that he had to take a taxi, and about how this must not happen again or he would be required to take appropriate steps—true, he did not say what these might be. Like schoolchildren, we stood along the wall of the enormous building listening to him in silence, and then the accused began to justify themselves, voices

FROM "On Both Sides of the Ocean—II," *Novy Mir* (December, 1962), as translated in *The Current Digest of the Soviet Press,* published weekly at Columbia University, Vol. 15, No. 10 (April 3, 1963), pp. 14–24. Copyright 1963 by the Joint Committee on Slavic Studies, appointed by the American Council of Learned Societies and the Social Science Research Council. Reprinted by permission.

gradually rose, and argument started, while Tadeusz Osipowicz stood apart and looked ironically at us. It was somewhat shameful.

Poor, poor Ivan Ivanovich. To some extent I understood him, and I was even a little sorry for him. After all, he had to keep track of all of us, and we were twenty—twenty people he didn't know and who had made one another's acquaintance only twenty-four hours previously, and we were not at home but in the City of the Yellow Devil ⟨Gorky's term⟩* with its gangsters, police, and FBI. How could one fail to sympathize with him? Still and all, our kind Ivan Ivanovich forgot one thing. The local citizens were drawn to us Soviet people, they were anxious to talk to us, and we had no right to cut ourselves off and retreat within ourselves. They watched our every movement and listened to everything we said, and therefore we had to act completely naturally, had to be ourselves. Excessive caution—let us call it that—does not bring people together, it drives them apart.

. . .

We spent all of five days [in New York]—a very short time. Strange as it may seem, one becomes used to this Babylon quite quickly. At first one is struck by the skyscrapers, especially in Manhattan, but quite soon one feels that one has been looking at them, walking about among them and riding up to the one-hundredth floor all one's life. The allegation that they are oppressive is nonsense (Hitler's Imperial Chancellery in Berlin oppressed me much more, in spite of its relatively modest dimensions), and many of them that have been built in recent years are very light (literally light!), airy, and transparent. There is a great deal of glass in them, and they reflect each other in an amusing way. In the morning and evening, when they are illuminated by the horizontal rays of the sun, they are simply beautiful.

. . .

The magnitude and beauty of man strikes one on the observation platform of the Empire State Building. After all, everything here was created by him, by his hands and his brain. One finds oneself asking the question: How many Empire State Buildings and Chrysler Buildings and bridges like the impetuous, light George Washington Bridge across the Hudson, how many useful things could be built with the money that is now spent on all sorts of Polarises, Honest Johns, and other jolly twentieth-century toys? (By the way, full-scale mockups of missiles stand in front of various military institutions in America, just as old cannons once did, and we even ran across one such missile in the concourse of Grand Central Station in New York. What is it doing there?)

. . .

We didn't go to the movies any more, but we still got an idea about them because there were 21-inch (the width of the screen) television sets in our hotel rooms. The stations operate twenty-two hours a day, and there are eleven channels. Did we ever see fights! In bars, on the street, in trains, in luxurious hotels, at sea, underground, in the air, with tables and cabinets turned over, rivers of blood and so many shots that they were still ringing in my ears after I had been home for two weeks. And how they fought! And the men, how nimbly they flew across the length of the saloon, somersaulting,

---

* Inserted by former editors.—Editor.

crashing through doors into the street and then, wiping off their noses, back they would go into the fight and escort their opponent out in the same style, but through the window. Then the races and the chases! Not since I was a child had I seen the like, only now the cars are longer, lower, and faster. We saw Rasputin, and Russian princes in troikas, some sort of hypnotizer, sybaritic women laughingly dealing with Tarzan-like men. The only trouble was that at the most intense and decisive moment a pretty girl would appear on the screen and for quite a long time would wash her hair with some sort of special soap mixture, or else some charming couple sitting on the banks of a beautiful lake would reveal that they could not kiss each other until the young man learned to take the right pill to kill mouth odor. These and other scenes like them interrupt every film every ten minutes. Every program means advertising, and the television companies live on the proceeds of this. Just imagine, it works. It even worked on us. All of us finally did buy the magical "Anacin" pills for headaches, although I, at least, do not suffer from this complaint.

Yes, American television is a fearful thing. I had heard a great deal about it, but only seeing it made me understand. Indeed, just try not to hit your neighbor, try not to knock him out with a well-aimed blow when from morning to night your television set shows you how to do it. If you don't do this yourself, others will do it to you. There was a great deal of talk about this at the writers' meeting in Florence. There is even the new term "semiculture" (polukultura)—what the English call "mass media" (means of mass communication) and the Americans "mass culture," which refers to a substantial part of Western films, comic books, pulp fiction, and illustrated magazines as means for drawing people away from the practice of thinking, and the first among these means, of course, is television, which has pushed out books and conversation.

Incidentally, if we are to talk seriously about this, television is not the scourge of America alone. We don't have the fights, the brawls or TV wrestling, that most monstrous of sports—if this mutual torture can be called a sport at all—but we do have something else: We chase our television viewers into the depths of boredom with endless interviews and amateur art shows that are as alike as two peas. Perhaps this must be done in order that the television studio fulfill its plan, but we don't have the energy to look at it any more.

.   .   .

America's second scourge is the broad dark stream of police and detective literature. It is literally an overflowing sea. A good deal has been written about this already—about all those books with a pistol pointed at you from the cover—so it somehow pricks the conscience to say any more about it; but it cannot be ignored. I don't want to say anything derogatory about American bookstores. There are a lot of them, and they contain a great many good, interesting, and serious books. But good books are expensive, while all the detective rubbish costs pennies and practically throws itself at you, and the worst thing of all is that it is eagerly consumed, especially by young people. I am very sorry for the American boy. In general he is a good, simple, and kindly sort, but I pitied him when I saw him sitting in the subway with an athletic bag on his knees and a publication in his hand that he had just bought for 25 cents at the newsstand and that he would throw away next day in one of the enormous trash baskets that stand on every street corner in New York. God, I pitied him. Of course, it is not obligatory to read Faulkner in the subway on the way to a training session or a game, but I fear that this boy does not read him at home either.

. . .

The American is nowhere near as interested in argument. In his pure state, the average—or rank-and-file, as they say nowadays—American (factory worker, office worker, student) is not very much given to cogitating and philosophizing. This is not primitivism, as some think, and not mental laziness; it is rather, I would say, a kind of infantilism (the American always even looks younger than his age), or, as one high-spirited Columbia University student said to me: "We don't like it when they fill our heads with all sorts of rubbish." Here, of course, it is necessary to decide what one is going to call rubbish, but, I repeat, the American—as opposed to the Italian, for example—does not like to argue. He prefers a friendly conversation over a glass of something strong, he likes jokes, jollity, fun. Generally he is by nature friendly, trusting, very simple and natural in his relationships, and if you are his guest he wants everything in his house to be simple and gay. He does not like tedium or anything official and formal.

I remember the black boredom that settled on our hospitable hosts and their guests in Buffalo when one of our tourist group (a university teacher) took out a notebook after the second glass of cognac and began a rather long recitation of figures on steel, iron, manganese, and coal production in the Ukraine. And I remember, on the other hand, how delighted everyone was with another member of our group (a young Moscow newspaperman), who won everyone over with the first words he spoke to our host: "I see you have the latest model Ford in your garage. Might I take the wheel for a spin at 160 km. an hour?" He took his spin and delved into the engine with our host, got into a discussion with someone about the latest baseball games, challenged someone else to a wrestling match. The Americans would not leave him alone, but our poor teacher sat in the corner with his figures in his pocket; everyone had forgotten him.

. . .

In general, there is no gainsaying that Washington is very beautiful. I am not much inclined to like eclecticism and all manner of reflected styles, but I must admit that the white, rose, and gold marble of the "Greek" porticos and colonnades of the buildings and museums buried in the green of the parks makes a striking impression. This is especially true at night, when illuminated fountains gush forth cascades of water of various shades and hues and the Capitol's dome and the Washington Monument seem to be lit from within. . . .

We strolled past the graceful fence around the White House, which was beautiful and calm in the shadows of ancient lindens and elms; on the next day, Nov. 8, there was to be a decision about who would be the next occupant of that house, Nixon or Kennedy. Under the Constitution, the Washingtonian has no electoral rights, but he may listen to the radio and watch the television set. On that evening we too sat at the television set and listened to Kennedy and Nixon.

Two young and energetic millionaires. Which of them would be the victor? What would the victory of either bring the world? . . .

For us Soviet people, this competition between two powerful capitalists had little meaning. Wasn't it all the same no matter which one won? One was supported by certain powerful trusts and monopolies and the other was supported by others. The struggle between the elephant and the donkey (the symbols of the two rival parties, the Democrats and the Republicans), a struggle that costs tens of millions, often seemed funny and naive to us. But Americans have a different opinion. The people of left-wing persuasion whom we met definitely favored the candidacy of Kennedy. He, they said, was younger (42 years old! There had never been a President so young), more progressive, had a good war record and in general, dear friends, it is rather difficult for you to figure out our democratic politics. Believe us, we know whom to vote for. On the evening of the ninth we sat before the television screen like all Americans and followed the counting of the votes, and we, too, "rooted" for Kennedy.

. . .

The same Kiev newspaperman—I will call him K. (the member of our tourist group who was worried because he did not have anything to write about, since they had not yet shown us the slums)—began to give lectures immediately upon returning home. There were posters all over town proclaiming "America, 1960." I went to one of these lectures. K. dealt very thoroughly with slums, unemployment, poverty, the New York streets that no light ever reaches, hard labor conditions, the high cost of apartments, low wages, and strikes. He was asked about the prices of goods. He replied that he had not looked into this. A whisper ran through the hall. A young man asked shyly what the alcoholism situation in America was, did they drink much there? K. answered:

"A great deal. In Washington—no, excuse me, in Chicago—we saw one drunk who could hardly stand up."

The audience burst into loud laughter. I was ashamed, although I understood that, thank God, one does not meet people like K. at every step.

Another Soviet journalist, who had lived in New York for about four years, said to me:

"America is truly a land of contrasts. The contrasts are extremely striking. Poverty and riches, beauty and monstrous ugliness exist side by side. But when one speaks of contrasts one must still retain some sort of proportions of black and white. I ask you when you write about America that you retain a balance of fifty-fifty, as they say here. Do not write that American young people are interested only in rock 'n' roll and baseball. They are interested in these things, even carried away by them, but, believe me, they also read newspapers and books and magazines as well. They will also read your article. Take this into account so you won't have to blush later."

. . .

Personally, I don't intend to keep to any balance. What is more, I am going to do everything I can to avoid generalizations (I saw too little), and I will attempt to figure out what I saw and to figure out those thoughts and associations that came to me from various phenomena or from various meetings in America. I don't pretend to anything more.

. . .

Those people who think that abstract art and so-called "left-wing" art in general is held in high esteem in America are very much mistaken. This has never been the case. It is true that at New York's Idlewild Airport there is a sort of many-bladed construction, said to be a sculpture, hanging from the vestibule ceiling and slowly turning (incidentally, I liked it very much for itself; there is something pterodactyl-like or helicopter-like about it—in other words, there is something of aviation in it); there is the Solomon R. Guggenheim Museum on New York's 5th Avenue, which is a museum dedicated to the latest and most left-wing art; and there are rich collectors in America who will pay any price for the latest ultra-left concoctions. But the masses of Americans don't like this art; they like art that "looks like something."

.   .   .

I have more than once been asked whether I like [American architecture]. Yes, I do, I've answered. And I now answer: I do like it. I see a somewhat surprised look. What? The Americans themselves don't know how to solve the problems they've piled up. Talk about an impasse, that's where you find it: transportation problem insoluble, no air, no sunlight, the elevated railroad in Chicago can drive the strongest-nerved man out of his mind, the skyscrapers look good only on postcards, and if anyone likes them it's only the tourists.

All this is so, and yet—

A friend and I were strolling along the shore of Lake Michigan in Chicago. The evening before a snow mixed with rain had still been falling; the city had been drowned in a mist reddish-yellow from advertising signs, and its wet asphalt had glistened. But now the weather had cleared, the sun was shining and the flat waves of the sea-big lake were plashing quietly in the very wide, deserted, cold beach. All around there was an amazing implausible absence of human life. There were cars whipping by—low, wide, noiseless—but there were no people. We were alone on that limitless lake front. There was no reason for a Chicagoan to be there: It was not summer, and the beach was closed. (And what a beach! We could do with one like it at Yalta.) And this absence of people, this almost idyllic stillness offered a chance to view the city—the most American of all cities, more American even than New York—to view it detachedly, without haste, without rushing to get someplace, seated on the parapet having a cigarette, lazily bandying occasional comments.

On one side lay the lake—the fourth largest lake in the world, if you exclude the Aral Sea; the wind had come up, and it was now covered with whitecaps. On the other side stretched the skyscrapers of the "Gold Coast," a fashionable section of Chicago. And among them stood two dark, well-proportioned skyscrapers. I knew them from photographs. They are famous. They were built by one of America's most celebrated architects—Mies van der Rohe! Beautiful! Really and truly beautiful. There's a city for you!

Then we walk across a bridge; below it dozens of railroad tracks, with moving trains, freight and passenger, signal lights blinking; cars racing noiselessly over the bridge, two workers in cradles screwing bulbs into the letter "o" of a gigantic "Coca-Cola" (we're silly to snicker at it—it's a delicious and really refreshing drink). Before us is a new panorama—the skyscrapers of Michigan Avenue. They stretch in a row for two kilometers. And at their head the recently completed Prudential Building. It's all ablaze at the moment—the low November sun is reflected in all the windows of its forty-odd stories. We walk along the lake front and, turning down Madison Street, land in the very center of town, the Loop (the elevated railroad actually does form a loop at this spot).

The advertising signs are lit up all the time, twenty-four hours a day; there is always semidarkness here; the shop windows are refulgent, with things shining in them, iridescent; on the corner, by the stairs to the elevated, is a pile of newspapers with the results of the presidential elections, and passers-by buy them on the run, putting five cents into a special little tin box, while overhead, stretching way, way up, are the gray skyscrapers; there was a time, some forty years ago, when Harold Lloyd was leaping from one to another.

What a city! A gigantic city. A great railway hub—1,700 trains a day! America's second city. Famous slaughterhouses, canning industry, iron and steel. The city where the American Communist Party was born. The city to which we owe May Day, instituted after the demonstration of 1886 was fired on. A city that 125 years ago had four thousand residents and today has five and a half million. A city that in 1871 burned almost to the ground and that still carefully preserves outside fire escapes on all skyscrapers. A city of financiers, magnates, clerks, workers. A real city! A gigantic city.

But the architecture? What has the architecture to do with it? And what is there to like here? Semidarkness in the streets, fire escapes?

My answer is that I, a city dweller, like the clear-cut urbanism of these cities. I like the skyscraper all of steel and glass, reflecting the clouds scudding across the sky. I like to throw back my head and look at its face, precise, like a mathematical formula. I like the higgledy-piggledy disarray of the skyscrapers, which destroys the regularity of the streets. I am talking about the look of the city, not about its tragedy—it is dirty, hot, crowded, and the gasoline fumes are suffocating; I am talking not about how well thought-out or haphazard is the layout of its buildings, or about the purity of their style, but specifically about its look.

·   ·   ·

I have seen many faceless cities in America, one like the other, indistinguishable: Buffalo, Detroit, and some others—they've all blended together. But I will not say this about either New York or Chicago; they have their own personality, alien to me, perhaps, but their own, their own charm, their own soul.

·   ·   ·

BUREAUCRACY AND THE INDIVIDUAL

Y. A. Zamoshkin

This article by Y. A. Zamoshkin in the Soviet philosophy journal *Questions of Philosophy* analyzes the impact of bureaucratization on American life, especially its destructive effect on individualism and other American ideals. The author demonstrates familiarity with the writings of Karl Mannheim, Max Weber, C. Wright Mills, David Riesman, and Erich Fromm, Western sociologists and psychologists who have dealt with the question of bureaucracy. With some facility, Zamoshkin uses their observations to level an attack on the alienation of the individual in a "bourgeois industrial society."

The antihumanist nature of modern monopoly capitalism becomes particularly apparent when we understand the effect which the process of bureaucratization inherent in this society has on the individual—bureaucratization in the economy, in politics, and throughout social life. The characteristic features of this process may be observed most clearly in the United States.

American corporations are models of bureacratic organization. The all-powerful rule of capital is concealed here behind the operations of a vast army of officials, administrators, and specialists of various grades and ranks. With the development of bureaucracy in private corporations there is a simultaneous growth of the bureaucratic machinery of the bourgeois state and its merger with the monopolies. Thus, while in 1900 there were only some 200,000 employees of the federal government, by 1950 the figure had grown to 2 million (not counting military personnel).

The bureaucratic inflation of the bourgeois state machinery proceeds in the first place through the creation of administrative bodies and organizations designed to provide economic and financial assistance to private corporations at the expense of the working people. The state tries in vain to protect the capitalist economy from constantly recurring crises by mobilizing the country's resources for the maintenance of the crumbling structure of the bourgeois system. Second, the development of the bureaucratic state apparatus is closely linked with the policy of militarization. Modern life in the United States is characterized by a sharp increase in the role of the military and their intervention in all spheres of activity: in the economy, in political life, in science and education, in the system of propaganda, etc.

But it is the private corporation which sets the basic tone of the process of bureaucratization of social life in the United States. Bourgeois political parties, reactionary organizations, and the state copy the forms and methods of bureaucratic management elaborated by the monopolies. This is emphasized, for example, by the well-known bourgeois journalist and sociologist Max Lerner in his book *America as a Civilization*. "The political 'organization,' " he writes, "has taken over much of the corporate structure." In his view the

FROM "Biurokratizasiia burzhuaznogo obshchestva i sud'by lichnosti," *Voprosy filosofii* (1961), as translated in *The Soviet Review,* Vol. 2, No. 8 (August, 1961), pp. 20–38. Reprinted by permission of the International Arts and Sciences Press.

government has adopted from private firms the key ideas of "scientific management," "classification of jobs," "standards of operation," and the like.

The process of bureaucratization has enveloped all spheres of life in the United States. It is also reflected in the trade unions, where the reactionary leadership has created its own hierarchy. It exists in the educational system, in the colleges and universities. It is a characteristic feature of church organization, and so on. All this is recognized by many leading American sociologists. C. Wright Mills in this connection speaks of the "managerial demiurge" in which "society becomes an uneasy interlocking of private and public hierarchies," and "more and more areas become objects of management and manipulation" [*White Collar*]. Max Lerner notes that ". . . the bureaucratization of life through the new managerial structures in business, the trade union, the government . . . are being extended through the whole culture." He characterizes bureaucracy as the "New Feudalism" and compares the hierachical system of command in corporations with the system of rule by the seigneurs in the society of the middle ages.

Modern state monopoly capitalism, a clearly reactionary society, in its attempt to retain the obedience of the masses uses forms of organization and administration which are very similar to those used by feudalism, i.e., a society against which the bourgeois revolution was directed (including the American Revolution). Bureaucratization reflects imperialism's typical tendency to reject the forms of bourgeois democracy.

.   .   .

In a society based on the exploitation of man by man, where the elemental laws of competition and the market prevail, the individual emerges as something quite accidental in relation to the bourgeois forms of group relations that emerge in this society. To the individual member of society bourgeois "collectives" appear as an alien and hostile force, indifferent to the individual's requirements and motives, and possessing their own completely different motives and requirements. These motives and requirements are the requirements of a production which is subordinated to capital, to the direct interests of capital, its strivings for profit and success in the competitive struggle, the economic and political interests of the reactionary ruling circles standing behind the bourgeois "collectives." Moreover, under the conditions of the growing bureaucratization of life it appears as though group activity is separate and distinct from the direct owners of capital. The combination of individuals into groups assumes an impersonal form, so that the individual member of society is confronted with and enslaved by something that appears to him as an external and unidentifiable social machine which exercises its own controls. For the individual American, the enterprise, i.e., the production unit in which he is included, [says C. Wright Mills] "is an impersonal and alien Name, and the more that is placed in it, the less is placed in man." Men "become cogs in a business machinery."

.   .   .

Bureaucracy is characterized above all by the tendency to *dehumanize* the individual, who becomes simply a means of serving the interests of the corporation or of some other bourgeois organization. This tendency is so apparent in the epoch of imperialism that it becomes noticed by those burgeois sociologists who criticize bureaucracy—even if they do so in the name of abstract bourgeois democracy. Thus one of the patriarchs and principal authorities of bourgeois sociology, Max Weber (whose work [*Images of Man*] is very popular in the United States at present), noted that the activities of the corporate apparatus and the bureaucratic state are conducted "without regard for persons." He wrote that this kind of organization "develops the more perfectly the more the bureaucracy is 'dehumanized,' the more completely it succeeds in eliminating from official business love, hatred, and all purely personal . . . elements." According to Weber this tendency constitutes the "specific nature of bureaucracy, and . . . is its special virtue."

. . .

Under these conditions the activity of workers and the overwhelming majority of employees is characterized by the absence of responsibility, the right to creative thought, initiative, the right to make independent decisions. Only a small number of individuals have these rights, those who stand at the head of the bureaucratic system—the "power élite" of the United States.

. . .

Under capitalism social relations and forms of intercourse are transformed into something external and alien to people. In the bureaucratic "collective," people are brought together not as individuals but as some kind of average magnitudes, as bearers and performers of particular, specialized functions and assignments in the process of production and management. And it is this specifically bourgeois method of linking people together that becomes the cause of their isolation as individual personalities.

Capitalism, as we know, prompts the individual to view himself and others as commodities, as possessing only exchange value and being involved in a system of purchase-and-sale. With the bureaucratic organization of state monopoly capitalism an additional feature appears in these relationships: contacts between people frequently assume those forms which are embedded in the system of bureaucratic rationalization. People become accustomed to dealing with one another as with individual, depersonalized links of a hierarchical system, subordinated to administrative rules, at the basis of which lie all of the same bourgeois laws of the exploitation of man by man. Relationships of purchase-and-sale are themselves bureaucratized, subordinated. They are distinguished by still greater callousness, official dryness, practicality, egoistic calculations.

These attitudes have produced frank dissatisfaction and protest on the part of many prominent sociologists in the United States. C. Wright Mills writes [in *The Power Elite*]: "When people's contacts with one another are only of this kind, their relationships become preconceived and stereotyped. The human essence of other people does not and cannot appear under these conditions." "Men," he points out, "are estranged from one another as each secretly tries to make an instrument of the other. . . ." To the question, "What is modern man's *relationship to his fellow man?*" [Erich] Fromm answers: "It is one between two abstractions ⟨values, function⟩,* two living machines, who use each other."

It should be noted that the criticism of these relations and of bureaucratiza-

---

* Inserted by the author.—Editor.

tion in general given by Mannheim, Max Weber, Fromm, and other sociologists has frequently been quite vivid and telling, but it has always been seriously limited because it has been bourgeois in its class essence. All of the sociologists cited above believe that the bureaucratic "dehumanization" of production and management, together with all of its consequences, stems largely from the increasing complexity of the production process, the growth of the division of labor in modern industry, the differentiation of technological processes, and the peculiarities of current technical and scientific thought. None of these sociologists understand that the "dehumanized" nature of society stems from the *production relations* of state monopoly capitalism. These relations increasingly alienate the individual from the "collective" which represses his individuality, give rise to bureaucratic connections in these bourgeois "collectives," and to a peculiar kind of bureaucratic rationalization which deprives the individual of initiative and cripples his personality. They transform the worker into an object of bureaucratic commands and produce a heartless, "impersonal" type of intercourse between people.

Not understanding this, even the most prominent bourgeois sociologists have been unable to offer realistic means of overcoming this tendency. They are forced, directly or indirectly, to recognize the fatalistic inevitability of this tendency, and thereby to become its apologists, for their bourgeois orientation does not permit them to conceive of the historical necessity of eliminating capitalist relations and replacing them by socialist relations.

The principal tendency of capitalism—to depersonalize production and administration—is increasingly accompanied and supplemented by another—the tendency on the part of the leadership of bureaucratic "collectives" to pay more attention to the personality of the worker. While superficially contradictory, these tendencies are part of a single phenomenon; they are two sides of a single process—the process of the suppression of the personality by state-monopoly capitalism.

.   .   .

An increasing number of people in the United States are dissatisfied, and protests against the all-powerful rule of the monopolies are becoming more distinct and widespread. That is why today, as never before, it has become particularly important for the ruling circles of the United States to work out a system of measures which the numerous bourgeois "collectives" could use to exercise "control" over the workers, "manipulating" masses of people, cultivating the bourgeois spirit in them.

The personality of the ordinary American has become an arena of a most serious class struggle, a struggle between bourgeois consciousness and psychology on the one hand, and the new, revolutionary consciousness and psychology on the other. This is what explains the concern with the human personality by the "collective" groups and organizations created by state monopoly capitalism in the United States.

At the same time it is clear that the very process of modern production, as well as the processes of accounting and control, impose new and greater demands on the spiritual and psychic nature of the worker. Labor productivity increasingly depends on the state of the worker's nervous system, on his character and attitude, on the extent to which he is personally interested (or uninterested) in his work, on his moral qualities. Thus, to increase labor productivity and thereby to attain higher profits, bureaucratic organizations of capital are forced to "concern themselves" with the personal spiritual qualities of the individual. But this concern is of a class nature; it has mercenary motives. It is inspired by the attempt to subordinate the personality not only in an economic and managerial sense, but also in a spiritual sense, binding it to forms and standards of behavior, thinking, feeling, experience, and character which serve capital.

. . .

In this respect a clear example is that sphere of activity of the corporation and the bourgeois state which has come to be called "human relations" policy. This policy is designed to instill in workers such artificial feelings as "the feeling of belonging" to the bourgeois "collective," "a sense of duty," to it. Its purpose is to work out various measures for transforming the worker into an obedient and devoted slave of capital. This objective is served by the organization of various kinds of "joint consultations" and "friendly" sessions led by specialists in the field of "social psychology," at which attempts are made to convince the workers that the economic position of the monopolies and the prospects for their growth require diligence and even enthusiasm in work. The same objective is served by "re-educating" managerial personnel, transforming rude supervisors and making them adept at deception and manipulation, smiling, considerate and, what is most important, having them win the confidence of their subordinates. Finally, this purpose is also served by such devices as the arrangement of "collective" picnics, dinners, entertainment, gatherings of workers, their wives and children, visits by the owners and managerial personnel to the homes of their workers, and so on.

. . .

In purchasing labor power, the capitalist corporation—usually tacitly, but sometimes openly—includes in the transaction not only the physical strength, work skills, and abilities of the hired worker, but also his personality, i.e., his character, emotions, attitudes. Purely personal traits become objects of exploitation. In American sociology this is sometimes referred to as "the personality market."

On this market the very personality of the hired worker becomes the property of those who purchase it. It is included in the process of bourgeois production and administration of things and people; it is molded and subordinated to this process. In bureaucratically organized capitalism, personal qualities are carefully appraised, thoroughly recorded, and then standardized depending on the peculiarities and tasks of the particular organization.

In order to manipulate the personality of the worker, capitalist machinery has created a whole series of special organizations intent on observing the personal lives of workers and cultivating in them a spirit that would conform with the requirements of this machinery. There are large staffs of "personnel supervisors," employees of "personnel departments" and psychologists in the United States for this purpose. The practice of giving various types of tests to workers and employees is constantly being extended, as well as the system of spying on the personal affairs of workers.

. . .

The government, the monopolies and various types of organizations connected with them organize—especially among the youth—a large variety of "human relations courses," issue a voluminous literature on the general topic "How to Develop Your Personality," and introduce special courses in schools and colleges. Chief emphasis is placed on cultivating loyalty to bourgeois "virtues," on the ability to appear "disciplined," a "charming" subordinate or supervisor in the system of bureaucracy, on developing the ability to "adjust" to prevailing forms of bourgeois behavior. Incidentally, hundreds of books have been written in the United States on the importance and rules of "adjustment." This is not mere chance. Fromm notes the following about the United States: "Virtue is to be adjusted and to be like the rest. Vice, to be different."

· · ·

A whole branch of spiritual production has been created in the United States—the production of patterns of behavior, standards of bourgeois character and feelings. These standards are enforced through a variety of administrative rules and instructions within the bureaucratic system, and are widely publicized on a national scale by means of radio, films, television, newspapers, etc., as the keys to success—success in the bourgeois bureaucratic sense.

Thus, in the state monopoly, bureaucratized capitalism of the United States the natural and personal characteristics of the individual who is drawn into the bureaucratic system are increasingly detached and alienated from him. For these personal characteristics are subordinated not to the normal requirements and inner peculiarities of development of the individual member of society, but to the purposes and requirements of the corporation and other bourgeois forms of organization. Thus, to the individual they often appear alien, as though tied to him from outside ruling over him. In the bureaucratic system of big business such personal qualities and characteristics as sociability, the ability to smile, enthusiasm, become professional skills—artificial and false. In the individual this necessarily breeds hypocrisy, mental and moral frustration, sullenness, and apathy.

· · ·

The United States has always been viewed as the citadel of individualism. Indeed, nowhere have the ideology, psychology, and morality of individualism been so openly expressed and widely diffused as in this country. To a large extent this is explained by the fact that capitalism developed there under especially favorable circumstances. In particular, bourgeois relations developed much more freely and intensively and without encountering serious resistance from feudalism. In America individuals were free from the fetters of feudal-bureaucratic and class constraints, and with the tremendous natural resources of the country there was scope for the appearance and development of aspirations for free enterprise and private initiative.

· · ·

The end of the nineteenth and particularly the twentieth century witnessed an intensive and stormy development of imperialism in the United States. This process of growth of giant monopolies was inevitably accompanied by the ruin of masses of the petty and middle bourgeoisie and a sharp decline in their importance in the country's economic and political life. In the middle of the twentieth century the majority of the population of the United States—more than four-fifths—worked as hired personnel exploited by 1 to 3 percent of the population (big capitalists and their privileged assistants).

The mass of farmers and individual entrepreneurs of the cities were transformed into workers and employees of bureaucratically organized capitalist and government agencies. Those few who were able somehow to retain private property became, as a rule, enmeshed in debt and so dependent on the monopolies, banks, and the government that it is really impossible to speak of freedom of private initiative as far as they are concerned. This is even more true of small holders of shares in large corporations.

.　　.　　.

This process, which millions of Americans are undergoing, is reflected in American sociology and psychology. This is particularly the case in the very popular books of David Riesman, *The Lonely Crowd* and *Individualism Reconsidered*. Riesman speaks of the transition from the earlier type of individual whom he calls "inner directed," to the new type—the "other-directed individual." Incidentally, these concepts have been very widely accepted in United States literature.

The "inner-directed individual" is the classic type of bourgeois individual of the epoch of "free competition." In his activities he is guided primarily by his own selfish, private-property motives and passions. But since the objective social causes of these motives and passions are rooted in capitalist production relations they are hidden from sight, and the specifically bourgeois motives and passions of bourgeois consciousness (bourgeois sociology and psychology) appear as something innate, permanent, as "natural" features of "human nature" in general, as some kind of subconscious impulses and biological instincts. The "other-directed individual" refers to the character-type of the bourgeois individual who is subordinated to bourgeois "collectivism," who becomes the servant of a corporation, the imperialist state, and other similar agencies. In such cases his actions are regulated primarily by rules (economic, administrative, and ideological, written and unwritten) established by those "collectives" and organizations in which he is a subordinate. He becomes an object of external compulsion and manipulation, and to a greater or smaller degree he must repress or limit his own private-property, selfish passions and strivings—a very painful process for this individual.

Reisman is close to neo-Freudianism. Freudianism and neo-Freudianism—both very popular in the United States—are particular illusory and mythical forms of expressing those real processes which occur in the character of the average American reared in the traditions of classical bourgeois individualism when he is confronted with new conditions, the conditions of imperialism. The basic Freudian idea—the idea of the "conflict" between the "subconscious" (the "id" or the "ego"), i.e., the inherent instincts of the individual, and the conscious (the "super-ego"), i.e., the system of external prohibitions and rules imposed by society—is a distorted expression (distorted by idealist and metaphysical concepts) of the actual conflict between individualistic habits, feelings, and instincts on the one hand, and the system of state-capitalist, bureaucratic "groupism" which represses these feelings and instincts in people on the other. However, Freudianism detaches this conflict from its roots—the evolution of capitalism—and assigns to it a false all-embracing character, treating it as something for which there can be no solution. Freudianism creates the myth of alleged age-old hostility between the inner feelings of "man in general" and his reason, thereby diverting the attention of the public from the actual, sharpening contradictions of modern capitalism. That is why Freudianism is a special form of apologetics for capitalism.

.   .   .

The breakdown of many traditional individualistic concepts and illusions affects different classes and strata in the United States in different ways. Among the working class this breakdown promotes the elaboration and development of the ideology and psychology of proletarian collectivism. This is most apparent in the workers' strike struggles.

However among sections of the population still permeated with bourgeois and petty-bourgeois forms of consciousness the breakdown of the old, individualistic illusions produces other results.

Here, for example, we may observe the phenomenon of a shifting of the center of gravity in individualistic consciousness from the sphere of production to the sphere of consumption. A bourgeois mode of life appears to be the last refuge for individualism in the consciousness of many ordinary Americans. Functioning as objects of exploitation and bureaucratic compulsion once they are outside their homes, they seek ways of exercising private initiative in their mode of life off the job, in the sphere of personal consumption.

Unable to overcome the routine in his work, deprived of any possibility of exercising creative initiative in the sphere of production, the "little man" seeks an escape in a well-appointed home, at parties and drinking fests, in sex, in the choice of his "own" particular heroes among movie stars, gangsters and the like.

.   .   .

FALSIFICATIONS OF
THE BOURGEOIS CLASS STRUCTURE

V. I. Ugriumov

V. I. Ugriumov's monograph *The Newest Theories of Contemporary Bourgeois Sociology,* published by the Higher School of the Soviet Communist Party, attempts to refute the work of American social scientists because it runs contrary to Marxist teachings. In this selection Ugriumov attacks American sociologists for obfuscating the nature of class stratification in American society. He also reasserts the standard Marxist analysis that as capitalism matures, society is increasingly divided into two antagonistic classes: the proletariat and the capitalists.

The history of human society, beginning with the slave-holding system, is filled with class struggle between the exploited and the exploiters. This struggle reaches special bitterness and great diversification in the epoch of imperialism, in the current stage of capitalist society which is the final class-antagonistic formation.

Having made a scientific definition of classes and having revealed the true causes of social antagonisms, Marxism pointed out that the class struggle is the moving force in the development of human society, which has been divided into antagonistic classes. In a bourgeois society, the class struggle inevitably leads to a dictatorship of the proletariat, the goal of which is the liquidation of all classes and the building of a classless, communistic society.

Life has fully confirmed the truth of the Marxist theory of social develop-ment. And, for this very reason, bourgeois ideologists attempt to "refute" it. Ignoring the objective laws of social development, they come out against Marxist teachings on class and the class struggle. Despite differences in detail, all of them uniformly maintain that for present-day problems Marxist teach-ings are obsolete and, as a result, should be rejected.

. . .

The bourgeois falsifiers of the class structure of capitalist society make the typical argument about "the limited applicability" of Marxist teachings about class and class struggle. They acknowledge the truth of Marxism for the past but deny its applicability for our epoch.

Marx was correct in much of what he said, they say, especially for his own time. But thanks to changing conditions, Marxism is obsolete, and like other "conditional truths" has become the property of the past. By the new condi-tions, to which Marxism supposedly does not conform, is meant the usual legend about the changing nature of contemporary capitalism and the argu-ment about the "leveling" economic positions of the various social groups. This supposedly leads to fundamental change in the social situation of the poor, as well as that of the rich, and also to the disappearance of social antagonisms. For example, one of the most prominent American representatives of contemporary bourgeois political economics, [J.] K. Galbraith, argues in this manner in his work *The Affluent Society.*

To capitalism, "under these new conditions," is attributed a special dyna-mism or "mobility," the consequence of which is said to be unprecedented mobility of its social structure. Thus has arisen the idea of "social mobility," the oldest of the constituent components of the newest methods of falsifying the class structure of bourgeois society.

By "social mobility" or the mobility of social classes, groups, and strata, bourgeois sociologists mean any shift of a man, differentiating in this connec-tion between horizontal and vertical mobility. Horizontal mobility is the move-ment from one place to another, changes in the place of work, in abode, and so on.

. . .

According to the assertion of bourgeois sociologists, social mobility is fundamentally changing the whole class structure of bourgeois society. It not

FROM "Fal'sifikatsiia klassovoi struktury sovremennogo burzhuaznogo obshchestva," *Noveishie teorii sovremennoi burzhuaznoi sotsiologii* (Moscow, 1961), pp. 7–18. Translated by the editor.

only transforms the former antagonistic classes, the bourgeoise and proletariat, but supposedly produces completely new, friendly "classes" or social layers.

In the principal capitalist countries, which ostensibly enjoy a particularly steady increase in the standard of living of the workers, bourgeois sociologists "reveal" the inexhaustable possibilities for the mobility of the population throughout the social structure. The highest degree of social mobility is imputed to the U.S.A. . . . supposedly typical of the society of an "open-class type." The increasingly active factor of mobility in this country, in the opinion of the American professor [Bernard] Barber, expresses itself in the further "strengthening of the American open-class system of stratification."

Such an "open-class" society is the forerunner of the society "devoid of exploitation." Class contradictions in this society are supposedly eliminated; the last classes, the proletariat and the bourgeoisie, are transformed and united into one "middle" class. The workers enter into this "middle class," which, as a result, becomes their own. The capitalists are also swallowed by the "middle" class because they stopped being owners of their own enterprises and were transformed into employees of manufacturing and financial companies. The "middle class" thus becomes predominant and in essence the only class.

Thus, we see that bourgeois sociologists, operating on the so-called theory of social mobility, falsify the class structure of bourgeois society, opposing the Marxist teachings on classes and the class struggle to the false theories of "social stratification" and "the middle classes."

.   .   .

The basic content of the theory of "social stratification" is the assertion that the social structure of bourgeois society is characterized today not by classes (in the Marxist sense of the word) but by social layers or strata, which do not have any connection with the relationship of property to the means of production. Barber, for instance, asserts that wealth or property must be considered "a secondary rather than a primary criterion of social stratification. Wealth and a high position in the system of stratification are not tied to each other."

.   .   .

The majority of sociologists consider social stratification as a product of any "social differentiation," that is, as the result of every difference between individuals. Insofar as individual differences are innumerable, bourgeois sociology has produced the notion of "multi-indexed stratification," according to which society breaks up into a multitude of completely independent systems of stratification based on very different criteria.

As a result of the manipulation by bourgeois sociologists of the notion of "multi-indexed stratification," one and the same individual might turn out to belong to different strata, and this conceals his actual class ties, based on his relationship to the means of production, and masks the actual class contradictions which exist in society.

.   .   .

In some cases bourgeois sociologists do not refrain from using the notion of class. But while utilizing this idea, some U.S. sociologists single out three classes (higher, middle, and lower) while others add a fourth or fifth.

The American sociologists S. Lipset and H. Zetterberg maintained, for example, at the Third Congress of the International Sociological Association, that in society it is necessary to differentiate among four classes. They are (1) the "professional classes" uniting people of one profession or occupation; (2) the "consumer classes" uniting people depending on the size of consumption; (3) "social classes" in which are found people who closely "associate with each other as members of society"; (4) "power classes" uniting those people with roughly identical degrees of power, and so on.

The applicability of the Marxist notion of class is not rejected everywhere and for all countries of the capitalist world, but only for those where there already supposedly exists "neo-capitalism" or "people's capitalism." The semantic idealist S. Chase, for example, declared that "class" is an abstract notion which does not have a definite meaning, especially in the U.S.A. where society is divided not into two basic classes, as Marxism teaches, but into six classes which are found to be constantly changing. "People who enter them," says Chase, "rise or fall as an elevator in a building." A professor at Washington University, J. Kahl, author of the monograph *The American Class Structure* which is well known in the West, goes even "further." He asserts that today in the capitalist countries there exist from four to eleven classes.

. . .

The growth in the numbers of specialists, employees, intelligentsia, and other middle strata of the population cannot hide the fact that capitalist society is becoming more and more polarized, more and more divided into two basic classes—the bourgeois and the proletariat—which leads to incessant struggle between these groups in order to attract the population to one side or the other.

The theory of "middle classes" and all the arguments of bourgeois sociologists about the erasing of class lines in bourgeois society not only do not agree with reality, but, on the contrary, are decisively refuted by life. They are disproved by diametrically opposed relationships to ownership of the means of production of the proletariat and of the bourgeoisie, and, moreover, by the property inequality of these classes. Indeed, it is well-known that millionaires make up 1 percent of the population, but in the U.S.A. they hold in their hands 55 percent of the national wealth. And in regard to the distribution of national income, the share of the toiling masses in the national income constitutes 34.6 percent while they make up nine-tenths of the population.

This and other data show the complete falsity of the assertion that the growth of the "middle class" in bourgeois society is wiping out class differences. The facts fully disprove this bourgeois-apologist device and completely confirm the truth of Marxist teachings on classes and class struggle.

. . .

WEST SIDE STORY IN MOSCOW

Ya. Varshavsky

The following review of *West Side Story,* published in the daily central newspaper of the Young Communist League, is notable for its praise of the artistic merits of the film and for its restraint in exploiting for propaganda gambits the movie's portrayal of life on New York City's West Side.

Here we have one of the most interesting and original films of the festival [the Third International Film Festival, Moscow, 1963]. Presenting *West Side Story* to the audience of the theater "Russia," director Stanley Kramer, a member of the U.S. delegation of cinematographers, called this film the most outstanding production of the American movie industry during the past year. Obviously it is.

Even in the prologue, by displaying on a wide molded screen the common sight of skyscrapers, superhighways, and bridges as contemplated so to speak from a bird's-eye view, the authors force you to descend from the heavens to the ground. And the descent is tangibly personified: as if you had examined the red cover of the magazine *America.* Then the authors land you at the doorstep of one of the innumerable workers' homes on the West Side.

Now you stare up close: there is a baseball lot squeezed between huge apartment buildings. Asphalt, mesh wire fences, a small strip of sky above one's head. Teenagers from the gang calling itself the "Jets" are sprawled on the asphalt, as if the light of life had been supplied according to some cruel minimum norm: less would be impossible.

And, I dare say, with feelings of the hottest resentment toward the whole world, the Jets want to inflict a severe blow on someone, to crush someone, to abase, to beat. Who? Of course, their nearest neighbors, whoever they may be.

Thus, the storm builds up on one of the side streets of the West Side. The spark that brings forth the outburst is the appearance of love—as in the tragedy of Shakespeare about the enmity of the Montagues and the Capulets. But, in this case, opposed to the unfortunate Jets are the still more miserable "Sharks"—Puerto Ricans, recently received into the bosom of American citizenship but treated like half-beggared stepsons of rich America.

The dance pantomimes, which do not need translation, tell about how they feel. . . .

Here is the paradox which so often occurs in the bourgeois world: it would seem that the poor Jets and the wretched Sharks should be on friendly terms and help one another in this strange city, in this concrete and asphalt jungle; but instead they pull knives on each other. And just then, when the young hero and heroine of the film have found happiness, when the backdoors, fire escapes, and stairways have been lighted up for them by the moonlight, like the heroes of Shakespeare Tony and Maria perish on the threshold of happiness.

FROM "Stolen Youth," *Komsomolskaya Pravda* (July 14, 1963). Translated by the editor.

Shakespeare told the story of Romeo and Juliet in order to condemn the dark ideas of the Middle Ages. For what reason is the tragedy of *West Side Story* told? Not so that the municipality will maintain order on the baseball lots. The authors of the film are shaken by the contradictions of life.

However, let us not guess at the thoughts of the creators of the film. The important thing is that the authentic tragedies are the realities bursting forth on the screen; and the film, through the mouth of one of its characters—the old druggist, before whose eyes young blood is spilled—angrily shouts to the youngsters in gabardine jackets and blue jeans: "Why do you live so terribly?"

This bitter "why" you will recall more than once when you see the films from distant countries playing at the festival. Very honest, very talented artists of the bourgeois world have found in themselves the strength to pose this question, but they are not able or do not consider it necessary to seek a precise answer, or they despair of doing so.

Let us not demand from the authors of *West Side Story* more than they dared to do. Let us not judge the film for what is not in it. Let us shake their hands for what they have done.

And they have done not a little. They have expressed a great theme in an interesting artistic form. There are no "contrived numbers," but, rather, very sharp moments of action expressed in both dance and song. "This is not a movie," some viewers say. Excuse me, we do not yet know all the possibilities of movies! This film . . . shows how unknown still are the diverse dialects possible in cinematic language.

Here it is necessary to say that Richard Beymer and Natalie Wood execute the main roles excellently, expressing honest and passionate love. And the supporting roles are also well done, making a strong ensemble.

Behind the unusually complicated artistic form of the film, we discern the emotional voice of the "collective artist"—the heartfelt pain and love toward the simple youths of America, so terribly deprived of youth and happiness.

I think that this is a significant film—in that it was born of the sincere love of the "collective author" toward the people living in the innumerable "west sides" of America.

.   .   .

WHY IVAN KNOWS MORE THAN JOHNNY

V. Strezikozin

Under the cultural exchange agreement between the United States and the Soviet Union several delegations of Soviet educators have visited in the United States. This report on American schools and schoolchildren by a Soviet educator appeared in a Soviet teachers' newspaper.

"Problem No. 1" of the American school is to teach the child to read his own language. Many times I felt that Americans did not believe me when I told them that Soviet schoolchildren can read their own language as early as in the second grade and that children who start to study English in the fifth grade are able to read simple texts in English quite presentably by the time they are in the sixth and seventh grades. The fact is that many American schoolchildren cannot read their own language well after six or eight years of study. I was told that in the secondary schools and sometimes even in universities one could find young people who are poor at reading.

American schools are now giving much attention to the teaching of foreign languages, and some of the pupils—still a small part, it is true—are studying Russian. Foreign language courses in the schools are constructed on an oral basis, and five thousand secondary schools have been provided with well-equipped laboratories where the pupil works independently for several hours a week with the help of the linguaphone.

Yet American schoolchildren are getting a poor knowledge of foreign languages.

One of the reasons is that foreign languages are studied in concentrated form—only in the upper grades of secondary school—whereas it is common knowledge that children most successfully master conversation in a foreign language at a younger age.

A considerable proportion of the American teachers clearly do not possess sufficient command of foreign languages.

It is paradoxical but a fact that although America is a country of high technical progress, it gives the overwhelming mass of pupils a starvation diet of mathematical knowledge. True, in recent years many schools have introduced the teaching of so-called "new mathematics." But in actuality only *Wunderkinder* are taught this.

Natural sciences are a weak spot in the training of American youth. The secondary school courses in physics, biology, and chemistry are primitive.

It would be sinning against the truth to say that the American pedagogical community is reconciled to the pupils' low level of knowledge. Problems connected with improving their knowledge are discussed at nationwide teachers' sessions of the National Education Association. Professors of education and psychologists are conducting interesting research. Much is being done to create visual aids and other teaching aids of modern technical quality.

Why, then, does this not yield the desired results? Why is the level of American schooling far below the level of the culture of our age? One cannot answer these questions without delving into some of the fundamental premises on which the American system of education is based.

DEMOCRACY OR DISCRIMINATION?

American education has developed and continues to develop along lines different in many respects from those of classical bourgeois educational systems.

FROM "Why Does Ivan Know More Than Johnny?" *Uchitelskaya Gazeta* (February 9 and 12, 1963), as translated in *The Current Digest of the Soviet Press,* published weekly at Columbia University, Vol. 15, No. 8 (March 20, 1963), pp. 17–18. Copyright 1963 by the Joint Committee on Slavic Studies, appointed by the American Council of Learned Societies and the Social Science Research Council. Reprinted by permission.

But it has the basic defect of the bourgeois school—the absence of equal educational opportunity. U.S. public education officials and other American educators deny this, of course. Inequality of education is carefully masked by slogans about the democracy of the American school. But it is the "democratic" conceptions of American education that in reality lead to limitation of the educational level for the majority of the pupils, chiefly the children of poor families.

"To create all the conditions for developing the individual, not to hold back the able pupil, to enable him to advance to the full measure of his capacities, to open the way for talent"—this credo of American education unquestionably sounds democratic and humanistic. But if one looks into the organization of instruction in the American school, its concealed true meaning becomes clear.

Hardly has the child crossed the threshold of the school when it becomes the chief concern of the teachers to determine his "intelligence level." Quite normal children are sorted into the gifted, the average, and the weak, on the basis of tests and brief observation. In large schools separate classes are set up for them, while in schools that do not have parallel classes the pupils are divided into separate groups. Each group has its level of education, its requirements, its teaching methods. True, you will be told that the weak pupil can be transferred to a different category if he improves.

The reference to inequality of intellectual potentialities in children or adolescents is the basic theoretical justification given for unequal education. School administrators, professors, and teachers constantly asked me such questions as: "How do you manage to teach all children with one and the same program? After all, children from an educated family and the children of an ordinary worker cannot have the same abilities."

This is what it is really all about. The myth of the limited intellectual capacity of children from "ordinary families" serves as the justification for ineluctable class differences in education.

No one disputes the need for an individual approach in education. In many American schools I saw this important pedagogical principle sensibly applied. I was interested, for example, in the way some teachers organized a class period so that, having assigned independent work to the whole class, they worked at a separate desk with a group of either strong or backward pupils. In the Hillside, New Jersey elementary school a special teacher is assigned to work only with children who have gaps in their knowledge. He works with a group of twelve to fifteen pupils of different grades (first to eighth grade) who have dropped behind their classes in one or several subjects, until they overcome their lag. Various ways of organizing individual instruction enable the teacher to work successfully with children of various levels of preparation.

.   .   .

It is also noteworthy that all newly built American schools have special reading rooms and study rooms for independent individual work with books and teaching aids. It is instructive that many American teachers try to conduct part of the studies in the school libraries, accustoming the children from an early age to work on their own with books and the library catalogue, finding the materials they want.

Also worthy of attention are such forms of bringing out and developing the schoolchildren's abilities as contests for the best work by children; displays of their research projects; national scientific assemblies of students; the establishment of a "junior academy of science," which helps talented schoolchildren to conduct research and write reports under the guidance of scientists; the holding of school seminars in the various branches of knowledge, enlisting scientists and prominent specialists to lead the seminars.

All this is certainly good. But at the same time one cannot fail to see something else: The American school, while opening up the road to science for a chosen few, plainly underestimates the learning abilities of millions of "average" schoolchildren. The consequence is extreme impoverishment of the school courses in the fundamentals of science.

In six years of instruction in elementary school the pupil receives little more than our schoolchildren easily assimilate in four years. One is amazed at the extraordinary wastefulness in the use of the period of study. Acquainting myself with the work of one elementary school in New Jersey, I was surprised that in the first year and a half of education the children only learn to letter the alphabet in pencil, and not until the beginning of the second half of the second grade do they start to write script capitals—also in pencil. In the preparatory period of teaching the child to read much time is spent on so-called recognition of objects and ability to name them.

A negative consequence of the American system of individualizing instruction is also the low demands made upon the student.

As is well known, study of the fundamentals of science in American secondary schools is, except for a few required subjects, a matter of choice and of the individual plan elected by the student himself. This causes the mastery of knowledge to be unsystematic, prevents any assurance of the necessary sequence of instruction, and inevitably leads to lowering the educational level.

The importance of constant current testing of knowledge is clearly underestimated in American schools. It is characteristic that the results of tests of the pupil's knowledge actually do not affect his promotion from grade to grade. One can fail to master a subject even by the time of graduation; in that case the student's educational record will carry a notation to this effect, and that will be all.

The promotion and graduation of pupils without regard to whether they have succeeded in mastering knowledge is also presented as a manifestation of the "democracy" of the American school. But it is one of the causes of American education's troubles: Lowering the requirements set for the student leads, in effect, to lowering the national educational level.

The principle of individualization of education underlies differentiation in American secondary schools. Various types of schools—academic, special, general, and trade—constitute one of the ways of legitimizing inequality of education. Only the students of academic schools obtain a higher-level education.

The American educational system, opening up the path to the heights of knowledge for the chosen (the so-called gifted), signifies in effect discrimination against millions of children and young people whose intellectual capacity is placed in doubt.

• • •

PRAGMATISM IN ACTION

Experimental foundations in teaching and the rejection of scholasticism proclaimed by American educators encouraged me greatly: I expected to see original methods of teaching that might be rationally used in our conditions also. But disillusion awaited me. It is particularly the methodological level of the teaching process that is the weak spot in the American educational system.

In the mass practice of the schools, the pragmatic foundations on which American teaching is erected have caused education to take on a descriptive character, as a rule: The pupil is made acquainted with phenomena and facts, but often without penetrating to their meaning. This applies both to the presentation of the material by the teacher and the independent work of the pupil.

. . .

Mrs. McIntosh, a professor who is one of the leading specialists in the federal Department of Education, said: "Our methodological ideal is to organize the learning process so that its foundation will be the independent creative searches of the schoolchildren. The teacher should merely guide the pupils, merely direct their independent work."

It must be pointed out that many leading American teachers follow this principle. The trouble is that the independent searches of American schoolchildren are primarily collecting information and describing facts but are not penetrating into their scientific essence.

American school textbooks delight by their fine printing and abundance of carefully selected illustrations. Another good thing is that they are generally produced in combination with educational films, film strips, and methodological aids for the teacher. The weak point of the textbooks is, again, the level of methodological theory. Neither the content of the articles nor the nature of the study assignments stimulates the pupils to delve deeply into the essence of the phenomena and facts being studied.

Such are the logical consequences of pragmatic teaching, the laws of which govern the educational process in the American school. This is likewise one of the basic causes of the low level of American school education.

ABOUT ORIGINALITY AND UNCRITICAL BORROWING

The experience of the American schools unquestionably contains much that can be used, critically and with regard for our requirements, in the practice of Soviet schools. I am thinking, for example, of the experience in designing school buildings, of introducing modern technical means in the teaching process, of creating new designs of school equipment. But acquaintance with the American educational system shows first of all how far ahead the Soviet school has gone and at the same time demands a very critical and thoughtful approach to some of the proposals for further perfecting public education in our country.

Each time I encountered the melancholy consequences of the differentiation of American schools, I recalled with alarm that sometimes voices are raised in our country for differentiation of Soviet secondary education almost on the American model.

Great caution and careful testing are called for in establishing special schools for so-called gifted children. I saw what such schools are in America. They are raising a caste of young people who are an élite but are developed essentially one-sidedly. This path is not for us.

.   .   .

THE FLAME OF THE NEGRO REVOLUTION

L. Velichansky

The Soviet press gives considerable attention to American racial problems. The following account of racial disturbances in Birmingham, Alabama, in the spring of 1963 and the activities of the Student Nonviolent Coordinating Committee was written by a Soviet journalist in the United States.

The article was published in the popular Soviet weekly magazine *Ogonok,* which presents both foreign and domestic news and feature articles and may be considered roughly the Soviet equivalent of *Life.* The tenor of this Soviet article should be contrasted with the Chinese description that follows it. The Chinese article explicitly links the Negro crisis to the Marxist class struggle—pictured as inherent in capitalism—and to Fascist imperialism. The Soviet interpretation avoids such an analysis and emphasizes local forces of resistance to integration.

For six weeks on the streets of Birmingham, Negro demonstrations have continued. For six weeks the attention of the whole world has been riveted on the events in Alabama, a state in the southern United States. The Birmingham authorities employed water hoses, which shoot water under enormous pressure, and special truncheons with electric batteries which until now have only been used in slaughterhouses to prod the cattle.

Police dogs were thrown against the demonstrators. The use of dogs was borrowed from the experience of former Hitlerite S.S. men who were invited from Western Europe to work in the South. But the American racists have introduced their own "innovation." They have taught the dogs to recognize people by the color of their skin and to attack only Negroes. In support of the dogs and the 350 Birmingham police were the armed forces of the state. The number of arrests has grown to 2,500. Half of this number are schoolchildren between seven and sixteen years of age.

The Birmingham jail and . . . all temporary armed enclosures are filled to overflowing. Several times the streets and parks of Birmingham have been

FROM "Flamia negritianskoi revoliutsii," *Ogonok,* No. 21 (May 19, 1963), pp. 2–3. Translated by the editor.

transformed into wild jungles. Chasing people with dogs and fire hoses continued until the last Negro was thrown back across the railroad tracks separating white Birmingham from black. But each time the next day saw the appearance of even greater numbers of demonstrators.

And it is just this fact, and not the unbridled terror, which is the genuine sensation of the Birmingham events. Terror against Negroes is not new in the southern states. It is constant. It is a distinctive facet of the American way of life.

What is new is that Negroes have stopped being afraid of terror.

I was not in the south of the U.S.A. (the State Department stubbornly does not allow Soviet correspondents into the southern states) but followed the events from the reports of American correspondents and television. The strongest impression made on me was a jail scene filmed by a television cameraman immediately after the arrest of the schoolchildren who had participated in the demonstration. Through the iron bars of the cells the eyes of seven- and eight-year-olds looked out at me. They had just been confronted by infuriated dogs, and white policemen had seized them and herded them into policewagons. In the large eyes of the children was bewilderment and an intense longing to know what would happen to them, but they showed no fear. The young ones didn't smile, but neither did they cry.

But the older children were jubilant. Clapping their hands, they chanted "Freedom, Freedom, Now!" They glowed with pride, for they had won a victory. It was the first time they had broken through the police barrier. The Chief of Police, Connor, decided not to use the dogs on them. This gendarme, well-known throughout America by the nickname "Bull," suddenly understood that neither water hoses nor dogs, but only the authority of the leader of the demonstration, Martin Luther King, could stop the Negroes from answering force with force.

In the hands of many of the demonstrators were rocks and empty bottles. If even one child were harmed in any way, then all the fury which had accumulated in the Negro community for centuries would rain down on the heads of the "defenders of order."

When the Attorney General of the U.S.A., Robert Kennedy, condemned the Negro leaders for using children in their street demonstrations and thus subjecting them to the danger of prison detention, one of the leaders of the Birmingham demonstrations, Wyatt Walker, said, "The Attorney General of the U.S.A. should be ashamed that in this struggle to make American democracy real, children have shown more courage than he has."

The name of Uncle Tom, the humble Negro in the important work of [Harriet] Beecher Stowe, has been known in America for a long time. On the lips of today's Negro youth it sounds like the despicable symbol of submission, like an insult.

I don't know whether Robert Kennedy was shamed by Walker's words, but the courage of the young people of Birmingham has made thousands of adult "Uncle Toms" who cared only for their own well-being blush, and will help them shake off their eternal fear before the violence of the white racists.

In the U.S.A. at this time several Negro organizations of "direct action" are operating. They have discarded the usual advice of patience, and they demand a variety of rights, now, today. "We have waited too long," they say.

I shall speak here of only one of these organizations. . . . This organization sprang up quietly. On the first of February, 1960, in the town of Greensboro, North Carolina, several Negro students entered a café for whites and announced that they would not leave until they were served. With the help of the police they were dragged out of the café. Their example was followed by students in all of the southern states. The participants of these "sit in" demonstrations were arrested and beaten, but on the next day, new groups of young people did the very same thing. By the end of the year about seventy thousand people had participated in the movement. In order to coordinate activities of these groups, the "Student Nonviolent Coordinating Committee" (SNCC) was created. In student circles it is called simply "Snick."

In 1961 the committee inaugurated a wide campaign against segregation in city transportation. These campaigns have had significant success. In ten southern cities racial segregation in cafés, libraries, museums, city parks, and buses has been ended.

In 1962, "Snick" began a campaign for the registration of Negro voters. This job is of great political significance. Southern Negroes almost never participate in elections. In the southern states there are 137 counties in which Negroes constitute a significant majority of the population, but on the voters' lists there are usually no Negroes, and they amount to only several score in all. Only the absence of political rights of Negroes can explain the fact that in the federal legislative organs, the southern states are represented by dyed-in-the-wool racists. So long as there is one-party rule in the South these gentlemen are automatically elected and can occupy their seats in Congress for life. And since activities of Congress are directed by the oldest members, this gives them the opportunity to occupy leading positions in the important Congressional committees. Together with the group of right-wing Republicans, the southern racists have built a reactionary coalition, in whose hands rests the legislative power of the country, independent of which party wins the election. This coalition not only blocks legislative measures directed toward guaranteeing civil rights for the Negro, but at present is the initiator of every antilabor law and other reactionary laws.

By inaugurating the campaign for voter registration, "Snick" has threatened the entire mechanism of political influence of the southern racists. The young men and woman who were sent by the committee to do this work were prepared to face every deprivation and danger. They have been shot at, jailed for "vagrancy" and "disturbing the peace" and beaten in police stations and jails. One of their leaders has been arrested and imprisoned twenty times. The white supporters of Snick have not fared better. . . .

But the worst thing was that the very Negroes who needed to be registered were afraid of even talking with the activists of "Snick." In Middlecounty, Mississippi, Herbert Lee, an old farmer and the father of twelve children, who only helped the students, was murdered. He was shot before the eyes of his neighbors by Deputy Garst, a representative to the State Assembly from that district, and he got away with it because none of the eyewitnesses would agree to give testimony, being afraid they would suffer the same fate as Herbert Lee.

It has been necessary to overcome centuries of fear. It has been necessary to explain to the people that for the sake of political rights everything must be risked: work, property, life. . . . But that has not been all. It has been necessary to learn all the tricks to which the pettifogging judiciary has recourse, such as not permitting the registration of Negroes on the basis of educational qualification. Finally, it has been necessary to make many people literate. One of the local secretaries of Snick, after a half-year of persistent work, persuaded three hundred people to go and inscribe their names on the voting rolls. But only one was allowed to register—a teacher with a university education. The rest were classified as "illiterate." All the preparation has had to begin again.

Such is the work required to build an organization. Headquarters have been set up in Atlanta, Georgia, and fifty active and courageous young men and women have become permanent committee workers. Snick concentrates its activities in two of the most racist states, Mississippi and Alabama. "Schools in Citizenship" have been organized in which students teach voter-registration candidates "reading, writing, and unity."

By the beginning of this year, the drive for registration had borne appreciable fruit. In Greenwood [Mississippi] registration assumed a mass character. There, 150 Negroes marched to the court to put their names on the list of registered voters. There, for the first time, the American police used dogs against the activists of Snick. The March demonstration and arrests in Greenwood were immediately preceded by events in Birmingham.

The demonstrations in Birmingham were led by a Christian organization headed by Dr. King, well known from the days of the bus boycott in Montgomery in 1956. But in this skirmish the Student Nonviolent Coordinating Committee also participated and left its mark on events. . . . Wide participation in the demonstration by Negro workers (Birmingham is a large center of the steel industry in the South) gave the movement a special stubbornness. One of the main demands was for the discontinuation of racial discrimination in the hiring of workers.

On the night of the twelfth of May, racists threw bombs at the homes of the Negro leaders of Birmingham, exploding the precarious armistice achieved between King and the representatives of the influential groups of whites in Birmingham. In the city widespread clashes between Negroes and the police continue. There are many wounded. And it has become even clearer that Birmingham is only the beginning.

"In America there is taking place an actual Negro revolution," wrote Max Lerner in the New York *Post* of May 10. "In the crowded Negro slums ticks a time bomb, which is ready to explode," wrote another journalist.

On Red Mountain, which rises above the blast furnaces, above the new sections of white Birmingham, and above the sections of Negro suburbs, stands the enormous figure of Vulcan, the God of Fire. By night the flames of the torch which he holds in his hand can be seen for miles. But the flame which has been kindled by the participants of the mass demonstrations in Birmingham can be seen today all over America.

RACISM AND THE CLASS WAR

Mao Tse-tung

In recent years Mao Tse-tung has made a decreasing number of statements in his own name. Thus, his declaration of August 8, 1963, on racial discrimination in the United States indicates the importance attached to this matter by the Chinese Communists. Mao carefully follows the Marxist analysis by linking racial discrimination to class struggle and the nature of imperialism. It is noteworthy that in the Sino-Soviet polemics of 1963, however, the Soviets charged the Chinese with fanning the flames of racism in a bid for leadership in Asia and Africa—an allegation that the Chinese denied.

An American Negro leader now taking refuge in Cuba, Mr. Robert Williams, the former President of the Monroe, North Carolina, Chapter of the National Association for the Advancement of Colored People, has twice this year asked me for a statement in support of the American Negroes' struggle against racial discrimination. I wish to take this opportunity, on behalf of the Chinese people, to express our resolute support for the American Negroes in their struggle against racial discrimination and for freedom and equal rights.

There are more than 19 million Negroes in the United States, or about 11 percent of the total population. Their position in society is one of enslavement, oppression, and discrimination. The overwhelming majority of the Negroes are deprived of their right to vote. On the whole it is only the most backbreaking and most despised jobs that are open to them. Their average wages are only from a third to a half of those of the white people. The ratio of unemployment among them is the highest. In many states they are forbidden to go to the same school, eat at the same table, or travel in the same section of a bus or train with the white people. Negroes are frequently and arbitrarily arrested, beaten up and murdered by U.S. authorities at various levels and by members of the Ku Klux Klan and other racists. About half of the American Negroes are concentrated in eleven states in the south of the United States, where the discrimination and persecution they suffer are especially shocking.

The American Negroes are awakening and their resistance is growing ever stronger. In recent years the mass struggle of the American Negroes against racial discrimination and for freedom and equal rights has been constantly developing.

In 1957 the Negro people in Little Rock, Arkansas, waged a fierce struggle against the barring of their children from public schools. The authorities used armed force against them, and there resulted the Little Rock incident which shocked the world.

In 1960 Negroes in more than twenty states held "sit-in" demonstrations in

FROM "Chairman Mao Tse-tung's Statement Calling upon the People of the World to Unite to Oppose Racial Discrimination by U.S. Imperialism and Support the American Negroes in Their Struggle Against Racial Discrimination," *Peking Review*, No. 33 (August 16, 1963).

protest against racial segregation in local restaurants, shops, and other public places.

In 1961 the Negroes launched a campaign of "freedom riders" to oppose racial segregation in transport, a campaign which rapidly extended to many states.

In 1962 the Negroes in Mississippi fought for the equal right to enroll in colleges and were greeted by the authorities with a blood bath.

The struggle of the American Negroes this year started in early April in Birmingham, Alabama. Unarmed, barehanded Negro masses were subjected to wholesale arrests and the most barbarous suppression merely because they were holding meetings and parades against racial discrimination. On June 12, Mr. Medgar Evers, a leader of the Negro people in Mississippi, was murdered in cold blood. These Negro masses, aroused to indignation and defying brutal suppression, carried on their struggle even more courageously and quickly won the support of Negroes and all sections of the people throughout the United States. A gigantic and vigorous nationwide struggle is going on in nearly every state and city in the United States; and the struggle keeps mounting. American Negro organizations have decided to start a "freedom march" on Washington on August 28, in which 250,000 people will take part.

The speedy development of the struggle of the American Negroes is a manifestation of the sharpening of class struggle and national struggle within the United States; it has been causing increasing anxiety to the U.S. ruling circles. The Kennedy Administration has resorted to cunning two-faced tactics. On the one hand, it continues to connive at and take part in the discrimination against and persecution of Negroes; it even sends troops to suppress them. On the other hand, it is parading as an advocate of the "defense of human rights" and "the protection of the civil rights of Negroes," is calling upon the Negro people to exercise "restraint," is proposing to Congress the so-called "civil rights legislation" in an attempt to lull the fighting will of the Negro people and deceive the masses throughout the country. However, these tactics of the Kennedy Administration are being seen through by more and more of the Negroes. The fascist atrocities committed by the U.S. imperialists against the Negro people have laid bare the true nature of the so-called democracy and freedom in the United States and revealed the inner link between the reactionary policies pursued by the U.S. government at home and its policies of aggression abroad.

I call upon the workers, peasants, revolutionary intellectuals, enlightened elements of the bourgeoisie, and other enlightened personages of all colors in the world, white, black, yellow, brown, etc., to unite to oppose the racial discrimination practised by U.S. imperialism and to support the American Negroes in their struggle against racial discrimination. In the final analysis, a national struggle is a question of class struggle. In the United States, it is only the reactionary ruling circles among the whites who are oppressing the Negro people. They can in no way represent the workers, farmers, revolutionary intellectuals, and other enlightened persons who comprise the overwhelming majority of the white people. At present, it is the handful of imperialists, headed by the United States and their supporters, the reactionaries in different countries, who are carrying out oppression, aggression, and intimidation against the overwhelming majority of the nations and peoples of the world. We are in the majority and they are in the minority. At most, they make up less than 10 percent of the 3-billion population of the world. I am firmly convinced that, with the support of more than 90 percent of the people of the world, the American Negroes will be victorious in their just struggle. The evil system of colonialism and imperialism grew up along with the enslavement of Negroes and the trade in Negroes; it will surely come to its end with the thorough emancipation of the black people.

4

The American Economy

MILITARIZATION OF THE ECONOMY

Otto Kuusinen et al.

Increasing militarization of the American economy is viewed in the following selection primarily as a result of the growing difficulties of a mature capitalist economy. In this "scientific" view, militarization appears almost inevitable although it will not solve any basic economic problems in the long run. This analysis is taken from the authoritative reference work *Fundamentals of Marxism-Leninism* prepared by leading Soviet academicians under the supervision of a committee headed by the late Otto Kuusinen, a member of the Presidium of the Communist Party. First published in 1959, it was designed "to present in popular form the fundamentals of Marxism-Leninism as a single and integral science."

Militarization of the economy in its developed form is typical of capitalism only in the period of the general crisis of capitalism, which is marked by world wars. It becomes possible because the government apparatus is utilized by the monopolies to redistribute the national income (by means of direct and indirect taxes, government loans, control over strategic raw materials,. etc.) in order to create a powerful war economy. The reason for such truly "total" militarization, exemplified by Germany in 1933–39 and the United States after the Second World War, is to be found in the sharpening basic contradictions of present-day monopoly capitalism. The big corporations persistently seek to solve the problem of markets by obtaining government war contracts. Moreover, their interest in the arms race is deep-rooted, for it is the source of super profits running into thousands of millions.

· · ·

It need scarcely be emphasized that from the moral viewpoint a society which uses the production of weapons of mass destruction as an economic "stimulus" is pronouncing its own death sentence.

FROM *Fundamentals of Marxism-Leninism* (London: Lawrence and Wishart, 1961) pp. 330–34. Reprinted by permission.

However, the question is not simply one of morals. This policy is not only criminal, but in the final analysis also futile, for it does not solve the basic contradictions of present-day capitalism.

An increase in state military orders sometimes acts as a lever for increasing overall production, including goods for civilian use. It can also *temporarily* promote a certain increase in wages, particularly of those employed in war industry. This takes place, as a rule, when war production expands and idle capacity and capital are put to use. The unemployed who obtain work in war industry increase the demand for goods. To satisfy this demand, it becomes necessary to increase production in other branches of the economy. Capitalist demand also grows, especially when old enterprises are expanded and new ones constructed in anticipation of increased war contracts, with the consequent need for building materials, machinery, and other equipment.

This was the situation in the United States during the Second World War, when inactive production capacity was brought into operation. From 1940 to 1943, the volume of industrial production increased by 90 percent, and the number of workers engaged in manufacturing rose by 70 percent. The outbreak of the Korean War in 1950 also served as a stimulus to industrial production. The example of the United States, however, also reveals the contradictions and limitations of a militarized economy. Even during the Second World War, the period of simultaneous growth of U.S. military and civilian production was short-lived. The level of civilian production soon began to fall. Long before the end of the war a situation had arisen in which civilian production could no longer be increased and had to be cut back. Beginning with 1944, a general decrease in industrial production could already be observed, for the increase in the output of war materials no longer covered the cut in production for civilian purposes. The same thing happened during the Korean War.

The short-lived stimulating effect of militarization for the general growth of production can also be explained by the methods used to finance it. In the early period, the government increases the military budget not only by levying taxes, but also by issuing government loan bonds, which are readily taken up by the bourgeoisie, who have the available financial means. Later on, however, more and more of the budget is met by increasing taxes on factory workers and office employees. The increase in government demand under such conditions is inevitably accompanied by a curtailment of the population's purchasing power, which leads to a shrinking market for civilian production.

From 1943 to 1957, U.S. industrial production increased by only 13 percent, which shows that the stimulus of the arms race in the postwar militarization of the U.S. economy was not very considerable. As a matter of fact, this rather small increase is by no means attributable to militarization alone. The role played by the mass renewal and expansion of fixed capital in industry and other branches of the economy was not less significant.

. . .

No matter how rich an imperialist country may be, militarization can only lead to a *gradual exhaustion of the national economy*. It inevitably retards the rate of growth of civilian branches of production and of the economy as a whole. . . .

Militarization of the economy leads to an unprecedented growth in the tax burden. The state buys weapons and pays for the maintenance of military personnel mainly by levying exorbitant taxes on the people.

In addition to taxation, the government obtains a certain portion of the means required for the army by state loans. The bonds of these loans are purchased primarily by capitalists who derive an important part of their incomes from the annual interest paid by the government. To pay interest to the capitalists and to redeem the bonds, however, the government must impose new taxes. Thus, the money supplied to the government by the bourgeoisie through the acquisition of state bonds is returned to them in full out of the pockets of the working people, and, moreover, with the addition of high interest.

An inevitable accompaniment of a militarized economy and one of its very important methods of operation is the *depreciation of money, or inflation.* The state is unable to completely cover its military expenditure by taxes and loans alone. The government's budget deficit is covered in part by issuing more paper money than is required for circulation. Furthermore, state bonds are used as a means of payment, as security on loans granted by banks to the capitalists, and this leads to an increase in the amount of money in circulation. The result is inflation—the usual consequence of wars and militarization of the economy. In 1957 the purchasing power of the U.S. dollar was one-half of its prewar level.

.   .   .

AMERICAN PLUTOCRACY TODAY

S. Menshikov

This selection deals with a subject that has always been close to the hearts of Soviet commentators on the United States: plutocracy. Menshikov is the son of a former Soviet Ambassador to the United States. He is currently on the staff of the Institute of World Economics and International Relations. Early in 1963 he toured the United States, interviewing business leaders. Here, he endeavors to trace the increasing wealth and power of the old plutocracy and the development of a new group of millionaire families.

Bourgeois literature provides extremely meager information about the life of the top ruling classes of the U.S. The vogue of expository works about the "robber barons," which reached its peak at the beginning of the twentieth century and which had a revival in the 1930's, is now past. The growth of

FROM "Amerikanskaia plutokratiia segodnia," *Mirovaia ekonomika i mezhdunarodnye otnosheniia,* No. 4 (1963), pp. 16–28. Translated by the editor.

finance capital and the strengthening of the rule of financial oligarchies in the realm of politics and economics, have had their inevitable consequences, a more careful and well-cultivated masking of the millionaires and billionaires. The standard explanation of the paid ideologists of imperialism is that the "old plutocracy" simply disappeared, "dissolved," "integrated," "reorganized"; made way for the impersonal and "democratic"; became the rich estate, devoid of pretension to power and fully "respectable," which still exists somewhere behind the scenes as an anachronism, but which no longer plays any essential role.

The facts refute all of these assertions. The American plutocracy today, at the beginning of the 1960's, exists and acts precisely as it did a quarter- or half-century ago. The old millionaire families who became rich during the dawn of monopolistic capitalism have essentially been preserved, and many of them have succeeded in significantly increasing the size of their wealth and the scale of their influence. Some, comparatively few, of the families have fallen into decay; but they have been replaced by new, large, energetic, and aggressive cohorts: the "nouveaux riches." The portion of the national wealth in the hands of the plutocracy has not fallen, but, on the contrary, has risen. "People's capitalism," those stylish words of contemporary imperialist propaganda, are now further from the truth than at any time in the past.

. . .

The results of a count (on the basis of capital income) show that the number of people having over $1 million has reached, at present, 300,000. "Petty" millionaires (who have from $1 million to $2–3 million) are now an extremely large category of the American bourgeoisie. As to the richer category (those having over $10 million), they constituted approximately 3,800 according to our count. In November, 1957, *Fortune* magazine, analyzing tax returns of specialists and millionaires and also materials in government archives and other data, printed the names of 155 people with personal capital of more than $50 million. "Within sight of this mark," noted *Fortune*, "are about another hundred." Thus, the magazine set roughly at 250 the number of individuals with capital of over $50 million. This corresponds to our count made on the basis of income data (230).

. . .

The portion of the total number of shares of stock owned by such people exceeds 50 percent. Conditions of a protracted boom on the exchange lead to the additional growth of the plutocracy's capital without any expenditure of their own energy. In the past thirty-five years, the average value of common stock in the U.S.A. has risen seven to eight times. Even after the market crisis of 1962, its market value was far and away higher than it was in the mid-1920's.

In spite of the assertions of bourgeois authors about "the excessive load" of taxes on the rich, their real significance is not so great. According to our reckoning (not considering illegal methods of avoiding taxes), the degree of taxation, in fact, on personal income of over $100,000 this year was from 42 to 48 percent, while under the official rate it should have been 75 to 90 percent. Capital gains are subject to a maximum taxation of 25 percent, or two-fifths of the gross income of the individual who receives more than $1 million a year. The tax laws allow a write-off of nine-tenths of each millionaire's loss at the expense of the Treasury, so that there is often a transformation of losses into profits.

American millionaires have radically improved the means of preserving their estates from eroding and being split up, and of transferring them to their heirs. An army of professional specialists is created for the supervision of capital wealth; it guarantees the maximum rates of enrichment to the financial oligarchy, producing the most advantageous strategy for investment, speculation, and the avoidance of taxes.

.   .   .

Never in the history of the U.S.A. have new multimillionaires been created as rapidly as they have been in the past twenty years. This is explained to a large degree by the prolonged period of industrial expansion which occurred from 1939 to the mid-1950's and was interrupted by only short crises. When the tempo of the growth of production sharply decelerated, the enrichment of new millionaires continued as a result of the market boom and the preservation of a sufficiently high tempo in a few new branches of industry. The high level of military spending and government orders led to the advancement of all the millionaires who had a great stake in the exploitation of this fiscal market. The scientific-technological revolution served as an endless feeding trough for those who succeeded early in taking root in the new branches of production and in profiting from the monopoly which resulted from the patent laws.

.   .   .

The colossal wealth of the plutocrats puts them in an exceptional position, isolated from society, shut off by an invisible barrier of gold, just as in the feudal period royal blood was, in the eyes of the retainers, like a "halo of divine origin." But, in fact, of course, the answer is not to be found just in a halo or just in bowing to the Golden Calf. The financial oligarchy consciously shuts itself off from society with the help of watchmen and bodyguards and an army of advisors and hired ideologists. For this the millionaires have their own class reasons.

They are afraid of the public and want it to know as little as possible about their affairs and their way of life, so that they will not suspect the real significance of their wealth and power. This yearning was unusually intensified in the 1930's with their colossal economic collapse and with the growth of the class struggle.

.   .   .

The plutocracy's fear of public shock has not killed the thirst for a rich and luxurious life. But more important than what happened in the past is that the members of the rich American families, consumed by their characteristic love of power, are trying to determine directly high policies and to occupy important governmental posts, utilizing these positions not only in their own class interests, but also for self-advertisement and self-enrichment.

THE AWAKENING WORKING CLASS

E. D. Vil'khovchenko and I. N. Zorin

The "Section on the International Working Class and Communist Movement" of the Institute of World Economics and International Relations published in 1961 a book entitled *The Working Class Movement in Capitalist Countries (1959-1961)*, devoted to explaining "the course and results of the class struggle of the working class in capitalist countries in the new stage of the general crisis of capitalism." The following selection is taken from the chapter entitled "The Working Class of the U.S.A. in the Struggle for Its Rights" by E. D. Vil'khovchenko, a Candidate of economic science, and I. N. Zorin. As Marxist-Leninists, Soviet writers view the working-class movement everywhere, at least potentially, as *ipso facto* "progressive," the embodiment of the best values in society, and that segment of society most sympathetic to the Soviet Union and its brand of "socialism." That the American labor movement has failed to match these standards thus far is attributed in large measure to "right-wing, politically opportunistic leadership," although some mention is also made of the special American conditions which have retarded the development of a true working-class ideology.

The ideologists of modern imperialism and reformists are making determined efforts to portray the U.S.A. as the country of "people's capitalism," where class struggle does not exist, where the interests of the monopolists and toilers do not contradict each other, and where arguments between employers and workers are settled in a spirit of "class cooperation." However, the facts refute these false theories.

In the largest country of the world capitalist system, social contradictions are intensifying, and the antagonism between labor and capital is growing.

Suffice it to say that, according to the quantity of strikes and the number of participants in strikes (based on official statistics), the U.S.A. surpasses the other capitalist countries.

. . .

In the postwar period, U.S. monopolies spent much effort to weaken and undermine the organized labor movement. The adoption of the anti-trade-union Taft-Hartley Act of 1947, the exclusion from the CIO in 1949–50 of a number of progressive trade unions, constant repression against Communists, and other measures of struggle with the labor movement added to the systematic propagation of reformism and conciliation on the part of the conservative trade-union leadership, which is in the service of monopoly capital.

In 1955, under pressure of the rank-and-file members of the trade unions, there occurred the unification of the two main trade-union centers, the American Federation of Labor (AFL) and the Congress of Industrial Orga-

FROM "Rabochii klass S SH A v bor'be za svoi prava," *Rabochee dvizhenie v kapital'-isticheskikh stranakh, 1959–1961* (Moscow, 1961), pp. 251–73. Translated by the editor.

nizations (CIO). But the reformist leadership of both organizations, headed by the reactionary trade-union leaders G. Meany and W. Reuther, attempted to utilize this important event to preserve control over the organized part of the labor movement, and tried to keep it within the bounds of pure trade unionism, subordinate to the policies of the bourgeois state. The rightist trade-union leaders did much, and are doing much, to implant hostility in the members of American trade unions toward the socialist countries, to persuade them that their destiny is bound to the successes of capitalist production and the militarization of the economy, and to create the illusion that their well-being is tied up with the aggressive course of foreign policy of the right-wing monopolistic circles of the country.

The strong pressure of bourgeois ideology on American workers and the relative ideological and political backwardness of the labor movement in the U.S.A. is conditioned by a number of historical and economic causes and, above all, it is connected with the place of American imperialism in the world capitalist economic system. Being international exploiters, American monopolies seize the economic opportunities to guarantee to certain categories of workers in the U.S.A. a higher standard of living in comparison with the rank-and-file workers of other capitalist countries, to create a wider stratum of labor-aristocrats, and to buy off the leadership clique of the trade unions.

Repression on the part of the reaction, suppression of the action of the working class, and the policy of "class conciliation" followed by the reformist trade-union leadership, led, in the estimation of the Communist Party of the U.S.A., in a short time to the weakening of the influence of the progressive forces in the labor movement and to the restricted character and perspective of the trade-union movement.

But today the situation is beginning to change. The growth of economic difficulties in the citadel of imperialism and the quickening of the crisis of overproduction are leading inevitably to a new aggravation of class contradictions.

During recent years the American working class has collided all the more sharply with the problem, the discussion of which has not been excluded from the agenda of all trade-union conferences and meetings, namely the problem of chronic unemployment resulting from the extension of automation and mass displacement of workers from production. Simultaneously, the exploitation of workers who have remained on the job has increased. The situation is aggravated by the constant under-utilization of productive capacity in American industry.

· · ·

In June, 1961, according to data of the Department of Labor, unemployment stood at roughly 7 percent of the working force. In numerous branches of industry in the first quarter of 1961, unemployment stood at between 6 percent and 22 percent of the whole working force.

More than half the unemployed are unskilled workers, and the percentage of unemployment is especially high among Negroes. Layoffs have also touched particular groups of skilled workers.

Attempting to shift the burden of the economic difficulties onto the shoulders of the toilers, monopolistic capital is strengthening its attack on wages and the trade-union rights of the working class. The monopolists demand noninterference by trade unions in questions of the organization of production and working conditions. They have obtained acceptance by many states of the so-called right-to-work laws which give to companies the right to hire workers who are not members of trade unions. In 1959 the reactionary, anti-labor Landrum-Griffin Act was adopted which, in essence, places American trade unions under state control.

. . .

A characteristic feature of the American labor movement of the past few years is the growth of activism among the rank and file of the trade unions and a noticeable increase in their pressure on the conservative trade-union leadership.

The activation of the rank and file of the trade unions has compelled the ruling class to resort to several new maneuvers in dealing with the workers. The United States government is seeking to utilize somewhat more broadly the governmental apparatus in an attempt to soften the sharpness of class conflicts. In February, 1961, a Presidential advisory committee, including representatives of capital, labor, and "the public" was created. The goal of this committee was to patch up the collaboration of trade unions and employers and to "guarantee industrial peace." In this way the Kennedy Administration is attempting, with the support of the right-wing trade-union leadership, to channel the growing class struggle of the workers into a less dangerous course.

But it is necessary to observe that the intensification of class contradictions in the U.S.A. during recent years is occurring under conditions of a general weakening of American imperialism, of a crisis in its foreign and domestic policies.

. . .

The striving of the workers for militant, unified action has strengthened from below the movement against the autocracy of the trade unions' executive organs, for increased rights of the rank and file, and against corruption and racial discrimination inside the workers' organizations.

At recent congresses of branch unions of the AFL-CIO, the policies of the trade-union bureaucrats were roundly criticised.

Most apparent is the struggle for increasing the rights of the rank and file and for altering the policies of the trade unions, which appeared in speeches of the opposition group of D. Rarik against the reformist leadership of McDonald of the Steelworkers' Union. In May, 1960, there sprang up "The Organization for the Struggle for the Rights of Trade Unionists" which demanded widening internal union democracy, instituting measures against the undesirable consequences of automation, etc. The militant character of the opposition, the challenge to the conservative leadership, and the intention of the Rarik group to nominate its own candidates for elections to the union leadership led, in February, 1961, to the persecution of this movement by McDonald, the president of the union.

. . .

An important change in the American trade-union movement is the relative strengthening of the political activity of the workers. The reformist leadership of the AFL-CIO, defending the principle of "neutralism" of trade unions in the political struggle, is trying to limit the growing activism of the workers to the realm of trade-union politics. They see the final goal of these policies as obtaining "liberalization" of Congress so that it will adopt more "just" legislation.

Now the American toilers have come forward more decisively against the antilabor laws, for a wider social security system, for a legal increase in the minimum wage, for an improvement of working conditions, and for more active participation by the workers in election campaigns, as well as for intensification of the struggle toward increasing the civil rights of the Negroes. Among the workers of the U.S.A., the movement to create their own mass workers' party is at last gaining strength.

This intensification of political activity by American workers has forced the AFL-CIO to accept ever wider participation in elections, although this participation has not yet gone beyond the limits of the two-party system.

In the Presidential elections of 1960, the unions came forward as a more significant force in the political life of the country than ever before.

· · ·

In 1960 many trade unions supported the candidacy of Kennedy as "the lesser evil," but several of them as, for example, the Carpenters [Union] and Miners [Union], which belong to the AFL-CIO, and some of the independent trade unions (the Electricians, the West Coast Longshoremen, the Teamsters, and others) abstained from officially endorsing either one or the other of the candidates. Explaining the position of the Longshoremen, their president, Bridges, wrote in the newspaper the *Dispatcher:* "Whichever candidate is elected, there can be no doubt that he will follow an antilabor policy."

In the U.S.A. there is an increasing tendency toward the creation of a mass workers' party. The decision of the Canadian Congress of Trade Unions to form the Labor Party of Canada met with a large response in North America.

· · ·

In the forefront of this struggle are the West Coast Longshoremen's [Union], the Teamsters [Union], and others, who created "committees of political action" during the election campaign of 1960. In the branch trade unions and regional organizations belonging to the AFL-CIO, as was shown by the conventions of 1959–1960, there is a growing desire to strengthen the committees of political education, to broaden their functions, and to found a political workers' organization based upon them.

In the New York organization of the AFL-CIO, the rank-and-file trade-union members demanded that the leadership pursue measures for the creation of a "permanent mass mechanism of political action," branches of which would be active in all electoral districts of the city and state. Similar resolutions were adopted by the trade-union organizations in the states of California, Illinois, and others.

The American workers are demanding more often that trade unions put up their own candidates for Congress. At the convention of the powerful union of automobile workers in 1959, the secretary-treasurer of the union, backed by many delegates, declared: "We no longer wish to see how our 'friends' in Congress betray us; we should nominate our own workers' candidates." The automobile workers demanded that the AFL-CIO leadership call a national conference of representatives of workers', Negro, and farmers' organizations for selecting workers' candidates and to work out a political program of the trade unions for the elections. The California Council of the AFL-CIO put forward analogous demands in March, 1960. Despite the negative stand of the leadership of the AFL-CIO, many workers supported these proposals.

·   ·   ·

The movement for the creation of a mass workers' party has met with great difficulties. One of the most serious obstacles is the strong trade-unionist tradition. "The American proletariat, which does not have a socialist ideology," wrote William Foster, "is inclined to value the minor concessions, gained by them with the aid of the Democratic Party, as the basis for participating in the two-party system." The reformist leaders of the AFL-CIO receive much help in this from the monopolistic bourgeoisie.

Nowadays, however, when the interests of the workers in political problems is growing, Meany, Reuther, Schnitzler, and other leaders of the AFL-CIO cannot openly promote nonparticipation of the trade unions in politics. They must do some maneuvering. Such devoted servants of the monopolies and mortal enemies of socialism as Meany do not want to hear about any type of trade-union political action. In 1959 the struggle of the workers against the anti-union Landrum-Griffin Act compelled Meany to recognize the inevitability "of the entrance of the workers into the arena of political struggle." On the eve of the 1960 elections he even mentioned the possibility of the creation of a workers' party in the future.

·   ·   ·

The working class is now participating more widely in the struggle against the attack of the monopolies on democratic freedoms. Not only the progressive, independent trade unions, such as the United Electrical Workers' Union, but several unions of the AFL-CIO (the workers of the meat-packing industry, the needle workers and others), have pressed demands for broadening civil rights, liquidating the House Committee on Un-American Activities, repealing the reactionary Smith Act, and others.

The development of the movement for the elimination of racial discrimination in the country once again confronts the working class with the question of its relationship to the Negro movement, one of the main questions in the struggle for democracy. The elimination of the system of discrimination would be a blow to the reactionary bloc of Democrat-Dixiecrats and Republicans and a blow to the monopolies. It would deprive big business of superprofits extracted from exploiting the cheap labor of the Negro workers in the South, and of the additional possibility of an attack on the standard of living and on the rights of the entire American working class.

·   ·   ·

The toilers of the U.S.A. are constantly becoming more actively involved in the movement for the defense of peace. The progressive, independent trade unions consistently and decisively speak out for peace and against the policy of "cold war." Thus, early in 1960, the United Electrical Workers presented to the government a program for peace that demanded reducing the burden of expenditures for arms and broadening the peaceful branches of the economy. The trade-union council of Minneapolis put forth a demand for the creation of a Department of Peace by the U.S. government.

Many trade unions in the AFL-CIO have come forward with demands for the reduction of military expenditures, a ban on nuclear arms, peaceful competition with the socialist countries, and an increase in trade with the U.S.S.R. and China.

. . .

THE MIXED ECONOMY

B. A. Denisov

The author of this selection, B. A. Denisov, attempts to prove that the basic nature of capitalism remains unchanged. He says that Western theories such as "democratic capitalism" and the "mixed economy" are incompatible with the correct Marxist-Leninist economic analysis. Some alterations in the "productive forces" (e.g., increased governmental regulation of the economy, the growth of labor power, and more widespread distribution of income) cannot basically change the nature of capitalism, which is defined by private ownership of the means of production and control over the state by monopolies. In fact, he asserts that these alterations merely mask the development of even more reactionary imperialism. It is noteworthy that Denisov feels obliged to refute the writings of specific American economists and historians, and in so doing exposes the main thrust of their thought to the Soviet reader. Denisov's monograph was published by the Higher School of the Soviet Communist Party, an institution that stands at the apex of the extensive system of Communist Party schools in the Soviet Union.

Many bourgeois scholars evaluate somewhat soberly the prospects of the theory of "people's capitalism" and its basic tenet that the future of capitalism belongs to its present. Not restricting themselves to arguments about the class harmony of "democratic capitalism," these theoreticians, together with their right-wing socialist allies, advance the idea that capitalism has accomplished its evolutionary movement to a "mixed economy," that is, to an economy composed of elements of capitalism and socialism.

The idea of a "mixed economy" was first advanced by the well-known American economist Chase as early as the Second World War. From that time on, this idea has achieved the rights of citizenship in many capitalist

FROM *Kritika sovremennykh burzhuaznykh teorii o budushchem obshchestve* (Moscow, 1961), pp. 22–25. Translated by the editor.

countries, and is the foundation of one of the current stylish theories, that of the "synthesis" of the two systems. The theoreticians of a "mixed economy" either speculate with the popular ideas of socialism among the working masses, lulling them to sleep with the song that capitalism already contains the elements of socialism, or they intimidate the capitalists with the spector of socialism, compelling them to fall back on drastic measures against the "Red menace.". . .

Arthur Link, an American professor at Northwestern University, says [in *The American Epoch: A History of the United States Since 1890*] that the outstanding feature of the development of the U.S.A. in the twentieth century is the systematic democratization of the economic and political life of society. As a result of this development, declares Link, American capitalism has been so transformed that it has ceased being capitalist and has been changed into something entirely unique. In the course of the twentieth century, the American economy has become a mixed economy that is impossible to label either capitalist or socialist. In this economy neither competition, monopolies, business, nor workers rule.

Professor Sumner Slichter, in his article "A Statement of Belief in Our Economy" [New York *Times Magazine*], undertook to prove that the following changes are occurring in the United States: (1) A significant portion of political power has been transferred from the businessmen to the workers, employees, and farmers. (2) The government has established wide control over the distribution of income, having achieved this with the help of the progressive income tax and large payments to the needy, pensions to the aged, unemployment benefits, general measures of aid, and compensation to workers who have been dismissed. (3) The government controls the prices on an ever growing number of goods. (4) There is a widening sphere in which the government has established more or less detailed direction—the direction and regulation of the mutual relations of workers and enterprises, for example. (5) The state, in the person of the government, has become a large proprietor in several branches of the economy (it is engaged in loaning money on a large scale and spends much money on state housing projects. (6) The government has created a system of distribution of subsidies (for example, subsidies to farmers for land reclamation, subsidies to the shipbuilding and aviation industries, and so forth). Slichter speaks of a "mixed economy," meaning an economy that the government directs to a significant degree and that to a certain extent "displays private economic initiative." Under the "mixed economy," which supposedly has been created in the U.S.A., centralized decisions play a limited role in the guidance of the economic activities of the country. Government intervention is of such a nature that each of the ten million independent producers (of which about 6 million are in agriculture) have the right to decide what and how they will produce.

Without considering in detail the theory of a "mixed economy," let us note its fundamental flaws. The defenders of this theory ignore the basic differences between capitalism and socialism. This is the heart of the matter. . . .

. . . Socialism is the very opposite of capitalism. To private property it opposes public ownership; to anarchy of production, a planned economy; to exploitation, free labor, and so on. This is why in the midst of capitalism there cannot arise the sprouts of socialist productive relationships. At best, the supporters of a "mixed economy" confuse productive relationships with the material preconditions of socialism. This confusion allows them to declare, for example, that state ownership of unprofitable businesses, and in general the use of socialist measures in the economic activities of the bourgeois state, is efficient. . . .

The attempt to find the embryos of socialism in the productive relationships in capitalist countries is fruitless. It is obvious and verifiable by historical experiences that in imperialist countries it is impossible for capitalist and socialist productive relationships to coexist. Of decisive significance here is the fact that the state acquires political power. The more powerful state monopoly capitalism grows, the less likely is the possibility of such coexistence. It is the nature of the development of imperialism to change over from democracy not only in the sphere of politics, but in the sphere of economics as well, where the capitalist monopolies stifle all possible competition. This is why socialist relationships in the midst of capitalism cannot arise, and therefore why all talk about a "mixed economy" is groundless.

.   .   .

5

American Foreign Policy

THE CUBAN CRISIS
AND PEACEFUL COEXISTENCE

Nikita S. Khrushchev

Before the Supreme Soviet on December 12, 1962, Premier Nikita S. Khrushchev discussed at length the Cuban missile crisis of late October, 1962. In the following excerpts from his speech, Khrushchev presents the Soviet version of American actions during the crisis and draws some general lessons about the nature of American foreign policy and the present operation of international relations. Khrushchev's job of explaining the emplacement and subsequent removal of Soviet missiles in Cuba was made more difficult because he had to defend the Russian actions against criticism from the Chinese Communists.

. . . Counterposed to the line of peaceful coexistence and the solution of international problems by peaceful means, followed by the Soviet Union and the other socialist countries, is the line of the aggressive circles of imperialism aimed at maintaining the cold war and increasing international tension.

It is their fault that crises flare up, one after another, aggravating the international situation and pushing mankind to the abyss of a world war.

The imperialist circles are trying to find a way out of their difficulties by organizing an attack on the living standards of the workers of their countries and stepping up the plunder of economically underdeveloped countries. After the collapse of the world colonial empires, the plan of the imperialist monopolies is to preserve intact and even intensify the economic enslavement of young national states, to keep in chains the peoples which are still in colonial bondage. Thus, we have on the one hand a growth of the national-liberation movement, which is supported by all progressive mankind, and on the other an intensification of the attempts of the imperialist powers to crush the movement by any means.

FROM "The Present International Situation and the Foreign Policy of the Soviet Union," report to the U.S.S.R. Supreme Soviet, December 12, 1962, as translated in *Documents of Current History*, No. 27.

The most aggressive and adventurist circles of imperialism are trying to resolve their difficulties through a further intensification of the arms race and the preparation of a war of aggression against the socialist countries and the young sovereign states of Asia, Africa, and Latin America.

It is becoming increasingly obvious that the seats of aggression created by the imperialists contain sparks which might produce the flames of an all-out rocket-nuclear war.

The aggressive forces of imperialism are tying knots of international tension which are fraught with dangerous consequences for mankind. The most acute point of this tension was the crisis in the Caribbean.

.   .   .

A large-scale military invasion of Cuba by counterrevolutionary mercenaries was launched in Cuba in April of last year. This invasion was prepared and carried out with full support on the part of the United States.

Further events have shown that the failure of the invasion did not discourage the United States imperialists in their desire to strangle Cuba. They began preparing another attack. In the autumn of this year a very alarming situation was created: everything indicated that the United States, resorting to its own armed forces, was preparing to attack the Cuban Republic.

Revolutionary Cuba was compelled to take all measures to strengthen her defense. The Soviet Union helped her build up a strong army standing guard over the achievements of the Cuban people. In view of the mounting threat from the United States, the government of Cuba in the summer of this year requested the Soviet government to render further assistance. Agreement was reached on a number of new measures, including the stationing of several score Soviet IRBM's in Cuba. These weapons were to be in the hands of the Soviet military.

What were the aims behind this decision? Naturally, neither we nor our Cuban friends had in mind that the small number of IRBM's sent to Cuba would be used for an attack on the United States or any other country.

Our aim was only to defend Cuba. We all saw how the American imperialists were sharpening knives, threatening Cuba with a massed attack. We could not remain impartial observers in the face of this bandit-like policy, which is contrary to all standards of relations between states and the United Nations Charter. . . .

. . . We were confident that this step would bring the aggressors to their senses and that they—realizing that Cuba was not defenseless and that American imperialism was not all-powerful—would be compelled to change their plans. Then the need for retaining rockets in Cuba would naturally disappear.

Indeed, had there been no threat of an invasion and had we had assurances that the United States would not invade Cuba and would restrain its allies from this, had the United States guided itself by this in its policy, there would have been no need for the stationing of our rockets in Cuba.

Some people pretend that the rockets were supplied by us for an attack on the United States. This, of course, is not wise reasoning. Why should we station rockets in Cuba for this purpose when we were and are able to strike from our own territory, possessing as we do the necessary number of intercontinental missiles of the required range and power?

We do not in general need military bases on foreign territories. It is known that we have dismantled all our bases abroad. All people who have any understanding of military matters know that in the age of intercontinental and global rockets, Cuba—this small faraway island which is only about thirty miles wide in some places—is of no strategic importance for the defense of the Soviet Union. We stationed rockets in Cuba only for the defense of the Cuban Republic, and not for an attack on the United States. Such a small country as Cuba cannot, naturally, build up such forces as could launch an offensive against such a big country as the United States.

Only those who are not "all there" in the head can claim that the Soviet Union chose Cuba as a springboard for an invasion of the American continent —the U.S. or countries of Latin America.

.   .   .

The developments in the Caribbean confirmed that there was a threat of such aggression. By the twentieth of October, a large-scale buildup of U.S. naval and air forces, paratroopers, and marines began in the southern part of the U.S., across from Cuba. The U.S. government sent reinforcements to its naval base at Guantanamo lying on Cuban territory. Big military maneuvers were announced in the Caribbean. In the course of these "maneuvers," a landing was to be made on Vieques Island. On October 22, the Kennedy Administration announced a quarantine of Cuba. The word "quarantine," by the way, was merely a fig leaf in this case. Actually it was a blockade, piracy on the high seas.

.   .   .

In the face of these stepped-up military preparations, we, for our part, had to take appropriate measures. The Soviet government instructed the U.S.S.R. Minister of Defense to alert the entire army of the Soviet Union, and above all the Soviet intercontinental and strategic rocket forces, the rocket anti-aircraft defenses and the fighter command, the strategic air command, and the navy. Our submarines, including atomic submarines, took up assigned positions. A state of increased military readiness was announced in the ground forces, and the discharge was halted of those servicemen of senior age groups from strategic rocket forces, anti-aircraft defense forces, and the submarine fleet.

.   .   .

In these conditions, if one or the other side had not shown restraint, not done everything needed to avert the outbreak of war, an explosion with irreparable consequences would have followed.

Now, when tension caused by the events in the Caribbean has been reduced, when we are in the last stage of settling the conflict, I should like to report to the deputies of the Supreme Soviet what the Soviet government has done to put out the approaching flames of war.

On October 23, immediately after the United States proclaimed the blockade of Cuba, the Soviet government, besides taking defensive measures, issued a statement resolutely warning that the United States government assumed a grave responsibility for the destinies of peace and was recklessly playing with fire. We frankly told the United States President that we would not tolerate piratical actions by United States ships on the high seas and that we would take appropriate measures with this object in view.

At the same time the Soviet government urged all peoples to bar the road to the aggressors. Simultaneously it took certain steps in the United Nations. . . .

However, the government of the United States of America continued to aggravate the situation. United States militaristic forces were pushing developments towards an attack on Cuba. On the morning of October 27, information from the Cuban comrades and from other sources, which bluntly said that the invasion would be effected within the next two or three days, reached us. We assessed the messages received as a signal of utmost alarm. And this was a well-founded alarm.

Immediate actions were needed to prevent an invasion of Cuba and to maintain peace. A message prompting a mutually acceptable solution was sent to the United States President. At that moment it was not yet too late to put out the fuse of war which had already been lit. Forwarding this message we took into consideration that the messages of the President himself expressed anxiety and the desire to find a way out of the obtaining situation. We declared that if the United States undertook not to invade Cuba and also would restrain other states allied with it from aggression against Cuba, the Soviet Union would be willing to remove from Cuba the weapons which the United States calls "offensive."

The United States President replied by declaring that if the Soviet government agreed to remove these weapons from Cuba the American government would lift the quarantine, i.e., the blockade, and would give an assurance on renunciation of the invasion of Cuba both by the United States itself and other countries of the Western Hemisphere. The President declared quite definitely, and this is known to the whole world, that the United States will not attack Cuba and will restrain its allies from such actions also.

But we shipped our weapons to Cuba precisely for the prevention of aggression against her! That is why the Soviet government reaffirmed its agreement to the removal of the ballistic rockets from Cuba.

Thus, briefly speaking, a mutually acceptable solution was achieved, which spelled a victory for reason, a success for the cause of peace. The Cuban question entered into the stage of peaceful talks and, as regards the United States of America, was, so to speak, transferred there from the generals to the diplomats.

. . .

Which side triumphed; who won? In this respect one may say that it was sanity, the cause of peace and security of peoples, that won. The sides displayed a sober approach and took into account that unless such steps are taken as could help overcome the dangerous development of events, a third world war might break out.

As a result of mutual concessions and compromise, an understanding was reached which made it possible to remove dangerous tension, to normalize the situation.

. . .

There are some who say that the United States allegedly compelled us to yield on certain points. But if this yardstick is applied, these people should say that the United States too was compelled to yield on the settlement of outstanding issues between states, without war, by peaceful means. This is exactly the policy of peaceful coexistence in action.

.　　.　　.

Among the ruling circles of the United States there are some politicians who are rightly called "madmen." The "madmen" insisted and insist now on starting war as soon as possible against the Soviet Union and the countries of the socialist camp. Is it not clear that if we had taken an uncompromising position, we would only have helped the camp of the "madmen" to take advantage of the situation in order to strike a blow at Cuba and to touch off a world war?

For the sake of justice it should be noted that among the leading circles of the United States there are also some people who take a more sane view of the situation and, considering the present balance of forces in the international arena, realize that, had the United States touched off a war, it would not have won it and would have failed to achieve its purpose. . . .

In our time, imperialists cannot disregard the growing might of the Soviet Union, the socialist countries. We have the necessary numbers of powerful intercontinental rockets which enable us to strike back if war is started against us.

The militarists who boast that they have nuclear submarines for use against the Soviet Union, with Polaris missiles and other "surprises," as they put it, on board, would do well to remember that we aren't rustics either.

Why do I recall such hardly pleasant things as intercontinental missiles and atomic submarines? Merely because we are compelled to do this by the irresponsible statements of certain leaders of the United States and their allies.

When the events around Cuba were at their height and danger was crackling in the air, many people in the West said it was necessary to seek a reasonable solution of disputes in order to prevent war. But now, when the shock has passed, so to speak, some of them are beginning to say that disputes should be settled on the basis of concessions by one side only. This is an unwise and dangerous policy.

.　　.　　.

Warlike calls for "toughness" have again begun to be made in the United States too. What can we say of such imprudent boasters? They remind me of the hero of one hunting tale.

A man once went hunting with his dogs. The dogs started after a hare. The hare kept ahead of the dogs for some time, but finally they began to overtake him. Suddenly the hare saw a hole in the ground and dove into it. Oh, horrors! . . . He found himself in a foxhole, and there were cubs in it. The hare was very frightened and asked in a tiny, timid voice:

"Little foxes, where is your mother?"

"Our mother went to get a chicken to feed us," the cubs replied.

The hare then recovered some of his courage and said—in a gruff voice this time:

"A pity. I'd have shown her."

In the same way, some Western politicians say now: A pity, we would have shown the Soviet Union. Well, gentlemen, try it!

It is not precluded that some madman may start a war. But if he starts it, then even a thousand wise people will be hard put to it to stop it. This is known from history.

Is a new invasion of Cuba possible? One cannot, of course, give guarantees for the demented militarists, but it can be confidently said that all madmen who dare start a war will meet with the same inglorious end as the Hitlers, the Mussolinis, and other barbarians who have plunged the world into war.

. . .

The critics of a peaceful settlement of the conflict say that, don't you see, one cannot believe the words of the United States, that history knows many instances when treaties have been violated. Yes, history knows such instances, but if one proceeds only from this, then one must acknowledge that people now have no other prospect except reciprocal extermination. To assert this means wittingly or unwittingly taking to the road of militarism, regarding war as the only method of settling disputes.

Are international disputes really bound to be settled through war and not through negotiations? No, the preaching of the settlement of disputes between states through war is madness, which holds out only suffering and calamity for the peoples. It has nothing in common with the teachings of Marx and Lenin. It is tantamount to denying the significance of international treaties and agreements, denying the principle of peaceful coexistence. Reasonable standards of international relations exist and we must not undermine but strengthen them. Cursing does not settle disputed issues.

Resting on the assumption that the nature of imperialism has not changed, some people say that it must be exposed, cursed. Imperialism, of course, must be exposed—it is an evil for the peoples of the world, but cursing imperialism alone, no matter how rightly, will not sap its strength.

It is, of course, true that the nature of imperialism has not changed. But imperialism today is no longer what it used to be when it held undivided sway over the world. If it is now a "paper tiger," those who say this know that this "paper tiger" has atomic teeth. It can use them, and it must not be treated lightly. It is possible in relations with imperialist countries to make reciprocal compromises, while, on the other hand, having all the means in order to smash the aggressors should they unleash war. . . .

THE SMOKESCREEN
OF PEACEFUL COEXISTENCE

Renmin Ribao's *Observer*

Chinese Communist views on the United States are closely connected with the disagreements between Moscow and Peking. In part the dispute rests on differing Chinese and Soviet perspectives on and evaluations of the world situation, particularly the nature of American policy. Moreover, the Chinese have attempted to discredit the Soviet position by asserting that the Russians are being duped by

United States policy and, in effect, are abetting the American cause. The attack on the policy of "peaceful coexistence" as an American deception is really a direct rebuff to the Soviet Union, for "peaceful coexistence" is a term long used by the Soviet leadership to characterize its foreign policy. Even more sinister, pointing to the test ban agreement, Soviet support of India, and the "hot line" between Moscow and Washington, the Chinese have implied in this and other statements that the Russians are beginning to ally themselves with a new reactionary "holy alliance" against the progressive world forces —i.e., the Chinese. Although these allegations are part of the endeavor to undermine Soviet leadership of international Communism, especially in Asia, Africa, and Latin America, they also reflect apprehension of the Chinese Communists about becoming increasingly isolated in the world.

The author of this selection is identified only as *"Renmin Ribao's* Observer," which indicates the authoritative nature of the piece.

On September 20 [1963] U.S. President Kennedy made a speech at the UN General Assembly. In the speech he talked a lot about "common destiny," "one world," "one human race," and said that "the Soviet Union and the United States . . . can find areas of common interest and agreement." These remarks of Kennedy, like certain of his previous speeches, sound very pleasant on first hearing; but a careful analysis of them enables one to discover without difficulty what he means to say and what he intends to do.

This is the background against which Kennedy's speech was delivered: the U.S. ruling clique considers that its "strategy of peace" backed up by nuclear blackmail has proved successful and that it holds promise of further successes. Unable to conceal their joy, many American government officials as well as the U.S. press have come out openly to egg on the Soviet leaders to go further along their present path. Now Kennedy has precisely used the rostrum of the United Nations to give a push in the same direction.

Kennedy glorified the tripartite treaty [on nuclear testing] as a guiding light. Changing the tune he has repeatedly used some time ago in propagating that the tripartite treaty could not restrain the United States from continuing her nuclear arms drive, Kennedy was now trying his hardest to brag about the great significance of the treaty. He called it a "milestone" in the relations between the United States and the Soviet Union. He gave official praise to the spirit of "partnership" displayed by the Soviet leaders in concocting the Moscow nuclear fraud. He urged the Soviet leaders to make further efforts in this direction.

KENNEDY'S TERMS FOR U.S.-SOVIET "PEACEFUL COEXISTENCE"

Don't the Soviet leaders want "peaceful coexistence" with the United States? O.K., said Kennedy. Don't the Soviet leaders want "peaceful competition" with the United States? O.K., said Kennedy. He even added with

FROM "A New Chapter in Kennedy's 'Strategy of Peace,'" *Renmin Ribao* (September 25, 1963).

emphasis that the United States considered such "peaceful coexistence" and "peaceful competition" necessary. "Speaking for the United States of America, I ⟨Kennedy⟩* welcome such a contest," said he. But he made it clear that the global strategical objectives of the United States could not be changed. These, according to Kennedy, are:

1. "The people of Germany and Berlin must be free to reunite their capital and their country." This means that Kennedy wants the Soviet leaders to go back upon their original position on the questions of Germany and Berlin and agree to the "reunification" of the German Democratic Republic into West Germany.

2. "The people of Cuba must be free to secure the fruits of the revolution that has been so falsely betrayed from within and without."

This means that Kennedy is bent on subverting the revolutionary government of Cuba and will not tolerate the existence of socialist Cuba. It will be recalled that responsible U.S. officials from Kennedy downwards have repeatedly proclaimed that the United States cannot coexist in peace with socialist Cuba. Recently they have also made it quite clear that Cuba is a big obstacle in the way of normalizing U.S.–Soviet relations. The Soviet leaders must agree to the removal of this so-called obstacle, they declare.

3. "In all the world—in Eastern Europe as well as Western, in southern Africa as well as northern, in old nations as well as new—people must be free to choose their own future, without discrimination or dictation, and without coercion or subversion."

The meaning of this is twofold. One is that capitalism should be restored in the socialist countries; and the other is that it is not permissible for the people of the capitalist countries to make revolution and still less so for the socialist countries to back the revolutionary movements in the capitalist countries. According to Kennedy, if the peoples of the world were given "free choice," they would all choose to join the "free world community" under the thumb of the United States.

4. "Our ⟨U.S.⟩ defenses around the world will be maintained for the protection of freedom."

In other words, the United States will continue its arms expansion and will maintain its global system for aggression. Nobody should interfere with U.S. intervention and aggression.

It is easy to see from these remarks of Kennedy's alone what he expects the Soviet leaders to do on a number of major problems. His intention is all too obvious. In his opinion, if the Soviet leaders are desirous of "all-round cooperation" with the United States, and look forward to further agreement, they must make substantial concessions on these problems.

U.S. "PEACEFUL EVOLUTION" POLICY

Thus, Kennedy has in fact dictated terms for the "peaceful coexistence" between the United States and the Soviet Union. His Secretary of State, Dean Rusk, declared in a speech on September 10 that "there can be no assured and lasting peace until Communist leaders abandon their goal of a world

---

* Angular brackets indicate insertions by *Renmin Ribao* editors.—Editor.

revolution." He asked the Soviet leaders to "go on from there, by putting aside the illusion of a world Communist triumph." Thus, the price set today by the U.S. ruling circles on "peaceful coexistence" is much higher than what they asked two years ago for a peace of twenty years. They have made it clear that the Soviet leaders must abandon Communism as an "illusion," and that they must furthermore compel the Communists and the revolutionary peoples of the world to renounce the objective of a world revolution, for only on such conditions will U.S. imperialism bestow peace. In that speech Rusk also made no secret of the U.S. ruling circles' hopes for "the peaceful evolution" of the socialist countries. He could hardly conceal his delight in finding "some suggestive signs of restiveness" on the part of the Soviet leaders "about the burdens and risks of their commitments to the world Communist movement." Therefore he held it possible to carry on with the policy of "peaceful evolution" until victory was won without having to fight a war.

But all the honeyed words of Kennedy cannot cover up the real intentions of U.S. imperialism. The so-called peaceful coexistence and peaceful competition which Kennedy has plugged so energetically are but a smokescreen behind which the U.S. imperialists hope to attain their strategic aim of "peaceful evolution."

Kennedy's UN speech is just another maneuver in his "strategy of peace.". . .

But the Soviet paper *Pravda* applauded Kennedy's speech lustily, saying that "the spirit of cooperation and understanding, which marked the President's statement, cannot but cause definite satisfaction."

What does this mean? Does it mean that the Soviet leaders regard Kennedy's conditions for "peaceful coexistence" as acceptable? Do they intend to agree to the U.S. plan to annex the German Democratic Republic? Do they intend to agree to the U.S. scheme to subvert the Cuban revolutionary government? Do they intend to agree to the U.S. plot to "liberate" the socialist countries in Eastern Europe? Do they intend to agree to let the United States have a free hand to suppress the revolutionary movement of the peoples? Do they intend to agree to the United States carrying out intervention and aggression throughout the world as it pleases? In a word, are they ready to seek "peaceful coexistence" with the United States at the expense of the interests of the German people, the Cuban people, the people of the socialist countries, and all other peoples of the world?

But the course of history is determined neither by Kennedy and his like nor by those who are obsessively seeking "all-round cooperation" with Kennedy. Under no circumstances will the German people, the Cuban people, the people of the socialist countries, and all the other peoples of the world permit them to get away with their crimes. . . .

·　　·　　·

U.S.–SOVIET RELATIONS
AFTER KENNEDY AND KHRUSHCHEV

Leonid Brezhnev

The sudden ouster of Party First Secretary Nikita S. Khrushchev in October, 1964, did not immediately result in dramatic new foreign policy initiatives. The cautious conduct of Soviet foreign relations can probably be attributed to indecision, differences within the post-Khrushchev leadership, and the serious difficulties posed for the Soviet Union by the continuing Sino-Soviet conflict and the escalating war in Vietnam. The conservative tenor of Soviet policy was matched by a reticence of the leaders to speak openly and at length on foreign policy issues in the manner of their predecessor. The following selection from First Secretary Brezhnev's address on the twentieth anniversary of V-E Day was one of the few public pronouncements on Soviet-American relations made by Khrushchev's successors during the first year of their tenure.

. . .

Our foreign policy is clear. Its goal is to ensure, together with all socialist states, peaceful conditions for the building of socialism and communism in our countries, to defend the cause of peace and progress. We are doing and shall continue to do everything in our power to strengthen the unity and solidarity of the socialist countries and to consolidate their friendship and brotherhood. We actively support and shall continue to support the liberation and revolutionary movements; we are developing and shall continue to develop all-round cooperation with the liberated states of Asia, Africa, and Latin America. We consistently champion the principles of peaceful coexistence in relations between states with different social and political systems. We shall do everything to thwart the plans of the imperialist aggressors and to save mankind from a new world war.

True, there are some people who are eager to misinterpret the policy of peaceful coexistence. American politicians, when speaking of relations between the U.S.S.R. and the U.S.A., seem ready to recognize the need for peaceful coexistence. But at the same time the U.S.A. crudely tramples this principle in its relations with other states, interfering in their affairs and committing acts of open aggression. The American politicians obviously are not being consistent here.

. . .

Comrades! The creation of the anti-Hitler coalition during the war was an example of the cooperation of countries with different social systems in the common struggle against an aggressor. What has happened to this coalition in the intervening years?

FROM "Great Victory of the Soviet People," *Pravda* (May 9, 1965), as translated in *The Current Digest of the Soviet Press,* published weekly at Columbia University, Vol. 17, No. 18 (May 26, 1965), pp. 10–11. Copyright 1965 by the Joint Committee on Slavic Studies, appointed by the American Council of Learned Societies and the Social Science Research Council. Reprinted by permission.

After the end of the great battle and the rout of the enemy, the chief participants in the anti-Hitler coalition did not set out on the common road of building a lasting peace, but took divergent paths. One might say that the ink on the declaration of the defeat of Hitler's Germany, signed in Berlin by representatives of the U.S.S.R., the U.S.A., Britain, and France, was not yet dry before our former allies began to break the ties that united the chief participants in the war against German Fascism.

Very soon after the rout of Fascism a new imperialist striking force was formed, headed by the U.S.A., which openly claimed "world leadership." As you see, the American imperialists had learned nothing from the fate of the German-Fascist pretenders to world supremacy.

The entire course of international events in recent times confirms the conclusion reached by the world's Communist Parties that the chief force of war and aggression in our days is American imperialism.

Having assumed the role of the bulwark of world reaction, the ruling circles of the U.S.A. are grossly interfering in the internal affairs of other countries and peoples, opposing the relaxation of international tension and creating more and more new breeding grounds for conflicts.

No sooner do the people of any country, be it in Latin America, Asia, or Africa, rise in struggle for freedom and independence before the international gendarme—American imperialism, with its warships, planes, or U.S. marines —immediately appears. This is what happened in the Congo. This is what is happening today in the Dominican Republic, where American soldiers by force of arms are suppressing the aspirations of the people of this country for freedom and independence.

Provocations are continuing against heroic Cuba.

The events in Vietnam serve as the most striking manifestation of the gendarme policy of American imperialism.

The American intervention in Vietnam has evoked wrath and indignation throughout the world. The professional bullies of the American military are cold-bloodedly repressing the patriots of Vietnam who, under the leadership of the National Front for Liberation, are struggling for the freedom and independence of their homeland. For several months now the American imperialists have been carrying out aggressive operations against the D.R.V. [Democratic Republic of Vietnam], raiding the republic's cities and villages from the air and engaging in piratical operations by their naval forces in its territorial waters.

In this situation, it is an affair of honor and the international duty of the socialist countries to give effective support to the fraternal country that is being subjected to attack by the imperialists.

The Soviet Union is giving the Democratic Republic of Vietnam aid in the cause of its defense against aggression. This aid will be increased if necessary. There is complete unanimity of views between the Soviet Union and the D.R.V. on the measures needed to rebuff the imperialist interventionists. Our country will sacredly fulfill its internationalist duty!

By its actions aimed at suppressing the liberation struggle of the Vietnamese people, U.S. imperialism is hurling an open challenge to the national-liberation movement of the peoples of the entire world. This is why support for the Vietnamese people, who are fighting against the imperialist aggression of the U.S.A., is a matter of honor, a matter of vital interest for all peoples who are defending their freedom and independence. Everyone who cherishes the preservation of peace on earth has an interest in this.

Today all peace-loving mankind is decisively demanding the cessation of American imperialism's aggression against the heroic Vietnamese people. And this demand must be fulfilled. The Vietnamese people are fighting for a just cause, and they will win!

As you know, just over half a year ago the present President of the United States, L. Johnson, campaigned for election under the slogan of allegiance to peace and fidelity to the traditions of Franklin Roosevelt. The American people voted for Johnson and against Goldwater, the representative of the pro-fascist circles. The voters, aware of the catastrophe a world war would mean for the United States in today's conditions, put their trust in the politician who in campaign speeches had spoken out for peace and a realistic approach to international problems.

The practical deeds of the present U.S. administration testify that it has embarked on a different path.

Apparently the ruling circles of the United States of America would like— on what grounds it is impossible to say—to assume the role of supreme arbiter over other peoples. They want to prescribe for the peoples of other countries what systems they should have at home and are trying to suppress by armed force those who do not kowtow before them.

What are the generally accepted norms of international law to them, the creators of such a policy! Without giving it a second thought they violate the solemn pledges recorded in the United Nations Charter and other international documents that the United States has also signed. This is a policy of violence and arbitrariness, a policy of aggression. And no pseudo-doctrines concocted in Washington can conceal this obvious fact. The course of suppressing the national-liberation movement of the peoples with the help of military adventures and *diktat* will bring the U.S.A. neither honor nor respect. This course is doomed to ignominious failure, for it conflicts with the will of the peoples who are rising for freedom, independence, and social progress.

More and more talk has been heard in the United States of late about the alleged U.S. "supremacy" in the area of nuclear weapons. Not a day goes by without one or another high-ranking American leader emphasizing in threatening tones that the U.S.A. has so-and-so many atom bombs, missiles, strategic bombers, and atomic submarines. They scrupulously calculate how many hundreds of millions of people will be annihilated in the course of a thermonuclear war.

What can be said about this?

No one can intimidate the Soviet people and the peoples of the other socialist countries. We know our strength and are confidently marching along the path we have chosen.

.   .   .

AMERICAN MILITARY STRATEGY

Vasily Sokolovsky et al.

This assessment of American military strategy was presented in *Military Strategy,* an authoritative and comprehensive book written by fifteen leading Soviet military theoreticians headed by Marshal Vasily Sokolovsky, who served as chief of the general staff from 1953 until his retirement in 1960. In this presentation of the broad outlines of American foreign policy and changing military strategies, the authors reveal considerable acquaintance with the pertinent American literature on the subject; the American reader, however, will have difficulty in recognizing the motivations attributed to United States strategists and policy-makers. It is difficult to assess the true views of the Soviet leadership about Western strategies and motivations because their public statements are highly tendentious, being designed to show Western intentions in the worst possible light.

· · ·

The ruling circles of Britain and the United States, who for well-known reasons found themselves in the same coalition as the Soviet Union, continued to pursue their imperialistic interests during [World War II], although covertly.

American and British ruling circles intended to undermine the power of Germany, Italy, and Japan—their principal competitors—but to preserve the regimes existing in these countries.

The political aims of the United States and Britain toward the Soviet Union found concrete expression in the military objectives pursued by the imperialist circles of those countries: to conduct the war as much as possible at the expense of the U.S.S.R., to weaken the U.S.S.R. in the course of the war, and to prevent the Red Army from entering the Balkans and Central Europe. Because of this policy, they delayed in all sorts of ways the opening of the second front, and made plans to launch Anglo-American operations in the Apennine Peninsula and in the Balkans, instead of in France where they would have hurt Germany the most.

These strategic aims, directed at prolonging the war in every way, were also responsible for the combat methods employed by British and American troops, and for the slow, passive, and indecisive nature of their operations.

· · ·

The United States, which had reaped fabulous profits during the war, exploited the postwar situation to strengthen its economic, political, and military position. The political aims of the American imperialists were and still are to enslave economically and politically the European and other capitalist countries and, after the latter are transformed into obedient tools, to unify

FROM the book *Soviet Military Strategy,* edited by V. D. Sokolovsky, pp. 145–46, 149–62. © 1963 by the RAND Corporation. Published by Prentice-Hall, Inc., Englewood Cliffs, New Jersey and reprinted by permission.

them in various military-political blocs and groups directed against the socialist countries. The main aim of all this is to achieve world domination.

.   .   .

During the first postwar years, American ruling circles attempted to encircle the socialist countries with a system of hostile military-political groups and blocs of capitalist states and to unite the latter into a single anti-Communist coalition. This policy was most clearly expressed in the organization of numerous military, air, and naval bases around the countries of the socialist camp; in the adoption by the American Congress of the essentially expansionist "Truman Doctrine"; in the "Marshall Plan," which made it possible for the United States to establish control over the economies and policies of the European countries; and in the "Eisenhower Doctrine," aimed at the enslavement of the Near and Middle Eastern countries.

.   .   .

Thus, shortly after the conclusion of World War II, the United States had created a closed ring of aggressive military groups around the Soviet Union and the other socialist countries. As a result, the American imperialists received the right to use the territories of the signatory countries as military bases. They also assumed control of almost the entire military and economic potential of these countries, including the organization, preparation, and possible use of their armed forces, in order to transform their partners into obedient instruments of their will.

The formation of aggressive military-political blocs under the aegis of the United States signifies the almost complete loss of political sovereignty of the countries participating in these blocs, and to a considerable extent the loss of the ⟨independent⟩* national character of their foreign policy and strategy.

In contrast to prewar years, when the strategy of the principal capitalist countries bore a distinctly national character, the postwar period has been characterized by a tendency toward uniformity in national military strategies and their combination into a single global military strategy, intended to assure the realization of American foreign policy aims. Therefore, under present conditions it is no longer possible to conceive of independent military strategies for the British, French, West German, or Japanese, for example. Bourgeois strategy is now unified; each country participating in one bloc or another contributes its own proposals, additions, or changes, on the basis of its national interests; this is not accomplished without sharp disputes, of course. However, when dealing with the political or ideological aspects of the struggle against the Soviet Union and other countries of the socialist camp, the imperialist circles, motivated by hatred of the socialist countries, always find a common basis for reaching agreement. . . .

The end of World War II coincided with the appearance of nuclear and, subsequently, thermonuclear weapons. This fact facilitated the consolidation of the imperialist forces under the leadership of the United States, and exerted considerable influence on the development of a unified imperialist military policy and strategy determined by American ruling circles. In the initial postwar period the American imperialists also initiated the policy of negotiating

---

* Angular brackets indicate insertions by RAND editors.—Editor.

"from a position of strength" in their dealings with the Soviet Union and other socialist countries. This policy on strategy was also reflected in official directives in which military strategy was defined as ". . . the art and science of using the armed forces of the country to achieve the aims of national policy by the application of force or the threat of force."

From this it follows that the American imperialists plan to attain their main political aim—world domination—by means of aggressive wars.

Until approximately the end of 1960, American leadership adhered to the strategy of so-called massive response, which derived from the policy of "deterrence," and acknowledged the possibility of conducting only total nuclear war against the Soviet Union. The strategy of "massive response" or, as it was also called, "massive retaliation" was adopted by the U.S. Government and the military command in 1953 at the beginning of the Eisenhower Administration. Its official adoption was announced on January 12, 1954, by Secretary of State Dulles, who declared in a speech to the Council on Foreign Relations in New York: "The basic decision was to depend primarily upon a great capacity to retaliate, instantly, by means and at places of our own choosing."

The terminology "massive response" and "massive retaliation" serves to conceal the general aggressive nature of American strategy. American imperialists, while hiding behind such phrases and terms, are really preparing a surprise nuclear attack on the Soviet Union and the other socialist countries. American poltical and military leaders have repeatedly stated this, directly or indirectly.

·　　·　　·

As is known, the strategy of "massive retaliation" was based on the assumption that the United States had overwhelming superiority over the Soviet Union in nuclear weapons and especially in strategic aircraft. Therefore, the United States could be sure of attaining its political and military aims only by threatening to initiate a general nuclear war, which the countries of the socialist camp could not risk because of their inferiority in offensive nuclear forces.

In accord with this strategy, the American government placed the main emphasis on the development of strategic and tactical nuclear weapons, to the detriment of conventional armed forces, especially ground forces; this resulted in sharp disagreement between the army on the one hand, and the air force and, to some extent, the navy on the other. Undoubtedly, such a trend in the development of the armed forces could not fail to cause great dissatisfaction among the representatives of the ground forces and the groups of monopolists who supplied these forces with arms and equipment. The victory of the proponents of the "massive retaliation" strategy was not only a victory for the air force and the navy, but also for the monopolies producing armaments for the air force and navy.

·　　·　　·

As a result of the spectacular Soviet success in the field of missile construction and in the conquest of space, the strategy of "massive retaliation" collapsed. Being completely unrealistic in its assumptions, it was soon rejected by its own creators. Dulles himself declared as early as October 27, 1957, that the United States and its allies must take necessary steps if a local conflict occurred, "without provoking by our actions a general nuclear war."

.   .   .

The main reasons for the failure of the strategy of "massive retaliation" were the overestimation of American strength and capabilities, and the obvious underestimation of the economic, technical, scientific, and military capabilities of the Soviet Union. As a result of the Soviet Union's significant superiority in intercontinental ballistic missiles, a real threat to American territory had arisen. Therefore, American political and military leadership was compelled to reassess its strategic position and capabilities.

.   .   .

Even President Kennedy himself was forced to admit the increased military strength of the Soviet Union and the loss of alleged American superiority in strategic weapons, when he stated in Seattle in November, 1961, that the United States was neither omnipotent nor omniscient.

Thus, under the conditions of today, when there is a "balance" (approximate "equality") in strategic weapons and Soviet superiority in conventional armed forces, the American strategists are forced to reevaluate their previous attitude toward general nuclear war.

They understand that when both sides possess very large stockpiles of nuclear weapons and various means of delivering them to targets, primarily strategic means, a general nuclear war holds great risks of complete mutual annihilation. Consequently, the greater the stockpiling of weapons of mass destruction, the greater becomes the conviction that it is impossible to use them. Thus the growth of nuclear-missile power is inversely proportional to the possibility of its use. A "nuclear stalemate," to use the Western expression, had arisen; on the one hand a tremendous increase in the number of missiles and nuclear weapons, and on the other hand the incredible danger of their use. Under these conditions, according to the evaluation of American and NATO political and military circles, both sides had attained the position of so-called "mutual deterrence."

All this led to the conclusion that the strategy of "massive retaliation" was inflexible and could no longer assure the attainment of the political aims of the American imperialists. Whereas previously the United States could, with almost complete impunity, threaten unlimited use of nuclear weapons in any situation, even the possible outbreak of a local (limited) military conflict, the change in the balance of forces had made it dangerous to engage in "nuclear blackmail" and to risk the security of one's own country.

This circumstance has had an especially strong effect on the European satellites of the United States. In particular, by the end of 1959 the Western European Alliance had already openly noted in its decisions that the European countries could no longer rely exclusively on the strategic nuclear forces of the United States, as they had previously. There was no reason to expect that the Americans would automatically become involved in an armed conflict in which there was a risk of exposing themselves to a nuclear blow from the Soviet Union. Thus the European countries raised the question of creating their own independent strategic nuclear forces.

On the basis of their assessment of the new situation, American political and military leaders began to consider the so-called strategy of flexible response more acceptable and expedient. In their opinion, this would permit the conduct of either general nuclear war or limited wars, with or without nuclear weapons.

. . .

The new strategic concept of the United States and NATO, therefore, was already essentially determined by the time Kennedy came to power, and the new President became its most fervent exponent.

In his messages to Congress on March 28 and May 25, as well as in his televised appearance on July 25, 1961, President Kennedy described aspects of the new strategic concept and the military program of the United States in some detail.

The strategic concept, the message of March 28, 1961, stressed, "must be both flexible and determined" and must prepare for the conduct of any war: general or local, nuclear or conventional, large or small. This concept is based upon the same idea as a "retaliatory strike," the only difference being that, whereas previously the threat of such a strike implied the unlimited use of nuclear weapons regardless of the scale of ⟨the existing⟩ conflict, i.e., a general nuclear war, now the "retaliatory strike" must be appropriate to the nature of the potential conflict.

The message noted that the United States must increase the capability of its armed forces "to respond swiftly and effectively" to any enemy action. In a world war this would mean that such a capability must be retained by that part of the armed forces which "survives the first strike." The message pointed out the prime importance of the ability to survive the enemy's first strike and to deliver a devastating retaliatory strike "in order to inflict unacceptable losses upon him." The President stressed that the ability to deter an enemy attack depended not only on the number of missiles and bombers but also on their state of readiness, their ability to survive attack, and the flexibility and sureness with which they were controlled to achieve strategic objectives.

Referring to the possible conduct of limited wars, the message stated that the United States and its allies must be capable of waging such wars with conventional weapons. If the forces with conventional weapons are unable to achieve the desired objectives, however, nuclear weapons could be used. At the same time, the probability of a limited war expanding into a general war was not denied, but it was stressed that all necessary measures must be taken to localize the conflict and to prevent it from causing the outbreak of a general nuclear war.

. . .

At first glance the following may seem strange. On the one hand, American and NATO political and military leaders believe a general nuclear war to be implausible, or more precisely, unpromising, in the sense that it would lead to mutual annihilation, ⟨a belief that explains⟩ why the former strategy was rejected. On the other hand, the newly adopted strategy, while more flexible, again provides primarily for the capability and readiness for general nuclear war. But this is only an apparent contradiction.

The admission of the possibility that they might conduct a nuclear war, despite its unlikelihood, proves that the American imperialists are ready to embark upon any monstrous crimes against mankind to prevent their own inevitable destruction. Such a war would be an extreme measure; it might be initiated by the aggressors when all other measures had failed to give tangible results in the struggle with the socialist camp.

The question is this: If general nuclear war is dangerous to both sides, then what must be done so that it can lead to the attainment of the desired objectives, i.e., the destruction of the enemy with the least possible losses and destruction for oneself? The American imperialists and their Western European allies answer this question as follows: first, sharply step up the arms race, especially missiles, and nuclear and space weapons; and second, achieve⟩ surprise. The first ⟨measure⟩ must assure overwhelming quantitative superiority over the enemy in the most advanced strategic weapons, primarily missiles, and nuclear and space weapons, in order to make possible a continuing policy of "intimidation" toward the Soviet Union and to facilitate negotiations with it from a "position of strength."

Surprise assures the seizure of initiative, the rapid destruction of the enemy's armed forces, in particular his strategic forces and weapons, the disruption of his control over troops and the country as a whole, the undermining of his economy, and the demoralization of the people. It is believed ⟨by the Western powers⟩ that the enemy could be paralyzed in all respects by a powerful attack and that his fate would be determined during the very first days of the war.

The U.S. Senate Foreign Relations Committee has made a complete appraisal of the role of surprise in contemporary war. Rejecting any talk of "peacefulness," ⟨the document⟩ openly calls for a surprise nuclear first strike against the Soviet Union and the other countries of the socialist camp:

The advent of the nuclear-missile weapons generation ⟨heralded by the Soviet ICBM test of August, 1957⟩* brought a drastic compression in the time required for the delivery of nuclear explosions at intercontinental ranges and a corresponding reduction in the attack-warning time . . . ⟨available to the victim of strategic aggression⟩.† These effects, added to the fact that there is as yet no active defense whatsoever against an intercontinental missile in flight, have gravely increased the temptation to strike first in a nuclear war.

Thus it is no accident that American military theorists are carefully studying the advantages and disadvantages of preventive war, a first strike, and a preemptive attack.

The theory of preventive war was first advanced at the end of the 1940's by the most reactionary representatives of the American political and military leadership, when America possessed a monopoly of nuclear weapons. However, propaganda for this theory subsided when the Soviet Union also acquired such weapons. Now the American military leaders and scientists have returned to the study of preventive war, viewing it as a possible and acceptable choice. . . .

Thus it follows that there is a very real threat of a preventive war being unleashed by the American imperialists against the Soviet Union and other countries of the socialist camp. The slogan of such a war is: "What was inevitable had better come early rather than late . . . because it would be less

---

* The Soviet authors omitted these words, without indicating an ellipsis.—RAND editors.
† The Soviet authors omitted these words, but indicated an ellipsis.—RAND editors.

devastating that way." This slogan has many temptations for them, since the aggressor picks the time he thinks most favorable to begin the preventive war. The American imperialists believe that the military potential of the United States is much more capable of destroying the Soviet Union now than it will be in the future, particularly by preventive war.

Some military ideologists such as Kissinger substitute the term "surprise (first) strike" for the term "preventive war." This is a purely formal distinction, since the first strike can also mean the beginning of preventive war. But no matter what the attack is called, its main feature is the achievement of maximum surprise.

Surprise can and must be achieved in a preemptive blow. Such a blow is defensive, according to American military theorists, since it is dealt to an enemy who is ready to attack (to initiate a preventive war or deal a first blow). It is considered to be the final and only means of avoiding disaster.

. . .

U.S. "AID"—AN IMPERIALIST SHACKLE

V. Rymalov

In this article, published in *International Affairs,* the journal of the Soviet Society for the Popularization of Political and Scientific Knowledge, V. Rymalov, a senior researcher of the Institute of World Economics and International Relations, argues that the American foreign aid program is merely an imperialist device to enmesh the new nations in the web of neocolonialism. He emphasizes the military aspect of the United States foreign aid program and argues that foreign aid does not even cover the losses of the new nations that result from imperialist exploitation.

Since the end of the war imperialist spokesmen have been vaunting so-called Western aid to underdeveloped countries as proof of the "unselfishness" of the policy pursued by the leading capitalist powers and as their "great contribution" to the efforts of these countries to achieve independent national development, to advance their economy, and to raise the living standards of their people.

The facts, however, show that the true purpose of such "aid," principally by the United States, which is the most powerful mainstay of contemporary colonialism, is not to promote the independent national development of the former colonies and dependent countries. Its real aim is to shackle the countries seeking a new and independent life in the disintegrating colonial system

FROM "'Aid'—An Instrument of Imperialist Policy," *International Affairs,* No. 11 (November, 1962), pp. 12–19.

with new economic and political chains. The monopoly circles render "aid" on such terms as would in one way or another impose fettering foreign control on the policies of the recipient countries. . . .

. . . Let us turn to the principal official document in this sphere, the Mutual Security Act of 1951. All the main "aid" measures of the United States to other countries conform in practice to this act, which has a special section graphically illustrating the selfish and aggressive nature of imperialist "aid."

Here are some excerpts from this act. Section 511 stipulates: "(a) No military, economic, or technical assistance . . . shall be supplied to any nation . . . unless the recipient country has agreed to . . . fulfill the military obligations which it has assumed under multilateral or bilateral agreements or treaties to which the United States is a party. . . . (b) No economic or technical assistance shall be supplied to any other nation unless . . . the supplying of such assistance will strengthen the security of the United States. . . ."

This policy of naked colonialism is pursued by U.S. imperialism toward countries already drawn into various military political blocs and alliances. In this case it acts on the principle "no more bait for a hooked fish." As regards other underdeveloped countries it applies a more subtle policy, but its ultimate objectives remain the same.

. . .

Throughout the postwar period the policy of U.S. foreign "aid" has been noted for its unashamedly militaristic character. It was above all designed to promote the strategic plans of American imperialism.

Official American propaganda, professing concern for other peoples, usually highlights the big figures of state appropriations for foreign "aid." But even the most general analysis of these figures, given in official documents of the U.S. government, reveals its truly aggressive character. Thus, President Kennedy's report to Congress of June 12, 1962, on the fulfilment of the "mutual security" program, pointed out that in the 1950's almost two-thirds of all appropriations under this program were used for direct military aid.

In addition to funds allotted for direct military aid, used to supply all kinds of weapons and war supplies to other countries, considerable appropriations for "support of the defense" of other countries are also directly bound up with the U.S. militarist policy. These allocations, which usually amount to about a third of the funds earmarked for the arms deliveries, are used to build and maintain American military bases in countries dependent on the United States militarily and politically, and also for other military installations: airfields, roads, communication lines, firing grounds, etc.

Of the $3,722 million assigned for foreign "aid" in the 1960–61 U.S. budget, $1,800 million was allotted for direct military aid (about $2,000 million was spent) and for "support of defense," another $675 million, of which more than 50 percent was earmarked for three puppet militarist regimes in Asia: the Chiang Kai-shek clique on Taiwan and the rulers of South Vietnam and South Korea. The balance of the $675 million was spent, as admitted by U.S. officials, on the maintenance of strategic bases and military installations in some other underdeveloped Asian countries located near socialist countries.

. . .

The U.S. militarists take pleasure in calculating how the huge scale of their military aid spurs on the arms race in other countries. They use this "aid" as the chief means of bringing pressure to bear on the recipient countries to increase their own military expenditure. It serves America's aggressive interests in wanting to reinforce the undermined system of imperialism by force of arms, to extend its sphere of influence, and to capture new positions. American experts have estimated that a "comparatively small outlay in military aid" by the United States has made its military allies spend "about six dollars of their own for every military aid dollar spent by the United States."

There was ample reason why William Randolph Hearst, Jr., the American newspaper tycoon, airing the views of the country's real rulers on "aid" before congressmen, had the following to say: "You don't have to be an Einstein to figure out that military aid is bargain-rate defense, whether given directly in the form of arms or indirectly to support the economy of nations which otherwise could not afford troops or modern weapons in the amounts needed for adequate defense of our vital world perimeter."

This statement exposes the full hypocrisy of the official American doctrine that the U.S.A. has no selfish imperialist aims and, moreover, it is of interest in that it underlines one of the major features of the American "aid" policy, the inseparable connection between the military and economic objectives of this policy.

.   .   .

The Western imperialists are loudly proclaiming their altruistic concern for the underdeveloped countries and are doing their utmost to convince the underdeveloped countries that it is private capital, i.e., capital of the imperialist monopolies, that is the main source of foreign assistance for their economic advancement.

The true value of imperialist "aid" can be seen from the fact that the capital they export is generally much smaller than the total profits extracted by the monopolies. The Brazilian journal *Estudios Sociais,* after making a study of the role of foreign capital in the country's economy in 1947–1958, arrived at the following conclusions: the influx of foreign capital amounted to $498 million during this period, while profits totaled $1,558 million, of which $1,033 million were transferred abroad and $525 million remained in Brazil. Consequently, Brazil lost $1,060 million.

The monopolists export capital not through any intrinsic interest in developing other countries or in raising living standards, but for the sole purpose of extracting large profits. Their main objective is to capture new spheres of material and manpower resources for exploitation. Senator T. Morton, speaking in the Senate in early 1962, cited figures which offer incontrovertible proof of this. Between 1950 and 1960, the United States monopolies invested $8,500 million abroad and withdrew $20,500 million in profits.

But even these huge sums do not cover all the profits obtained by the imperialist monopolies abroad, because a considerable proportion is reinvested in other countries. To appreciate the scale on which the underdeveloped countries are being robbed through the export of capital, it must be remembered that American statistics gives official figures on profits, based on the financial reports of the monopolies themselves. But calculations made by the well-known American economist Victor Perlo from governmental sources, show that the actual profits of the monopolies on foreign investments are twice as high as those declared.

In the light of all this the question arises: who is "helping" whom, who is "financing" whom: the imperialist monopolies the underdeveloped countries or vice versa? The answer no doubt will not be in favor of the underdeveloped countries. Capital exports, however, are only one of the ways in which the industrial states of the capitalist world rob the economically backward countries.

The monopolies use their dominating position in the world capitalist market and the economic dependence of the underdeveloped countries to expropriate regularly a substantial part of their national income through nonequivalent foreign trade, through monopoly-high prices for industrial goods sold to these countries and monopoly-low prices on raw materials and food bought from them.

It was estimated by Alencastre, economic adviser to the Brazilian Labour Ministry, in the middle of this year, that the Latin-American coffee-exporting countries have sustained losses of $7,000 million during the last five years through the application of this policy by the European Common Market. The Common Market inflicted similar losses of $3,000 million on Asian and African coffee-exporting countries.

B. R. Sen, Director-General of FAO [Food and Agriculture Organization], stated at the end of 1961 that an economic survey of Africa by his organization showed that, as a result of lower export prices and poorer trade conditions, the African countries lost $600 million on exports in 1959 as compared with 1955, or twice as much as the total outside "aid." If this is aid, then it would be interesting to hear the imperialist definitions of robbery and exploitation.

. . .

THE PEACE CORPS—
AGENTS OF NEOCOLONIALISM

V. Kudryavtsev

V. Kudryavtsev, a frequent contributor to *Izvestia,* the all-union governmental newspaper, characterizes the Peace Corps as merely another, more insidious instrument of American imperialism. This article is similar in tone and content—even to the point of citations —to a number of pieces in *New Times* and other Communist publications which appeared in 1962 and 1963.

There are some anniversaries that do not deserve commemorative articles but still must be written about, because the peoples must draw lessons from negative phenomena too, sometimes.

Doubtless the second anniversary of the founding of the American Peace Corps belongs to this category. Let us say right away that it has no more to do with peace than magic with science. In two years this corps has extended its feelers to many states in Asia, Africa, and Latin America, which are usually counted among the economically underdeveloped countries. U.S. government agencies give special attention to the sending of members of the corps to African countries.

When this corps first came into being, the U.S. propaganda agencies gave special emphasis to the idea that it was created exclusively to fill a serious shortage of national cadres in the underdeveloped countries and that the members of the corps would live in the conditions prevailing in the given country and would receive no remuneration for their work. In brief, when American propagandists described the activity of the corps members, they even ascribed to it a certain amount of self-sacrifice. In actuality things are completely different.

The Peace Corps has its own budget of tens of millions of dollars, and in the U.S. budget it comes under the important heading of the maintenance of "mutual security." This fact alone gives the lie to American propaganda.

The Peace Corps is the offspring of neocolonialism. Whereas in the past American imperialism planted its influence in Latin-American countries through the dollar and the marines, the situation has now changed and it has become risky to operate in so crude a manner. This applies especially to Africa, where the United States has had almost no base of operations.

The American monopolies have not yet gained a firm economic foothold on African soil, even though after the Second World War they made considerable success in squeezing out British, Belgian, Portuguese, and, to a lesser extent, French capital. Therefore they are concentrating heavily on exerting ideological influence on the leaders of African states, on the intelligentsia, and, above all, on the young people. It is true that deviations from this stand have been made; when difficulties are encountered, American imperialism is not averse to resorting to the old coercive methods of implanting their influence. The events in the Congo, where the U.S.A. used the UN armed forces in its own interests, can serve as an example. Nevertheless, the basic method of penetration into Africa is, for the American neocolonialists, capital investments (according to some data, they had reached $3 billion by 1963, as against $100 million in 1939) and ideological infiltration. And the Peace Corps serves the latter purpose.

Members of the corps have an opportunity to penetrate where by dint of usage the roads are closed to embassy and mission officials. To say that corps members pass on experience to the local population in remote regions of a country would be an extreme exaggeration, since the majority of the members are young, just out of college, as a rule visiting Africa for the first time, and thus ignorant of local conditions. But for purposes of reconnaissance and

FROM "Deep Reconnaissance of Neocolonialism," *Izvestia* (March 1, 1963), as translated in *The Current Digest of the Soviet Press*, published weekly at Columbia University, Vol. 15, No. 9 (March 27, 1963), pp. 22–23. Copyright 1963 by the Joint Committee on Slavic Studies, appointed by the American Council of Learned Societies and the Social Science Research Council. Reprinted by permission.

propaganda this "fifth column" doubtless has great value. It is not for nothing that, when all is said and done, the Peace Corps is subordinate not so much to the State Department, not even to the Pentagon, as to the Central Intelligence Agency. They even undergo training as intelligence agents: At intelligence camps they are trained in the use of light weapons, take long hikes over very rough, swampy, and wooded terrain, etc. Besides, they represent a still greater value in the future, when they have learned the local language, living conditions and traditions, have established the appropriate contacts, and can enlist agents.

Aside from intelligence, the corps members engage in political propaganda among the population. The young African states are confronted with a choice of courses along which to steer the development of the economy, and these countries, having known the bitter experience of colonialism, are inclined toward the noncapitalist path of development. Therefore, the propaganda of the corps members is focused on these questions. The Ghanaian newspaper *Spark* has noted that the Peace Corps is directed against the noncapitalist path of development. The Somali newspaper *Al-Kifah* has stressed that "the task of the Peace Corps is to struggle against the progressive ideals of the national-liberation movement in Africa, Asia, and Latin America in order to assist the implanting and strengthening of American influence." To put it simply, the Peace Corps is a weapon in the hands of the American neocolonialists who want to take the place of the old colonial powers in Africa.

If the American ruling circles really wanted to fill the present lack of national cadres in Africa, they would have to subordinate the corps members completely to the appropriate governments and not interfere in their activities. But the way the matter stands is entirely different. When they arrive on the scene, the corps members remain completely under the command of corps headquarters, or more precisely, the Central Intelligence Agency, and fulfill its orders. Consequently, the corps members are microbes of American neocolonialism in the living but still not hardy organism of the young independent African countries. To spot this threat in time means to strengthen national security and to prevent the gradual subordination of the country to the interests of American monopolies. This danger is all the greater in that in African countries, under the influence of an extreme need for trained specialists, an illusion is at first created that the corps members are really people who are making available their knowledge for the benefit of the young states. But actually, as the Indian newspaper Delhi *Times* writes, "the facts attest that the loud talk about the philanthropic and humane character of the Peace Corps is a lie from first to last."

The anniversary of the corps affords an opportunity once again to assure oneself that this is a dangerous offspring of American neocolonialism; the decisions of the Third Afro-Asian Solidarity Conference, held recently in Tanganyika, passionately call for a stubborn struggle against this neo-colonialism.

III

VIEWS FROM THE DEVELOPING NATIONS

Until the emergence of many newly independent nations in the last decade, the attitudes of Africa, Asia, and Latin America were considered reflections of those of Europe and the United States, under whose political, economic, and cultural influence they lay. Such leaders as they had were educated in the West and seemed to be part of the West culturally and politically. America had been accustomed to criticisms from Europe, and since the 1920's it has heard the Communist critique of American political and economic institutions, but only in recent years has it discovered a third source of criticism and evaluation of things American—the developing nations of Africa, Asia, and Latin America.

Those familiar with the differences among the countries of Asia, Africa, and Latin America are aware that any attempt to describe the common attitudes of a group of nations which demonstrates such a diversity of background, geography, politics, economics, and social organization is fraught with difficulties. Charles Malik, in a section of a recent book (which is excerpted in this part), rightly notes the important differences between Latin America and the Afro-Asian world with respect to historical and cultural links to the West. One might add that even the term "Afro-Asia" itself is something of a misnomer when it attempts to encompass under the same general heading countries as diverse as India, Iraq, and Upper Volta.

The term "developing nations" may also be inaccurate for some of the countries to which the term is applied, but, if it does not describe the reality, it corresponds to the common ideal of the countries of Asia, Africa, and Latin America—the wish to transform themselves from backward, poor, largely agricultural, dependent territories to advanced, industrialized, independent nations. This common aspiration links the diverse nations represented in this collection and influences the content of their evaluation of America. It explains the priority given to economic development over political democracy and their preference for neutralism in international relations. A consciousness of their own inferiority in technology and military power also intensifies the critical attitude of representatives of the developing nations toward the more powerful countries—in particular toward the United States.

The economic situation of the developing nations explains why their representatives make their comments and criticisms only on selected aspects of American life. There is little interest in how American democracy and capitalism really work, since in many areas these institutions are regarded as completely inapplicable to conditions of underdevelopment. American foreign aid, on the other hand, impinges directly on nearly all the countries of Africa, Asia, and Latin America, and the American race problem is often seen as related to the open or concealed racism of the former colonial rulers. It is therefore understandable that the topics of foreign aid and race relations appear often in the selections that follow.

Another aspect of American life that is often noted—more a matter of style and approach than of substantive content—is the influence of the frontier on American life. Three writers included in this part allude to this influence—either directly as a reason for American moralism, readiness to shoot it out, and directness of personal approach, or indirectly through the restriction of economic opportunity and mobility that has resulted from the disappearance of the frontier. Whether because of the pervasive interest in "westerns" or because we have a Texan in the White House, what was originally an interpretation of American history by Frederick Jackson Turner has now become an explanation for many contemporary features of American life.

America may be strong materially and economically, some of the critics argue, but it lacks the superior moral, spiritual, and cultural attainments of the older non-Western civilizations. American values are materialistic, utilitarian, and dedicated to the worship of the machine. (See the opening selection by José Enrique Rodó). Its principal concern today is a negative one—a hysterical obsession with the evils of Communism—that affects both foreign policy and the character of American politics. (See the selection by Manuel Pedro González.)

Yet there are other values for which America stands that are viewed favorably from the perspective of the developing nations. The traditional American ideals of equality, national self-determination, and democracy still have revolutionary implications for areas where hierarchy, colonial or feudal control, and autocratic despotism have long been the rule. The Declaration of Independence and the writings of Jefferson and Lincoln are still read and quoted in Asia, Africa, and Latin America—as often as not to berate the United States for not living up to its avowed beliefs.

While the leaders and the intellectuals of the developing areas are committed to the ideal of democracy, the meaning they give the word differs widely from that which it has in the United States. They maintain its etymological sense, rule by consent of the people, but they often assume popular consent to be what the people *should* want rather than what they actually *do* want, their real rather than apparent will. In Africa and the Middle East, in particular, this real will is understood to be that of the single party or of the leader rather than that expressed through the interplay of interests, opposing parties, and the arbitration of the ballot box, as understood in the United States. It is only as a result of experience that a number of observers in these areas are becoming disillusioned with the single party as a permanent political institution and are taking a second look at the arguments for the existence of an organized opposition. Others, however, still defend the single party as more democratic and more efficient in the new nations. (See the selection by Julius Nyerere.)

Except for defenders of the Cuban United Revolutionary Socialist Party, Latin Americans do not argue for the single party as a system, although at least one Latin-American country, Mexico, is effectively under the control of one party with no more than token opposition. Many Latin-American constitutions reflect American influence in such institutions as a strong presidency and the separation of powers. Some American political institutions and practices—federalism, a written bill of rights, and the power of judicial review of legislation—have influenced the authors of the new institutions of Asia and Africa as well. (See the selection by M. Ramaswamy.)

The American example of two parties that are relatively similar in program and social composition is puzzling to the ideologically conscious intellectuals from the developing countries, and at times our system appears to be a confirmation of the Marxist theory that bourgeois democracy is merely a façade for control by outside economic forces. The evident shift of U.S. policy toward the developing areas under Kennedy (notably the Alliance for Progress and the opposition to Katangan separatism) seemed to cast some doubt on this thesis, but the Johnson Administration's support of Tshombe in the Congo and intervention against a constitutionalist revolt in the Dominican Republic confirmed the view (for those who wished to believe it) that the election of a Democratic Administration did not mean a fundamental change of policy. As this example indicates, judgments on American politics are made on the basis of certain symbolic acts in foreign policy as it affects the developing countries rather than on any profound understanding of the operation of American domestic politics. Only one domestic problem, the race issue, arouses great interest in the countries of Asia, Africa, and Latin America—intensified, of course, by the fact that most of the inhabitants of the developing areas are not Caucasians.

The relatively slow progress in the solution of the racial question in America has also focused attention on the nature of the American federal system—an aspect of American politics that foreign critics find difficult to understand. While some countries in Asia, Africa, and Latin

America have federal structures (e.g., Brazil, Nigeria, Venezuela, and India), in none is there so much power in the hands of the state and local authorities as there is in the United States. In most countries the drive for modernization requires considerable centralization, and if the degree of local autonomy that prevails in the United States were permitted, they would probably split apart. Still, the fundamental reason for the developing nations' criticism of American federalism is not that it differs from their own systems but that they are impatient with the exploitation of federalism by opponents of the emancipation of the American Negro.

No other aspect of American society receives so much attention as the racial question. Especially in Africa, the smallest incident in the South receives banner headlines, and the largest single obstacle to the acceptance of the American claim to have established true equality is the delay in granting it to the Negro.

But when observers from Asia, Africa, and Latin America get beyond this topic, they are often impressed by the relative equality in social relations and economic opportunity (at least for white citizens) in America, which contrasts with the often narrowly circumscribed and hierarchical relationships in their own more traditional societies. These observers hope to achieve economic development and social change in their own societies and at the same time to avoid the loss of traditional social values that has, in their view, accompanied the emergence of the affluent society in America. This is one reason that so much stress is placed on the revival of traditional culture, on "the African personality," and the development of native crafts and industries. The same pattern can be traced in reactions to American individualism and competitiveness. It is appreciated that these characteristics have much to do with the success of the American economic system, but the leaders of the developing nations define as their objective a more socially concerned and cooperative society—involving a less drastic break with the pattern of traditional society in which the group is more important than the individual.

Much of the criticism of the American economic system from the developing areas resembles that of the orthodox Marxists, and there is no doubt of the considerable appeal of the Marxist analysis in the developing nations. Yet the Marxist view of American society as foredoomed to depression and proletarian revolution has found little favor among observers from the developing nations, for they are impressed by the high living standard of the American worker and the affluence of our society. Admiration for the accomplishments of our economic system, however, has not led to any desire on the part of intellectuals and leaders in the developing countries to adopt a capitalist or free-enterprise economy. With the exception of certain groups in Latin America, the word "capitalism" has a negative connotation in the developing areas. It is associated with exploitation, selfishness, materialism, greed, and in particular, with the attempt to extend control over weaker and less developed areas for the purpose of securing raw materials, cheap labor, and a ready market for surplus production—in short, Lenin's description of imperialism. American worldwide economic influence and certain of the practices of American business firms, particularly in Latin America, sometimes seem to conform to this description, and it is not only Communist-influenced groups which refer to American "imperialism." Yet at the same time, developing nations, driven by the overriding objective of national development, are eager to encourage private economic investment in their countries by American business.

Despite their criticisms of American imperialism, the leaders of the developing nations have no hesitation about accepting foreign aid from the United States. Often one of the first acts of a newly independent nation is to send a mission to Washington to request aid, while insisting that it will accept assistance only if there are no political strings attached. Most of these leaders would reject the Marxist assumption that the interests of capitalist and proletarian nations are inevitably opposed, and, at least in their appeals for American aid, they stress the mutuality of interest in economic development. In other forums, however, the need for the less developed nations to band together to counterbalance the economic power of the developed nations, especially the United States, is a common theme. (It should also be noted that as neutrals, the leaders of the developing nations often consider the Soviet Union, and more recently China, at least as materialistic, exploitative, and disinclined to end the cold war as their capitalist opponents.)

A frequent complaint about United States foreign policy is its emphasis on the cold-war power struggle, and America's corresponding inability to understand the preference for neutralism among the developing nations. Neutralists are particularly critical of the American effort to build up anti-Communist alliances through military pacts such as NATO, CENTO, and SEATO. (See the selection by Gaganvihari L. Mehta.) If only the East and West would negotiate their differences and end the cold war, argue the developing countries, the vast amounts of money now devoted to armaments would be available for economic and social development. Perhaps because of our own tradition of moralizing in foreign policy, Americans, now confronted with responsibilities as a global power, resent this kind of sermonizing on disarmament, neutralism, and the evils of American power politics. Moreover, events have demonstrated that the critics in developing countries have sometimes seriously underestimated the dangers of Communist expansionism. The missile crisis in Cuba in the fall of 1962 and the Chinese invasion of India in the same period revealed to the developing countries that the danger of Communist aggression was not simply a fiction invented by the Americans.

The fundamental problem in the view of American policy held by the developing nations is that on the one hand, they are acutely conscious of the importance of power considerations in the relations

RECENT CARTOON VIEWS FROM THE DEVELOPING NATIONS

Marcha (Montevideo)

"What a nightmare—
I dreamt
that Domingo troops
landed in New York."

Landru in *El Mundo* (Buenos Aires)

(The octopus is labeled
"Red conspiracy.")

Ultima Hora (Lima)

Marcha (Montevideo)

Roma in *Novos Rumos* (Rio de Janeiro)

Bunzo Kai in *Yomiuri Shimbun* (Tokyo)

Don Quixote in Vietnam

Osorio in *Caretas* (Lima)

Dizi in the *Free Press Journal* (Bombay)

between a powerful United States and the relatively weak countries of Asia, Africa, and Latin America, but on the other hand, they do not recognize the power factor in the relations between the United States and the Soviet Union. Leaders of the developing nations assume that all differences are negotiable and that somewhere there is a harmony of interests if only men would look for it—except when their own national interests or ambitions come into play. The developing nations expect negotiation to settle East-West problems, but not the Arab-Israeli, Indonesian-Malaysian, or Indian-Pakistani conflicts.

Anti-colonialism is another common theme in the criticisms of U.S. foreign policy by Asians, Africans, and Latin Americans. The United States did not develop a large colonial empire, and it has given independence to the Philippines, commonwealth status to Puerto Rico, and statehood to Hawaii, but they charge that for political and economic reasons, it has not been sufficiently active in bringing about the liquidation of the colonial empires of its allies. (See the selection by Ronald Segal.) In addition, the term "neocolonialism" has been invented to describe the continued maintenance of political and economic domination after the grant of independence, and the United States is sometimes regarded as the leader of the "neocolonialist" forces. (See the selection by Kwame Nkrumah.) A related criticism denounces American willingness to aid dictatorial regimes provided only that they are opposed to Communism. This is a frequent theme in Latin-American writing on U.S. foreign policy, and it is often cited to substantiate the charge that in its struggle against Communism, America has been false to its original vocation as the prophet of equalitarian democracy to the world.

Despite their criticisms, observers from Asia, Africa, and Latin America admire much about America. The Peace Corps is an example of American generosity and moral sense that has made a deep impression in many parts of the developing world. The picture of a selfish, power-mad, racist, wealthy, but ignorant Uncle Sam is balanced by the image of an intelligent, humane, tolerant, generous, and liberal America, typified for the citizens of the developing countries by the late President John F. Kennedy, as their reactions to his death indicated.

At this writing, President Lyndon B. Johnson has not been able to inspire the same confidence in Asia, Africa, and Latin America. For all the current and past criticisms, however, a basic reservoir of good will toward the United States remains, and we can expect that the dialogue between the United States and the developing areas that has just begun will continue and one may hope, result in an increase in mutual understanding and cooperation.

1

American Ideology

ARIEL: A COMMENTARY ON THE SPIRIT OF AMERICANISM

José Enrique Rodó

It may appear puzzling that this section should begin with a translation from a work that was first published in 1900. However, *Ariel,* by José Enrique Rodó, has been republished many times, and it is still influential in shaping Latin-American attitudes toward "the colossus of the North." It reflects a general attitude common among educated leaders in many developing countries. The American gospel of hard work, energy, and practicality is at the same time envied and rejected by those who feel that it has been acquired at the sacrifice of higher ideals and spiritual values. The assertion of moral superiority also acts as a compensation for technical inferiority vis-à-vis the United States and the more developed nations. Rodó was a Uruguayan essayist and classical scholar. "Ariel" (from Shakespeare's *The Tempest*) symbolizes the cultural ideals of Greco-Roman civilization, which Rodó contrasts with Caliban, the symbol of the materialism of North American democracy.

·   ·   ·

A belief in utility as the goal of human destiny and a social norm of equality in mediocrity, these together comprise what in Europe is called the spirit of Americanism. It is impossible to regard either of them as inspirations for human conduct or society, or to contrast them with their opposites, without their bringing to mind that formidable democracy there in the North, in all its prosperity and power—a dazzling proof of the efficacy of the ideas and institutions of democracy. If one could say of utilitarianism that it is the expression of the English spirit, the United States may be considered the incarnation of that expression. Its gospel is spread everywhere, teaching the triumph of materialism. And Spanish America, in her relation to the United States, is not wholly unsympathetic to its message. The mighty federation is carrying

FROM *Ariel, Obras completas,* Vol. 2 (Montevideo: Barreiro y Ramos, 1956), pp. 167–68, 172–89, 192. Translated by the editor with permission.

out a sort of moral conquest of us. Admiration for its greatness and its strength is a sentiment that is growing rapidly among our governing classes and even more, perhaps, among the masses, who are easily impressed with success. And admiration easily becomes imitation. . . . So it happens that many who are sincerely interested in our future already dream of a Latin America "delatinized" by its own free will, not by force of arms, and reborn in the image and likeness of its Northern archetype.

. . .

Any critical judgment about the North Americans should begin with a formal salute to them, as the knights of old saluted their adversaries. This is easy enough for me. Failing to recognize their faults seems to me less culpable than denying their good qualities. Born . . . with the innate experience of liberty, they have remained faithful to the principles of their birth and have developed their country's fundamental principles with a mathematical precision that gives their history a unity which, while it has not permitted the acquisition of differing aptitudes and accomplishments, has the beauty of logical consistency. Their traces will never be blotted from the pages of human history, for they were the first to convert the modern idea of liberty from an uncertain experiment and an imaginary utopia into an imperishable living reality. By their example they have shown that it is possible to extend the authority of a republic over a large nation. Their federal structure has revealed —as De Tocqueville put it—the way to combine the brilliance and power of the large states with the happiness and peace of the small.

Theirs are many of the most audacious deeds for which this century will be remembered over time. Theirs is the glory of having fully demonstrated the greatness and dignity of labor—thereby emphasizing the finest element of moral beauty of our civilization—that blessed force which antiquity abandoned in abject slavery and which today we identify with the highest expression of human dignity, based on the conscious exertion of one's own effort. Strong and tenacious, holding inactivity in contempt, they have placed in the hands of the mechanic in the shop or the farmer in the fields the mythical keys of Hercules. They have given to human genius a new and unexpected beauty— girding it with the leather apron of the smith. Each one of them presses on to conquer life as the Puritans of old conquered the desert. Persevering devotees of the cult of individual activity, which makes each man the architect of his destiny, they have modeled their social structure on a kind of imaginary meeting of Robinson Crusoes who have developed their personalities in the practice of self-help and have begun to weave the threads of a strong state. Without sacrificing that sovereign conception of the individual, they have known how to make their gregariousness a useful instrument of their grandeur and empire. They have obtained from the sum of their human efforts, as directed to research, philanthropy, and industry, results which are the more marvelous in their testimony to the absolute integrity of individual autonomy.

They possess an insatiable and lively curiosity, an impatient eagerness for enlightenment, and a love for public education which they profess with a monomaniacal obsession that has made the school the surest guarantee of their prosperity and the mind of the child the most cherished of their precious possessions. Their culture, which is far from refined or intellectual, is admirably organized for the realization of an immediate practical goal. They have not added a single law or general principle to the findings of science, but they have done wonders in its application. They have made giant strides in the practical domain. They have given the world, in the steam boiler and the electric dynamo, billions of invisible slaves that are a hundred times more powerful in the service of the human Aladdin than was the magic lamp. The increase in their greatness and power will astonish future generations. With their prodigious gift for improvisation they have been able to accelerate time itself so that, by an act of their powerful will, they can produce in one day in the heart of the desert the cultivation which is normally the work of centuries.

The Puritan liberty that gave them light in the past was also accompanied by the warmth of a lasting piety. Next to the factory and the school, their strong hands have built churches from which ascend the prayers of many millions of free consciences. They have been able to preserve, in the collapse of ideals, the highest ideal of all; keeping alive the tradition of a religious feeling which, if it does not rise to the heights of profound spirituality, at least preserves the firm restraints of a moral sense amid the harshness of the pressures of utility. They have known how to preserve a certain primitive robustness in the midst of the refinements of civilized life. They hold to the pagan cult of health and strength. In strong muscles they consecrate and refine the precious instrument of their wills, and, obliged by their insatiable ambition to cultivate all human energies, they combine the fine body of the athlete with the heart of the free man. Their civilization and culture produce a dominant impression of optimism, of confidence, and of faith; which makes them face the future with a proud and stubborn assurance—the characteristics of the poems, "Excelsior" and "The Psalm of Life," which typify the philosophy of force and action that their poets have produced as a balm for the bitterness of life.

Thus their titanic greatness impresses even those who are repelled by the distortions of their character and the violence of their recent history. And, for my part, you can see already that although I do not love them, I admire them.

.   .   .

If after sincerely recognizing what is brilliant and great in the genius of that powerful nation, I have now acquired the right to complete the picture in the interest of fairness, I will pose one central question: Does that society realize, or at least try to realize, an ideal of rational conduct which corresponds to the legitimate spiritual and moral requirements of our civilization? Is it there that we can find the most approximate model of our perfect state? Is the feverish intensity which seems to multiply within that society the intensity and movement of life? Does that society have an end that is worthwhile and a goal that is sufficient to justify it?

Herbert Spencer, speaking with sincerity of American democracy . . . marked as the fundamental characteristic of North American life that same unlimited restlessness which is manifest in an infinite passion for work and a pride in material expansion in all its forms. Later he observed that this exclusive preoccupation with activity directed toward immediately useful goals . . . which was tolerable no doubt for a new country as the first task of civilization, should be modified if it tended to make useful work the supreme end of life, when in fact it is only the accumulation of the elements which make possible the total harmonious development of our being. Spencer added that it was necessary to preach the gospel of rest and recreation to the North Americans—and we, identifying those words with the *otium* [leisure] of the ancient moralists, will include in the gospel to be preached to those restless workers, any ideal concern, any disinterested use of time, any object of meditation that rises above the immediate goal of utility.

North American life effectively forms that vicious circle which Pascal described as the continuous pursuit of well-being with no goal beyond that pursuit. The prosperity [of the United States] is as great as its incapacity to satisfy even an elementary conception of human life. Titanic as it is in its enormous concentration of the human will and its unprecedented triumphs in all spheres of material aggrandizement, as a whole that civilization produces a singular impression of emptiness and insufficiency. After thirty centuries of evolution under the worthy guidance of the classical and Christian spirit, we rightly ask what is [America's] guiding principle, its underlying ideal, the ultimate goal beyond the immediate preoccupation with physical interests which moves that mighty multitude. [In reply] we will only receive as the expression of that definitive ideal the same absolute preoccupation with material success. Orphaned from the profound traditions which produced them, the [American] people have not been able to substitute any high and disinterested conception of the future for the inspiring idealism of their past. They live for the immediate reality of the present, subordinating all their activities to the egoism of individual and collective well-being. . . . Not even the selfishness of national patriotism, lacking higher impulses, nor the exclusiveness and pride of race which transformed and exalted the harshness of life of ancient Rome can provide a glimmer of the beauty of idealism for a people in whom the confusion of cosmopolitanism and the atomism of a misunderstood democracy hinder the formation of a true national consciousness.

One might say that when the positivism of the mother country was transmitted to its emancipated children in America, it lost all the elements of idealism which had tempered it, reducing it to the crudeness which exaggerated passion or satire have attributed to English positivism. There is no doubt that the English soul, beneath its rough, utilitarian exterior, its commercial cynicism, and its puritanical severity, conceals a rare poetic genius and a deep respect for sensitivity. . . . In the primitive Teutonic depths of that race, even when modified by the influence of its conquests and the habit of commercial activity, there was an extraordinary exaltation of emotion. The American people have not inherited this ancestral poetic spirit which gushes like a limpid stream from the British rock whenever a gifted Moses touches it. The English people have the institution of aristocracy—however anachronistic and unjust it may be from a political point of view—an ancient and impregnable bulwark against the spirit of commercialism and the pervasiveness of the prosaic world—so lofty and impregnable . . . that, since the time of the Greeks, history has not created a society more suited to produce men of elevated spirit. In the American context, there are no heights which are inaccessible to the spirit of vulgarity, which is spread and propagated as over the flat expanse of an endless plain.

Sensitivity, intelligence, manners—all are characterized among that mass of people by a complete incapacity for selection. The mechanistic order of their material activity and political life is combined with a profound disorder in the realm of the ideal. It is easy to find examples of this lack of selectivity—starting from its external and obvious manifestations and going to more essential and intimate activities. Prodigal with his riches—for meanness has no place in his code—the North American has been able to satisfy fully his vanity and desire for material luxury, but he has not acquired the selectivity of good taste. In such circumstances, true art has been able to exist only as the result of the rebellion of the individual. Emerson and Poe are examples of fauna expelled from their true habitat by some geological catastrophe. . . . The successful North American . . . has never been able to conceive of [art] except as a new way to satisfy his restless vanity. . . . Despite the munificence which he scatters to encourage the development of a delicate sense of beauty, despite the splendor of the museums and expositions which his cities boast, despite the mountains of marble and bronze sculptures which decorate his public places, he does not understand the artistic principles of disinterestedness and selection. And if we wished to characterize his taste it would have to be with a description which is the negation of art itself—strained brutality of effect, insensibility to soft tones or delicate manner, worship of a false grandeur, sensationalism incompatible with the noble serenity that is the opposite of the pressure of his hectic life.

The ideal of beauty does not appeal to the descendants of the austere Puritans, nor does passionate devotion to truth. They despise as vain and useless any exercise of thought which goes beyond an immediate purpose. They do not bring to science a disinterested regard for truth and they have given no evidence of prizing it for itself. Research is carried on not for itself but for its utilitarian application. Their glorious efforts to spread the benefits of material education are motivated by the praiseworthy purpose of communicating the rudiments of knowledge to the masses. But they show no indication that, while there is that increase in the number of the educated, there should be any concern with selection or with encouraging those superior qualities which rise above the general mediocrity. Thus the result of their untiring war on ignorance has been a universal semiculture and a profound indifference to higher culture. Along with the decline of ignorance at the base of that mass democracy goes a parallel decline of higher learning and genius. This is why the intellectual history [of America] is one of progressive deterioration in brilliance and originality. While in the period of the Declaration of Independence and the establishment of the Constitution, many famous names represented the thinking and will of that nation, a half-century later De Tocqueville could observe that, in this respect, the gods had departed. When De Tocqueville wrote his great work, however, Boston, the city of the Puritans and of the tradition of learning, still boasted a glorious circle which is universally famous. Who has followed in the footsteps of Channing, Emerson, and Poe? The leveling effect of the middle classes pressing on with their work of destruction has tended to eliminate what little remains of the intelligentsia. Their books have long since ceased to soar to the heights. Today the best example of American taste in writing is to be found in the gray pages of a journalism which in no way resembles that which once produced *The Federalist Papers*.

As to moral sentiments, the mechanistic impulse of utilitarianism has been moderated by a strong religious tradition. But this does not mean that their conduct has been directed by any unselfish principle. The religious life of Americans is an extreme version of that of the English—no more than an auxiliary aid to the criminal law. It would cease to have any force on the day that it was found possible to give to utilitarian morality the religious sanction that Mill desired for it. The best example of their morality is that of Franklin —a philosophy of conduct which goes no further than general honesty and a utilitarian prudence that will never give rise to emotions of sainthood or heroism. Fit only to support the conscience in the common affairs of life, [the morality of Franklin] is like the cane he used in walking, incapable of giving more than fragile support in the effort to reach great heights. Yet he was the culmination—below we must seek the reality. Even if our moral criterion were no more than Franklin's sound and moderate utilitarianism, the inescapable end of a society educated in such a limited morality would certainly not be, as De Tocqueville observed, the noble, satanic beauty of the decline of empire, but a kind of pallid and mediocre materialism and finally an exhausted and colorless collapse in the silent decay of all the mainsprings of the moral life. In that society in which morality tends to regard the highest manifestations of self-sacrifice and virtue as beyond the area of the obligatory, realism will keep reducing the limits of obligation.

.　　.　　.

Public life certainly does not escape the effects of that moral disintegration in society in general. Any casual observer of the political habits [of Americans] will tell you how their obsession with material success weakens and destroys the respect for law in their hearts. The civic virtue of Hamilton has become a rusty sword, forgotten in the cobwebs of the past. Venality, beginning at the polls, spreads to all their political institutions. Government by the mediocre replaces the rivalry which exalts the character and intelligence. . . . Democracy not subject to the controls of a higher notion of human excellence has always tended among [Americans] to become the brute force of the majority that despises the greater moral benefits of liberty and destroys all respect for the dignity of the individual.

.　　.　　.

Their own character has made it impossible for [Americans] to be leaders. Nature has not granted them a genius for propaganda or an apostolic calling. They lack the great gift of likeableness—in the loftiest sense—that extraordinary power of sympathy which Providence has given to those races destined for leadership, producing in their culture a beauty like that of Helen in which all think they see their own traits. [North American] civilization can and does have many suggestive and admirable examples. It can inspire admiration, astonishment, and respect, but it is difficult for the foreigner seeing Bartholdi's Statue of Liberty holding her torch high over the port of New York to feel in his heart the profound religious emotion that the ancient traveler felt on seeing in the distance the luminous marble and golden spear of Athena on the Acropolis.

.　　.　　.

Let us hope that this massive social organism which until now has stood for will and utility may one day also represent intelligence, sentiment, and idealism, and that from that mighty forge may arise that generous, harmonious, chosen human figure that Spencer anticipated in the speech to which I have referred. But we will not find him in that people now or in the immediate future, and we must give up hope of seeing an ideal civilization where there is only a rough and misshapen outline that still must pass through many changes before it acquires the firm serenity of a people who have arrived at the fulfillment of their genius.*

. . .

THE NEED FOR A WESTERN REVOLUTION

Charles Malik

Not all observers from Asia, Africa, and Latin America are critical of American ideology. Some have been very strongly influenced by Western values and continue to defend them vigorously. Charles Malik, former United Nations representative from Lebanon, has spoken out in a recent book for the reassertion of the Western and American ideals of freedom, truth, and religion, and for an awareness of their revolutionary implications for the new nations. For him, these values are not only Western but universal, and should not be sacrificed for the sake of economic development and progress. It is the developing countries that are the materialists in Malik's view, since they are willing to surrender human freedom for the sake of material advancement. If his opinions are compared with most of the others in this part, it will become evident that he expresses a viewpoint that is in a decided minority.

One understands how international Communism lumps Latin America indiscriminately with Asia and Africa: they are all "underdeveloped," in the strictly Marxist-economic sense. But the lumping now is taken over by the West, so that all three are usually mentioned in the same breath. This one cannot understand, for the community of background, history, religion, art, language, and law, and culture and civilization in general, between Latin America, on the one hand, and the United States and Europe, on the other, does not exist between either of these and Asia and Africa. Here is one instance of how the West sheepishly falls for Communist slogans (one can make a list of twenty or thirty loaded Communist expressions which have

* The influence of "Arielismo" on Latin-American thought is discussed in Kalman H. Silvert, "*Ariel* and the Dilemma of the Intellectuals" in *The Conflict Society: Reaction and Revolution in Latin America* (New Orleans: Hauser, 1961).—Editor.

FROM *Man in the Struggle for Peace* by Charles Malik, pp. 212–19. Copyright © 1963 by Claremont Graduate School and University Center. Reprinted by permission of Harper & Row, Publishers.

crept into uncritical Western usage since 1917), a "falling for" which only expresses a deeper existential "falling into" or "conversion to" the Communist ontological interpretation of man and things. One wonders if there has been anywhere near a corresponding Communist "falling," not only nominally, but in meaning and intention, "for" the Western language of freedom. We seem to have here a fruitful field of research as to who has held and retained "the terminological initiative"—the Communists or the West. To stress what unites Latin America with the West rather than what divides [them] is quite revolutionary these days, when all that people seem to care for is material values and "stages of development."

.   .   .

It is a shame that the West has been on the defensive all these years. The time has come to pass to the offensive on every front. The initiative should be seized in a dozen fields, especially the political, moral, personal, intellectual, and spiritual. To think of vigorously and relentlessly challenging the Communists on their theory of man, government, and history, on whether the mind is really free in their realm, on why they broke away from the wonderful spiritual heritage of their peoples, and on why they persecute those who believe in God and Christ is quite revolutionary these days when the utmost that people seem to be capable of thinking of is "systems," "societies," "gross national products," and who is going to reach the moon first.

It is necessary to think of economic and technical assistance, mutual security, meeting "the revolution of rising expectations," and raising the standard of living of the masses. But to think *only* of these things is to imitate the Communists and to play into the hands of their revolution. It is to confirm people in their thinking (they are already prone to this by nature) that these are the only things that matter, and this is precisely what the Communists love to have you mean and convey to them. In so-called peaceful competition one cannot be too wary lest one become so mesmerized by one's competitor as to turn into an exact copy of him. Hunger, poverty, and disease are depicted as the worst enemies of mankind; actually, there are far worse enemies. When will the West move onto the plane of the fundamental spiritual values of freedom? When will it think and talk and act in terms of freedom of thought and conscience, free inquiry and free criticism, the dignity of man, the supremacy of reason, the ultimacy of the human person, personal depth and personal freedom, freedom of choice in the selection of the government, the rule of law, the conception of law as something not arbitrary, not determined by that fiat of the will, but as something natural, universal, inherent, objectively just, and independent of partisan interests? All this is quite revolutionary.

It is quite true that America and the West in general cannot be secure if they remain an oasis of abundance amidst a world desert of privation. A thousand people, both from the East and the West, have on a thousand occasions and in a thousand and one different ways given expression to this persuasion. But if this truth should cause America and the West to develop a guilt complex with respect to their wealth (and this is exactly what the Communists love to see take hold of Western conscience), then, weighed down by this sense of guilt, the West will not be free to think and talk in intellectual, moral, personal, and human terms. Allowing for all the possible "exploitation" (even in the exaggerated Marxist sense) that may have occurred, both internally and between the West and the rest of the world, it is certainly true that Western abundance is the independent creation of Western science, industry, and foresight. The West owes its affluence, with all its attendant ills, to nobody but itself. Those who suffer from privation today, especially if they have freely chosen to break away from the West politically, economically, and socially, have no strict moral claims on the fruits of Western industry. The mechanical equalization of merit, purely on the basis of counting heads and without any regard for personal-moral-intellectual-cultural worth, is one of the great fallacies of this age. To help the needy materially, not because you owe them anything nor because you wish to bribe them, but in freedom and joy and liberality and out of sheer human solidarity, is quite revolutionary these days, when foreign economic assistance is so guilt-ridden and so politically determined.

Consider the following statement: "We are pledged, realistically, to defend freedom where there is a will to have it. There was no such will in Laos. There is some of it in Thailand." [Ralph McGill, Washington *Evening Star*.] You hear and read these days a thousand different variations on this same theme. This is completely unrevolutionary. A genuine revolution does not wait for people to will it: it creates in them the will to its major theme itself. "Existence-as-usual"—this is the great enemy today. You "have" "freedom"; others do not "have" it and do not seem to "have" the "will to have it." This is the existing state of affairs, and so let us leave it at that! You do not want to be bothered; you do not want to be disturbed; essentially, you want to be left alone; essentially, if the "unfree" were not falling one by one to an enemy who at this rate will one day isolate, engulf, and destroy you, you would not give a hoot for them; therefore, you will not so deeply bestir yourself as to make others, whether or not they are falling piecemeal to your enemy, see and love and seek your deepest values. You do not then have an independent, original, distinctive, universal message yourself: your message depends on your enemy's being and action; it is a function of his will. And then you wonder why Communism moves in and takes over! "Existence-as-usual" is the exact antithesis of any revolutionary spirit. Existing-as-usual, you dread to return radically to yourself. But only in this radical return can you "meet" your ground from whence all help, all hope, and all movement start. The will to freedom should be aroused, trumpeted, called forth. If it does not exist, it is not the fault of those who do not "have it"; it is the fault of those who are free. For it is right that man everywhere should be free, and if you do not believe this, then you do not know freedom yourself, and Communism has already won in your soul. How can any revolution start anywhere if it *begins* with lack of faith in its highest values? And the highest values of the West are man, freedom, truth, and God.

If you really believe in the values of freedom, you must remain faithful to freedom's lovers everywhere. Wherever there is the least trace of freedom, you must rejoice and do what you can to strengthen it. This is quite revolutionary these days, when the West treats almost equally the free and the slave, those who are attached to its values and those who hate them, nay, when it often delivers those who believe and love its values to the tender mercies of the dark and despotic.

.   .   .

There is much that is good and true and of enduring value in non-Western cultures. The West can only approach them with love and the utmost respect. All men share a common human nature and a reason that, under conditions of confidence and love, can by its natural light distinguish between right and wrong, true and false. And no matter how limited or colored, prejudiced, distorted, or warped his reason might be, no man is ever in principle hopeless so far as the possibility of seeing the right, the good, and the true is concerned. How to love the non-Western cultures without pampering them, how to learn from them without becoming their slave, how to challenge them without causing them to lose confidence in their genuine values, how to help them without sentimentally confirming them in their outworn customs and habits of mind, how to establish relations of equality, dignity, and mutual respect with them without either weakening yourself in your hold on the deepest you know or making them feel that everything is as good as everything else—all this requires a hard, revolutionary bent of mind that knows what it believes, what it wants, and how to get it. . . .

ANTI-COMMUNISM IN THE UNITED STATES

Manuel Pedro González

The psychological mechanism in the developing countries that leads to assertions of moral superiority such as the one associated with Rodó's *Ariel* also tends to produce an ideological neutralism that is just as critical of the political ideals and practices of the United States as it is of those of the Soviet Union. The following selection by a Mexican writer argues that the cold war, McCarthyism, and more recently the Goldwater movement and the emergence of the radical right have turned the United States into a police state with an ideology of hysterical anti-Communism.

. . . Like the subjects of an imperial power in any age and continent, the American of today is imbued with a pronounced superiority complex combined with a strong Messianic impulse. Both these characteristics confront identical complexes on the part of the Communist camp, specifically the Soviet and Chinese messianisms. Each of the two sides—capitalist and Communist—thinks it is superior and destined to save humanity from the evil designs of the other. Both think that they possess absolute truth, revealed and unshakable. And since both have enough atomic and hydrogen bombs to annihilate each other and at the same time to destroy all life on this planet, the power of the two sides to make war is balanced, and the great superiority

FROM "El panorama norteamericano," *Cuadernos Americanos,* Vol. 24, No. 1 (January–February, 1965), pp. 7–14. Translated by the editor with permission.

in the number of A- and H-bombs that the United States has accumulated relative to the Soviet Union is of no use. Humanity lives, then, not so much under a balance of power as of terror, since the lethal consequences of atomic war will affect all the peoples of the earth equally.

Its enormous wealth on the one hand and its rivalry with the Communist powers on the other have had dangerous consequences for freedom and democracy within the frontiers of the United States and, as a result, for the Western world. The Communist advances in the last twenty years have frightened the American people, especially the middle and upper classes. . . . From this have followed a huge armament effort, repressive legislation, limits on the freedoms and rights of the individual, hysterical propaganda against Communism, the proliferation of more or less clandestine organizations and groups that are radically nationalist, reactionary, and warlike in spirit, the appearance of politico-social phenomena as ominous and alarming as McCarthyism and Goldwaterism, the creation of new secret agencies for subversion and espionage, such as the CIA, etc.

No Western capitalist nation is so brainwashed today as America. The anti-Communist propaganda which has been turned out in the last fifteen years has permeated and impregnated everything—the press, literature, TV, films, radio, the university, the pulpit, the school, and the home. In this propaganda, Communism is more than a theory or an economic, political, and social system which now governs nearly half the human race. It is something monstrous, diabolical, evil, atheistic, and noxious that must be destroyed as a dangerous plague at whatever price and by whatever means. To make it still more odious and repellent in the eyes of the ignorant and credulous masses, a religious element has been injected into the campaign, and there is much insistence upon the atheism [inherent in Communism]. The fact that the Soviet Union and other Marxist countries allow various religions to operate freely alongside the national or Orthodox religion is carefully omitted in this campaign. It is never mentioned that the Communist government in Poland gives a subsidy to the Catholic Church. Instead, every day there is insistence on the official atheism of those regimes. In this war, which is beginning to cease being a cold one, God is an efficient ally. (God has been a useful associate of all modern imperialists.) In fact, the American mentality today with respect to Communism reminds us of the warlike and fanatical psychosis of the Spanish people under Philip II with respect to Protestantism and the Reformation. If we put Marx and Lenin in place of Luther and Calvin, and Communism in place of Protestantism, the fanaticism is identical. This anti-Communist obsession has reached the point that the average American confuses the terms "socialism," "Marxism," and "anti-imperialism," and identifies them with "Communism." For him they are all one and the same. This hatred and fanaticism justify and condone any action if it serves to combat the hated dogma, and the individual who dissents from this mental attitude is regarded as suspect. Like the Catholics and Jesuits of the sixteenth century, those American fanatics think that "the end justifies the means." Even the language has been contaminated with this hysteria and hatred. The verb "to hunt," for example, is constantly employed with reference to Communists as if one were discussing rabbits, rats, or vermin—not to mention the names and epithets which the daily press uses for them. Having arrived at the conclusion or "infallible" conviction that the government and the American people are in possession of the absolute revealed truth, that theirs is the only legitimate moral position, it is necessary to complete and justify this ethical posture and self-persuasion of absolute moral rectitude by declaring the enemy an ignominious outcast. The more diabolical, atheistic, and execrable they are, the more justified will be the procedures which are employed against them, and the more tranquil will be the conscience. How else can one justify the horrible napalm bombs—one hundred times more inhuman and cruel than the atomic bomb—which the American army is dropping on the South Vietnamese Communists ten thousand miles from the American borders? How else can one justify before one's conscience the tremendous effort which the United States has made to starve the Cuban people to death, including women and children—except by declaring that the Marxist regime which prevails in Cuba today is evil and accursed by God? In America today, a Communist is a criminal and a priori is assumed to be a potential traitor and little less than a public enemy. (This has come to such a point that in certain states to call a person a Communist is libelous and a crime punishable by law—unless the one who puts forward the charge can prove it.) In the United States, capitalism and what is called there "the American way of life" have attained the status of quasi-religious dogmas and of a hierarchy of immutable and eternal truths—exactly like the dogmas of Catholicism in Spain under Philip II.

But the most absurd thing about this frantic anti-Communism is the fact that in that country there are hardly any Communists. In a population of 188 million people, there are only some twenty thousand affiliated with that doctrine and party. There is not the remotest possibility there of a revolution or of Communist subversion or of insignificant groups posing a threat to the stability of the democratic and capitalist regime. Yet in no country in the world can one see the fear, hysteria, and anti-Communist fanaticism which have gripped the American people. . . . It is likely that out of 188 million Americans, at least 160 million have never seen or spoken with a Communist in their lives. But the press, the TV, the McCarthyite politicians, the official police, the espionage agencies, and the industries that profit from the cold war and enrich themselves from armament-making have found a gold mine in the anti-Communist hysteria; they foment and exploit it, masked as superpatriots. (Two centuries ago Samuel Johnson said that patriotism was the last refuge of scoundrels.) More tragic for the world and for American democracy is the fact that the artificially fomented propaganda has taken effect and the people believe it and accept it as incontrovertible proof of the imminent and grave danger their country faces. The people do not see nor are they aware of the real danger. I refer to the danger, if not immediate, at least very serious and probable, that the nationalist and Fascist-like activity will result in a particular form of Fascism, masquerading as nationalism. This is a serious menace to democracy and freedom in the country.

. . .

With their enormous wealth and unequaled war potential, Americans should feel secure and happy. Yet they do not. Large elements of the population are consumed with hatred, fear, and frustration. They are principally the sectors of the extreme right that support Barry Goldwater, but there are also Democrats among them. . . . These disoriented and fanatical elements . . . include reactionaries with very little education, but among them are also many doctors, engineers, lawyers, dentists, and professionals in all fields. . . . I should also say that this type of noisy and aggressive superpatriot is more common in the South, the Middle West, and the Southeast than in the North and East of the country. Texas and California are the principal bastions. One can establish an inverse ratio between the level of culture and the proliferation of these groups. The more ignorant and wealthy the average level, the more the extreme right groups flourish. For this reason, Los Angeles, Pasadena, San Bernardino, Dallas, Houston, Phoenix, Atlanta, etc. have large numbers of this patriotic type. The principal object of their hatred is the Negro, of course. Some of those who hate Negroes are believers in racial superiority, but Negro-haters are found in great numbers in the North for economic reasons. It is not only the Negro whom they hate and believe to be inferior. This feeling extends to other minorities—Mexicans, Italians, and Jews. But the minorities of a differing nationality and culture are not the only ones hated by those professional patriots. They hate the Supreme Court with the same intensity because in the last ten or twelve years it has given a series of decisions that are just and correct. They also hate whatever signifies liberalism, progress, absolute equality before the law, etc.

A feeling of frustration is no less intense among those elements—a frustration which frequently is joined to fear. Why frustration when the country has reached the high point of its history in every sense? This is not their belief. Certainly we have more A- and H-bombs than any other country and we are the most powerful in the world; yet, they argue, not only have we not overcome Communism but it is still advancing. . . .

This type of nineteenth-century frontier mentality is incapable of understanding that the military power of a country can be measured in absolute or in relative terms. For them there is only the first of the two alternatives. If we consider the war capacity of America in absolute terms, that is to say, in itself, it must be admitted that it has increased many times in the last twenty years. But if we measure it in relative terms, as we should, that is to say, in relation to the potential enemy or enemies, we will discover that the United States was at its greatest power in 1948, and since 1949 it has declined. Such are the ironies which the arms race between the giants presents. . . . But many millions of Americans who support Goldwater cannot and do not wish to understand [this change in the balance of power] because he offers the solution of force, a simplistic and absurd solution in the world today.

AMERICA AND THE NEW NATIONS

U Thant

This section concludes with a more balanced assessment of American ideological thinking. U Thant, the Secretary-General of the United Nations, discusses the profound effect upon Asia of American ideas of equality and human rights and compliments the American people for their generosity to the new nations. However, he criticizes the American failure to understand the socialism and neutralism of many of the nations of Asia and Africa (including his own country, Burma), and like most of the leaders of these nations, he does not feel that the United States has taken so active a role in opposing colonialism as its own tradition of freedom demands.

. . . A reborn nationalism of formerly dependent areas has risen in revolt against the domination of the world by the West and is now defying the latter's leadership. This postwar phenomenon is not properly understood in many countries, including America, and this lack of understanding is at the root of occasional frictions in Asian-American relationship. The newly resurgent nationalism of Asia is sometimes misconstrued in America as pro-Communist and anti-American. But the plain fact is that all the countries of Asia, with the exception of China, North Korea, and North Vietnam, are not Communist and are not likely to turn Communist so long as their economic and political stability is maintained and promoted. In this great task of maintaining and promoting stability in Asia, the United States of America can play a signficant role. There is no fundamental incompatibility between [the] American outlook and the nationalism of newly awakened nations of Asia, and the closest cooperation between them is essential to a greater future for both of them.

The vitality of the American people is reflected in the extraordinary pace of your everyday life, the vehemence of your reactions and your feelings, and the fantastic growth of your economic enterprises. This vitality, this vigor, and this exuberance of your national character have been in the past both an asset and a liability in your relations with Asia, which is emotionally calm, contemplative, and proud. On the credit side the United States of America has been a pillar of a dynamic form of democracy and your contributions to the methods of mass democracy have been impressive. You have also given proof of vigor and inventiveness in the realm of foreign policy. This [has been] especially true since the 1930's, when you began to give up isolationism and entered the arena of world politics.

A large number of intelligent Asians think of the Americans as a great people because of your vigor, your history, your traditions, and your devotion to the principles of freedom and democracy. These ideas and characteristics have been the inspiration and hope of Asia for more than half a century. They had a tremendous impact on Asia where there was no recognition of the equality of man; where there was little recognition of the fundamental rights of man; where governments were generally imposed from above and had as their primary objective the exploitation of the people. It is true to say that these ideas played a leading part in inspiring Asia's fight for freedom from colonial bondage.

This is not the only reason why Asians think highly of the American people. Your glorious record in the two world wars in which you undoubtedly saved the world from tyranny and dictatorship, at great sacrifice and expense,

FROM "A Burmese View of the World," *Toward World Peace* (New York: Barnes, 1964), pp. 36–41. Reprinted by permission.

cannot be ignored or made light of even by your most severe critics. Finally, your post–World War II record, in which you have contributed so much towards the relief and rehabilitation of the war-devastated countries, is entirely without precedent in the annals of history.

Yet, in spite of this most impressive record behind you, you have not won as many friends and influenced as many people as you should in Asia. The explanation, I think, is your extraordinary vigor, the vehemence of your reactions and your feelings, and your failure to see the Asian mind. The incompatibility, though not fundamental, is emotional. In several respects this incompatibility is due to other factors than mere emotion. Your historical association with the West, your sympathy for Western institutions and attitudes, and your close identity with Western policy have been a hindrance in Asian-American relations. The equivocal attitude which you seem to have taken in recent years on colonial issues has been regarded as surprisingly reactionary by the progressive Asians. To an Asia which had come to regard America as the symbol of freedom, the spearhead of the attack against colonialism, and the champion of the underdog, this has indeed been a disappointment. Some hard-thinking Asians have begun to wonder whether you had abandoned your precious heritage and your honorable tradition. Explanations which have been given to the effect that colonialism is dying and that a new and even greater danger has emerged have left nearly all of Asia unconvinced. On many occasions we Asians feel that leaders of American life and thought—administrators, legislators, journalists, and educators—fail to make a distinction between nationalism and Communism. Many underdeveloped countries of Asia, the moment they regained their independence from the colonial powers, chalked out their own policies and built their own future. Many believe that the launching of agrarian reforms, the operation of state enterprises, and the adoption of "neutral" policies in respect of foreign relations are in the best interest of their own countries. Burma, for instance, has chosen a democratic, parliamentary, and nontotalitarian type of socialism.* In America, I understand that the term "socialism" is anathema. You find it difficult to think of "socialism" in terms of democracy and individual freedom, but in our socialist Burma we enjoy the fruits of parliamentary democracy and fundamental human freedom. We enjoy freedom of speech, freedom of expression, freedom of association, and freedom of belief as you do here. But the newly resurgent nationalism and this sudden adoption of so-called socialism put you into confusion. You are apt to think that a certain Asian nation has gone to the other camp when that nation refuses to toe your line. With your traditional vigor and the extraordinary vehemence of your reactions you then alienate many of your most sincere admirers. I think that your attitude towards colonialism and your failure to distinguish between nationalism and Communism are mainly responsible for the present lack of warmth in Asian-American relations, although of course they are generally friendly. Perhaps your attitude is born out of youthful dynamism not yet restrained by experience and tradition.

This dynamic quality and vigorous application of policies are responsible for your all-out support to certain regimes simply because they subscribe to all your views without questioning. It is a fact that you are pouring your precious

---

* Since this was written, a military government has taken power in Burma. However, the government describes its program as the establishment of "Burmese socialism."—Editor.

millions into the coffers of regimes which by no stretch of the imagination can be regarded as "governments of the people, for the people, by the people." You are vigorously supporting certain of those regimes in spite of the fact that they are undemocratic, corrupt, and discredited. The effect of this on some Asian minds has been to build up the impression that America is against change and that it wishes to preserve the status quo. Let me hasten to add that this is a view not *generally* held, but that it *is* held cannot be doubted.

Another source of misunderstanding between America and Asia stems from the activities and statements of some of your leaders and a section of your press. These are the people who are responsible for building the impression abroad that America is bellicose, subjective in her views, and fond of distortion. If some of your leaders and a section of your press try to understand "the other fellow's point of view" then there is sure to be greater understanding and better relations between America and Asia. No doubt it is a two-way traffic. Some of the Asian leaders and a section of our press are equally guilty of this shortcoming. It is up to both Asia and America to make the necessary psychological adjustments, to become themselves once again, to live up to their respective heritage, and to the great moral principles which each of them spawned.

As a well-wisher of better Asian-American relations, let me say that American leadership tends to limit itself to grants of material aid to the needy. It is far from my intention to underestimate its importance. The Marshall Plan aid to Europe and the Economic Cooperation Assistance to Asia have been an indispensable help in restoring the two continents' economy after the war. To raise the living standards of the millions who still exist in the barest poverty and squalor is one of the main challenges to American wealth and American generosity. But this humanitarian act alone is not sufficient to create better understanding and closer friendship between America and Asia. No self-respecting nation will accept another's guidance and appreciate another's motives merely because the other is wealthier and prepared to share some of his wealth with him. On the contrary, the sad truth is that between nations, as between individuals, this seems to make for resentment rather than for gratitude. The battle for the minds of the millions will not be won by just holding out to them better drinks and faster cars, particularly in countries of Asia where spiritual values are always paramount. America and the West possess two spiritual values which can be put across with immense benefit to Asia: religious devotion and democracy. The whole Asian continent is thirsting for a religious renaissance, the rebirth of cultural values, and the improvement of moral standards. America can certainly help fill the need.

2

American Politics

THE MONOPOLIES AND AMERICAN POLITICS
Juan José Arévalo

One of the strongest and most widely read Latin-American attacks on the United States in recent years was *The Shark and the Sardines* by Juan José Arévalo. In the section on American foreign policy, an excerpt is presented from the fable satirizing the establishment of the Organization of American States, which gives the book its title. The selection below, taken from a later part of the same book, views the American political system as a vehicle that permits the Pentagon and Wall Street to control American domestic and foreign policy. The Democratic and Republican Parties are identical in practice, Arévalo asserts, and both are dominated by the wealthy. (For an American reply to Arévalo's charges, see the book review of *The Shark and the Sardines* that appears in Part IV, p. 320.)

Arévalo, President of Guatemala from 1945 to 1951, has been living in exile since a U.S.-supported revolt in 1954 drove President Jacobo Arbenz, his left-wing successor, from office. While Arévalo is a Marxist-socialist, it should be noted that the suspicion that American politics is motivated primarily by economic interest is widespread in Latin America, Africa, and Asia, even among non-Marxists.

. . . Attempts to expose the colossal monopolies that deform life inside the United States cannot be brought about through those publication media that operate under the trademark "free press."

This world press in the hands of the National Association of Manufacturers (and in the hands of their subaltern, the American Society of Newspaper Editors) regards as the most precious of values *their* freedom of the press, *their* sacred freedom of opinion. And one of the forms of this freedom consists of being silent when they so choose: to choose not to say a word about matters that jeopardize the industrialists of the industries that produce the paper, the mats, the ink, the linotypes, and the news itself. In *their* press they

FROM "The Den," *The Shark and the Sardines* (New York: Stuart, 1961), pp. 231–35. Reprinted by permission.

say what they please. The sacred freedom belongs to—is the property of—the millionaires.

It would be necessary, then, to turn our eyes to other sources, to other horizons, to other support. Better said, to the authorities. We in Latin America still have the habits of our Spanish heritage. Romantic, liberal, legalistic as that heritage may be, we cannot get out of our heads the notion that there is an authority to cope with cases of exploitation, cases of abuse, cases of banditry, cases of corruption, cases of treason.

The notion of an impartial authority—superior, competent, and *above* all nondiscriminatory—is at the very roots of our public life. This is a simple and clear premise—so simple and for that reason so great. In the villages, the constable; in the cities, the mayor. In the provinces, the governor. In the country, the president or monarch.

Spanish democracy is made up of elementary ideas. It would seem to us that the United States authorities, elected by the people and elected to be changed every twelve months in the cities (and every four years in the country) must be of unique decorum, of absolute honesty, of superior culture. For us, the government has all the attributes of a judge. And when we see ourselves injured by an injustice, humiliated by an abuse, victimized by robbery, we take recourse to the government in the certainty that whichever organ comprises the government will take up the problem with sobriety and with the dignity appropriate to the judiciary.

It occurs to us, then, that to straighten out matters like the anomalies and the blatant crimes in economy, finances, trading, industry, and banking and to denounce the collusion of the press with the monopolies, the most natural thing for the Yankees to do would be to turn to their government: to the federal government, to the Department of Commerce, to the Department of Justice, to the Department of State, and to Mr. President of the nation.

The phrase is decisive and common all over the world: "The government should take a hand in the matter."

.　　.　　.

However, we suspect that this is no longer possible in what was the great democracy of the past century—the United States. For eighty years the possibility of [the] government's taking a hand in the matter with severity, with independence, with a spirit of justice, with grandeur of spirit, without commitments to the monopolies has become very limited—limited to a few judges . . . limited to a few senators and representatives who still act as though they were in a state of law.

There's the rub. While in the little Central and South American *republiquettes* the state continues to be a juridic power, in the United States the state as a juridic power has disappeared, caught up slowly and implacably in the claws of the industrialists and the millionaires. *"L'état, c'est moi,"* shouts Wall Street. *"L'état, c'est moi,"* shouts the Pentagon. "I am the Pentagon," corrects General Motors.

Those few representatives and senators and those few court judges are the ones who uphold the privilege of being independent in the face of the millionaires' syndicate. These few good men are the last remains of a juridic state of law that was the greatest stronghold of democracy at the beginning of the nineteenth century. They are the enfeebled heirs of one of the world's great men, named Lincoln.

They are the idealists of the old school. They do survive, but they are backed into a corner as a ridiculous minority. (From idealism to pragmatism, and from pragmatism to mercantilism: a 180-degree turn.)

Unfortunately, such men do not carry a majority on any occasion. The overwhelming and vociferous majority is nowadays made up of senators and representatives who are lackeys of monopolies and judges who "interpret" the laws in an attitude of protection and paternalism—protection and paternalism of the powerful.

.   .   .

The Democratic Party is no more independent with respect to Wall Street than the Republican Party—with its dinosaur division. Both have their home base in Wall Street.

So any candidate who is elected will have a great deal for which to thank the golden oligarchy—and, for that very reason, much to keep quiet about and much to obey. It is superfluous to point out the danger that the millionaires might get wise and become candidates themselves, taking advantage of the "authority" that comes from the apportioning of electoral funds. In 1949 —for just one example—Mr. G. Mennen Williams was chosen Governor of Michigan. He was on the ticket of the Democratic Party, but he was a millionaire who had prospered by manufacturing the Williams Shaving Cream and mentholated Mennen cream, to be used after shaving.

Since then, Nelson Rockefeller has been elected Governor of New York.

Let us not be surprised that the Congress of the United States should, in the long run, turn out to be a conglomerate of captains of business or gentlemen of industry, improvised statesmen, men with hair on their chests, regional bosses, repentant politicians—all of them as disciplined, as constructive, and as collaborationist as the members of the Congress that in 1961 existed in the Dominican Republic under the regime of the multimillionaire Trujillo (who, at the time of his assassination, was said to have stolen 60 percent of the total wealth of his country) or like those that can exist in Nicaragua, under that country's principal businessman, Somoza, who happens to be President of the Republic.

.   .   .

THE SYSTEM OF JUSTICE
IN THE UNITED STATES

Mauro Almeida

Full of misconceptions and errors of fact as it is, the following selection, by a Brazilian who studied journalism at the University of Missouri, provides a useful insight into the confusion created by the American federal system in the minds of foreign observers. Almeida errs in asserting that any state can pass legislation in violation of Supreme Court rulings, yet the frequent defiance of court rulings on segregation and occasionally on other issues make it appear that this is the case. Local municipalities do not have the power to set the driving age, as Almeida says, yet on such questions as liquor prohibition, local option often does prevail (although by permission of the state legislatures). The Federal Bureau of Investigation was not created solely to aid the state police, but it is true that its functions have expanded in recent years. Almeida's assertion that the FBI has become an anti-Communist Gestapo repeats the theme of the González article in the preceding section.

. . . As we shall see in our discussion of racial segregation, the conflict of laws is extremely common in the United States. Every State in the federal union can legislate as it sees fit even if this comes into direct conflict, as often happens, with decisions of the Supreme Court. Relying on the theory that they are the ones who delegate power to the central government, the states feel that they have the right to establish the judicial norms that should govern their own internal relations. Thus the state courts decide not only on the maintenance of the death penalty but also on the way to carry it out. The majority of the states execute criminals in the barbaric electric chair; others prefer the classic formula of the firing squad, while still others have discovered a new method of legalized killing, the gas chamber.

A very natural consequence of this "independence" on the part of the states is the way it is reflected in the actions of local governments. The local authorities have also elevated themselves to the status of legislators of their own destinies, even on matters concerning the civil code. One curious aspect of this which still exists today is the maintenance in many local areas in America of "dry laws" like the well-known national Prohibition Law which forbade the manufacture, sale, and transport of alcoholic beverages. I had a chance to verify this in the town of Lampasas, Texas, which had voted prohibition in its territorial limits. Yet a few miles away the bars continued their regular business. Thus the regular drinkers had little difficulty in satisfying themselves. This very natural eagerness to regulate their own affairs in accordance with the needs of the local community sometimes results in absurd and curious laws. In the town of Gury, the local council approved a law which says, "It is forbidden to travel in a bus or train for four hours after eating." Another city allows anyone who is at least seventeen years old to drive, while a third considers that a couple is officially engaged if they have kissed seven times, even on different days. Killing dogs and cats is a crime punishable with imprisonment in some towns while others punish anyone who spits in the parks.

The organization of the judiciary is very different from our own. If a city is the county seat, this does not automatically mean that it has a permanent court to decide the cases that arise there. The country is divided into 3,047 counties, reminiscent of the English political organization. The number of these is not a function of the number of towns or of the area of the state. Thus, for example, Missouri has 114 counties although it is one of the smaller states. Many towns have a court without a judge. When necessary, a traveling

FROM "A justiça," *E.U.A.: Civilização empacotada* (São Paulo: Editora Fulgor, 1961), pp. 147–54. Translated by the editor with permission.

judge comes, and after deciding a case, he leaves the town and goes to another county. The Court of Appeals in each state hears appeals concerning these decisions while the federal Supreme Court is at the top of the judicial system. The classification of crimes is not uniform. Some are federal and some come under the states. On this basis, counterfeiting, avoidance of military service, robbing the mails, income tax evasion, and treason are judged by federal courts. However, a crime can cease to be under the state jurisdiction if the criminal crosses the borders of the state where the crime was committed and takes refuge in another state. This diversity sometimes has curious results. If a train goes from one state where the sale of alcoholic beverages is permitted and crosses into a state where it is not allowed, the moment that it enters puritan territory the dining car or bar immediately stops serving.

One of the most criticized aspects of American justice is the speed with which its decisions are made. Although this permits a practical distribution of burdens and avoids the rancorous and superfluous formalism of Latin justice, which is no doubt a considerable advance, it also involves serious inconveniences. The most serious and complex cases are often brought before the courts a few weeks after they have been committed, with [the result that] many of the circumstances [are] still uncertain and unclarified. Paradoxically, some cases drag on for years after being decided, while the accused goes in and out of jail a number of times depending on the progress of his case through the increasingly complex maze of laws. Another distressing aspect of the rapid implementation of justice is the fact that often individuals have been executed for capital crimes of which they were later found to be innocent. The existence of appeal courts does not always lessen the danger of unjust sentences.

As for the penitentiary system, there are about thirty federal prisons scattered throughout the country while two hundred others are under state jurisdiction. . . . As a result of the multiplicity of laws referred to above, various states still employ prison methods long since abandoned in all other countries of the civilized world. Thus Georgia abolished chain gangs only in 1943, while other states maintain corporal punishment and similar methods far more than necessary. Fortunately there are strong forces in favor of more modern prison methods, sometimes employing techniques that are very advanced compared to other [prison] systems.

. . .

Concerning the bearing of arms, I should note that it is rare for ordinary citizens to own a revolver. It is rarer still for them to wear them. The only persons who do so are those who must go armed because of their profession (guards, bank cashiers, etc.). To carry a revolver is nearly always a reason for arrest and fine. The police must be on the alert because the crime rate is constantly going up. The recorded total [last year] was 7.5 percent higher than the number of crimes registered the year before. Gangs like those that made Chicago notorious still exist, although they act differently. If they are not engaged in bootlegging as during Prohibition, they engage in gambling, prostitution, stealing cars, etc. To give an idea of the commercial value of crime, it is enough to say that it comes to twice the value of the annual production of General Motors, one of the largest businesses in the world with control of much heavy industry all over the world.

One aspect which is cited by many who visit the United States is the excessive importance of the police. It is not that they are trying on their own initiative to increase their power. This is not the case. American policemen are very helpful. They never deny assistance to anyone who seeks it. Policemen have taken numerous specialized courses and nearly always have had a high school education. They are solicitous and courteous, and they always approach a person respectfully even if he has committed an offense or crossed the street against a red light. They receive salaries that, even if they are not large, make bribery a serious crime and permit them to live in middle-class comfort. Nevertheless, the anti-Communist hysteria that is growing stronger every day is making the police force too important. In particular, the FBI constitutes a super-police force today. Until just before the Second World War, its principal purpose was to aid the state police in the solution of crimes committed in their respective territories. It has fabulous equipment, ultramodern laboratories, and complete files and has rendered incalculable service in the fight against crime. With the recrudescence of an anti-Communist policy, this body has become a kind of Gestapo, involving itself in everything in the name of national security and acquiring a power unprecedented in American history. Classical legal rights, such as access to automobiles and the right to cross-examine the evidence of accusers before a jury, have been denied the defense, which has aroused strong protests on the part of the more enlightened men in the country. Attitudes of this kind have created in some cities of the country a certain "police-state" climate to the point that in many of them someone who is unknown is considered suspect of some crime.

·   ·   ·

FEDERALISM AND THE BILL OF RIGHTS

M. Ramaswamy

Some observers from the developing nations have taken a more careful look at American political institutions and have found some features worthy of imitation. M. Ramaswamy, an Indian legal scholar writing for a study prepared in 1946 in connection with the creation of a constitution for the new state of India, urged the establishment of a federal system and legally enforceable guarantees for human rights similar to those in the United States. The model that India actually adopted departed from the British example in incorporating these two American practices, with some modifications. The constitutions of the Philippines and several Latin-American countries also reflect American influences.

Constitutional safeguards alone will not ensure to a people the enjoyment of basic liberties. The ultimate sanction which preserves to a people the benefits of a free regime rests upon the determination of the people themselves not to give quarter to the forces that may threaten to imperil it. The question naturally arises whether it would not be better for the people to rely upon their own efforts to stave off encroachments upon their basic liberties instead of leaning upon constitutional provisions. My answer is that, while a people cannot afford entirely to depend upon constitutional safeguards but must exercise an eternal vigilance to prevent invasion of their basic freedoms, the help which the courts by their power of judicial review can give them, even though in a limited field, is so very precious that they would do well to have binding constitutional safeguards incorporated into their constitution. The experience of the United States in working with a Constitution containing guarantees for fundamental rights has made it clear that, in the matter of protection of basic liberties, the courts generally, and the Supreme Court of the United States in particular, have rendered invaluable service. . . .

That the United States, comprising a vast assembly of minority groups, has become welded into a great and prosperous nation ought to serve as a beacon light for all humanity. In race, religion, and in traditions, the people differ from pole to pole. Every nationality of Europe is represented in its population. There is an important Negro element in its population texture. Yet, out of all this diversity, the United States has evolved a basic unity. Two important factors, in my view, have contributed to this happy result. The first factor is the federal system operating in that country which has been able to harmonize national unity with regional freedom. In fact the United States has demonstrated beyond doubt that national strength is not incompatible with local autonomy. If what is now the territory of the United States had been parceled out among half a dozen or more independent states, it is more than probable that North America, like the continent of Europe, would have become the cockpit of national rivalries and jealousies. And since the federal union functions as a single economic unit without any restrictions being placed on the free flow of commerce across state frontiers, the country has gained immeasurably in economic strength. In fact, the United States is the greatest single free market in the world. The second factor which has contributed to the great success of the country is the cardinal faith of every American in the worth and dignity of the human soul and in the need for a free atmosphere for the individual to rise to the full height of his powers. It is this faith in human liberty which shines through the pages of that great document which Thomas Jefferson drafted in 1776 to serve as the spiritual banner of the American Revolution. It is this faith again which animates that historic message which the late President Franklin D. Roosevelt sent to the Seventy-seventh Congress on January 6, 1941, pledging his nation's support to all those who were struggling for the establishment of the Four Freedoms everywhere in the world, namely, freedom of speech, freedom of worship, freedom from want, and freedom from fear.

The guarantees for fundamental rights contained in the Bill of Rights of the United States Constitution are a visible expression of that nation's faith in

FROM "The Case for a Constitutional Bill of Rights," *Fundamental Rights,* issued under the auspices of the Indian Council of World Affairs (Bombay, 1946), pp. 37–39. Reprinted by permission.

the worth and value of human beings as persons. The attempt is rather to reconcile the two so that everybody may have the largest freedom consistent with the demands of social order to lead his own life free from hampering restrictions. In so favorable an atmosphere it is not surprising that minorities feel secure and give of their best to the country. . . .

ONE-PARTY AND TWO-PARTY DEMOCRACY

Julius Nyerere

In contrast to the preceding selection by M. Ramaswamy, Julius Nyerere, President of Tanzania, opposes the adoption of the British and American political institutions by the new African states. He asserts that the two-party system is appropriate for the West because it reflects the divergent class interests there. But it is not necessary in African countries because class antagonisms do not exist in independent Africa. (He is thus implicitly criticizing the Marxist doctrine of the inevitability of the class struggle.) If freedom of discussion and criticism is maintained within the single party (a big "if"), he believes it can preserve democracy and strengthen national unity against the divisive tendencies of tribalism.

The African concept of democracy is similar to that of the ancient Greeks, from whose language the word "democracy" originated. To the Greeks, democracy meant simply "government by discussion among equals." The people discussed, and when they reached agreement the result was a "people's decision."

. . .

To minds molded by Western parliamentary tradition and Western concepts of democratic institutions, the idea of an organized opposition group has become so familiar that its absence immediately raises the cry of "dictatorship." It is no good telling them that when a group of one hundred equals have sat and talked together until they have agreed where to dig a well (and "until they have agreed" implies that they have produced many conflicting arguments before eventually agreeing), they have practiced democracy. Proponents of Western parliamentary traditions will consider whether the opposition was organized and therefore automatic, or whether it was spontaneous and therefore free. Only if it was automatic will they concede that here was democracy!

FROM "One-Party Rule," in *The Ideologies of the Developing Nations,* edited by Paul E. Sigmund (New York: Praeger, 1963), pp. 197–99. Reprinted by permission.

Basically, democracy is government by discussion as opposed to government by force, and by discussion between the people or their chosen representatives, as opposed to a hereditary clique. Under the tribal system, whether there was a chief or not, African society was a society of equals, and it conducted its business by discussion.

It is true that this "pure" democracy—the totally unorganized "talking until you agree"—can no longer be adequate; it is too clumsy a way of conducting the affairs of a large modern state. But the need to organize the "government by discussion" does not necessarily imply the need to organize an opposition group as part of the system.

I am not arguing that the two-party system is not democratic; I am only saying that it is simply one form which democracy happens to have taken in certain countries, and that it is by no means essential. I am sure that even my friends in the Labour Party or in the Conservative Party in Britain would admit that if their party could succeed in winning all the seats, they would be perfectly happy to form a one-party government. They—the winning party, that is—would not be likely to suspect themselves of having suddenly turned Britain into a dictatorship!

Some of us have been overready to swallow unquestioningly the proposition that you cannot have democracy unless you have a second party to oppose the party in power. But, however difficult our friends in Britain and America may find it to accept what to them is a new idea—that democracy can exist where there is no formal opposition—I think we in Africa should think very carefully before we abandon our traditional attitude.

It is often overlooked that the Anglo-Saxon tradition of a two-party system is a reflection of the society in which it evolved. Within that society, there was a struggle between the "haves" and the "have-nots," each of whom organized themselves into political parties—one party associated with wealth and the status quo, and the other with the masses of the people and change. Thus, the existence of distinct classes in a society and the struggle between them resulted in the growth of the two-party system. But need this be accepted as the essential and only pattern of democracy?

With rare exceptions, the idea of class is something entirely foreign to Africa. Here in this continent, the nationalist movements are fighting a battle for freedom from *foreign* domination, not from domination by any ruling class of our own. To us, "the other party" is the colonial power. In many parts of Africa, this struggle has been won; in others, it is still going on. But everywhere the people who fight the battle are not former overlords wanting to reestablish a lost authority; they are not a rich mercantile class whose freedom to exploit the masses is limited by the colonial powers; they are the common people of Africa.

Thus, once the foreign power—"the other party"—has been expelled, it is by no means certain that democracy will adopt the same machinery and symbols as the Anglo-Saxon. Nor, indeed, is it necessarily desirable that it should.

.   .   .

3

American Society

A GENERAL VIEW OF AMERICAN CULTURE

Alceu Amoroso Lima

Alceu Amoroso Lima is a Brazilian writer, journalist, and Catholic intellectual who has represented his country at many international meetings and has lectured at New York University and the Sorbonne. This excerpt is taken from the final chapter of a long essay comparing Europe and the Western Hemisphere. Amoroso Lima describes American cultural life as characterized by three traits—decentralization, diffusion, and heterodoxy—and he contrasts the general availability of a rather primitive *"Reader's Digest* culture" in the United States with the restricted high culture developed by an intellectual and literary élite out of touch with the masses. This is only one of the many contradictions that Amoroso Lima, like Hailou Wolde-Giorghis, the author of the following selection, found in American life.

. . . [One] characteristic [of American culture] is its decentralization. Writers live in different places, often in small towns or abroad. Generally they do not stay in the large centers. And this means that they can live on their writing once they have attained a certain reputation. Precisely because they live in isolation in different areas, they meet from time to time in congresses and small gatherings to study particular aspects of their profession. The United States is an extremely professionalized culture. Everyone has a profession and possesses the skills of that profession. This is reflected in the culture as a whole, which is therefore also completely professionalized. But there is no group spirit in the cultural media. It is an individualistic culture, with a great deal of cultural freedom. Today, as we have observed, there is a conspiracy against cultural freedom in the name of "thought control." But this does not affect the general quality of liberty or the isolation and dispersion of cultural activity. Hence it is difficult to get into contact with cultural groups. They are

FROM "Panorama cultural norte-americano," *Europa e América: Duas culturas* (Rio de Janeiro: Livraria AGIR Editôra, 1962), pp. 59–62. Translated by the editor with permission.

so varied, so different from one another, so shut off, so scattered through the whole country that no one can say which city is the cultural center of the United States. Is it Boston or New York? Other cities, too, can claim the same thing for themselves without any of them, including these two, deserving it. Decentralization is the norm.

Another characteristic of American culture is its diffusion. This accounts for the primitivism which dominates the mass culture and which is combined with its extreme opposite among the élite. There is a mass culture as there is a mass production. Hence the mass publication of cheap little magazines available to everyone. Hence the symbolic triumph of the *Reader's Digest* or, as we know it, *Seleçôes*. The history of this effort is widely known today; in ten years it has produced one of the most impressive examples of American cultural vulgarization. This undertaking began with the excellent idea of offering its readers a sample of the best articles published in other magazines. But today this practice has changed completely. Instead of choosing articles already published, they arrange to have articles written that will please the mass of readers, and then they are placed in other magazines with the understanding that these articles will then be extracted from them as if it were a spontaneous operation. . . . Everyone in the United States reads a great deal—but for recreation rather than for education. There is an enormous circulation of detective stories and badly written literature, which means that letters, properly speaking, are only one sector of American life, unlike the situation in the European countries, especially France, where culture is the center of life and not a specialized area. Yet an interest in culture is universal in the United States, and in all these ideas we see the democratization of culture. Nothing is more incorrect than to speak of a lack of culture in America. There is a strange coexistence of an extreme diffusion of culture among all levels of the population with the most highly developed cultural sophistication among the more refined groups.

A last characteristic is that of heterodoxy. Just as the extreme diffusion of culture leads to a spirit of conformism, the existence of a very refined cultural élite is expressed in an absolute heterodoxy on the part of writers. They live alone in different places and frequently in opposition to the spirit of the times. Consider, for example, the cases of Henry Miller, Ezra Pound, Mencken, Steinbeck, Sandburg, Hemingway, and John Dos Passos. All these and dozens of others—I am referring only to names already universally known—live in complete disagreement with the spirit of the times. In a puritan society, Miller is a permanent scandal. In a democratic society, Ezra Pound became a Fascist to demonstrate his disapproval. In a society based on a spirit of reciprocity and mutual understanding, Mencken was a kind of Bernanos without faith. In a conservative society, men such as Steinbeck, Caldwell, or Sandburg represent a permanent rejection of bourgeois pharisaism. In a strongly (but with important qualifications) technical civilization, Hemingway returns to primitive forces. In a capitalist and socialist society (the rule of big business is always a kind of hidden socialism, which for that reason runs into considerable resistance from the universal spirit of liberty), John Dos Passos ends up defending private property, just as in the land of cities, [Louis] Bromfield preaches the return to the country. . . .

At the same time, then, a primitive mass culture and a refined intellectual élite exist, the one academic and conservative and the other complex and isolated. In painting, for example, abstractionism is very much in fashion, and all the large museums organize exhibitions of the most modern and original esthetic forms. At the same time, bad taste also finds much support.

.   .   .

In any case, the cultural intensity [in America] is considerable. This diversity of aspect is very typical of a civilization expanding in every direction and presenting the most flagrant contradictions. But it cannot be said that there is apathy or cultural vacuity.

MY ENCOUNTER WITH RACISM IN THE UNITED STATES

Hailou Wolde-Giorghis

Observers from Africa, Asia, and Latin America are concerned to the point of obsession with the racial problem in the United States. It is the most widely discussed and the least understood aspect of American society. In the following selection from a Ugandan journal, an Ethiopian student who visited the United States under State Department sponsorship recounts his experiences with racism in both the North and the South. The author notes the recent progress in the struggle for integration but is pessimistic about the future, because of the deep economic and psychological roots of discrimination in America.

Invited with a Guinean student by the State Department to visit the U.S.A. for forty-five days, I did not hesitate long. I went. I wanted to get to know this country where, according to what is said, men are broken down by clever machines, and not vice versa, as is the case in our "underdeveloped countries," where it is the machine which loses nuts and bolts—something always less serious than the destruction of a man.

.   .   .

Let us then relive together a part of this great adventure, for it is impossible to talk about everything that I saw. I shall present only the human side of this testimony and try my best to avoid the truth of numbers and statistics in the hope of substituting a more palpable truth, a truth lived from day to day.

"Negroes are dirty," say the whites, but in nearly all restaurants I saw

FROM "An African Encounters the United States," *Transition,* Vol. 4, No. 15 (July–August, 1964), pp. 23–25. Originally published in *Présence Africaine* (Third Quarter, 1963). Reprinted by permission.

Negro waiters and cooks. "They're lazy": I noticed that it is the Negro who does the hardest manual work. They are also said to be uncultivated, and are therefore denied access to culture. As George Bernard Shaw said, "The haughty American nation makes the Negro shine its shoes, and then demonstrates his physical and mental inferiority by the fact that he is a shoe-cleaner."

But why should this racism exist? Some will tell you that it's because the white man is ignorant of the Negro: he doesn't know him and has never tried to understand him. Why should the master bother to know his Negro cook? Certain whites advance reasons relating to tradition and custom. In the course of a discussion dealing with activities of the National [Student Association], a white, southern student admitted to me that until the age of seventeen he had himself been a racist, first of all because his parents were, and secondly because he really believed that there were two existing orders, the white and the Negro. When an individual from one of these orders wanted to mix with the other, he had thought to himself that "something in society was cracking."

The last and perhaps most important explanation of racism relates to the economy: the white worker is afraid of the competition represented by the Negro. The latter is offered only the most degrading work, such as shining shoes and working as porters (at the airport in New York, for example, I saw only one white porter). When the Negro has other capabilities, he is victimized by discrimination. Thus the federal court had to intervene on behalf of a Negro pilot who had been refused work by a commercial airline company. The most inflexible American racists are precisely those belonging to the lower class. It is for them nearly an intellectual comfort to be able to say. "It is true I haven't succeeded in life but, thank God, I'm better than the niggers."

But how, in practice, do the whites manifest their racist sentiments? It is no secret that southern cinemas, public gardens, restaurants, toilets, golf courses, bars, and even shops do not admit Negroes. I had before my departure vaguely heard about all this, and I admit that my feeling then was nearly one of indifference, but once I arrived I met with several painful experiences.

When speaking with an ex-racist or quite simply an honest Southerner, I noticed that when I spoke to him of certain injustices or of the white man's exploitation of the Negro, he would immediately ask me what I thought of Communism. In the South, for example, all anti-racist demonstrators are accused of being Communist. Therefore, in fighting the Negro the Southerner must also fight this twentieth-century "sickness." Nor is the United Nations exempted; it is "Communist," and if it is successfully to carry out its mission it must first be purged of all Negro nations and all eastern countries. In New York Negro delegates regularly receive offensive but anonymous letters asking them to leave the United States. The Ethiopian diplomat who told me this has himself read several of these letters addressed to the leader of the Ethiopian delegation.

It is often said that the racial problem does not exist in the North. Listen to the story told by this Nigerian diplomat, a delegate to the United Nations, whom I met in New York. Invited by a gracious American family to a very congenial dinner, he was telling them what he knew about the African climate and the folk-dances of his tribe when, from one of the other rooms, there suddenly appeared a young girl who bounded toward her mother and said, "But Mother, you told me that all Negroes were dirty! Why is this one clean?"

Curiously enough, American Southerners are generally in favor of the independence of African countries, not because they condemn colonialism but because they are hoping for the "repatriation" of all American Negroes.

．　　．　　．

Certainly the American Negro is resigned and, with the exception of occasional "insubordination," has, in spite of himself, accepted this humiliating situation. He has unhesitatingly opted for integration; an eventual return to Africa is chimerical. He has been taught since early childhood that his African ancestors have remained savages and that, as a gardener, he is earning one hundred times more in America than what he would be earning in Africa. This he believes and will choose a very clear-skinned woman to be his bride and in order to make himself "presentable" will have his hair uncurled, possibly grateful that he hasn't had to have it dyed.

I asked a Negro intellectual what he thought about all of this. "For us," he answered. "Africa is a distant mother that we love very dearly. We are all for the final independence of African states because, among other things, that would enormously influence the attitude of the white American extremist, but we anticipate no return to Africa. We have been cut off for three hundred years. We would feel uprooted in Africa, and if we have to lead the fight against injustice, we will do it here, where we live. One of your distant great-grandfathers must have sold one of mine, and now that we're face to face, I wonder whether I should hit you or thank you."(!!!)

What is known as integration in the South is the ability of a Negro to enter a shop and buy a record, or the fact that, of ten thousand students enrolled in a university, two of them are Negroes. "A miracle!" they cry. Real integration, however, does not exist, not even in the North, and by real integration I mean interracial communication, complete equality in the strict sense of the word. Still another example drawn from the South: the manager of a television studio told me in frigid terms that he could not hire Negroes; there would be a scandal and all his sponsors would protest.

One of the consequences of this discrimination is obviously the Negro's economic situation; with the exception of a few wealthy Negroes in show business or sports, or businessmen (in Atlanta, for example, some of the more important banks are owned by Negroes), most belong to the lower class. I could talk a little here about the southern slums, which I personally saw, where thousands of Negroes are housed in quasi-military camps. I was told at great length—the way one profusely excuses oneself—that there were whites living in the same conditions. This is very possible, but I myself did not see any.

There are occasionally completely segregated quarters consisting of old wooden houses, many of them shacks built with soapboxes. In most of them there is neither water nor electricity (and remember that this is the United States in the twentieth century); sanitary conditions are frightful, similar to those of many African countries. When at "play," the children—very dirty and sickly and often without shoes—roll themselves on the several square yards of dust that constitute their garden. Old men, themselves equally thin, sit on rickety chairs in front of their tumbling shacks, somnolently smoking their pipes as if awaiting death. Younger muscular men whistle or chatter in the narrow streets, and one feels that they have been devoured by boredom. This pitiful sight struck me all the more when not more than a stone's throw away in the same city I found myself visiting a well-to-do white family. This gave me a taste not [only] of *their* view—an extensive and breathtaking land-scape—but of that inimitable and famous "southern hospitality." Their house, in reality a villa whose large picture window overlooks a nearly exotic moonlit garden, is decorated à la Picasso. They have a garage, three cars, no television (a sign of affluence in the United States), a private swimming pool, a beautiful library, and so on. Please understand that I am in no way against the success of this gracious family, but the sense of injustice is very apparent when you think of the number of human beings who have not had the same chance.

However, there are some Americans who are very conscious of this fact and who are fighting to improve things. It was, for example, a white professor of political economy, teaching at the Methodist University of Dallas, who initiated my visit to the Negro quarter of that city.

.   .   .

What, then, is America? I think the word "contradiction" is the word which best expresses my thoughts; racist and not racist, nothing resembles anything on this continent. However that may be, and passing over the racial problem, there remain the wonders of the machine, the generous hospitality, the beautiful collections in the museums . . . so many riches to welcome one!

With its qualities and its defects, it remains a country to be seen and known. If you have the chance I had, do not hesitate. Go! Even for a Negro, it is a wonderful trip.

IF THE VIETCONG WERE IN ALABAMA

J. B. Adotevi

The following selection, from a Senegalese newspaper published under Catholic auspices, indicates the intensity with which racial developments in the United States are followed in Africa. This article could also have been included in the sections on American politics or American foreign policy; it attributes Johnson's reluc-tance to intervene with federal troops in Mississippi to the power of Southern congressmen and contrasts this reluctance to the speed with which the President was willing to escalate the war in Vietnam and to intervene in the Congo in November, 1964. Both actions were opposed by most Asians and Africans, as well as by some Latin Americans.

The situation would undoubtedly have changed in Alabama if Johnson had decided to escalate in Mississippi as he did in Vietnam. We would not have had to deplore the death of the white minister, James Reeb, attacked by white racist hooligans.

In the city of Selma, Reverend Reeb was demonstrating along with American pacifists, protesting the obstruction of the registration of Negro voters by the administration of George Wallace. Since the white racists of the United States have always thought of the white integrationists as pariahs, they could not tolerate the presence of members of their race among the Negroes. It was thus necessary to avenge this insult to the "chosen race." So, a gang challenged the young minister; he died at the hospital a few days later as a result of multiple fractures of the skull.

This crime, like so many others which are never punished, aroused justifiable indignation in the American nation. The demonstrators' courage increased; even the White House was assailed by pacifist organizations.

Then President Johnson decided to act. He telephoned Wallace to have him come to Washington. After the interview, President Johnson assured the nation that the government would utilize all available means to assure justice to men of all races. He promised to propose to the legislature a new law for Negro voting rights. We must conclude that the preceding law which aroused so much enthusiasm is no longer adequate in the present situation. Will the new law prevent new obstructions by the segregationists? In any case, Wallace himself has finally promised to obey the federal laws and to refrain from any action which could be detrimental to them.

But the mayor and the sheriff of Selma do not consider themselves defeated. They denounce the "outside racial agitators." They swear that the laws of city and county will be strictly enforced, to the detriment of federal laws.

A little less than a month has passed since Malcolm X fell under bullets from his own people. [At that time] the conclusion was hastily drawn that violence breeds violence and that Malcolm X was not representative of the majority of the people whose cause he defended. . . . To say that he deserved this fate would have been unseemly; but a great many people thought so, and this was evident in their statements. Today, it is an advocate of nonviolence . . . who has died, he too killed by his own people. But there were many other young people before him, black and white, whose only error was to believe that the democracy of their country meant something. Under cover of darkness and with the cooperation of corrupt policemen, they have disappeared in the stench given off by the Deep South. Their deaths, like Malcolm X's, were also a settling of scores. In America scores are always settled with those who hold different opinions. Whereas Malcolm X was killed for having hated too much, Alabamians and Mississippians disappear for having loved too much. . . . The "Gandhis" are not always understood; hatred understands only the "Malcom X's," because in them it can see itself: Malcolm X's racism had white racism as its father.

But the United States of America continues to be the leader of "democracy," to claim justice for the Asians of the Gulf of Tonkin. Bombers are sent to destroy the nests of the Vietcong in Ho Chi Minh's country, just as

FROM "Si les Vietcongs étaient en Alabama," *Afrique Nouvelle*, No. 919 (March 18–24, 1965), p. 10. Translated by the editor with permission.

yesterday bombers were sent to Stanleyville.* But in Alabama and Mississippi juries acquit the assassins of the "niggers." "Go free, you have deserved well of the country."

It is true that in Vietnam it is the "government" and the "Vietnamese people" who called on the Americans to save them. It is however easier to hear voices from one's own country, especially if those voices have been calling for more than one hundred years. Why then is the federal government satisfied with ineffectual laws while a majority of the nation clamors for its intervention. It is certainly unnecessary to introduce a new law in the Senate; escalation in Mississippi would largely suffice. But since the representatives of the people of Mississippi are neither Indians, nor Negroes, nor the Vietcong . . . the facts of the problem are no longer the same . . . The odor of the [gas] bomb only makes the whites sick . . . so no escalation in Mississippi!

AN INDIAN IN AMERICA

Deb Kumar Das

The following selection by an Indian poet, Deb Kumar Das, gives an original interpretation to the well-worn theme of American conformity by relating it to the American desire to test different group values in a sincere search for truth. The author also cites the heritage of the American frontier (mentioned previously by Manuel Pedro González)—a theme that has been given new vitality by the Texas origins of President Johnson. Kumar Das sees the closing of the American frontier as a significant development that led to the retreat of American culture into insularity and materialism, and to the manufacture of self-defeating myths like those that still impede progress in India.

America is not really a place, nor a country, nor is it, to use a metaphysical cliché, a state of mind. America, in fact, makes sense only as a way of looking at human experience. This is why so many Indians fail to find it, or lose it in the act of discovery. It is out of reach of the traveler who has his own self-conscious identity. It can only be found by an act of courage, the willingness to gamble one's own personal world for the chance of discovering another.

Part of the Indian's problem, of course, is of his own making. Every Indian "knows" that America is crassly materialistic, that sex is the mainspring of American life, that America will spiral into neurosis and anarchy without an

* United States transports, not bombers, were used in the Stanleyville paratroop rescue mission in November, 1964.—Editor.

FROM "An Indian in America," *The Century*, Vol. 1, No. 45 (New Delhi, March 28, 1964), p. 18. Reprinted by permission.

Oriental philosophic detachment. The more orthodox Indian can even persuade himself that Eastern mysticism is the only answer to Western crisis: or, to borrow a phrase, that the Bhagavad-Gita is the only answer to *La Dolce Vita*. This leaves little space in the Indian's mind to search for America's meaning except in confirmation or denial of his own hypotheses. If he falls for American temptations, he ends up in a cultural no man's land, his assumptions swept away and little to put in their place except borrowed values. If he can protect his inclusiveness, he goes back with a kaleidoscope-eye view of a cultural ferment whose patterns are those of his inner vision. Either way, he fails. The truth has eluded him, though the facts were always within his grasp.

Prosperity—the first dazzling chimera of American life—is, surprisingly, not the most important thing about America. It is, at best, its most conspicuous symptom. True, the abundance of goods and services creates an overpowering impression on a mind used to thinking of such things in terms of conspicuous scarcity. But the significant point is not the abundance itself, but the facile transformation of luxury into a common and universal aspiration. The American appeal, through its mass media, is the essentially self-contradictory thesis that "everyone" can be "best"—status symbols, ultimate conveniences, prestige, and exclusive goods are universally accessible to "everybody" who wants them. This self-contradiction is turned by the hard-sell of advertising into nearly believable myth and makes a self-sustaining affluence possible. American prosperity could never exist unless there was this inner tension, a mass culture created by the process of denying its own existence. Yet this same process makes America seek local boundaries of difference and differentiation, so that a hundred separate "bests" can live together by insulating themselves from each other and the rest of the world by rationalized status: the district, the area, the income level, the cultural mainstream, the attitude to life. America would have to invent the Negro even if he did not exist—so vital is discrimination and differentiation to its current existence.

It is useless, of course, for the tradition-steeped Indian or European to look down his nose at the unbelievable "commonness" of American culture; useless also to remark, as did a German friend, that Karl Marx would have shut up for all time if he could have seen what the common man can do to a culture when given the importance of a cult. No honest person can forget that three-quarters of the human race would give up much more than culture to enjoy even such a plebeian prosperity: nor can he forget that it is the surplus from this prosperity that assists, in whole or part, in sustaining his own traditions.

American conformism is as deceptive a phenomenon as American prosperity. The secret is that the human race perversely constructs a philosophy even where there is no need for one; and conformism in America is no more than a result of that restlessly irrational drive. In the absence of traditional guides, values are defined out of thin air or circumstance, and become (in time) the principles of local action: having arbitrarily defined themselves as a mythical series of differentiated groups, Americans set about inventing group norms with a zeal that would interest an anthropologist. Mass communication helps the process in the short run, but sometimes destroys it over time by making the norms too easily accessible: this is what creates the "fads" that sweep the country to disappear without a trace—Buddhism, the Beat Generation, un-Americanism, Twist, the Beatles—the list is endless. Some are more conditionally viable than others and take on the form of "tradition," like Mother's Day or Civil Rights. But even these are rather tentative: America is either too sincere or too naive to believe all its own stories about itself. So its conformism goes hand in hand with a deeper search in the undefined shadow of what (for want of a better name) can be called truth. And the dual nature of American conformism creates the anxiety that is endemic to American life, the tension between outward goal and inward search. The paradox is that it is American *sincerity* that invites the uncomprehending sermon from the Indian pseudo-mystic, and the impatience of the Indian intellectual; if America were less sincere, she could act out a far more fool-proof conformism that would absolve her from both charges. Certainly there is nothing unintelligent about American conformism, as some of our superior philosophers in India would have us believe: only an intelligent culture can test out such "consciously" derived moralities, ready to reject them when found unworkable.

However, American sincerity does not answer a deeper, far more disturbing question. How much of America is myth, built out of related myths? How far has sincerity carried America deeper into the backwaters of self-deception?

. . .

Fortunately, at least at first, America [had] its western frontier as a counterpart to its eastern gates. This allowed a magnificent conception of America, which is one of the hardest things for an American to live down. Those who came to America were the social and spiritual nomads, carrying their Old World needs for fuller fulfilments in the New; their children lost what Old World characteristics their parents possessed and picked up only the expedients of language and law-and-order for the freedom to define themselves. They moved, searching. There was lust and greed and simple security, yes, but more than that to the movement: it was elemental human need, given the vast canvas of a fertile continent to find expression in.

Today, there is no western frontier, only another ocean to define its end. There is no eastern gate, only jealous steel barriers at New York harbor. Faced with the loss of its limitless physical horizon, America drew its meaning tightly around itself like a cloak and refused to share its search. It discovered that it had a great deal to lose, and it let the elemental human need that once defined it lapse into elemental greed as it allowed itself the exercise of insularity in the absence of other consistent motives. This retreat into material inclusiveness was not American. It was a lapse into humanity, much more petty and trivial than the American concept. Few cultures share their own gains without a price. And America, in retreat from itself, was just beginning to make the mistake of thinking about itself as what it was not—a culture.

But the process was bound to backfire on America—as indeed it has done. America cannot separate itself from the world without regressing into myth, as a more internally viable culture might have in the past; it is an entirely contemporary product of an age of growing interdependence, [and] has little meaning beyond the extension of the hopes of Old World cultures that gave it birth. It is easy to sense in many Americans the underlying bewilderment of their condition. They will still talk about their backgrounds—Scandinavian, German, Irish. But, in not understanding *which* Scandinavian or German, they can never understand the alienation that their supposed European cousins feel towards them. For, by enacting for themselves the myth of a culture called America, they have betrayed the quest of their ancestors, their faith. They have denied their meaning.

Can America rediscover humanity—and, in rediscovering the world, rediscover itself?

.　　.　　.

4

The American Economy

THE AMERICAN ECONOMIC SYSTEM

Ömer Celâl Sarc

The author of this selection is a Turkish economist and educator
who has taught at Columbia University and has worked for the
United Nations. In this basically sympathetic discussion of several
aspects of the American economic system, Sarc replies to those
who accuse Americans of being mercenary and materialistic.
He observes that the American tendency to put a price tag on everything is merely a manifestation of a basic economic rationalism that
others would do well to imitate. He is impressed by the high living
standards of the American worker and contrasts the equality made
possible by the American economic system with the inequities of
his own society. He notes that while American capitalism is subject
to more governmental controls than most foreign observers believe,
its basic character remains that of a free-market economy.

Americans are generally characterized as materialistic, in contrast to other
nations, particularly those in the East. The meaning of this word is not very
clear. It seems to be used mostly to mean that material welfare is given
priority over spiritual interests. Several indications appear to support this
contention, but reflection shows that important qualifications are needed if
the charge of materialism, so defined, implies fundamental differences in this
respect between the United States and other countries.

Among the indications of American materialism is the widespread tendency
to evaluate things in money terms. Thus people like to speak not only of $40
million bridges or of the $100 million damage caused by an insect but also
of a $300,000 El Greco painting and a $100,000-a-year man. A second
factor that may appear to support the contention is the extreme cost-
consciousness one [notices] in the country. In all fields it is customary in

decision-making to evaluate with the greatest possible accuracy the probable costs and returns, and to compare them carefully with each other, a tendency that is much less pronounced in many other countries, especially in mine. Moreover—to use the slogan of a well-known American department store—"It is smart to be thrifty," while for a great number of people in my country, even for many in the lower income groups, lavishness still rates higher than thrift.

But to a large extent these American attitudes represent manifestations of rationalism rather than of materialism. Cost-consciousness is entirely attributable to a rationalistic mentality, and if it is very marked in the United States this reflects in no way the primacy of material interests—even a person who prefers temples and museums to factories may be cost-conscious—but solely the fact that people there have learned to think more sharply. And thrift, which is more pronounced in some European countries than in the United States, is again a phenomenon of rationalism since it denotes careful foresight.

The same is true to a certain extent of the tendency toward monetary evaluation. One of the main trends in modern civilization is to translate qualitative phenomena as far as possible into quantitative terms in order to make them measurable. Perhaps it has rendered the world less colorful, but it has contributed to great advances in science and technology. Thus the the American's inclination to "price" all values can denote a materialistic attitude only if he neglects to distinguish market prices, costs, incomes, and the like from intrinsic values, such as a person's usefulness to society or a painting's aesthetic value. It is wrong to assume that the practice of putting price tags on all values necessarily implies a failure to make this distinction. True, the failure may well be more common in the United States than in other countries. Prestige in society depends there to a greater extent than abroad on wealth and income. Thus businessmen apparently rank much higher in people's eyes than scholars, while the reverse is probably the case in Turkey. But I think one easily overstates the differences in this respect between America and other countries. It is often overlooked that everywhere social scales of value seem now to be evolving toward the American pattern.

.   .   .

It was a great surprise for me not to find in America marked class differences, allegedly a fundamental attribute of a capitalistic society. Some poverty certainly exists. I know of the "Tobacco Road" conditions in the deep South and the hillbilly regions in the Appalachians, and have seen destitute quarters in cities. Before the Second World War about 40 percent of the population appears to have had only enough income to make possible bare subsistence—measured, of course, by American standards. But since then the amazing increase in national income has mostly benefited the poor, and there has been a sharp decrease in the percentage of families unable to provide more than mere subsistence. At the same time the very rich have become somewhat poorer, mainly because of sharply progressive income and inheritance tax rates and to some extent through a decline in the interest rate. As a result, a large-scale equalization has taken place, which manifests itself in the tremendous absolute and relative expansion of the middle class. At present the income of perhaps two-thirds of American families appears to be above the level necessary to assure adequate diet and clothing, some medical and dental care, and a certain amount of entertainment and comfort. Many enjoy in addition the benefits of social security.

Of these families only a very small proportion are really rich, say with a yearly net income of $15,000 or more, and among the remainder, constituting the bulk of the population, differences in living standards are slight. The families in this large group can afford neither servants nor custom-made suits, but practically all own a motorcar and a refrigerator and have lodgings that are adequate in at least certain respects, for instance well heated in winter. In this immense middle class the main difference in living standards seems to be that certain durables (television, air-conditioning sets, movie cameras) and certain possibilities (trips to Europe, college education for children) are available to some but not to all.

This relatively equal distribution of income constitutes at present one of the distinguishing features of American society. . . . In America the difference between a university professor's standard of living and that of a factory worker is one of degree, but in Turkey it is fundamental, affecting housing, furniture, clothing, and medical care, not to speak of the education given to children. . . . Since marked disparities in living standards are an important barrier to genuine fraternization between individuals, it can be said that the equalization of income distribution has greatly consolidated democracy in America.

Moreover, this has been achieved mainly by an upward leveling. Though the average income of the very rich has somewhat declined, the increment in that of the masses has come very little, if at all, from taxes collected from the rich. Its principal source has been the large increase in national income; both legislation and trade-union action have provided labor with a growing proportion of this increase.

It is noteworthy that the greater equality in income distribution was brought about without giving up basic principles of capitalism. To be sure, capitalism in the United States today is something greatly different from what it was in the nineteenth century. "Rugged individualism" has been harnessed and the "laissez faire" principle to a great extent abandoned. Very strong controls exist with regard to such activities as railroad transportation, banking and finance, [and] monopolistic combinations, while extensive regulations govern working conditions and wages. The government incurs large welfare expenditures and levies very heavy taxes on high incomes. But basic principles of capitalism have been maintained. The principle of private ownership is largely intact. Direct economic activity by the government is very limited, consisting of the postal service and the operation of some airports and water, gas, and electricity works. There has been an expansion into production of hydroelectric power, but not into manufacturing. Military plants built during the war were later sold or leased. In this respect there is a sharp contrast with Turkey, where 55 percent of the net value of large-scale manufacturing was derived from public establishments in 1954, and some fields, such as iron and steel and sugar production, are de facto under government monopoly.

Moreover, despite all the government regulations the American economy is not a planned economy. Its functioning is governed to a large extent by decisions of individuals, though these are of course indirectly influenced by government measures, for instance in the field of monetary policy. Thus some major targets of socialism have been attained without much damage to the mechanism of the free-market economy, and society continues to enjoy certain benefits this mechanism provides, particularly those arising from competition.

Some characteristics of the American economy and of American production methods are [noted] even by visitors who are not professional economists. The enormous turnover in shops and the uniform standardized type of most merchandise sold are indicative of mass production. One not only hears of the high level of wages but soon sees many of its manifestations. In the huge amount of consumer purchases it is striking that everything with a large wage component in its costs (particularly services, such as repair of watches, custom-made suits, doctors' fees, even shoeshining) is much more expensive than abroad, while the reverse is true of goods that are produced mainly by machinery and thus have a low labor component. But there are also some aspects of the economy which are puzzling to the foreign visitor. The huge sums spent for advertisement appear wasteful, as does the lavish use of various materials. Packaging, for example, is very elaborate, but practically all containers and wrapping material go to the wastebasket as soon as the merchandise is unpacked. Stockings and shirts are rarely mended, because new ones are cheaper than the time mending requires. Only a deeper scrutiny reveals that some of these phenomena are explainable by the immense natural resources with which America has been endowed, and that others entail advantages outweighing in importance the waste incurred.

Visiting foreign economists are puzzled by the farm policy, which has led to an enormous accumulation of stocks and will probably contribute to their further increase. They wonder about the outcome of labor-union efforts to continuously boost wages. They ask themselves whether latent inflation is inherent in the American economy, and of course particularly whether economic depressions will recur. But American rather than foreign economists are entitled to treat these questions.

PRIVATE PROPERTY IN AMERICA

John Pepper Clark

John Pepper Clark, a former exchange student at Princeton, is a Nigerian poet and playwright. Like González and Kumar Das, Clark refers to the closing of the frontier, noting the resulting limits on the freedom of the individual American, now dependent on the large corporation for his livelihood. Along with many Asians and Africans, he is a socialist by conviction, and he criticizes the American belief in the virtue of private enterprise, the success of which has depended, in his view, on government action. The familiar theme of the contradictions in the American federal system is also briefly asserted.

Nobody denies that the early American founders and pioneers . . . did in spite of their rapacious tendencies have a creed to live and fight by. Thus one of them, John Quincy Adams, could proudly say: "Revolution took place in the minds of the people in the fifteen years before Lexington."

An unshakable belief in the personal ownership of property and the right to protect it with all the means possible as never enjoyed by his fathers and brothers back in Europe lay behind it all. "I was drying my saddlebags," says the gentleman in Pound's *Cantos,* "and four yeomen in the bar room were talking politics: 'If,' says one, 'they can take Mr. Hancock's wharf and Mr. Rowe's wharf, they can take my house and your barn.'" So he was ready to take up gun at once not only in the unequal fight with the original owners of the land he was tilling by the labor of another, but also as soon as Congress cried out against tax prerogatives of an imperial master overseas.

And if things got too hot and uncomfortable in Boston with the whole town hunting him down as a witch or disciple of the devil, the old, intrepid American tiller could always sell up his farm or brewery, hitch the family fortune to a wagon, and with the Bible and a two-barreled gun in hand, set out further afield to carve a new place for himself in the sun and virgin country still unexplored and open to the claim and title-deed of first-come, first-served. There was always the chance of moving out to try again one's luck and pluck if the initial strike and hope that brought in the first instance the settler out of oppressive Europe happened to prove vain. Today, however, the frontier has vanished forever from the reach of descendants of men and women who trudged miles into hostile forests and deserts leading nobody knew where. "Oh, you exaggerate!" said the political professor. "Surely an American still enjoys today a degree of mobility and choice obtainable nowhere else in the world." Yes, if an American packs his job up in one state or city, the chances of a break for him in another may still show reasonably even. But that is not saying his trail will parallel that walked by his forebears. The very fact that he would be looking up to another for employment belies the comparison. The pioneer before him was his own master with God himself as confidante. The automobile may be a wonderful improvement upon the wagon, and the fact that one can always stop a few nights today in motels, however synthetic their hospitality, is a prospect less dangerous than walking into the righteous ambush of red Indians. But arrival at last would be at a stereotyped industrial center into whose inevitable whirl and pull the presentday adventurer soon gets sucked, and if he is not fast and firm with his grip, a clean sweep-out into the vast cess-pit of more than 6 million unemployed and bums may well be the wages, for all his independent striking out. In the cold light of this vision of a horizon really already lost, President Kennedy's slogan of New Frontiers opening out to Americans suddenly falls into proper perspective.

. . .

At Edison, a real industrial hub off New Brunswick [New Jersey], I had been put on the carpet . . . by a group of big industrialists and businessmen gathered there for the opening of a new factory making new types of electric-lamp shades that diffuse light evenly about a room. . . .

FROM "The American Dream," *America, Their America* (London: Deutsch, 1964), pp. 123–31. Reprinted by permission.

"You come from Nigeria?" They all swamped me, making me look very big indeed.

"Yes," I said, turning to as many of them as I could take in at once. "And when are you going to market your wares there?"

"Not immediately," said the managing director of the new plant. "Our plans don't extend even to Europe yet."

"Tell me," some big shot cut in. "Why do all you new African states go for state ownership of business?"

"Oh, not really," I said.

"Of course so," another cut me short. "I happen to know in Nigeria the railways, ports, power, mines, and even broadcasting are run by government. And isn't that the pattern all over Africa and Asia today?"

"Don't you think those industries you have mentioned are too vital to leave in private hands?"

"A real Communist fellow," someone muttered at the outskirt of the crowd about me.

"One thing you don't know—" I began.

"And what's that?" an impatient director snatched at my tongue.

"Well," I said, "those state industries you speak of were really opened by the British."

"Oh, the British!" Several there stamped their feet. "Why couldn't they let the citizens themselves develop their own resources?"

"What of capital?—"

"And of the know-how?"

"No those fellows just love fouling up things so the Communists can make a quick takeover."

There was much more musing among those men of money assembled there that day to prospect for profits, none of which they were prepared to risk on the African market.

"I know your politicians are corrupt fellows," one patted me on the back, "but tell your President—you are a journalist, aren't you?—Well, tell him industry is safest and best in private hands. See us here in the U.S.? That's what we have gone for all our lives, and today we'd do it all over again."

I thought of the U.S. Postal Services run by the government and I could not agree less with the man. Letters are delivered only once a day, and unlike Her Majesty's mail that must go on, any local holiday is enough to hold up progress of the U.S. Mail. At that moment too, two lines of Pound came into my mind:

> and the fleet that went out to Salamis
> was built by state loan to the builders

but I thought better of it and kept them to myself.

The old credo of the right to private property and of the inherent ability and right of man to exploit an existing opportunity for wealth sounds as good as ever in the American ear. It little matters that with the collapse of the frontier the chief articles in the creed have also lost all their foundations. The Vanderbilts and Stanfords have built for themselves and their heirs all the transcontinental railways for which Congress in Washington, D.C., granted them sole rights as well as all resources above and beneath the ground ten miles on either side, thus spelling the ruin and rise of many a city and state in the Union. Similarly, and side by side, if in cutthroat competition, the Rockefellers and Andrew Carnegies have tapped all the vast wells and mines even though thousands found in them their common grave. And so did the J. P. Morgans unto their heirs forever

> Robbing the public for private
> individual's gain . . .

with their worldwide chain of discount banks binding government and individuals alike fast about their feet. In such circumstances what equal opportunity to wealth and power is there left for the present generation American to exploit in the true spirit of his fathers when all the corporations, accounting for a preponderant proportion of the nation's resources, are long since safe and sound in the hands of a few families and females estimated to be no more than a mere 6 percent of the entire people? But this again is a futile query to throw at any American.

Once on a trip from Ford's Mahwah assembly complex, the largest in the whole world, situated at where New York State stands shoulder to shoulder with the State of New Jersey, I recall asking [my guide] about the ownership of America's giant corporations like General Motors. "Why, we Americans," he said promptly, and with obvious pride added for the peace of my mind: "My wife and I own a number of shares of General Motors. And so do thousands of Americans." Now to be fair to the . . . man, I remain quite ignorant of how large his holdings are with the Chevrolet people. But it is not unusual to meet a proud American investor who, because of the ten or so shares he has bought in a huge corporation, claims equal ownership of it with a Ford and the true heirs of a Du Pont. So accommodating is the heaven of property and free private enterprise, everybody within enjoys absolute happiness even though one capacity may be no bigger than a jug's and another as large as the Atlantic.

Against such a backdrop it becomes doubly fascinating to overhear the debates now going on, in the hollow halls on Capitol Hill, over new vistas of wealth like aeronautics and satellite communication. Who is to own them? Is an industry valued at billions of dollars and developed with taxpayers' money to be signed away by government to a private monopoly group? It had been done before, when General Ulysses Grant of Civil War fame granted perpetual concessions to the Robber Barons who exploited their mines and railways at public expense and with public bonds. And in this present day and age the same principle has been in full operation since and during the war, with the granting of sole manufacturing rights of nuclear and other heavy military equipment to a closed cartel. This is free private enterprise, indeed not unworthy of that saying by Christ that unto them that have more shall be given, and from them that have not even the little they have shall be taken away and added to them that multiply their talents abundantly.

It would be interesting to watch how the advocates of state ownership fare further in the debate, especially now that one of their most outspoken men, Senator Estes Kefauver, has fallen, mortally wounded in action, so to speak. And if the Kennedy Administration, as in many other issues, refused to show its claws, it may well be on account of the simple fact that a strong central government is a red rag to the champion American bull who will charge and pull out all such administrative claws, at any sign of their showing. That surely was

the cause of racialist state governors like Ross Barnett and Wallace, of Missis-·
sippi and Alabama. But federal troops moved in all the same as a worthy
band of matadors, and probably the whole world outside South Africa was
their *aficionado!* But resistance to government advance is certain and unbend-
ing on other fronts more vital to the American, if less celebrated. I quite
remember once an advertisement carried in a national newsmagazine. The
message? Rally round the banner of private enterprise, it exhorted all true
Americans. The federal government has made inroads into the power supply
business other than with its damned Tennessee Valley project. If you don't
take a stand now and dislodge all those socialist agents, you sure will lose the
entire field!

Now, the fun in this hue and cry was that more than 80 percent of the
power supplied in the United States has always been in the control of private
hands. It is also significant that it was in this very industry that some of the
most notorious antitrust prosecutions have been made in the United States.
Top-ranking executives in the nation's largest electrical houses were probably
at that time still serving sentence in Philadelphia for fixing equipment prices,
sharing out the market among themselves, and keeping out all others from
contract awards in a tight monopoly vise. As a result and part of this free
enterprise frenzy and craze, the American housewife has had to pay for her
electrical services (which goodness knows she needs in the factory of her
kitchen) at a rate that has risen by more than 60 percent since the war as
against an increase in other consumer fields ten times less than that.

But as De Tocqueville well stated in his testimonial, America is one vast
house of chance and contradiction, with a structure unwieldy beyond understanding. And truly as that French noble predicted, the house so divided
deeply against itself was, a few years after, one vast hall of death. Of course,
the slaughter of brother by brother exhausted itself in five years, but the outcome proved so delirious that the victors abandoned the stand for the defeated
who went further and dug themselves in deeper than before. Since then,
although the terrible mess was all cleared up, ghosts have haunted its gilded
halls and walks. And to this day, as family members from Massachusetts
engage themselves in a running row with others from Mississippi over the
natural rights guaranteed the individual, black or white, by the American
Constitution, birthrights which the school song innocently proclaims are
enjoyed from the city of New York to Birmingham, the visitor from abroad,
not won over by the conducted tour and the lavish board, may well wonder
how long this union of several disparate, self-repellent elements can last. But
then many a marriage has survived on some rock of convenience undiscovered
to the gossip columnist!

. . .

THE AMERICAN ECONOMY
AND LATIN AMERICA

Eduardo Frei

In September, 1964, Eduardo Frei won the Presidency of Chile on the Christian Democratic ticket by the largest plurality in Chilean history. This selection was published in 1956 while he was a member of the Chilean Senate. Here, Frei pays tribute to the great advances in the American domestic economy, the high wages for the worker, and its success in maintaining farm price levels. However, he criticizes the inequities of economic development between the United States and Latin America, attributing these imbalances to "the structure of international commerce." Frei is referring to the long-run decline in the price paid for raw materials, on which the developing countries depend for foreign exchange, as contrasted with the increase in the price of manufactured goods produced in the highly developed countries—a problem that has received increasing attention in recent years. Frei calls on the United States to make an effort (not unlike the later Alliance for Progress) to improve living standards in Latin America and argues that economic advances in Latin America will benefit the United States economy as well.

The United States definitely has succeeded in creating a life for its people of which it can be proud—the American way of life. Keeping in mind the relativity of human accomplishments, it can be said that the [American] people live in a real democracy where the material conditions have been created for their happiness. There is a characteristic peace and security in action in the very life of every man and woman, and, what is especially indicative, of every American child as well.

Americans believe in their way of life and hope that the world will consider it a good approach to problems, but they cannot live in a continent in which half the population hates and opposes them. This will be the inevitable result if the differences become more pronounced and Latin America is regarded as only a good source of business, raw materials, and profits. The strength of the American position will come from the extension of its living standard to the whole continent so that one can speak of democracy in Latin America and not of a struggle between Latin America and the United States. Otherwise it will appear that the American way of life depends solely on the structure of international commerce and cannot be shared.

The American people can be of decisive assistance in arriving at this objective. The problem is that they do not wish to be. The United States has given its people a high living standard, but in foreign policy it must avoid committing the same errors as other nations that have occupied a dominant position in international relations. Having arrived prematurely at world responsibility, the Americans see themselves pressured by events and losing

FROM "America tiene un destino," *La verdad tiene su hora* (Santiago: Editorial del Pacifico, 1956), pp. 141–46. Translated by the editor with permission.

their freedom of action. Like Janus they have two faces, one turned inward and the other directed at those outside, particularly at Latin America.

The American people are nationalistic, but they have shown little inclination to imperialism in the situation in which they find themselves. We should reflect on what would be the lot of South America if the United States were a nation of 150 million Frenchmen or Germans or Englishmen or Japanese or Russians. It is not daring for me to say that we would be in much greater difficulties. No doubt the United States exerts a pressure in proportion to its size, riches, and power, and there is no question that its economic enterprises seek profit; this is perfectly logical from a business point of view. Yet the people as a whole are not imperialistic. Rather, their basic tendency, which has been reflected in blind isolationism, has been to withdraw from foreign affairs and to interest themselves in their own domestic concerns in the search for a satisfying way of life. Only the dramatic power struggle that they have undertaken has turned them away from this course, and this has not been without unexpected resistance.

Hence, despite what is said by those who make a profession of hatred and who lack integrity, we can develop a constructive policy which can lead to a worthwhile association. Apart from the conflict that would result from any systematic opposition, there is the reality of geography and historical proximity, that is, the facts that answer those who pretend to deny that this is the only possible way. This association implies equal treatment, an increasing equality of opportunity, mutual interest, equal dignity, and, for those who participate, freedom to develop their own institutions within the association.

There is no opposition in theory to this position, which seems logical and unobjectionable. Unfortunately the same thing is not true when it comes to translating it into a practical and coherent policy. Because we two Americas are not equal, the inequalities tend to become more pronounced with [Latin-America's] relative position one of greater dependence due to the very structure of international commerce and the [comparative] economic development of North and South America. The result is that we must be aware of the inherent obstacles to this great cause, which will be all the greater if our relations are left to investors whose natural concern is only with profit.

Nevertheless, these obstacles can be overcome because the establishment of a true economic complementarity would generally constitute a greater source of wealth and security. It remains to discover the effects of such a large market with the high productivity that would come from equal living standards. An economic system that has given such possibilities of expansion to forty-eight states would be extended to the whole continent.

. . .

In the last few years two peaceful revolutions of the utmost importance have taken place in the United States. The first is that the American worker has reached a high standard of living based on real wages with great purchasing power. American capitalism has been convinced that, far from undermining its efficiency, this [growth] has permitted an enormous development as a result of the increased capacity for consumption. It has produced an evolution in the structure of American capitalism which makes it different from the form that it had in the past century.

. . .

For the American, the word "capitalism" describes a system which scarcely resembles that of the era of the great captains of industry, of the monopolies, and of the westward movement. Present-day American capitalism is a system in which the forces of that earlier age still operate, but they are balanced by new forces that have substantially modified it, such as the tax and antitrust laws and, especially, the power of the labor unions.

. . .

The second revolution, perhaps unique in history, is that the farmer has obtained a high price level for his products and, as a result, a living standard that is as high as that of the industrial worker. This is worth noting since usually in the past, progress in the social condition of the urban industrial masses was made at the expense of those in the rural areas.

. . .

The third step in this revolution should be the realization by Americans that a Latin America with an increased power to consume, a high level of production, and improved social conditions is a necessary premise for the development of the American economy, for understanding and cooperation between the two hemispheres, and for its own strength and continued existence.

5

American Foreign Policy

THE FOREIGN POLICY OF DULLES
Gaganvihari L. Mehta

As the following selection indicates, India is friendly toward the United States but critical from a nonaligned position. A dominant theme in the criticisms of United States foreign policy by spokesmen for Asia, Africa, and Latin America has been its excessive reliance on military pacts for security. In a sympathetic but critical article on the foreign policy of John Foster Dulles, Gaganvihari L. Mehta, Indian ambassador to the United States when Dulles was Secretary of State, analyzes the development of this policy under Dulles' auspices. Like many Indian observers, Mehta objects to Dulles' moralistic black-and-white view of East-West relations, but on the other hand he is critical of India's naive policy of exclusive reliance on peaceful coexistence and its reluctance to build up its military strength. (The article was written at the time of the Chinese invasion of India in 1962.)

. . .

What were the determinant motives and objectives of Dulles' foreign policy? He was firmly convinced that Communist ideology, as preached and practiced by Soviet Russia and China, menaced not merely American interests and its "way of life" but also the freedom and independence of men everywhere. He would have reconciled himself to coexistence with a "national Communist" regime such as that of Yugoslavia, which he visited and courted despite its atheism. But the Kremlin and the Cominform (or the Comintern) had the same ultimate objectives—the domination of the world by Communism, whether by conquest, subversion, or infiltration. The tactics might change but the goal never. Indeed, so firmly rooted was his antipathy that he thought it preferable for the Western powers not to arrive at a long-term agreement with the Soviet Union until under unremitting pressure—political, economic,

FROM *The India Quarterly,* Vol. 19, No. 1 (January–March, 1963), pp. 4–20. Reprinted by permission.

and moral—the Soviet leaders revised their policies. "Under the pressure of faith and hope and peaceful works," he wrote in 1950, "the rigid, top-heavy, overextended structure of Communist rule could readily collapse." So distrustful was he that when Moscow smiled instead of frowning, in referring to summit meetings he said that "The cement of Western unity disintegrates when there is less fear." In other words, the isolationist and intractable Stalin would be preferable to the extrovert and flexible Khrushchev, if only to keep the West united and in trim.

This "grand alliance" was to be maintained, in Dulles' view, by a system of collective security. America had traveled far from the edict of George Washington against "entangling alliances" with other nations and the implications of the Monroe Doctrine about nonintervention in European affairs in return for European nations not interfering in the affairs of the American continent. Instead of the isolationism favored until the commencement of World War II, the United States made defense commitments to forty-two countries in both the hemispheres and had bases in thirty-five countries. For Dulles believed that the United States could keep out of war only by preventing war breaking out, which had to be done by building up adequate collective strength as well as by making explicit along with the Allies that open aggression would be resisted by force. It was widely believed in the United States that Dean Acheson's statement about placing Korea outside the defense perimeter of the United States had emboldened Stalin and Mao to conclude that Korea could be attacked with impunity. Dulles shared this view and was determined to avert war by miscalculation of the intentions of Western countries by Communist rulers. Some issues, in this view, were negotiable and might be negotiated but fundamentals were not, for which even the risk of a war might have to be taken. And these fundamentals must be clear to avoid misunderstanding. It is, no doubt, a matter of judgment as to which issues are basic and which subsidiary.

.   .   .

Granting the ultimate Communist objectives and the single-minded strategy of Soviet Russia, it still remains true that Dulles' approach was too narrow and rigid, tactically and psychologically. Indeed, as Mr. Edward Crankshaw has recently pointed out, the face of Communism is changing, and Soviet Russia is no longer purely Communist nor entirely totalitarian but is evolving new patterns and systems of which the West has yet to take a proper measure. Mr. Khrushchev may want to keep alive tensions but he does not want war which would destroy the remarkable achievements in education, technology, and social equality of the Soviets. If he wants domination without victory, a military posture to oppose him may be and, indeed, has been overdone. It is not enough for the West to improve its military posture to meet the multiple challenge presented by the Soviet Union to the international status quo. Informed persons—statesmen, diplomats, authorities in international affairs—who were as antipathetic to Communist ideology and Soviet aims as Dulles, believed that the Western countries would gain rather than lose by endeavoring to achieve a détente or a modus vivendi between the two sides; and that relaxation of tensions would strengthen and hasten the forces of democratization within Soviet Russia and liberalization of mutual relations within the Communist bloc. When Mr. Khrushchev launched an ambitious and long-range program of economic and technical aid to underdeveloped countries and established friendly relations with the leaders of independent countries, the construction of military bases and forging of alliances by the U.S.A. with reactionary and corrupt regimes was no adequate answer. This is not to deny that firm action by the United States in Europe and on one or two occasions in Asia has frustrated the aim of overrunning Berlin and Southeast Asia. Nor is it a plea for total unilateral disarmament. But it should be recognized that if there is a time to stand up to the Russians, there is also need to sit down with them. Impatience is seldom a virtue in international affairs, and rigid minds go ill with world responsibilities. Dulles, who was an accomplished diplomat, frequently forgot Talleyrand's wise dictum, "Above all, not too much zeal." If the Communist faith that it is the mission of Soviet Russia and China to rid the world of capitalism is wrong, the belief of many (although by no means all) Americans that the United States has a mission to rid the world of Communism is no more right. Dulles looked upon the conflict between the Communist and the "free world" as an eternal struggle between the forces of Good and Evil, between the gods and the satanic elements. There were no intermediate shades between white and black. Yet it is undeniable that this conflict is due to the power rivalries of the two blocs and not merely to pure ideology. The "free world" has contained such horrible dark spots as Algeria until recently, and even now there are Angola and South Africa and Rhodesia. If it is a question of dictatorship versus democracy, there are Spain and Portugal and the dictators in Latin America and West Asia* as members of this "free world." The fact is that the Western countries are opposed not to dictatorship as such but dictatorships which they believe—and with justification—threaten their interests, values, and very existence. But Dulles gave the impression of being "a wearisome moralist" in defending and interpreting his policy. Labourchère said that Gladstone, like other politicians, had a card up his sleeve, but unlike other politicians he believed that the Lord had put it there. Dulles' self-righteousness was on many occasions not very different. This quality of unctuousness created not merely in many uncommitted countries but even in Europe the image of an unduly intransigent and bellicose America which was impervious to the deep yearnings for peace among the peoples of the world and which accentuated and prolonged the cold war instead of helping the relaxation of tensions. This was in many respects an unfair and misleading picture, but it was due in no small measure to Dulles' exposition of his policy, his habit of oversimplifying issues, and the high ingredient of bombast in his speeches and pronouncements. No doubt he tried subsequently to clarify and amplify his statements as by stating that he had not threatened "massive retaliation" but had only said that "we must have the capacity for massive retaliation," or that it was not the United States but Russia which had dragged the West to war so that he was "forced to the abyss." But like most politicians and diplomats, he became the prisoner of his own slogans while some of the crises were of his own making. And the effect of all this on a Europe—which was war-weary (no doubt, initially through its own internecine conflicts)—and on Asia and Africa—which were frightened of being the helpless victims of a nuclear holocaust—[was] singularly unfortunate. Not only in Britain but on the continent of Europe, a growing volume

* West Asia is the Indian term for the Middle East.—Editor.

of opinion favored disengagement and even nonalignment in the titanic struggle in which the two nuclear giants were locked.

. . .

The sphere in which Dulles' overemphasis on the military aspect of resistance to Communist powers was least successful was the Far East and West Asia. Like several foreign ministers of Western countries, his outlook was predominantly European. He did not have adequate appreciation of the many forces at work among the emergent nations, and he lacked an imaginative insight into the psychology of the peoples of Asia and Africa. He was thus prone to apply rigid black-and-white standards so that frequently to be anti-Western was regarded by him as being pro-Communist.

In regard to the Peking regime, Dulles, like most Americans, was intensely emotional. He looked upon China's turning Communist as almost a breach of faith with the United States. This is not to deny that of all the Western powers the United States was the most disinterested in its relations with China in the past nor the massive help it had rendered China in the war with Japan. Nor, indeed, should it be forgotten that it was the Peking government which first broke the ties with the United States by asking it to close down its embassy and inprisoning American nationals. But while American refusal to recognize Peking is understandable, its resistance to admission of China in the United Nations was hardly justified. This question is not free from difficulties, especially because of an émigré government in Formosa and the threat of Chinese expansionism, the grim reality of which gave a rude shock to us in India after years of "wishful thinking" and complacency. Yet I cannot help feeling that the nonadmission of China in the United Nations has probably made China's rulers more irresponsible and intransigent and has maintained an illusion of Formosa as a world power with a permanent seat in the Security Council. I should, however, add that to the best of my knowledge, the U.S. Government *might* have modified its policy in this respect but for the Chinese intervention in the Korean War.

. . .

Dulles' policy in West Asia was no more fruitful. He borrowed the concept of a "northern tier" from the British Foreign Office and endeavored to encourage the forging of a military alliance on the periphery of Soviet Russia without, however, the United States joining it. This led to the Baghdad Pact, which in its original form proved within three years to be perhaps "the most abortive alliance of the century." On the one hand, Dulles did not relish being associated with Britain in the Middle East; on the other, he was anxious to build "a ring of steel" around the Communist world. This ambivalence was considered "devious" by Eden. How in the days of jet planes and nuclear weapons any invulnerable barrier could be constructed that would stem Soviet Russia is incomprehensible. Clearly, Dulles considered the problem in predominantly military terms and was influenced by Pentagon thinking. Pineau, France's Foreign Minister, opposed the Pact and argued that the force to be derived from the Baghdad Pact would be less than the Russian counterforce it would provoke. In July 1958, the Baghdad Pact was blown sky-high by Baghdad itself. Here, as elsewhere, the United States was in a dilemma. Countries outside the Central Treaty Organization (CENTO) accused the

United States of supporting "reactionary" regimes or of "imperialism" to protect its oil and other interests. Members of the alliance, on the other hand, felt aggrieved that the U.S. government's support was only halfhearted, and they continuously demanded more and more money and arms. Mr. Michael Howard has observed [in the *New Statesman*] that if Communism is an alien tyranny irrelevant to the real needs of the peoples, Communist attempts to penetrate popular movements of liberation should not cause the Western countries to play into their hands by attempting to suppress those movements and seeking military gimmicks to prop up crumbling and unpopular governments.

There is one aspect of this problem which deserves mention. Delay in the grant of independence to a country usually throws the national movement in the hands of the extremists who nowadays are either "leftists" or who turn to Soviet Russia for arms and aid. But American apprehension has been that the grant of independence to a country whose peoples are not prepared through levels of education, administration, and minimal unity would throw the country into a state of anarchy which would be exploited by the Communists. This argument has some force as the Congo, among others, has shown. Yet the post-independence history of almost all newly freed countries shows that a national government is more capable of dealing with internal subversion— Communist or otherwise—than alien rule. It is, of course, of little avail for Communists to protest against "undemocratic" regimes when the very first step they take everywhere they capture power is to abolish free elections and parliament, liquidate all opposition, and muzzle the press. Unfortunately, in the highest official circles in our country there has been a tendency to suspend judgment in such cases and to condone such tyranny as "a new system."

So, too, another link in the "ring of steel" was the Southeast Asia Treaty Organization (SEATO), which was not of much avail in countering Communist infiltration into South Vietnam or in Laos. SEATO, like any other military alliance, could only provide protection against external, open aggression, not against subversion or infiltration. Here again, the manner in which Dulles brought about the agreement seemed devious and was resented by Eden. To deal with domestic problems and internal forces, some kind of constitutional authority and responsible government are necessary and economic welfare has to be ensured; this cannot be done by arms and planes. In this respect, American military aid to Pakistan should serve as a warning rather than as an example. This aid, in my view, was the worst mistake the Eisenhower Administration made in its relations with India. It did not stabilize Pakistan politically nor did it make a more loyal ally of the West—as evinced by its continued threats amounting to blackmail in relation to Kashmir, its protests against the U.S. economic aid to India, and its flirtations with China. It [U.S. aid to Pakistan] undermined good will in India and helped to strengthen Communist as well as Hindu communalist forces. And, above all, it started a futile and costly arms race between two neighboring countries. . . . Dulles and his colleagues knew that they were antagonizing Indian opinion, but they wanted to take a calculated risk since the U.S. wanted some vital bases in this region and Prime Minister Nehru had repeatedly declared that India would remain neutral in case of a world war.

In regard to SEATO, Dulles [told me] . . . that it had not been sufficiently noted that the United States had promised aid only in case of Communist aggression; in other words, the United States did not want to get involved in internecine quarrels in the region. If Pakistan, for instance, attacked India, the United States was not bound to assist it. It may be argued that the dividing line in such an eventuality might become rather thin. If, for instance, Cambodia gets embroiled with Thailand and American opinion is persuaded that Cambodia is acting under Communist instigation or is under Communist domination, the United States would have to go to Thailand's assistance. Nevertheless, the qualifying condition is important and should not be lost sight of in criticizing the SEATO or the CENTO.

Dulles was of the view that Western powers must free themselves from the stigma of colonial rule to win the confidence of Asian peoples. Such repudiation of nineteenth-century colonialism was embodied in what was rather pompously called the "Pacific Charter," jointly enunciated by some Western powers and a few Asian countries. At the same time, in Dulles' view, free Asian nations could be helped if they were prepared to help themselves, and a widening system of collective security was the only foundation on which their continued independence could be ensured.

.   .   .

In the summer of 1954, when Dulles appeared before the Senate Foreign Relations Committee, he was asked why aid should be given to India when the Indian government nearly always supported the Soviet view, and the leader of the Indian delegation at the General Assembly of the United Nations never missed an opportunity of opposing American and Western policies and assisting the Soviet Union to undermine them, Dulles replied that "Freedom involved and accepted diversity." He said that because India and the United States were free countries, they could differ on international issues and yet cooperate for common purposes. India, a sovereign democratic country, was seeking to raise the standards of living of its masses through a democratic program of planning and should be assisted. In the last conversation I had with him before I left Washington in May, 1958, Dulles told me in reply to my query that the U.S. Government, having agreed to give aid ($225 million in February of that year), would be "foolish" if it did not continue to do so, since development was a long-term process. One could not have asked for a clearer indication of American interest and commitment for the future.

.   .   .

It is a stale cliché that judgment on the policies and work of a statesman may be left to the verdict of history. . . . We are yet deeply involved in the great struggle which will decide not only how we shall live in future but whether we shall live at all. Not all the facts are known, not all the different knots untied, not all the deeper issues sufficiently clear, not all the personal equations solved. We should seek to understand, as Mr. George Kennan has said, "the way in which diplomacy really works—the marvelous manner in which purpose, personality, coincidence, communication, and the endless enormous complexity of the modern world all combine to form a process beyond the full vision or comprehension of any single personality." I have, therefore, endeavored here to present a picture, inadequate as it may be, of one of the leading personalities who represented his powerful country in world affairs at a crucial period.

NEOCOLONIALISM IN AFRICA

Kwame Nkrumah

This selection by another neutralist, Kwame Nkrumah, former President of Ghana, reveals a much less favorable attitude than that of the preceding article. Nkrumah sees the United States as attempting to expand its influence in Africa for "financial, industrial, and military considerations," and he calls upon Africans to unite in order to resist the efforts of American and NATO neocolonialism. While Nkrumah's views represent the radical left in African politics and although his own personal bid for leadership in the unity movement has been rejected, his fears about American interference in African affairs are shared by other Africans, as was shown by the United Nations debate on the Belgian-American intervention in the Congo in November, 1964.

The pattern of imperialist aid to Africa is set not only to draw the unwary back into the neocolonialist relationship but to tie them into cold-war politics. This has been amply explained by Walt Whitman Rostow, counselor and chairman of the Policy Planning Council of the U.S. State Department, in an interview given to the weekly journal *U.S. News and World Report* [May 7, 1962]. Asked what America is doing about the underdeveloped areas, Mr. Rostow refers to the "gradual creation of a pattern to succeed the colonial period. We helped pioneer this pattern in our relationship with the Philippines." After commenting upon the new relationships established with their former colonies by Britain, France, and Belgium who "is making an important continuing contribution to the Congo," he states that: "As the residual problems are solved we look, as I say, to a new partnership based on the common interests of the northern and southern parts of the free world." This, Mr. Rostow admits, is a long-term process. "In playing the game in the underdeveloped areas you must be prepared to play for a long time," and hence, in some of the underdeveloped countries, "as in most of Africa, we have to start from a very low level—*with specific projects, not national plans of a sophisticated kind.*"* For, says Mr. Rostow, using the examples of Italy and Greece in the Marshall Plan period, "we were buying time to protect crucial pieces of real estate—and the possibility of human freedom for those who lived there. And in the end we sweated it out and won. . . . Buying time is one of the most expensive and thankless things we do with our money—as in South Korea."

This is perhaps one of the most cynical but clear-cut summings up that has ever appeared in print of the approach of a rich power to the needs and hopes of the new nations of the world. There is no need to underscore the intention it so blatantly exposes in "playing the game" of "buying time." It should be an object lesson for all those African statesmen who think that associations

---

FROM *Africa Must Unite* (New York: Praeger, 1963), pp. 183–84, 191–92. Reprinted by permission.
* Italics added by K. N.—Editor.

with non-African powers will foster their true interests and give them the opportunity to prosper their nations within continuing independence of action.

.   .   .

We cannot afford either to ignore the sinister chain of interests which unites events in the Congo and Angola to East and South Africa. These interests are also connected with the East-West battle for world supremacy and the frenzied efforts being made to drag the newly emerging countries of Africa into the orbit of the cold war. The contest for ideological influence over the new states of Africa is throwing into confusion and complicating even more what is already a complex enough struggle for freedom from imperialist political and economic dominance and the unification of the continent. Any difference, any kind of fissure among Africans is seized and turned to the imperialist and cold-war interests. The Congo offers perhaps the most striking example of how tribal dissensions and political careerism are exploited in order to fragment united territories and exacerbate divisions. The aim of the marionette control of local careerists like Moise Tshombe, besides the maintenance of economic power, is to cut across the African determination to secure continental unity in full independence. It was unfortunate that the United Nations was maneuvered into a position where at one time it appeared to be weighing its influence against the legitimate Congolese government on the side of those who were responsible for throwing the country into upheaval and for the murder of Patrice Lumumba.

We must be forgiven, I think, if we also see some connection between events in the Congo and Angola and NATO. The dominating powers joined in this organization—Britain, France, the United States—are all influenced by financial, industrial, and military considerations in maintaining in Africa regimes that will support their interests. The means used for doing so are, if the evidence is to be believed, dubious in the extreme. It would be difficult to convince most people of what can only be described as the criminal intent behind certain actions that are employed to upset the stability of states trying to sustain their national unity and integrity against subversive forces.

.   .   .

As we examine the multifarious dangers to which the new states and the freedom fighters of Africa are exposed, the more it becomes certain that our best, indeed our one, protection is in unity. For it is that very unity which all the imperialist designs and actions are intended to prevent. It should, therefore, be glaringly obvious that these designs can only be circumvented by achieving the end they are planned to frustrate.

.   .   .

THE FREE WORLD'S OTHER FACE

Ronald Segal

Lest we forget that despite the emergence of many independent African states, there are still colonial areas that have no prospect of freedom and Africans who are subject to white domination, Ronald Segal, an exiled South African editor and publisher, reminds us that United States support for Portugal, its NATO ally, and for South Africa, a major American investment market, in effect condones the violation of the rights of Africans by the South African and Portuguese governments. He calls on the United States to take more vigorous action on behalf of the ideals of equality and national independence which inspired the American Revolution, the first revolt against colonialism.

There is little doubt that the United States has discovered Africa. During a lecture tour of the States that I staggered through at the end of 1958, I found everywhere an interest and even an excitement, always a recognition that the African tomorrow must be America's as well, that what happens in Accra and Lagos will inevitably reverberate in Boston and Montgomery. Yet it seemed to me then—as it seems to me still—an ignorant and easy recognition, requiring a minimum of effort and intervention. With few exceptions, those I spoke to at the time and those whose statements and articles I have read since appear aware of only the more superficial of the issues. Their interest is opulently in uncomplicated Africa, in the black states which have achieved— or are very soon likely to achieve—their independence. The overall American recognition seems a distant benevolence, the good wishes of a family friend at the christening of independence.

It is a comfortable limitation this; it so obviously makes friends without having to make any enemies. Black Africa can only be grateful for the enthusiasm with which its triumphs are greeted and look forward to the presents in their brightly colored wrappings which belong to such ceremonies. But stretching over vast areas of the continent suffers multiracial Africa, the territories dominated by white settler minorities. For the black inhabitants of these areas, self-determination appears only as the accomplishment of struggle, desolate and interminable, to be pursued in anguish and neglect. And to these peoples, the United States pays only the sporadic attention of discomfort. There is nothing here to be easy about; benevolence has to be officious, and one cannot make friends without making strenuous enemies at home as well as abroad.

There can be few subject peoples as sunk in degradation and despair as those of Angola and Mozambique, the Africans existing forgotten under Portuguese rule. For them, no independence has been promised; and the United States will have to wait long to make friends and influence people if she looks to the independence celebrations as the occasion for her benevo-

FROM James Duffy and Robert A. Manners, eds., *Africa Speaks,* pp. 204–06, 221–23. Copyright 1961, D. Van Nostrand Company, Inc., Princeton, N.J. Reprinted by permission.

lence. Yet she cannot intervene before [then] without antagonizing Salazar; and Portugal under Salazar is one of the string of fortresses with which the free world proposes to defend itself from attack. The dilemma is absolute: if the United States is to make her presence felt in Africa, she is going to have to collide with some of her staunchest strategic allies; if she persists in sacrificing the doctrine of self-government to power politics, she is going to breed a bitterness against the West in Africa that will poison the peace of the world for decades to come. Fundamentally, of course, her choice is not between Africa and Europe; it is between the two sides of herself. As the United States will help to decide the future of Africa, so inevitably in the process she will be deciding her own.

It is in South Africa that the dilemma is at its crudest and its most cruel. Almost daily, Americans arrive in the Union [of South Africa] to open new branches of banks and investment houses or establish new suburbs of American industry. Direct American investment in the Union outstrips her total investment in the rest of the continent and must amount, with the disguised funds flowing through the London Stock Exchange, to little less than a billion dollars already. The official figure for direct investment is £250 million ($700 million). The South African government is appreciatively polite to foreign capital, covering every puddle with its cloak. And, as everyone knows, South Africa not only produces most of the West's gold supply and a substantial slice of its uranium, as well as nearly all its diamonds, but its administration is anti-Communist to the point of derangement. Here in truth is a Gibraltar of the West. Yet on this rock 3 million whites dominate some 10 million Africans, over 1 million Coloreds, and just under 500,000 Asiatics; and the dominion is not only absolute, it is malevolent. Stripped of all franchise rights and all but a mockery of civil liberties, the Africans are hounded by "pass" laws into silent serfdom on the white-owned farms or slow starvation in the suffocated Reserves. The 2.5 million in the towns and cities are kept a rightless proletariat, without security of residence or employment. . . .

Connivance would be less uncomfortable if such people were only sullenly still, helpless before the baton-swinging intransigence of their oppressors and sinking ever deeper into the apathy of despair. Yet of all the peoples of the continent, among the most vital and vigorous are the 10 million dispossessed Africans of the Union, striking out more strongly with each blow they receive.

· · ·

The *Wall Street Journal* may remark upon South Africa's attraction for foreign investment, and visiting bankers, their ears filled with the clamor of government apologists, may continue to decry the prejudiced press that South Africa gets overseas, but the country is already waist-deep in revolution and the coming years are big with the retribution of three centuries of race insanity. The Congress Movement* will continue to organize the mass of the nonwhites for defiance of the law and industrial action, laying the only possible foundations of discipline and direction on which the coming South Africa must rest. But violence too will continue, and it will grow, following the pattern of Cyprus and Algeria, condemned by the responsibility of the

---

* Segal is referring to the African National Congress, an organization of Africans and Coloreds (those of mixed blood) who oppose the government policy of *apartheid.*— Editor.

Congress leadership and fed by the fury of the Congress rank and file, till South Africa hangs from the thinnest ledge or falls with a scream into chaos.

.   .   .

Yet all this is not finally unavoidable. One cannot expect the outside world to intervene directly, to overthrow the de facto government of the Union, and force the whole society back to sanity at the point of a gun. But what the United Nations Organization can legitimately do is to serve notice upon the Nationalist government of the Union that wholesale retaliation against the unarmed masses of nonwhite South Africa will not be tolerated by world opinion. The revolution in South Africa must be left free to take its self-disciplined course, and any attempt to drown it in blood will call in the troops of civilization. With the degree of retaliation limited by outside pressure, non-white South Africa will soon enough accomplish its destiny through the dynamics of an industrial society. The United States may not shirk her part in this. The choice is patently before her. She can continue to connive at the "safe" tyranny of apartheid, cashing her dividends and contemplating intercontinental strategy. She risks, after all, no more than numberless lives and the moral disfigurement of Africa for generations to come. Or she can give life again to the ideals which fashioned her beginning, giving to Western culture a meaning that it so often claims and so very seldom deserves. And her reward will be the Africa she will live with and the world of tomorrow she will live in: her reward will be herself.

THE SHARK AND THE SARDINES

Juan José Arévalo

An excerpt has already been given (pp. 217–19) in the American Politics section from *The Shark and the Sardines,* by Juan José Arévalo, the former President of Guatemala. The selection below reproduces the central portion of Arévalo's satirical fable about the attempt to establish legal equality between a shark (the United States) and a sardine (a Latin-American country). In addition to attacking American domination of the Organization of American States, the fable hints at the usefulness of involving the Soviet Union (represented by the swordfish) in Latin-American politics. (See Part IV, p. 320, for an American book review of *The Shark and the Sardines.*) While the view expressed here is representative only of the left wing in Latin-American politics, references are now often made to the problem of "the shark and the sardines" by others who feel that the overwhelming power of the United States in relation to the Latin-American states makes inter-American cooperation difficult.

"I am here as Apostolic Nuncio. I bring you the new word—civilization, legality. I bless you, shark and sardine, in the name of the all-powerful Guardian of the Seas, punisher and avenger, who both builds and destroys, who is both kind and cruel. From this day on you will be little brothers, facing life together, allies in days of adversity and partners in the time of harvest.

"Little sardine, the shark will be your big brother, your protector. You will be the little sister, the protected. . . . Common perils will be overcome by uniting your forces."

(The sardine knit her brows.)

The speech continued: "Common needs will be satisfied by sharing your possessions."

(The shark seemed not to understand or not to have heard, and changed his posture, tilting an ear.)

"You, shark, will place at the disposition of the sardine your energetic capital, your speed, your power, your ferocity, your many teeth, your experience as a pirate, your technique as butcher of the seas. Now, no longer, shark, will the other beasts of the sea or the voracious small fish with an appetite for purée of sardines and anchovy paste bother your little sister. Your obligations to her will guarantee that no other beast except you will be able to come near her. . . ."

. . .

"You and only you, Oh shark, will keep watch around the sandbar where your little sardine-sister, ally today and always, will sleep and rest, free now from danger, free from anxiety, free from uncertainty, in full enjoyment of her sovereignty as an untouchable member of your world, shark—the Free World."

. . .

The sardine, with eyes full of tears, took advantage of the speaker's pause. Approaching him, almost on her knees, she said:

"And I, Oh Prophet, the most humble of the creatures of the sea, how could I return such great favors on the part of the shark whom you present to me as though he were the son of all the gods?"

"My child," the Prophet answered, "do not disparage yourself. Saturn endowed you with all the possibilities for expressing gratitude and has reserved for you a monopoly [in] being a good servant. You must know that there is no such thing as a small friend nor a contemptible favor. Your usefulness lies in your small size.

"For example, you will keep watch around the shark's cave or haunt, and in the neighborhoods he frequents, you will eavesdrop on his friends to determine whether they are or are not really his friends. You will listen to his enemies without their recognizing you. You will take care of the glory and the prestige of the shark as though he were a priest of Neptune, and you will say that he has changed his villainous habits, that his licentious ways have been reformed and replaced by the piety of the monk and the gentleness of the angels.

FROM "The Fable," *The Shark and the Sardines* (New York: Stuart, 1961), pp. 31–38. Reprinted by permission.

"You will proclaim to the four winds his good will, the transparent character of his intentions. You will swear that he is a person of good will and that he is an agent of good idealistic causes. You will learn by memory his Fourteen Points and the Four Freedoms. And you, too, will read the Bible! You will be his spokesman and, in the choice of his friends, you will be choir master. And if by force of habit, the shark should again take to his old ways, your spirit of loyalty will be shown by saying that this is a lie, that it is a slander by his enemies, that it is the echo of their constant envy of him. These are services, sardine, that cannot be rendered by the giants of the sea; these are services that can be lent only by mobile, small sentinels like you."

. . .

"As you see, sardine, destiny reserves for you the glory of serving, of serving well, of serving in all things, of giving ever more and more service to this giant of the sea, one-time criminal, bandit, master delinquent, and model pirate—today converted to the religion of Law. And he will be willing to control you, to help you, to protect you, to have you very near, every day nearer, until one day you become encrusted as an oily granule in his grotesque skin. Nobody but a knave could deny that, from today on, the shark has ceased to be a threat to you. Nobody but a rogue can deny that from today on, the shark, when he looks at you, will be inspired by the noblest of appetites, as befits a convert to oceanity."

. . .

A swordfish of enormous proportions created a disturbance when he drew near, wanting to offer the sardine his professional services against the shark. But when he came within a short distance of the scene, he was told about the legal equality between the sovereign shark and the prisoner sardine.

"Charlatan! Hypocrite! Panderer!" he charged, and went away, snorting, growling and muttering.

. . .

In his own handwriting, the notarizing priest began with the sacramental words:

"The high contracting parties, with full legal capacity, making use of their sovereign will and dispensing with preambles—" The bearded and robed one paused to explain that solemn terms and rhetoric had gone out of fashion in these documents; then he continued "—agree to protect and to mortgage themselves mutually."

Here, in reference to the mortgage, the sardine jumped up, alarmed, because from the laughter among the public she began to understand that everything was not rose-colored.

After mental excuses [to] Neptune the Terrible, she asked the lawyer: "But if the shark does not live up to the pact, who will help me capture him?"

. . .

"If you become very alarmed, we will set up a Pan-Ameroceanic Society of Sardines, with headquarters in the very cave of the shark. A society to which the shark can belong, temporarily impersonating a sardine. This society of prisoner sardines will be your protection and guaranty against the sovereign shark—for a possible eventuality that I presume will never arise."

THE ALLIANCE FOR PROGRESS
IS NOT THE ANSWER

Carlos Fuentes

Carlos Fuentes is a well-known young Mexican novelist. In recent years he has published five novels, the best-known of which are *Where the Air Is Clear* and *The Death of Artemio Cruz.* His views reflect the opinions of pro-Castro leftist students and intellectuals who believe that only a revolution can solve the problems of Latin America. While some who hold this belief are Communists, others cite the Mexican Revolution of 1910 and the Cuban Revolution of 1959 (before the United States, in their view, forced Castro into the Soviet bloc) as authentic Latin-American revolutions that have tried to deal with the problems of agrarian reform, economic development, and national control of minerals and other wealth. These problems, they argue, cannot be solved by evolutionary means such as those envisaged by the Alliance for Progress.

. . . The key question is this: How can the causes of underdevelopment in Latin America be chopped away? There is no room for doubt in the answer: stabilization of prices of raw materials in the short run, and economic diversification—industrialization—in the long run. But you want it to be done through peaceful evolution and the Alliance for Progress. And we think: through revolution. Let us examine both solutions.

The only structural reform foreseen in the Alliance for Progress is agrarian reform. Now, please consider that in Latin America the base of political power is the landlords. Do you sincerely believe that a leading class whose roots are in the ownership of land is going to let go of its reason for being? Agrarian feudalism is the basis of the wealth and political dominion of the governing classes in Central America, Chile, Peru, Argentina, Brazil, Venezuela, Colombia, Ecuador. Do you believe these classes are going to commit suicide voluntarily? A Peruvian oligarch recently told me: "If the gringos force us to divide the land, we will answer by expropriating their mining companies." No, my American friends: an agrarian reform in Latin America, as demonstrated by Mexico and Cuba, is only made through revolution, with weapons in hand. This is what the sharecroppers of Peru, the peasants of northeastern Brazil, the pariahs of Chile, Ecuador, and Colombia are beginning to do. They are not allowing themselves to be cheated by "false" agrarian reforms: the distribution of sterile lands, without credit, without machinery, without schools or hospitals. Those governing classes can deceive you, but they are not going to swindle the peasant masses or stifle their revolutionary impetus.

The Alliance is going to be used by governments that do not truly represent their people, by governments representing the old feudal order whose only interest is to keep its privileges. Look where your dollars are going to go: as

---

FROM "The Argument of Latin America," in *Whither Latin America,* by Carlos Fuentes *et al.* (New York: Monthly Review Press, 1963), pp. 13–20, 24. Reprinted by permission.

in South Vietnam, as in South Korea, as in Iran and Spain—to the bank accounts of a handful of people, to the importation of luxurious automobiles, to the construction of apartment houses.

The Alliance does not even mention one of the basic factors of backwardness in Latin America: the economic deformation imposed by foreign domination of our economies. Ah, you jump at this point. You refuse to admit this. You have helped the development (what development?) of Latin America. You unselfishly give us dollars and technical aid.

We have already spoken about the domination of natural resources: iron ore, copper, tin, coal, lead, zinc, oil. These resources, in your hands, enter your economy: they are not employed in the internal development of our countries. The Alliance does not even speak of that. It does not foresee that the iron and oil of Venezuela may contribute to creation of heavy industry there, that the copper of Chile or the lead of Peru may be motors of national industrialization. At any rate, our industrialization must be light, for refining, but nothing more.

You are also proprietors of Latin American foreign trade. Sixty percent of our foreign trade is with you, in accordance with the prices you set. American companies manage 75 percent of our commercial movement. You impose the conditions and the prices. Last year, the Alliance gave $150 million to Colombia; but in that same year, Colombia lost $450 million because of the decrease in coffee prices.

Ask the great cotton concerns how much they pay for a bale of Mexican cotton, at what price they resell it to the English monopoly in Hong Kong, and how much they charge the Communist government of China, which you detest, for it. The Anderson Clayton Company in this operation makes five times the amount that the Mexican grower does. And ask the Department of State why it forbids Mexico to sell its excess oranges to Czechoslovakia in exchange for machinery we need, machinery you either do not sell us or sell us for too high a price; ask the Department why the whole crop went rotten on the docks of Tampico while you traded happily with Communist countries and allowed Adenauer's Germany to be the principal Western market of that very same Czechoslovakia.

Investments? You have invested $10 billion in Latin America. It is a curious thing: we have always received your investments, and we are still poor. You speak about *your* property in Latin America and call us thieves when we expropriate it. But why don't you ask your investors? Ask them how much they invest and how much they take back to the United States in profits. Do you want to know? Between 1950 and 1955, you invested $2 billion, made $3.5 billion, and took back to the States $1.5 billion. In a single year, 1959, you made $775 million, only reinvested $200 million and sent $575 million back to the United States. In the last seven years, Latin America lost, because of these shipments of money, $2,679 million. You take out too much, leave too little, and even this little is distributed unfairly: where is the real benefit for our economies? Is it just that these profits do nothing, not a single thing, to alleviate the horrible misery, ignorance, and illness of the great majority of the Latin Americans who, with their slavery, made them possible? You, as Americans, tell me if that is just.

And tell me also whether you have not recovered more than your investments, whether it is not right that this squandered wealth should be recovered and directed towards improving the lot of everyone, because it was created by the work of everyone though today it benefits only a dozen corporations.

Finally, in its year of life, the Alliance for Progress has been accompanied by acts of political aggression that prostitute it completely. These acts are the Cuban invasion in April, 1961, and the violation of the inter-American law in Punta del Este in January, 1962.

PLAYA GIRON AND PUNTA DEL ESTE

American responsibility in the invasion of the Bay of Pigs is not debatable: President Kennedy assumed it completely, with full knowledge that in this way he was violating not only inter-American treaties but the internal laws of the United States itself: the Neutrality Act and the U.S. Code. You pride your- selves on living in a state of law. Why did you allow your government to violate it? Don't you count on representatives of the people to defend it? Is there not a process to call to account—impeach—the President who violates it? Why do you permit an apparently irrational act by your government, your CIA, and a band of mercenaries recruited from the assassins and sadists of the Batista government? Or do you agree with your government in consider- ing the law a dead letter when faced by political necessities? In this case you yourselves are justifying Goldwater, the John Birch Society, and all the Fascist forces that, beginning with McCarthy, have been growing in the United States of America.

You killed women and children in Playa Giron. You bombed the first decent houses, the first schools, the first hospitals of Cubans who never before, during the long American protectorate over Cuba, had a roof, an alphabet, or their health. And you did it in the name of liberty, democracy, and free enterprise. What do you want us to think of these nice-sounding words when in their names a population is murdered and the first proofs of concrete wel- fare are destroyed? We think the same as Simon Bolivar did 150 years ago: "The U.S.A. seems destined by Providence to plague us with all kinds of evils in the name of liberty."

In Punta del Este, the second aggressive act in the name of the Alliance took place. Maybe for you the standards of inter-American law are not important, but for us they are the result of a long struggle. It took us a whole century to win these standards. We won them with the invasion of Mexico and the annexation of half our territory, with the mutilation of Colombia, with the Platt Amendment, with the murder of Madero, with the occupation of Veracruz and the punitive Pershing expedition, with the interventions in Haiti, Nicaragua, and Santo Domingo, with the death of Sandino, with the campaign and the pressure against the Mexican Revolution, with the violation of Guatemala. It cost us a great deal of blood to set these standards: self- determination, nonintervention, respect for territorial integrity, equal rights for natives and foreigners, peaceful solutions of controversies, the right of each American state to organize as it thinks best. In Punta del Este, all these standards were violated by your government. A century of judicial construc- tion collapsed. It does not matter, said Secretary Rusk: "It is not the role of foreign ministers to discuss judicial matters, but to make decisions in the field of politics." The OAS ceased to be a legal organization because it was converted, now without any disguise, into a political weapon of the United States of America.

And the Alliance for Progress looked like the soft loincloth of naked intervention in favor of the concrete political and economic interest of the United States in Latin America.

REVOLUTION, YES

For years, many Latin Americans put faith in a gradual change of American policies towards Latin America; they also put their faith in the ability of the inter-American organization to support the minimum principles of our sovereignty. It is necessary to thank President Kennedy who, in only a year, has destroyed those illusions. The New Frontier turned out to be identical to the Republican Old Guard. Today, Latin Americans know they must no longer trust in the possibility of a change in the American government or in the OAS: they must trust only in themselves, in their capacity to destroy, by themselves, the old feudal structure and replace it with a radically new society, from which they can build for themselves.

.   .   .

Revolution! You cry to heaven, wring your hands, weep before violence and bloodletting. Yes. Unfortunately, it has never been possible to persuade the leading classes of a feudal country that their last hour has come. The Count of Arana, in the eighteenth century, could not persuade them, and President Kennedy, in the twentieth, cannot either. Porfirio Díaz and Fulgencio Batista were convinced only at gunpoint. This is the only way the Peruvian landlords, the Argentine militarists, and the Colombian landlords are going to be convinced. Blood? Yes, historical backwardness is paid for in blood. Injustice is paid for in blood. Remember Jefferson.* From Spartacus to Fidel Castro, going through the Protestant, English, French, American, Mexican, and Russian Revolutions, revolutions have been accomplished by violence. Mickey Mouse does not make revolutions. They are made by hungry men, valiant, angry, desperate men.

But you complain: what about democracy and liberty? Why, instead of bringing representative democracy, human rights, elections, and a free press, do Latin-American revolutions impose a leftist dictatorship in the place of a deposed rightist dictatorship? Why do they impose a single party, start a wave of political emigrants, suppress freedom of the press and elections? Why do they invite the protection of extracontinental powers?

Ah, this is what is worrying you. This is what you do not understand. You should start remembering. You have a very bad memory. You would do well to remember your own revolution in the eighteenth century. You also had your traitors, your deserters, and your execution walls. Like all revolutions, yours begot a counterrevolution. In those times, you had 3.5 million inhabitants; 70,000 fled the United States to find shelter in Canada. You expropriated the belongings and lands of exiled people without paying them anything. You suppressed the pro-British press. You won the revolution with the help

---

* A reference to Jefferson's statement, "The tree of liberty must be watered from time to time with the blood of patriots."—Editor.

of a foreign power, France. Without Rochambeau's French troops and De Grasse's fleet, you could not have defeated the British. You suffered shameful press campaigns, were labeled "bandits and savages" by the royalist European press. You used "exotic doctrines"—those of the French encyclopedists—to form a republican government, a heresy against the status quo imposed and defended by the Holy Alliance. You were the devils, the heretics, the non-conformists of the eighteenth century. You had to resist the counterrevolutionary invasion of 1812, your own Playa Giron, with Andrew Jackson's improvised militia. But you, during the colonial period, had already practiced representative democracy. You did not live under feudalism; you were already Protestants and capitalists; you were not struggling along as an exploited, illiterate, hungry mass of people.

In our day, a true revolution in Latin America is equivalent to a war of independence. It means starting from the bottom and creating conditions that, at least, will permit the exercise of democracy. A democracy cannot exist, you know, with empty stomachs, empty minds, and empty shacks. Democracy is not a cause; it is a result.

. . .

We are different from you. Our problems are not your problems. We have to make decisions and walk on roads different from those you believe to be universally valid. Try to understand the diversity of the world. Try to understand that we want progress that is real, not the unjust lie of today. . . . We want to be free of slavery, and we want to save you from a destiny worse than that of a slave: that of the lord, of the master.

Latin America knows its own path. Nobody, my American friends, is going to stop those 200 million people.

THE ALLIANCE FOR PROGRESS—
AFTER KENNEDY

Alberto Lleras

Perhaps no area of the world was more deeply grieved by the death of President Kennedy than Latin America. This article, written by the former President of Colombia now serving as one of the members of the Inter-American Committee for the Alliance for Progress, is an attempt to answer those who feel that since Kennedy's death the Alliance has been doomed to failure. Lleras notes the resistance that the Alliance is currently meeting in both the United States and Latin America, and he calls on Americans to draw on the resources of idealism and generosity symbolized by Kennedy to work with Latin Americans to reform their antiquated social and economic patterns. Many of his arguments apply with equal validity to the United States foreign aid programs in other parts of the world.

For me, who had been a personal friend of the late President and Mrs. Kennedy and had worked closely with him, the young President's unexpected and tragic death was a shattering blow, as it was, indeed, for the whole world. The task in which I had the privilege to work with John Kennedy was the quest for a more fruitful inter-American policy, chiefly the creation and the development of the Alliance for Progress. . . . John F. Kennedy had been not only the President of the United States, but the vigorous spokesman for a new policy of understanding and joint endeavor designed to transform the entire hemisphere into a genuinely new world. Such a world would be less weighed down by prejudice, obsolete traditions, injustice, poverty, broad disillusionment, the clash of aspirations and realities, demagogic fallacies, inaction, and indolence.

The proposal for the Alliance for Progress, which was approved by nineteen Latin-American countries without complete sincerity and without full understanding of its scope and by the United States with perhaps inadequate powers of implementation for the appropriate agencies, meant a new decade for the Americas; a decade of energetic action, discipline, and austerity and of placing the common interest ahead of individual interests—a decade unequaled since the shining and legendary years of our struggle for independence.

But on the very same day after the historic agreement had been signed, the effort to obstruct it began—openly or surreptitiously, here and in Latin America. It is a miracle that at least we still honor the existence of the commitment itself—a commitment without parallel in the history of international relations, a commitment not fully understood by our peoples nor implemented in complete good faith.

President Kennedy understood fully and clearly the significance of the agreement we had reached. He realized the heavy burden of its obligations, the urgency with which it had to be put into effect, the need to defend it against its adversaries in Congress and against the thoughtless and unrelenting hostility of private interests both here and in Latin America. These private interests have tried since the first day to twist the program around—to convert it into a protective screen for the operations of big business. The Alliance also had to be defended against attack from political opponents, who were criticizing it from varied and contradictory vantage points with the aim to hurt one of its most outstanding authors.

I must pay profound tribute to John F. Kennedy—a tribute that reflects the gratitude of millions of Latin Americans, steeped in poverty and anxious for a better life, who saw the imaginative concept of the Alliance as a means to break the chains that hold back progress and that go under the name of underdevelopment. They sensed that the solution of the national problems of each country was charted in those fundamental documents of the Alliance for Progress and that only the united determination of the entire hemisphere could make it a solemn obligation to carry out this important program of social improvement and economic development.

But it is also a fact that these vast and varied hopes reposed mainly in the young Chief Executive of the United States—not because we in Latin America are, as has been said, addicted to leader worship any more so than the

FROM *The Two Americas,* edited by William Manger (New York: Kenedy, 1965), pp. 133–44. Reprinted by permission.

people of the United States, but because the same man who had spoken out with generosity and without fear about the vital problems of Latin America had also wanted greater freedom, more justice, less poverty, and full equality of opportunity and treatment for his own people.

Why is it that the Alliance for Progress, of all our inter-American policies, is best suited to cope with the current situation of the developing nations of Latin America? It is because it has unique virtues, which were distilled out of the very extensive experience of the relations between this country and the vast, complex, and contrast-ridden region south of the Rio Grande and, to the east, the islands of the Caribbean. Above all, it is not a unilateral policy but a freely chosen approach to multilateral action. Secondly, because it offers a broad path to progress designed to promote the deepest aspirations of all Americans, north, center, and south, embracing all our nations and economic groups without exception or discrimination. Finally, the Alliance represents a policy which will benefit social sectors which in the past never have benefited directly or indirectly from inter-American cooperation.

This policy, furthermore, is based on principles which were not recognized as essential in the past. In fact, the failure to recognize the importance of these principles for inter-American relations has made a shambles of more than one attempt at cooperation and mutual understanding. One of these principles is the concept that genuine and lasting prosperity for Latin America can be accomplished only by developing greater economic solidarity among the Latin-American countries and through a higher degree of social justice and progress within each of our countries.

Prior to the Alliance for Progress, inter-American cooperation was based on a different philosophy. The idea was that the underdeveloped nations of Latin America were to move forward along the same road which the United States had traveled to achieve prosperity. The feat was to be accomplished by the free or perhaps licentious action of private enterprise functioning undisturbed in the vast reaches of a new and savage continent. In a completely different world situation, our peoples were arrogantly asked to perform exploits similar to those of private enterprisers of many decades past.

Only a few years ago, shortly after the spectacular launching of the Marshall Plan, the very Secretary of State after whom this plan was named told us in Bogotá that the United States was unable to concern itself with the vital needs of Latin America. The best suggestion he could make was that we should fling open our doors to private foreign capital. In other words: Go West, young man!

It took a growing economic and social crisis, catalyzed in a new political phenomenon—the Cuban Communist revolution—to find new approaches to the totality of Latin America's problems. This fact by no means diminishes the highmindedness of those who embraced the Alliance program while there was still time, nor does it reflect even on those many Latin Americans who undoubtedly accepted it out of fear. It is a sign of good health when reflexes respond promptly under the stimulus of external events. If the Alliance for Progress had not been developed, proposed, and adopted as opportunely as it was, the situation today would be very different.

But the question is not whether the Alliance is heading off a revolt of social discontent or a revolution of rising expectations. Rather, it is whether the Alliance is moving ahead toward its objectives with all the consequences that such progress implies. The Alliance today is being attacked under the cover of intellectual obscurity.

The attackers do not spell out the real motives of their opposition. Those who obstruct its progress say that it has not moved forward very much, implying that it is not a successful program, or they denounce it as unrealistic. The reason why it has not moved ahead faster is that it is being resisted in the United States and in Latin America by men in government, by vested interests, by big business, and by commercial empires whose operations extend throughout Latin America or the United States or both. All of them hide behind the banner of private enterprise, which in their view is being treated unfairly under the Alliance.

I cannot think of a single instance of greater blindness to reality than to be indifferent to or hostile toward the only program capable of saving the peoples of Latin America from anarchy and its inevitable consequence: the drift of a large part of this vital region of the Western world toward radicalism and Communism. I am amazed to see that at the same time that we hear people speak with disdain of the "failure" of the Alliance for Progress (with ill-concealed hope that it *will* fail), orators and newspaper columns are bursting forth with praise for an auxiliary and secondary program, the Peace Corps, good in itself and admirably conducted, but incapable of accomplishing revolutionary structural changes in our societies or those of any other region.

The best instrument that was available to the Kennedy Administration or that is available to the present Administration to bring about an almost miraculous transformation in Latin America is the Alliance for Progress. Yet no other program has been treated with as much misapprehension and dislike. The very forces which are most bitterly opposed to it and which it was designed to curb are being allowed to distort and twist its true image.

How has this image been distorted? First of all, it was stripped of its multilateral quality. The Alliance was conceived as an international commitment to undertake a gigantic development effort over a ten-year period. The idea was that the Latin-American countries, with financial and technical assistance from the United States, would carry out concrete and well-thought-out plans for social betterment and economic development which would help them to emerge from the final stages of underdevelopment. If this is not the commitment that all our nations have undertaken, the program is of no value—nor will it enlist the interest of the peoples whom it is designed to benefit.

If the Alliance is merely a United States foreign aid program with discreetly attached strings and indiscreetly applied discrimination or "selectivity"—used to benefit United States business firms and to help entrenched United States interests in Latin America—then it will encounter only distrust, skepticism, and resistance. Unfortunately, the legislative strings attached to the program by Congress and the speeches of individual senators and congressmen and even of some officials of the executive branch have put a stamp of their own on the Alliance. It is being promoted as a new United States policy toward Latin America, run from Washington and to be used as an instrument for the pragmatic pursuit of United States interests. This is a legitimate policy, but it is not the Alliance for Progress. It may be a good policy for the United States to place its national interests ahead of all other considerations, but this surely is not good policy for nineteen other nations who also must think of their national interests.

There was only one way for the Alliance to become effective at the very outset and to overcome the obstacles which were bound to be put in its path by a wave of reaction: that way was to stick to the concepts spelled out in the preamble to the Charter of Punta del Este. This meant the unlimited and unstinting dedication of the governments and the peoples of the Americas, including those of the United States, to the objective of wiping out all forms of backwardness and misery in the hemisphere. To accomplish such an objective, it was necessary to generate a truly revolutionary spirit which could enlist a supreme effort and innumerable sacrifices from free men and to sustain this effort until the goals of the program's first stage had been achieved.

It was another purpose of the Alliance to demonstrate that it was possible for a generation of free men to undertake tasks of social improvement and economic development never before attempted in a joint program, either in the free or the totalitarian world. What was needed was a thorough shakeup of the fossilized social structure of Latin America—to jolt it just as powerfully as the more modern and more just society of this country is being jolted. This was to be the final assault in the age-old battle for the equality of all men.

There—in Latin America—the objective was to force the entrenched interests of economic privilege to give way. Here, it was the quest of millions of people suffering grave injustices for first-class citizenship. Obviously, trouble and unrest were bound to ensue in Latin America, as we have witnessed. But the reforms are being made and nobody will be able to stop their completion.

But the more constructive phase of our joint endeavor—the job of creating conditions conducive to economic development—requires planning, which prior to the Alliance was ignored in Latin America, and it requires skilled personnel, of whom we have all too few. It also takes a sustained flow of financial support from abroad, at least in the volume envisaged in the Charter of Punta del Este. And all this, as well as the truly revolutionary spirit, has lagged behind or has been diluted by bureaucratic slowdowns. The result is dismay and cynicism among the great masses of people whose faith was the basic premise of the entire undertaking.

The Alliance for Progress was, moreover, [unlucky] in its early years at a time when a major financial effort was required of each of the Latin-American nations. Their financial capacity was weakened by a grave economic crisis in the region, brought about chiefly by the steady drop of Latin-American commodity prices on the world markets and especially on the United States market. This price drop started at the end of the Korean War and continued until the last part of 1963. In short, Latin America was suffering from a financial crisis at the very time when the Alliance for Progress called for major financial investments.

At the same time, just as the United States was committing itself to invest considerable sums through loans and other forms of assistance for the full-fledged development of the Alliance program, this country's balance of payments entered a critical stage. The restrictions with which the United States hedged its commitments under the Punta del Este Charter caused incalculable damage to the program. Another problem was the misguided manner in which the United States manifested its interest in the structural reforms which the Latin-American countries had offered to make on their own initiative, such as tax and land reform. An image of *do ut des* was created, making it appear that financial aid was to be granted in return for changes in Latin America's constitutions. Thus, objectives designed to be attractive to the masses of Latin America became unpopular.

But all this belongs to the past. Fortunately, a major change has come about through the creation of the Inter-American Committee for the Alliance for Progress. This is a strictly multilateral organ, an authentic voice for Latin America as well as for the interests of the United States, with the single purpose of accelerating progress toward social betterment and economic development. If this new instrument does not accomplish the desired results, then we will have to agree that the countries of the Americas neither understand nor are able to carry out the one truly great and important program which has been conceived for the solution of the internal conflicts of their economic and social life.

I have heard it said that a more pragmatic policy toward Latin America is either needed or will be carried out or is already being carried out. Surely the word "pragmatic" is not being used as Peirce or James understood it. Rather, it seems to have a more common meaning: to do business by taking care of concrete problems without looking too far ahead and without idealistic elements. This is another implied criticism of the Alliance. What it intends to convey is that the Alliance is not a realistic program, that it has set itself goals which are either impossible or very difficult to accomplish.

But of course this is not being said in so many words. It is the same thing that we hear over and over again from businessmen and landowners in Latin America—among them not a few North Americans. These people do not think it is very realistic to increase taxes in order to build more schools or to distribute land that is not being used productively among those who *can* use it well. But has the United States pursued a pragmatic policy of this type in other parts of the world? Is it to be a privilege for Latin America to be rewarded with a policy of pragmatism designed to serve North American interests in our countries?

The Marshall Plan, which was designed to rebuild the European nations—both friends and foes—out of the ruins of World War II with the unconditional aid of the United States, neither appeared to be nor was pragmatic until its results were seen by all the world—results which were unexpectedly amazing. The United Nations and, earlier, the League of Nations—American concepts which emerged out of the experience of the association among the nations of this hemisphere—were by no means pragmatic initiatives. Rather, they were frankly, openly, and, I dare say, almost madly idealistic.

But the world today is living with concepts and institutions which when first conceived had to be viewed as utopian and boldly unrealistic. The Alliance for Progress was going to be something like that, and it can still be something like that. But it cannot be such a concept and such an institution if it is going to function like a business which must yield dividends from the first day of operations. It can be such an institution only if it rises to the grandeur of the great international ventures of this country in our time—ventures which bear the stamp, the creativeness, and the image of a great people filled with optimism, inner strength, and a missionary spirit on behalf of great purposes.

On the other hand, there is nothing less pragmatic from any point of view than to conduct foreign policy strictly on the basis of narrow self-interest. It was possible in the days when we relied on force of arms. It was the policy of Rome, of France in the days of Napoleon, of Bismarck's and Hitler's Germany. But to pretend that the philosophy of such political movements—the exclusive interest of a city, in the case of Rome; of a country, in the case of France; or of a supposedly super race, in the case of Germany—could command the attention and arouse the support of other supposedly inferior peoples and races, or of other nations, is sheer insanity.

If there is any desire to preserve or to develop quickly a posture of respect, support, and affection in the world, a nation must do what the United States did in the First and the Second World Wars and what it did to organize the peace instead of enjoying its victory. It might be said that the United States must now return to a policy of narrow self-interest—and the interests of its business firms, of individual Americans, of commercial and other enterprises. To return to such a policy over and above other considerations could be indeed a new policy. But it would be a policy totally incompatible with the American tradition and with the principles proclaimed in the Alliance for Progress.

That is why I do not believe that there is a new policy or a new pragmatic spirit or any element different from the original purpose of the Alliance, even though some of the momentum and the mutual confidence that President Kennedy was able to call forth among the Latin-American peoples with the warmth of his personality may be missing. We must return to that mutual confidence. Consistency of policy within the framework of the regional hemispheric organization can accomplish much more than coping with the concrete problems of Latin America one by one in line with the political exigencies of the moment and with the quickly improvised interpretations of such needs.

Thus I do not believe that the relationships between the United States and the Latin-American countries have suffered real deterioration. There is perhaps a crisis of confidence, and there are the kind of doubts that often arise in a climate of uncertainty and of unjust criticism of every action of the government in this country, especially during electoral campaigns. Surely it is unfortunate that the greatest power in the world must periodically devote all its energies to the very important task of electing its administration and that during all this time everything that is being said or done is related to the political campaign. On the purely international level much of this discussion has neither importance nor value. In other words, the nation which is called upon to be the leader of the free world takes a vacation from its responsibilities of world leadership every four years, when in fact its indispensable function as a great power should go on uninterrupted.

But democracy calls for such sacrifices. And it has its compensations, such as an alert, tolerant, intelligent public opinion willing to listen to everyone, even to foreigners, and to do so with the same or even greater interest when they criticize this nation's conduct than when they praise it.

Thus we must not believe that there is a change in policy, nor judge too severely the actions of the political parties or of the government itself, until this country can again move forward along the established path which it has chosen clearly to follow before in history: the path of the most generous nation, the country most conscious of its responsibility to humanity and most faithful in its conduct abroad to the concepts it professes at home. This is the greatest praise that can be bestowed on this nation at any time in its history.

IV

AMERICAN REACTIONS TO FOREIGN COMMENTARY

The three preceding parts have explored the predominant views of the United States that one finds today in Western Europe, in the Communist world, and among the developing nations. Our principal purpose, as noted earlier in the Preface to this book, was to examine the international image of this country in three reflecting pools, representing the three major ideological approaches of the contemporary international community. Now, the time has come to examine American reactions to our image abroad and to understand the process by which national images are created and reflected. For, however fascinating foreign views of America may be by themselves, it is even more fascinating—and challenging—to put these foreign judgments into perspective.

The first revealing perspective is that of history. Some Americans today assume that harsh critical comment by foreign observers is primarily a cold-war phenomenon. Before that, apart from the writings of Fascist or Communist spokesmen during the twentieth century, it is thought, foreign views of America were predominantly friendly and fact-filled accounts of the "land of opportunity." The foreign commentators who are remembered are authors like Alexis de Tocqueville and James Bryce, whose interpretive works on nineteenth-century America, and those of their twentieth-century counterparts such as Denis Brogan, have been essentially favorable estimates of the American political system and American ideals. Thus many Americans begin their concern over current foreign commentary with the guiding belief that the United States was once widely "respected" and "admired" throughout the world, and that something has happened in recent decades to transform our image into a controversial one in the nontotalitarian forums of literate foreign opinion.

Alongside this assumption has developed a related current belief— that Americans today are more sensitive about foreign commentary than were their forefathers. According to this view, pre-cold war Americans cared little what foreign observers said about them or their system; they pursued their goals with an independence born of firm convictions and an understanding of the ideological and emotional hostilities that lay behind much of the critical foreign judgments of their day. Only recently, in the day of insecure "other-directed" Americans worried over the use of national power and obsessed by the status of their "image" abroad has foreign commentary attracted such nervous attention from the American press, officialdom, and intellectuals.

Both of these assumptions, of course, are the sheerest historical fiction, as any student of American history can easily demonstrate. A steady stream of "anti-American" books and articles by foreign commentators began in the earliest days of the American nation, featuring such nineteenth-century celebrities as Captain Basil Hall, Francis Trollope, and Charles Dickens. Although many European travelers wrote favorable accounts of American life, and although millions of Europeans paid the United States the supreme compliment of emigrating here, a procession of British Tories, French aristocrats, German military officers, Italian counts, and other members of the European privileged classes came to see—and mock—the young democracy. By the late nineteenth century, these aristocratic critics were joined by European socialists and anti-capitalists: the twentieth century simply added to this stream the attacks of Fascist, Communist, assorted "European culture" critics, and colored critics of white America and her racial policies. Thus, from the launching of the American republican experiment to the present, the United States has been the target of foreign attacks, from the subtle and sophisticated to the strident and broadside. There were always some foreigners who visited America and loved her, and, what was even rarer, those who understood and explained her accurately. But the foreign verdict on America was far from unanimous in the 1820's, or 1860's, or 1920's, and the presence of foreign attacks is as old as the United States herself.

By the same token, Americans read, worried about, and rebutted such critical foreign commentary from the start. As the *North American Review* lamented in 1815:

Few nations have received more provocations from [European] travelers than the United States; these have sometimes created greater irritation than such attacks should have excited, when it is considered from what sources they commonly originated. A certain degree of feeling, however, . . . is not without salutary effects. . . . A proper susceptibility on the score of national character may inspire others with respect for what is watchfully defended, and in the mutual intercourse now existing between nations, the professed libelers of another nation may be brought to shame in their own [countries] by a manly exposition of their calumnies.

Allan Nevins [in *American Social History as Recorded by British Travelers*] called this "nervous attention of Americans in the impressions formed of them by visiting Europeans" a continuing "national trait," well established by the late eighteenth century and a key feature of nineteenth-century American life and letters

One friendly English traveler, James Silk Buckingham, pronounced this sensitiveness to be our principal fault; and if we view it as a product of our American boastfulness, as Tocqueville did in condemning our "irritable patriotism," a decided fault it was. But it may be regarded in a kinder light; not as a product of our conceit, but as a set-off against it, a defensive armor— an admission that we were not so sure of our national merits as we liked to appear.

To trace the progress both of foreign commentary in the past and of American responses to it, we open this American part of *Views of America* with an essay by Henry Steele Commager that surveys the basic patterns of nineteenth- and early twentieth-century foreign writing about the United States.

Of course the great bulk of this historical foreign commentary on America consisted of travelers' accounts, social notes, and amateur political science analysis. However, with the publication in 1835 of Alexis de Tocqueville's classic study *Democracy in America,* foreign commentary began to include the occasional "great work" of interpretation by a foreign philosopher, historian, political scientist, or sociologist. In each of these, Americans—and foreign intellectuals of the day—felt they had been given a mature and penetrating insight into American society, and the interpretive volumes were received accordingly. Later generations have also accepted these works as valuable studies of American manners and institutions of that period, especially because foreign observers often discussed aspects of American life that native writers took for granted or glossed over as commonplace. In addition, students of American history and culture have found in the great works and the better foreign-traveler volumes a source of historical material with which to test assumptions about changes in American national character, such as whether Americans were really "inner-directed" during the nineteenth century or were just as "other-directed" then as in the contemporary era.

To explore the "great works" we begin with an article by Arvid Brodersen, who discusses three of the most important great works— de Tocqueville's *Democracy in America,* James Bryce's *The American Commonwealth,* and Max Weber's *The Protestant Ethic and the Spirit of Capitalism.*

Unfortunately, we have no great works of foreign interpretation on America in the 1960's; many would say that we have not had any that gained general acceptability since Siegfried, or even Bryce. We have many works of "middle-level" insight, such as Denis Brogan's several books of the 1940's and 1950's, Geoffrey Gorer's *The American People* (1948), and Herbert von Borch's *The Unfinished Society* (1963). But even middle-level works are missing from the Afro-Asian and Latin-American commentators, since there have not been as yet sustained books of analysis on American society by interpreters from the developing nations. There are books on particular aspects of American policy, such as foreign policy or race relations, but most of these works tend to be stringently ideological pieces such as Juan José Arévalo's *The Shark and the Sardines* (1962). The attention of the developing nation leaders and intellectuals is still focused so directly on the handful of problems that affect their prospects as new societies that broader-range analyses of the American "Goliath" are not really to be expected.

To present a sampling of current American reactions to foreign commentary on the United States, we have included representative reviews from leading American magazines of three books that were excerpted in earlier sections of this volume. Thus, the ways in which the works of Francis Williams, Juan José Arévalo, and Herbert von Borch were viewed in the New York *Times,* the *Saturday Review,* and *Commonweal,* respectively, provide a fair indication of American judgments about such foreign works in the 1960's.

This part turns next to the works of social scientists. In recent decades, students of public opinion, psychology, sociology, and political science have turned with increasing interest and concern to national-character analysis and the process of image formation from nation to nation. William Buchanan and Hadley Cantril's *How Nations See Each Other* (1953) and Richard T. Morris', *The Two-Way Mirror* (1960) are examples of this work. At its simplest, the social science approach seeks to collect and classify enough foreign commentary by spokesmen from a particular geographical or ideological area in order to permit careful analysis of the central themes voiced by such spokesmen. Finding the patterns and tracing their roots in the cultural, political, and governmental agencies of that country or area is the goal, and such analysis may aid Americans in knowing what policies and presentations of the American viewpoint would have the greatest chances of reaching and affecting foreign judgments. Examples of such content and source analyses have been included in Frederick Barghoorn's essay on the Soviet image of America in the Khrushchev and post-Khrushchev eras and in the "sensitive-area complex" thesis advanced by Richard D. Lambert and Marvin Bressler to explain judgments on America by visitors from "low-status" nations such as India. Other selections in this section deal with broader explorations of stereotype formation and national images, such as William Buchanan's survey of this field of research and of the UNESCO poll into national images, and Bryant Wedge's examination of the roots of common misconceptions held by African, Latin-American, and Soviet visitors to the United States.

The part on American reactions to foreign commentary closes with two selections that present different ways in which Americans can respond to foreign criticism. The two essays by Dean Acheson and C. L. Sulzberger constitute something of a debate over American options in responding to short-run world opinion. It is important to note that what Acheson and Sulzberger are discussing is *not* the measured judgment of foreign books and survey articles but the more volatile and immediate reactions to American policies and American words. Yet this, too, is part of foreign views of America, and no volume dealing with this topic could properly ignore it as a matter for discussion.

Thus the selections printed in this part show the patterns of foreign commentary from early republican decades to the present and suggest both the sources of these judgments and the variety of American responses to them. During the nineteenth century, when criticisms (accurate and inaccurate) were made of American intentions and institutions, thoughtful American writers often remarked that our imperfections were primarily the result of our central virtue. This was a land of opportunity, equality, and democracy, and the frontier manners, the lack of literature, the political spoils system, and the rest were only growing pains in the process of achieving freedom. Thus when nineteenth-century travelers visited the sites of Athens, Babylon, or Rome, they were seen as looking through a microscope to see the causes of decline in the record of the past. But when travelers came to America, as the *New York Review* remarked in 1840, they had to reverse their glass and use a "mental telescope," for they were peering into the future. In Europe, "The present is a ghost; here, it [is] a prophet. . . ."

There was a sweeping assurance—even an arrogance—about such nineteenth-century responses. We are less sure today that American institutions are the model of the future, or even that our own survival is preordained. We have come to know the power of totalitarian systems and to realize that the economic and social preconditions for our brand of democracy do not exist in most of the new nations of the world. We know more today about how unlikely it is that the country that wields international power will be loved by those who are lesser allies or dependent objects of that power. We are more sophisticated about the effects of propaganda, distortion, cultural conflict, and stereotyped thinking on the judgments of one nation by the government and people of another. We are far more self-conscious about the gap between American ideals and practices, especially in the area of race relations—so important in forming the estimations of the non-white peoples of the world.

Yet, despite all of these chastening realizations, we continue to pay an astounding amount of attention to what others say about us. At its worst, this may be vanity or cold-war apologetics. At its best, it represents a desire of Americans to "know themselves"—and to debate the images of their "selves" held by foreigners out of a continued respect for world opinion.

1

Foreign Commentary in Historical Perspective

HISTORICAL PATTERNS OF FOREIGN COMMENTARY ON AMERICA

Henry Steele Commager

As one of the most eloquent and distinguished historians of the American past, from colonial settlement to cold-war struggles of the 1960's Henry Steele Commager, professor of American history at Amherst College, had unique resources to draw upon when he decided to write an essay about the basic patterns of foreign commentary on the United States. He set out to explore why foreigners came to look, who they were, and what things they tended to consider the topics worth discussing about the American Republic. In addition, Commager offers some judgments on how the predictions of foreigners about American prospects have compared with the record of history. This essay, written in 1946, concentrates primarily on nineteenth- and early twentieth-century views of America.

·   ·   ·

No other people, it is safe to say, was ever so besieged by interpreters; none had its portrait painted, its habits described, its character analyzed, its soul probed so incessantly. The practice started before Independence and has continued unabated to the present day. . . .

What is the explanation of this apparently insatiable curiosity about America? Is it that America was the most interesting of all countries, or the most attractive, or the most hospitable? Matthew Arnold, to be sure, thought not: his criticism of America was precisely that it was not *interesting*—the italics are his—yet even he found it necessary to write a book about it. But interesting, as William James remarked, is not a substantive term: nothing is really interesting in itself, only in relation to some thing or some body. Surely

FROM the Introduction to *America in Perspective: The United States Through Foreign Eyes,* edited by Henry Steele Commager, pp. xii–xxi. Copyright 1947 by Random House, Inc. Reprinted by permission of Random House, Inc. and Penguin Books, Inc.

the 35 million immigrants who crossed the Atlantic to find homes in the New World found America interesting. And just as surely to the thousands of visitors who wrote books about it, it was interesting—as a curiosity or an entertainment, as an asylum or a refuge, as a catalytic agent or an experimental laboratory, as an object lesson in political depravity or an example of moral virtue, or, more frequently, as a combination of all these things.

The interest in America which animated the best of them—and their number is large—was profound. For they saw, from the beginning, that America held the key to the future: some, like the Italian Loria, thought that she held the key to the past as well, and that the newest of nations would reveal the history of the oldest. "I confess," wrote the incomparable Tocqueville, "that in America I saw more than America; I sought the image of democracy itself, with its inclinations, its character, its prejudices, and its passions, in order to learn what we have to fear or to hope from its progress." And he added that "the question here discussed is interesting not only to the United States but to the whole world; it concerns not a nation, but all mankind."

It was no idle prophecy. All mankind was, perforce, interested in the American experiment. Here was the largest, the best equipped, of all laboratories, and one whose findings were compulsory, as it were. What would be the consequences of political democracy, of social equality, of universal free education, of the intermixture of peoples and races, of new standards of material well-being? Could a federal system so extensive and so artificial endure? Could a democracy avoid degenerating into a tyranny of the majority? Could the arts and the sciences flourish in a society that was committed to the doctrine of equality? Could morality prosper without an established Church? The answers to these, and to scores of questions no less momentous, were to be found, it was thought, in America. And it was to these great and enduring questions that the most thoughtful and responsible foreign observers addressed themselves.

Nor were they, for the most part, disappointed. If the answers were not always clear, some of the confusion was in the minds of the observers, nor is it given to mortals to find ultimate answers to the most profound questions. Many of those who came over found what they were looking for, or merely confirmed what they already knew, for as André Maurois has observed, "A people is a mirror in which each traveler contemplates his own image." Yet others . . . were edified. What they saw, and reported, was relevant to the future, and because that future is with us, is relevant to our own day.

Our interest in these commentators is not so much in what they had to tell their own people as in what they have to tell us: in this matter we are justifiably parochial. Some of the interpretations were directed, in fact, to us: Grund, Gurowski, and Munsterberg, for example, wrote for their American audience, and Bryce and Brogan, it is safe to say, have been more widely read in America than in Britain. Most of our interpreters, however, looked for what was of interest to their own people. It might be supposed that they could tell us little that was relevant to our problems, little that we did not already know. Yet such a supposition, however logical, runs contrary to experience: biographies are usually more revealing than autobiographies and portraits than photographs. What they can, and do, tell us are mostly the obvious things, for it is in what a people take for granted that their character can be read—in the unformulated assumptions, the spontaneous reactions, the inevitable responses, the articles of faith. Americans, like any other people, are often in the position of the dullard who discovered with delight that all his life he had been writing prose.

We take for granted our pervasive social equality and do not appreciate the nature of class distinctions until we go abroad—until we go even to democratic England and discover the importance of the public-school accent. We take for granted the exalted status of women and the almost universal pampering of children, until we discover how these things alarm or horrify our visitors. We take for granted universal public education—until we familiarize ourselves with the statistics of secondary-school and university education abroad. We take for granted a political unity which enables us to travel from New York to California without customs barriers or change of money—until we travel over comparable distances in Europe. We take for granted, alas, a double standard of private and public morality, personal integrity, and political venality—until we learn how that double standard shakes faith in democracy abroad. It is because foreign observers can see America without the assumptions and presuppositions that becloud the American vision, because they can, in fact, see America in perspective, that they are helpful.

What then do they tell us, these commentators who look at America from the perspective of the Old World? There are, altogether, several thousand of them, spread over a century and a half, representing every country, every point of view. At best the view which they seem to present to us is kaleidoscopic, at worst chaotic. Can we draw any conclusions from such disparate interpretations, can we find any unity in such diverse points of view? Can we, in any event, find common denominators in a selection of over a score of representative interpreters, a selection necessarily meager and inevitably arbitrary?

Surprisingly enough a real unity emerges. . . . We know that in all outward matters America has changed profoundly in the century and a half since Independence, and that these changes have been continuous and complex; we are sometimes inclined to suppose that there have been comparable changes in the national character. That is not the conclusion to be drawn from the findings of these foreign observers. They report diversity, to be sure, but they conclude, too, in the words of one of them, that "over confused diversity there broods a higher unity." To the visitors of the 1770's and the 1940's, to Britons, Frenchmen, Germans, and Swedes, America *meant* much the same thing.

What then was the permanent rather than the transient in the American character as seen by these observers? What was the abiding meaning of America in history? What were the recurring themes, the persistent traits? America was the land of the future, and held the key to the future. "Westward the course of empire takes its way. . . . Time's noblest offspring is the last," Bishop Berkeley had written, and the prophecy was re-echoed decade after decade. "Americans are the Western pilgrims," said Crèvecoeur, "who are carrying along with them that great mass of arts, sciences, vigor, and industry, which began long since in the east; they will finish the great circle," and one hundred and sixty years later the Swedish journalist Victor Vinde concluded that the American "knows there will be a tomorrow. He believes in tomorrow." Throughout their history Americans have insisted that the best was yet to be, and they have rarely been disappointed. America was the land of opportunity. Here the poor of the Old World were given a second chance, here men achieved a new stature, were endowed with a new dignity. "God made America for the poor," said Dicey; "there is no other country on earth which in so short a time has accomplished so much," asserted Mackay. America was, above all, the land of equality. This was the great theme which Tocqueville elaborated with consummate mastery, and the theme to which his ablest successors, Mackay and Bryce and Munsterberg and Brogan, recurred. That equality was political; it was, until the twentieth century, economic; it was, above all, social and psychological. Much of that equality stemmed from the frontier, and America was a land molded by the frontier. "He who would see America in its proper light must visit our extended line of frontiers," wrote Crèvecoeur a century before Turner, and the Norwegian jurist, Ole Munch Raeder, who came over in the forties, observed the leveling influence of the American west on judges, courts, and law. America was the land of experimentation. Everything here was new, as Francis Lieber discerned, everything had to be measured by new yardsticks. "In America," said the Pulszkys, "the spirit of progress is bold, and often encroaching; . . . new ideas easily get a chance of being practically tried; the public at large does not shrink from testing at once different solutions of a problem." Equality, too, as Tocqueville pointed out, encouraged experimentation, for equality rejected the sovereign authority of the past, or of the great, and permitted every man to be his own authority—even on matters of language. Bryce more elaborately than any other commentator analyzed the American contribution to political experiments, and in the twentieth century Brogan returned to the theme. America was the land of industry, of energy, of vitality. "Excitability," wrote Gurowski, "is omnipotent in the American character," and George W. Steevens discovered that the American was an electric Anglo-Saxon. The explanation varied: climate, the frontier, the principle of equality, the intermixture of races—but whatever the particular explanation, the generalization was accepted by almost all observers from Crèvecoeur to Brogan. It was the combination of industry with natural wealth which accounted in large part for the material well-being of the American, and America was preeminently the land of plenty. "You are not much pressed to eat and drink," wrote the English reformer William Cobbett, who returned to America in 1817, "but such an abundance is spread before you . . . that you instantly lose all restraint." Perhaps no theme recurs more frequently, but it afforded few opportunities for philosophical interpretation and is not stressed here. It was the lush abundance of America that accounted, in part, for the generosity of its people, and America was the land of hospitality. The earliest visitors met it in the farms and in the villages; later visitors had to contend with it in mansions and banquet halls. Cobbett found it in rural Pennsylvania and Raeder in frontier Wisconsin and Harriet Martineau in Boston; Bourget thought it so extravagent as to be a national vice, but Birmingham thought that it contrasted happily with the prudence of the Old World and George Steevens delighted in it wherever he found it. The materialism which such physical well-being and such hospitality reflected could be interpreted as a virtue or as a vice, but whatever the interpretation, most observers were agreed that America was the land of materialism. "It would be well if they loved the real less and the ideal more," thought Dickens, but perhaps fame had brought him more hospitality than he could endure. Tocqueville explained

American materialism as a consequence of equality, and Gurowski as a consequence of industrialism and commercialism; the first looked upon it as something to be overcome, the second as something to be proud of. "Money-making," wrote the Polish critic, "continually extends the area of culture. It conquers the rugged face of nature, transforms the wilderness into a habitable and cultivated soil. In proportion as prosperity increases and expands, general civilization increases and expands." And Munsterberg too thought the American interest in money on the whole creditable. Notwithstanding the pervasive materialism of Americans, America was, most observers agreed, the land of exalted morals. This was a tribute all the more striking in the light of the general attribute of lawlessness. Tocqueville had analyzed the phenomenon, especially in its relation to the family, and he had found it, as usual, a manifestation of the principle of equality. Francis Grund found the explanation rather in religion which "presided over their councils"; Bryce traced it to more diverse factors. All agreed that sex morals were purer in America, female virtue safer, family relations more wholesome, than in Old-World nations. All agreed, too, on the elevated position which woman held in this country. America was the land of chivalry. "The age of chivalry is not gone," wrote Munsterberg; "until America it never came," and in one form or another a hundred commentators echoed this observation. Only the novelist W. L. George suggested that women relieved from domestic duties and large families were to be pitied rather than envied. That there was a chasm between private and public morality was, however, argued with increasing insistence as the decades passed. Crèvecoeur thought that "we are the most perfect society now existing in the world," but Dickens, who was revolted by the licentiousness of the press, did not agree, nor for that matter did the judicious Bryce, who more tellingly than any other exposed the venality of American politics. Political immorality was, indeed, the most pervasive of American vices, and few observers were able to extenuate it as they extenuated the American passion for money or American restlessness or American manners. Yet there was a paradox here, too, which the more astute interpreters did not fail to note. It was on his institutions, and particularly his political institutions, that the American fixed his patriotism. American patriotism was as new as American democracy, and dependent on it. It was not attached primarily to the soil, to a particular locality; it was not symbolized by a king or a nobility; it was inspired by abstractions—and this in the most practical of people—by the Constitution, equality, democracy, liberty. For these institutions Americans confessed a reverence otherwise alien to their character, nor were they deeply troubled by the gap between the ideal and the real, for in their minds the ideal assumed reality. For America was the land of perfectionism. The American knew that nothing was impossible, in his brave new world, and history confirmed his intuition. Progress was not, to him, a mere philosophical ideal but a commonplace of experience, and he could not understand why foreigners should see vulgar realities where he saw visions. He was outraged at any failure, at any imperfection even, could not tolerate a depression or a military defeat, could not acquiesce in any inadequacy of culture or, as Roussy de Sales pointed out, even of marital felicity.

It all added up to a flattering picture, and this is, perhaps, one of the more gratifying surprises of our investigation. For familiar as we are with the animadversions of a Trollope or a Dickens, or a score of lesser commentators, we have supposed that the foreign verdict on America was unfavorable. "The feelings of the American people," as Mackay observed, "have been wantonly and unnecessarily wounded by successive travelers who . . . have generally viewed them on the ludicrous side," and every American schoolboy knows Lowell's famous essay on a certain condescension in foreigners. The wanton attacks, the envy, the misunderstanding, the patronage, are all to be found readily enough—Arnold is an example here—but jaundiced criticisim came from the second-rate commentators rather than from the magisterial ones. The most judicious, the most learned, the most perspicacious, the most profound interpreters of America returned a verdict that ranged from sympathy to enthusiasm.

That there were faults was acknowledged by even the most friendly of our visitors, and the faults, like the virtues, seemed to persist from generation to generation. What were the major criticisms of the American experiment? The passion for equality, it was charged, made for mediocrity, for a general leveling down of distinction and of talent. The concern for material well-being produced a materialistic civilization, one in which the arts flourished only by indulgence, as it were. The passion for work, or for mere activity, left little time for the amenities of life, and Americans were rude. An easygoing tolerance played into the hands of the vulgar and the corrupt, permitted the invasion of privacy, the exaltation of the mediocre, the violation of law and order. An excessive nervous vitality made for instability and rootlessness, gave an air of impermanence to almost everything that Americans undertook. The excessively high value put upon woman led to a matriarchal society, and the conviction which animated all parents that their children must have a better and easier life than they themselves had enjoyed produced successive generations of pampered brats. Most serious of all, perhaps, was the charge of Tocqueville, reiterated by many later interpreters, that democracy invited the tyranny of the majority and that in the end popular rule might be metamorphosed into mob rule. Curiously enough not until almost the twentieth century— Bryce is perhaps the earliest example—did foreigners note the danger to democracy that came from the wealthy minority rather than from the underprivileged majority.

Yet the dour prophecy of the tyranny of the majority was confounded, and a hundred years after Tocqueville Americans still observed the proprieties of the Constitution and cherished their system of checks and balances. The observation can, without fatuousness, be enlarged to a generalization. America has, on the whole, confounded her critics where they were pessimistic rather than where they were optimistic.

FOREIGN TRAVELERS' ACCOUNTS AND
THE AMERICAN NATIONAL CHARACTER

Seymour M. Lipset

Foreign travelers' accounts have long been a rich source of contemporary observations on historical events, biographical episodes involving American leaders, data on social customs, geography, and scientific life, and similar material. Because foreign reports were written from outside American cultural and political frames of reference, they could balance American records of historical events, as long as the historian took into account the biases of the foreign observers.

In recent years, sociologists, political scientists, and others concerned with analysis of changes in American society have realized that foreign views of America offer an ideal body of material for measuring judgments about supposed shifts in American values. One of the best such uses of foreign material was made by Seymour M. Lipset, professor of sociology at the University of California at Berkeley, in his study of early American national development, *The First New Nation*. The question Lipset asked was whether American national character was more constant than changing in the past century and a half, and his answer, drawn from foreign commentary, follows.

Foreign travelers' accounts of American life, manners, and character traits constitute a body of evidence with which to test the thesis that the American character has been transformed during the past century and a half. Their observations provide us with a kind of comparative mirror in which we can look at ourselves over time. It is important to note, therefore, that the type of behavior which Riesman and Whyte regard as distinctly modern, as reflecting the decline of the Protestant Ethic, was repeatedly reported by many of the nineteenth-century travelers as a peculiarly American trait in their day. Thus the English writer Harriet Martineau [in *Society in America*] at times might be paraphrasing *The Lonely Crowd* in her description of the American of the 1830's:

⟨Americans⟩* may travel over the world and find no society but their own which will submit to the restraint of perpetual caution, and reference to the opinions of others. They may travel over the whole world and find no country but their own where the very children beware of getting into scrapes, and talk of the effect of actions upon people's minds; where the youth of society determine in silence what opinions they shall bring forward, and what avow only in the family circle; where women write miserable letters, almost universally, because it is a settled matter that it is unsafe to commit oneself on paper; and where elderly people seem to lack almost universally that faith in principles which inspires a free expression of them at any time, and under all circumstances. . . .

FROM *The First New Nation* by Seymour Martin Lipset, pp. 106–21. Basic Books, Inc., Publishers, 1963. Reprinted by permission.
* Angular brackets indicate insertions by the author or by former editors.—Editor.

There is fear of vulgarity, fear of responsibility, and above all, fear of singularity. . . . There is something little short of disgusting to the stranger who has been unused to witness such want of social confidence, in the caution which presents probably the strongest aspect of selfishness that he has ever seen. The Americans of the northern states are, from education and habit, as accustomed to the caution of which I speak, as to be unaware of its extent and singularity. . . .

Few persons ⟨Americans⟩ really doubt this when the plain case is set down before them. They agree to it in church on Sundays, and in conversation by the fireside: and the reason why they are so backward as they are to act upon it in the world, is that habit and education are too strong for them. They have worn their chains so long that they feel them less than might be supposed.

Harriet Martineau is only one observer of early American life, and not necessarily more reliable than others. But it is significant that her comments on American "other-directedness" and conformism do not flow, as do those of other nineteenth-century visitors who made comparable observations, from fear or dislike of democracy. Many upper-class visitors, such as Tocqueville or Ostrogorski, saw here a threat to genuine individuality and creativity in political and intellectual life, in that democracy and equalitarianism give the masses access to élites, so that the latter must be slaves to public opinion in order to survive. Harriet Martineau, as a left-wing English liberal, did not come to America with such fears or beliefs. She remained an ardent admirer of American democracy, even though she ultimately decided that "the worship of Opinion is, at this day, the established religion of the United States."

The most celebrated post-Civil War nineteenth-century English visitor to America, James Bryce [in *The American Commonwealth,* 1888] saw inherent in American society "self-distrust, a despondency, a disposition to fall into line, to acquiesce in the dominant opinion. . . ." This "tendency to acquiescence and submission" is not to be "confounded with the tyranny of the majority. . . . ⟨It⟩ does not imply any compulsion exerted by the majority," in the sense discussed by Tocqueville. Rather Bryce, like Harriet Martineau fifty years earlier, described what he felt to be a basic psychological trait of Americans, their "fatalism," which involved a "loss of resisting power, a diminished sense of personal responsibility, and of the duty to battle for one's own opinions. . . ."

Although Harriet Martineau and James Bryce stand out among nineteenth-century visitors in specifying that these other-directed traits were deeply rooted in the *personalities* of many Americans, the general *behaviors* that they and Tocqueville reported were mentioned by many other foreign travelers. For example, a summary of the writings of English travelers from 1785 to 1835 [Jane L. Mesick, *The English Traveller in America, 1785–1835*] states that one important characteristic mentioned in a number of books "was the acute sensitiveness to opinion that the average American revealed." A German aristocrat, who became a devotee of American democracy and a citizen of the country, stated in the 1830's that "nothing can excite the contempt of an educated European more than the continual fears and apprehensions in which even the 'most enlightened citizens' of the United States seem to live with regard to their next neighbors, lest their actions, principles, opinions, and beliefs should be condemned by their fellow creatures" [Francis Grund, *Aristocracy in America*]. An interpreter of nineteenth-century foreign opinion,

John Graham Brooks, mentions various other writers who noted the unwillingness of Americans to be critical of each other.

. . .

The foreign travelers were also impressed by the American insistence on equality in social relations, and on achievement in one's career. Indeed, many perceived an intimate connection between the other-directed behavior they witnessed and the prevalence of these values, such that the behavior could not be understood without reference to them. An analysis of the writings of hundreds of British travelers in America before the Civil War reports [Max Berger, *The British Traveller in America, 1836–1860*]: "Most prominent of the many impressions that Britons took back with them was the aggressive egalitarianism of the people." If one studies the writings of such celebrated European visitors as Harriet Martineau, the Trollopes (both mother and son), Tocqueville, or James Bryce, it is easy to find many observations documenting this point.

Baedeker's advice to any European planning to visit the United States in the late nineteenth or early twentieth century was that he "should, from the outset, reconcile himself to the absence of deference, or servility, on the part of those he considers his social inferiors." A detailed examination of the comments of European visitors from 1890 to 1910 reports general agreement concerning the depth and character of American equalitarianism [Robert W. Smuts, *European Impressions of the American Worker*]:

Whether they liked what they saw or not, most foreign observers did not doubt that America was a democratic society. . . . Different occupations, of course, brought difference in prestige, but neither the occupation nor the prestige implied any fundamental difference in the value of individuals. . . . The similarity of conclusions based on diverse observations was simply another indication of the absence of sharp class differences. Even hostile visitors confirmed this judgment. . . . Some foreign observers found the arrogance of American workers intolerable.

. . .

American emphasis on equalitarianism as a dominant value is significant in determining what to many of the Europeans were three closely related processes: competition, status uncertainty, and conformity. Tocqueville, for example, argued that equalitarianism maximizes competition among the members of a society. But if equalitarianism fosters competition for status, the combination of the two values of equality and achievement results, according to many of the travelers, in an amorphous social structure in which individuals are uncertain about their social position. In fact, those travelers who were so impressed with the pervasive equalitarianism of American society also suggested that, *precisely as a result of the emphasis on equality and opportunity,* Americans were *more* status-conscious than those who lived in the more aristocratic societies of Europe. They believed, for example, that it was easier for the *nouveaux riches* to be accepted in European high society than in American. British travelers before the Civil War noted that Americans seemed to love titles more than Englishmen. European observers, from Harriet Martineau and Frances Trollope in the 1830's to James Bryce in the 1880's and Denis Brogan in recent years, have pointed out that the actual strength of equality as a dominant American value—with the consequent lack of any well-defined deference structure linked to a legitimate aristocratic tradition where the propriety of social rankings is unquestioned—forces Americans to *emphasize* status, background, and symbolism. As Brogan has remarked [in *The English People*], the American value system has formed "a society which, despite all efforts of school, advertising, clubs, and the rest, makes the creation of effective social barriers difficult and their maintenance a perpetually repeated task. American social fences have to be continually repaired; in England they are like wild hedges: they grow if left alone."

Status-striving and the resultant conformism have not been limited solely, or even primarily, to the more well-to-do classes in American society. Many of the early nineteenth-century travelers commented on the extent to which workers attempted to imitate middle-class styles of life. Smuts notes that visitors at the turn of this century were struck by "what they regarded as the spend-thrift pattern of the American worker's life"; Paul Bourget, a French observer, interpreted this behavior as reflecting "the profound feeling of equality [in America which] urges them to make a show." As Werner Sombart, the German sociologist and economist, put it, "since all are seeking success . . . everyone is forced into a struggle to beat every other individual; and a steeple-chase begins . . . that differs from all other races in that the goal is not fixed but constantly moves even further away from the runners." And in an equalitarian democracy "the universal striving for success ⟨becomes a major cause of⟩ . . . the worker's extravagance, for, as Munsterberg ⟨a German psychologist⟩ pointed out, the ability to spend was the only public sign of success at earning." And lest it be thought that such concerns with conspicuous consumption emerged only in the Gilded Age of the 1890's as analyzed by Veblen, sixty years earlier a medical study of the "Influence of Trades, Professions, and Occupations, in the United States, in the Production of Disease" described and analyzed behavior in much the same terms:

The population of the United States is beyond that of other countries an anxious one. All classes are either striving after wealth, or endeavoring to keep up its appearance. From the principle of imitation which is implanted in all of us, sharpened perhaps by the existing equality of conditions, the poor follow as closely as they are able the habits and manner of living of the rich. . . . From these causes, and perhaps from the nature of our political institutions, and the effects arising from them, we are an anxious, care-worn people.

While some Europeans explained American behavior that they found strange—the sensitivity, kindliness, concern for others' feelings, and moral meekness—by reference to the nature of political democracy or the overbearing desire to make money, others saw these traits as consequences of the extreme emphasis on equality of opportunity, the basic American value which they properly regarded as unique. Many argued that this very emphasis on equality, and the constant challenging of any pretensions to permanent high status, has made Americans in all social positions extremely sensitive to the opinions of others, and causes status aspirants greater anxiety about the behavior and characteristics indicative of rank than is the case with their counterparts in more aristocratic societies. Discussing the writings of various travelers, John Graham Brooks [in *As Others See Us*] states:

One deeper reason why the English are blunt and abrupt about their rights . . . is because class lines are more sharply drawn there. Within these limits, one is likely to develop the habit of demanding his dues. He insists on his prerogatives all the more because they are narrowly defined. When an English writer (Jowett) says, "We are not nearly so much afraid of one another as you are in the States," he expressed this truth. In a democracy every one at least hopes to get on and up. This ascent depends not upon the favor of a class, but upon the good-will of the whole. This social whole has to be conciliated. It must be conciliated in both directions—at the top and at the bottom. To make one's self conspicuous and disagreeable is to arouse enmities that block one's way.

One may find an elaboration of this causal analysis among many writers at different periods. Thus Max Weber, after a visit to America in the early 1900's, noted the high degree of "submission to fashion in America, to a degree unknown in Germany" and explained it in terms of the lack of inherited class status. Seven decades earlier another German, Francis Grund, who saw in American equality and democracy the hope of the world, nevertheless also believed that the ambiguous class structure made status-striving tantamount to conformity. He presents both sides of the picture in the following items:

Society in America . . . is characterized by a spirit of exclusiveness and persecution unknown in any other country. Its gradations not being regulated according to rank and title, selfishness and conceit are its principal elements. . . . What man is there in this city ⟨New York⟩ that dares to be independent at the risk of being considered bad company? And who can venture to infringe upon a single rule of society?

This habit of conforming to each other's opinions, and the penalty set upon every transgression of that kind, are sufficient to prevent a man from wearing a coat cut in a different fashion, or a shirt collar no longer *à la mode,* or, in fact, to do, say, or appear any thing which could render him unpopular among a certain set. In no other place, I believe, is there such a stress laid upon "saving appearances."

James Bryce, a half-century later, also linked conformity to the ambiguity of the status system, particularly as it affected the wealthy classes. He pointed out that it was precisely the emphasis on equality, and the absence of well-defined rules of deference, which made Americans so concerned with the behavior of others and seemingly more, rather than less, snobbish toward each other than were comparably placed Englishmen.

It may seem a paradox to observe that a millionaire has a better and easier social career open to him in England than in America. . . . In America, if his private character be bad, if he be mean or openly immoral, or personally vulgar, or dishonest, the best society may keep its doors closed against him. In England great wealth, skillfully employed, will more readily force these doors to open. . . . The existence of a system of artificial rank enables a stamp to be given to base metal in Europe which cannot be given in a thoroughly republican country.

THREE VISIONS OF AMERICA:
DE TOCQUEVILLE, BRYCE, AND WEBER

Arvid Brodersen

In the history of foreign views of America, there are perhaps a dozen acknowledged "classics," works that in their day and since have been accepted as penetrating studies of American life and institutions. Here, Arvid Brodersen, professor of sociology on the graduate faculty of the New School for Social Research, summarizes and discusses three of these classics, by a Frenchman, an Englishman, and a German: Alexis de Tocqueville's *Democracy in America,* published in 1835 when the United States was in the excitement and turmoil of the Jacksonian revolution; James Bryce's *The American Commonwealth,* published in 1888 when the United States was just entering the industrial age and trying to adjust its political and social institutions to that new environment; and Max Weber's *The Protestant Ethic and the Spirit of Capitalism,* containing Weber's reflections on the dynamic and rough American capitalism he had seen during a visit to the country in 1904. Brodersen, who has written books about Thorsten Veblen and Max Weber, has taught at the University of Oslo and has directed the Social Sciences Department of UNESCO.

. . . The perspective in which the foreign commentator sees America is not always that of a student bent on understanding the country and the American people in their own terms and for their own sake. More often, in fact, the perspective is one of partisanship with regard to issues in the commentator's own country or beliefs in his personal philosophy, and in some cases his interpretation of America is but a convenient language in which extraneous views and prejudices can be expressed with impunity. Hence the liberal's picture of America is apt to differ radically from the conservative's, the socialist, working-class picture from that of the middle class, the artistic and literary person's from that of the businessman.

Each sees America in his own perspective, and some will for their own reasons praise America for her freedom and democracy—or condemn her for them; some will perceive the cultural creativity and the spirit of idealism in America, others deny its existence; some will admire America's industrial and business enterprise, others deplore it as materialism. All these views are recurring themes in the image of America as it has emerged in the perspective of foreign visitors over the last two hundred years. They sprang from the minds that produced them as much as from the subject, and whatever truth they contain therefore nearly always refers to two realities, in part the reality of the perspective, in part that of America.

In exploring some major themes in the interpretation of America, I propose to discuss the writing of three well-known commentators of the past. . . .

FROM "Themes in the Interpretation of America by Prominent Visitors from Abroad," *The Annals of the American Academy of Political and Social Science,* Vol. 295 (September, 1954), pp. 21–28. Reprinted by permission.

The visits of Tocqueville and Bryce fell in very different periods of this nation's history. The former saw America still in a preindustrial stage, with a population of 12 million, mostly farmers, craftsmen, and traders; the latter when she had grown to a great industrial nation of 62 million people. Tocqueville was the first observer to form a comprehensive view of American civilization—not just random "opinions," but a systematic interpretation of America, seen as a whole. Bryce was his true successor in this respect, and while their images differed in some ways, the continuity and the fundamental agreement in their interpretations of American democracy remain a most remarkable fact.

ALEXIS DE TOCQUEVILLE

In 1831–32 Alexis de Tocqueville, twenty-six at the time, spent nine months traveling in the United States on a commission from the French government to report on the American prison system. The fruit of that visit (aside from the prison report) was the first great study of American society and culture ever written, the four-volume work *De la démocratie en Amérique* Vols. I and II, 1835; Vols. III and IV, 1840). Few books have won such immediate and widespread fame.

In Tocqueville's interpretation of America one grand theme governs the entire analysis of sociopolitical institutions. This theme, in one word, is equality. What really motivated Tocqueville's passionate interest in the study of America was not the problem of democracy in general, but that of a new society founded upon equality among its members. He saw the movement toward equality as a universal historical trend, the manifest destiny of his own people. His perhaps most urgent concern in studying America was the charting of the inevitable future course of France. He wrote in the introduction to the first volume, "It appears to me beyond doubt that, sooner or later, we shall arrive, like the Americans, at an almost complete equality of conditions." Tocqueville himself was deeply rooted in the other, aristocratic type of society and did not welcome its passing; but being convinced that this was "a providential fact" at this stage, he proceeded to find out, in America, what good could possibly come of it.

The latter part of *Democracy in America* (Vols. III and IV), generally considered the more profound, presents in many variations the one theme that the human mind under conditions of social and political equality will develop a new and specific creativity, new and specific modes of social actions and attitudes differing from those of an aristocratic society, but of a certain value if considered in their own terms. This is in fact the counterthesis to the often expressed view that "real culture" (philosophy, art, and literature) is possible only in the old type of society, and that consequently "America has no culture"—a view which seems to be held as strongly in some quarters today as it was almost universally a hundred years ago. Tocqueville has, by virtue of interpreting the American mind in its own terms, the power and also the right of critical evaluation, and while he is as often negative as positive in his judgment, the Americans themselves could not but accept him and learn from him. He has harsh things to say of their "passion to get rich," their crude tastes, and their lack of intellectual refinement. On the other hand, he is struck by "the extreme equality of social relationships. The plutocrat and the lowly worker shake hands in the street." And he confesses to envying America her moral climate, the people's respect for the law, and their faith in human equality, in wisdom and good sense, in man's perfectibility, and hence in universal education.

The themes that dominate the first part of *Democracy in America* relate primarily to the subject matters of government and politics. In the following I shall be able to point to but some of the major motifs.

In the first place, Tocqueville affirms that egalitarian democracy as government by the people—by all the people—is possible only through the people's active participation in their own local affairs. Such participation, however, can become politically effective only under a system of administrative decentralization, that is, one diametrically the opposite of the French centralized system of his time, in which all major decisions were handed down to the local communities from the capital ruling power at the center, and no policy-making authority was vested in the so-called provincial institutions. While admitting that the American system has its weaknesses, Tocqueville eloquently pleads in its favor. Decentralization he considered one of the most important lessons he derived for France from the study of democracy in America. If his arguments failed to sway the rulers and people of France, they greatly impressed an influential reader in England: John Stuart Mill later confessed in his autobiography that he "owed his rescue from a thoughtless belief in centralization to Tocqueville's book. . . ."

Tocqueville found the American federal system a particularly happy construction just by virtue of its combination with local self-rule. This dualism he considered "one of the greatest inventions known to political science," since it permits the American people to enjoy the "happiness and freedom of small nations" while simultaneously wielding "the power of great nations," or in other words, "combining the different advantages which result from the magnitude and the littleness of nations." It should, however, be kept in mind that in making this statement 120 years ago, he did not anticipate a world situation in which America would become a great military power. On the contrary, his assumption was that the "American Union . . . placed in the center of an immense continent . . . is almost as much insulated from the world as if all its frontiers were girt by the ocean," and consequently "has no great wars to fear." Nor did he perceive the explosive potentialities of the domestic issue of slavery which already was looming ominously on the American horizon.

An aspect of American democracy which Tocqueville studied with interest was the selection of men for public office, on the policy-making as well as administrative level. In his view, partly because the most distinguished individuals would keep away from public affairs and partly because the electorate itself would by "the natural instincts of democracy . . . reject distinguished citizens as their rulers," equality tended to favor mediocrity. The lack of an established civil service, with its social order of prestige and status as well as security of office, made—in Tocqueville's opinion—for a poor selection of talent and an unfortunate instability and discontinuity of administration: "No one cares for what happened before his time; no methodical system is pursued." His criticism was concerned mainly with the technical efficiency and intellectual standard inherent in American administrative practices, rather than the problems of political ethics.

Tocqueville's principal criticism of American democracy, to which he devotes two full chapters, is summed up in one phrase, "the tyranny of the majority." The irresistible and absolute rule of the majority which he observed on the American scene was based—according to his analysis—upon a system of government which was no longer genuinely representative, but rather a direct rule of public opinion through agents elected for very brief terms and acting under continuous control of the people in its majority. "A proceeding is becoming more and more general in the United States, which will, in the end, do away with the guaranties of representative government: it frequently happens that the voters, in electing a delegate, point out a certain line of conduct to him, and impose upon him certain positive obligations which he is pledged to fulfill. With the exception of the tumult, this comes to the same thing as if the majority itself held its deliberations in the market place." Tocqueville with these and numerous other observations demonstrated the tremendously important difference between representative and direct democracies, and again contemporary political thinkers like John Stuart Mill acknowledged their debt to him. Later observers, stressing other aspects of the American system (especially Lord Bryce), could not agree with Tocqueville's diagnosis of a trend toward direct democracy. More recently, however, it appears that the introduction of new techniques of mass communication, mainly radio and television, into the political process may well have promoted the development he predicted.

JAMES BRYCE

James Bryce visited America, mainly for the purpose of studying her political institutions, more than fifty years after Tocqueville. His subsequent two-volume work, *The American Commonwealth* (1888), ranks second only to *Democracy in America* as a political and philosophic treatise on its subject, and second to none as a systematic analysis and interpretation of American government. It is a classic in the world literature of political science, and is currently used as a textbook in many countries. No book better serves serious students of American politics. Its influence, nonetheless, could but be less profound than that of its great predecessor, for it is largely descriptive and factual, its political message being—British style—carefully understated, rather than eloquently and imaginatively elaborated, as in Tocqueville. Bryce in some important respects carried forward into the present time Tocqueville's fundamental conceptions of American democracy. Simultaneously, he contributed significant new features to the total interpretation. Again, only a few major motifs can be mentioned here.

Bryce shares and restates many of Tocqueville's views regarding the strength and weaknesses of American democracy. Like Tocqueville, he praises the people's spirit of legality and obedience to the law; the reliance on law rather than officials; the restriction of official authority; the simplicity and consistency in public affairs; and the people's faith in liberty and in their own institutions. In addition, Bryce emphasizes certain characteristics which are hardly or not at all to be found in Tocqueville's analysis, since they had not yet developed in the America of the 1830's. The extraordinary stability of the national community; the fundamental unity of the people; its ability to close ranks, on which Bryce comments, became fully visible only after the acid test of the Civil War. The relative freedom from political class struggle, which he emphasizes, became a truly remarkable feature only through the tremendous industrial growth of which Tocqueville saw only the faintest beginning but which fifty years later had produced an unmistakable cleavage in terms of socioeconomic classes in American society.

Bryce lists a third feature among the positive characteristics of the Americans: he says democracy has taught them "fraternity," and defines it as a certain "kindliness, a sense of human fellowship, a recognition of the duty of mutual help, owed by man to man . . . the natural impulse of every citizen . . . to respect every other citizen." Of course, Tocqueville had made similar observations. Yet there seems to be a difference in the feeling tone. Bryce feels closer to the Americans, and occasionally calls them "the English of America." Tocqueville in his time perceived American social manners as "grave, deliberate, reserved," rather than cordial, and human relations as almost devoid of real pleasure: "They laugh mighty little on this side of the Atlantic." Bryce on the contrary refers to "the humorous tendencies of the American mind." The spirit of fraternity which Tocqueville saw was a certain simplicity of heart ("If their demeanor is often cold and serious, it is never haughty or constrained") rather than a genuine kindliness and fellowship.

It is hard to tell whether the difference here lies in the minds that observe or is due to changes in the object observed. Charles Dickens, who visited America ten years after Tocqueville and forty years before Bryce, voiced a curiously ambivalent view. In his *American Notes* he describes the Americans as "by nature frank, brave, cordial, hospitable, and affectionate," while at the same time finding in them a spirit of "Universal Distrust," a lack of "lightness of heart and gaiety," and a generally "prevailing seriousness and melancholy air of business." Was this a true reflection of an America different from that of the two famous observers just discussed, or a subjective view conceived by a different temperament?

In describing the weaknesses of American democracy, Bryce again follows Tocqueville in important respects. His criticism concerns the level of political life in America, the intellectual standard of leadership, and the technical efficiency of government. Like Tocqueville, he finds a certain commonness and lack of dignity among the people's representatives (they "behave as ordinary men"), as well as lack of knowledge and judgment in legislative and administrative matters. The best talent does not enter the field of public affairs, and in consequence government in all its branches is below the level to be expected in a nation like the United States. "In no country is the ideal side of public life, what one might venture to call the heroic element in a public career, so ignored by the mass and repudiated by the leaders."

Bryce points to two defects of American democracy which had received little or no attention in Tocqueville's analysis: the corrupt and unethical practices occurring in party politics and in city governments, and the formidable power of wealth in America. Not only did Bryce penetrate much deeper into these problems as such (Tocqueville's treatment of party politics was one of the few rather weak parts of his study), but he was also, of course, confronted with a political situation in which a merely technical, moral judgment was no longer meaningful. Both corruption and big business had become inescapable issues in the America Bryce studied. He condemned the cynical selfishness and venality of many politicians and branded the system of machines, rings, and bosses as "the ugliest feature" in American politics. He attributed it to historical causes, and believed that it would decline when people, particularly the masses of new immigrants, learned more and developed an active sense of political responsibility. Civil service reform and better ballot and election laws would also help.

Unlike Tocqueville, Bryce did not consider a "tyranny of the majority" a danger inherent in American democracy. "The features of mob-rule do not appear in her system, whose most characteristic faults are the existence of a class of persons using government as a means of private gains, and the menacing power of wealth. Plutocracy . . . has shown in America an inauspicious affinity for certain professedly democratic institutions." Yet Bryce was convinced that American democracy was strong enough to avert this menace and to overcome any other weaknesses. Toward the end of his life he wrote: "No Englishman who remembers American politics as they were half a century ago, and who, having lived in the United States, has formed an affection as well as an admiration for its people . . . will fail to rejoice at the many signs that the sense of public duty has grown stronger, that the standards of public life are steadily rising, that democracy is more and more showing itself a force making for ordered progress, true to the principles of Liberty and Equality from which it sprang."

MAX WEBER

Approximately a quarter of a century later, Max Weber turned his keen mind to an examination of American democracy and the American people. Weber in 1904 was already near the peak of his career as an outstanding German social scientist. The occasion of his visit was an invitation to lecture at a congress held in conjunction with the Universal Exposition at St. Louis; the more important motivation was his desire to see the country which long had been a main object of his scholarly interest. At that time he was concentrating on the great problem of the nature and sources of Western industrial and business civilization, the historical phenomenon referred to as capitalism; on the eve of his departure he had sent to the publisher the first part of what was to become his most famous work, *The Protestant Ethic and the Spirit of Capitalism*.

To Weber, America was the society of modern capitalism, the country where the original sources of capitalism could be studied as nowhere else. What interested him primarily was not the spirit of capitalism itself, not the spirit of business enterprise, hard work, and moneymaking, often called materialism, but rather its deeper roots which he discovered in the ethic of Protestantism. From that religious source originated, in his view, the particular discipline of mind and the methodical way of life which created modern capitalist civilization. He demonstrated this thesis with a rich material, not the least of which was from American thinkers, especially Benjamin Franklin, whom he considered a prototype of the Protestant translating his religion into a code of capitalist practice.

America to Max Weber was the stage upon which the drama of the modern world was enacted in its purest and most consistent form. In his St. Louis lecture he characterized the American farmer as a businessman, "an entre-preneur like any other," in contradistinction to the Old World peasant who exists in a precapitalist relationship under the dominance of traditional ruling classes. This meant to him that America was as yet a society without an aristocracy. He was not certain that it would remain so, and at the end of his lecture predicted that America might experience a structural change in the distant future, and develop its own form of nobility based on land monopolies, as an effect of the power of capitalism.

Years later, in one of his political essays of the First World War, Weber returned to this theme with a remark in passing: "Unlimited political 'democ-racy' in America, for instance, does not prevent the growth of a raw plu-tocracy or even an 'aristocratic' prestige group, which is slowly emerging. The growth of this 'aristocracy' is culturally and historically as important as that of plutocracy, even though it usually goes unnoticed."

Another major theme heralded in the St. Louis lecture is that of bureau-cracy and its role in modern societies. "The importance of the stratum of state officials is and must be much greater in Europe than in the United States. The much more complicated social organization makes a host of specially trained officials, employed for life, indispensable in Europe. In the United States only a much smaller number of them will exist, even after the movement of civil service reform shall have attained its aims." This relative freedom from the bureaucratically formalized type of administration was, to Weber, one of the most valuable aspects of American democracy. Its main strength, however, he saw in the positive use Americans made of that freedom. The lack of formal organization did not mean to Americans an organized individualism, as people abroad, and particularly in Germany, often believe, but on the contrary, a fuller and richer type of community life: "In the past and up to the very present, it has been a characteristic precisely of the specifically American democracy that it did not constitute a formless sand heap of individuals, but rather a buzzing complex of strictly exclusive, yet voluntary, associations." This sentence, written in 1906, sums up what was perhaps Max Weber's crucial experience and his main orientation point during the American visit. The voluntary associations of free men in clubs, religious sects, and other groupings of all kinds which he found flowering in this country were to him the heart and core of American democracy, and a topic to which he returned again and again in speech and writing for the rest of his life.

After 1917, when America had entered the war and Weber realized far more clearly than most of his compatriots that Germany inevitably would be defeated, he worked feverishly on ideas for the establishment of a new, demo-cratic government and way of life in his country. In two important respects he presented American democracy as a model. He pointed to its pattern of voluntary associations, the club system, as a type of social order within which human freedom and creativeness could thrive in spite of the progressive bureaucratization of modern society. And he proposed the adoption of the American practice of electing the chief executive by direct vote of the entire nation, a provision which in fact was embodied in the Weimar Constitution of 1919. . . .

One important trend which Weber predicted with certainty was the ascent of the United States to world-power status. Long before America entered the war "he saw that sheer prolongation of the war would bring world industrial supremacy to America." At the end of the war he remarked that America's political supremacy was now, after the German defeat, as inevitable as that of Rome after the Punic War, and he added: "I hope America is not going to share it with Russia." He had long seen America and Russia as the two great centers of gravitation in the modern world, and as early as 1906, still under the impression of his American journey, he wrote: "Irresistibly the point of gravity of the population of Western civilization advances toward the great inland areas of the North American continent on the one side and of Russia on the other."

.   .   .

2

American Reactions
to the Great Works

ON DE TOCQUEVILLE'S
DEMOCRACY IN AMERICA

De Tocqueville's *Democracy in America* (1835–40), which has been summarized and discussed in the Commager and Brodersen selections, was received in the late 1830's in the United States with wholesale approval. After the barrage of carping and critical volumes by French and English writers in the 1820's and '30's and a deskful of friendly but ignorant volumes from other foreign travelers, the thoughtful, relatively accurate sociological analysis of De Tocqueville seemed to Americans, at last, an honest and just appraisal, not least because it defended democracy and predicted its triumph as the "coming" form of government. Laudatory notices in the *North American Review* (1836), the *American Quarterly Review* (1836), and the *New York Review* (1840) typified their warm responses. "We regard his work," the *North American Review* wrote, "as by far the most philosophical, ingenious, and instructive which has been produced in Europe on the subject of America."

After the publication of *Democracy in America*, De Tocqueville became active in French politics, serving as Minister of Foreign Affairs in 1849 and publishing several other books of historical analysis. He died in 1859.

The article from the *New York Review* of 1840, printed here, indicates the first wave of American reaction. The second article printed here, from the *North American Review* of 1866, records a different American estimate of De Tocqueville, however. Many Northerners had seen De Tocqueville's pessimistic conclusions about the viability of the federal Union as a major aid to southern propaganda in Europe. Here an anonymous northern writer paid De Tocqueville back after the Union triumph of 1865.

DE TOCQUEVILLE:
THE ABLEST VIEW THAT HAS EVER APPEARED

New York Review

The first part of M. de Tocqueville's *Democracy in America* presented the ablest view by a foreigner, of our government, and political and administrative systems, that has ever appeared. It fixed the eyes of all Europe upon the practicability of self-government and gained for its author a distinguished reputation, which he has more than sustained in this second and concluding part of his work, which we have just received.

. . .

The second part . . . undertakes to illustrate the influence of democracy upon the progress of opinion, and upon our social condition, feelings, sentiments, and manners. That such causes are capable of producing positive effects upon communities, and are beginning to assume a definite shape and color upon our own national and individual character, is undeniably true and, therefore, needed no proof; but M. de Tocqueville is the first writer who has attempted to point out their origin and tendency, or estimate their value, and to contrast them fairly and impartially with those effects which are produced under the aristocratic forms of government existing in Europe. The task is one of great extent and perplexity, and required five years of meditation and study to execute it in a manner which, although not satisfactory to the author, merits in our opinion the praise of candor and ability. No author of our age has looked deeper, or with a more prophetic eye, into the destinies of mankind, and the mighty causes which are now in progress to change the future political and social condition of our race.

. . .

Had we gone into a discussion with him upon principles and their practical application, we should have endeavored to show that it is unsafe to adopt a system of universal generalization as he has done, and determine all moral results with the certainty of mathematical. That grand abstraction, democracy, which, to his mind, stamps an unvariable impress upon society, is seen in our country to be essentially modified by the circumstances under which it acts, just as all great causes always are. It is not the single element, as he allows, upon which alone a calculation may be safely based; it does not of itself determine the kind or degree of refinement, cultivation, or social improvement generally, that exists among a people. M. de Tocqueville recognizes as a fact that democracy, in its present form, is a new state of society, and he should, therefore, admit that its influences are not yet fully developed, especially in this country, when so many causes are cooperating with it in molding our social institutions. Of these institutions, as they now are, we freely acknowledge that he has given an exact delineation; the great features of our existing society he has drawn with a masterly hand, but he has erred in think-

FROM *"Democracy in America,* Part the Second," *New York Review,* Vol. 8, No. 15 (July, 1840), pp. 233–48.

ing that democracy has been so great an agent in forming them, or that they have obtained an adult and fixed character. If we were called upon to name the most operative of all the causes, which have contributed to produce our national peculiarities, we should fix upon the rapidity with which everything among us moves and changes: we are nomadic—hence our habitations are tents, not substantial houses—we adapt everything to a temporary want, because we know that the future will demand something higher than that which answers for the present—we are constantly outgrowing our clothes, and are, therefore, obliged to get new ones—the youngest parts of our country are in their infancy, and the oldest have not advanced beyond childhood; none have yet hardened into the bone and gristle of manhood."

.   .   .

THE CRUCIAL ERROR OF DE TOCQUEVILLE

North American Review

Many among us are old enough to remember the visit of Messrs. de Tocqueville and de Beaumont, and the sensation produced throughout Christendom by the appearance of *La Democratie en Amérique,* from the pen of the former of these gentlemen. . . . Much as he studied and well as he understood our institutions,—and he studied them deeply and with great fairness—he signally failed, as late events have shown, to discover the real secret of their nature, or to fathom the character of our people. His book has been so much read, and has had, as we think, so considerable an influence in Europe, and particularly in England, as to have led to great misunderstanding in relation to the late Rebellion. Under this persuasion, we believe that a little time may be well spent in pointing out, and accounting for, a very grave mistake of the writer in a most important particular.

.   .   .

It is . . . very important, in forming a judgment of the value of M. de Tocqueville's work, to keep in mind the state in which he found things among us at the time of his visit in 1832. It was, as we all know, most critical. The prologue was then being recited of the great drama on which the curtain has just fallen. John C. Calhoun was then at the acme of his doleful career; the cry of nullification was then at its loudest, to be succeeded in no long time by the more appalling watchword of Secession. State rights, the true construction of the Constitution, the Virginia Resolutions of 1798, tariffs, and the "forty-bale" theory were the standing topics of angry discussion in all parts of

FROM "The Error of De Tocqueville," *North American Review,* Vol. 102, No. 211 (April, 1866), pp. 321–34.

the Union. While the controversy was carried on at the North with quite enough of eagerness and warmth, it was raging south of Mason and Dixon's line with a degree of bitterness which might well cause astonishment to a foreigner newly come among us, and tend to mislead him in his estimate of the people and government. It was at such a period that M. de Tocqueville set foot on our shores, with a sincere desire to form an impartial judgment of the nature of our institutions, and of the probable destiny of our country.

.   .   .

The result of M. de Tocqueville's mode of proceeding is just what might have been looked for. So long as he discusses the origin and history of our government, which he gets at by consulting historical and other documents, nothing can be more fair or more trustworthy than what he has to say. Not only are his facts indisputable, but his manner of stating and elucidating them is all that could be wished. Not so when he comes to deal with the questions of the day, and the future of the United States. That section of his tenth chapter which is headed, "What Are the Chances of the Duration of the American Union, and What Are the Dangers Which Threaten It," is a standing example of reasoning refuted by events. . . . He assumes at the outset that the United States are a mere confederation of sovereignties. In this section, he says:

If a contest should arise today between the states and the Union, it is easy to perceive that the latter must succumb. I question even whether the struggle could ever be brought to a serious issue. Whenever an obstinate resistance shall be made to the federal government, it will give in (*on le verra céder*). Experience has proved thus far that, whenever a state has obstinately insisted upon anything, and was resolved to obtain what it asked, it has never failed to succeed; and when it has refused point-blank to act, it has been let alone.

This statement he undertakes to prove by a course of reasoning which, though now quite worthless otherwise, is not without its use in showing how the wisest men may deceive themselves when arguing in support of a foregone conclusion. He lays down with great minuteness the distinction between the prerogatives which belong to the national government and those which belong to the separate states, and concludes that the latter must needs prevail over the former; that the local sovereignties are constantly gaining ground, so that the national government, growing daily more and more weak, must finally die of inanition. He follows up the argument with a cogency of logic which defies all refutation, winding up the whole with an axiom from which, he ventures to affirm, there is no escape.

It seems then certain to me, that if one portion of the Union wished seriously to separate from the other, not only would it be impossible to prevent it, but that prevention would not even be attempted. The existing government will therefore last only so long as every one of the states composing it shall continue to wish to form a part of it.

.   .   .

He then goes into a minute examination of the inducements the states have to remain together; which, in the existing state of things, is, to say the least, amusing. A favorite notion of M. de Tocqueville was, that the state governments, being more immediately connected with the domestic interests and everyday concerns of men, would in time become the great objects of ambition, and would eventually gain the ascendency over the national Congress. Now, nothing is more notorious than that the fact is just the other way. As the concerns of the nation become more vast, and the offices, diplomatic and domestic, more important and desirable, a seat in Congress is the constant aim of every aspirant for political distinction; the local legislatures being, for such men, merely stepping-stones to that object.

.   .   .

We might go further, but we think our readers will by this time agree with us that M. de Tocqueville's "religious terror" of social equality, imperceptibly to himself, warped his judgment. We propose to show presently some of the effects of his false conclusions.

With his hereditary prejudices, it is perhaps unfortunate that his visit to this country took place just at the moment when the great convulsion, whose heavings have not yet subsided, was beginning to stir the minds of men. Assailed on all sides by the clashing doctrines of contending parties; misled, or bewildered, by the specious fallacies of Calhoun and his adherents; alarmed at the growth of leveling ideas which had, not long before, rent his native country— he was but too ready to seek, in the probable preponderance of state rights, a last hope for the old conservative doctrines which were struggling at home against the two extremes of popular license and the despotism of a single ruler. He accordingly misunderstood the vacillation of the executive when the state of South Carolina boldly put forward pretensions to a right to nullify the decrees of Congress and asserted the sovereignty she claimed never to have parted with. He attributed the unwillingness of Congress to deal summarily with such a case to a consciousness of weakness, whereas it grew out of love of the Union, and the desire to stave off as long as possible, by temporizing and compromise, the dreaded moment when the question of nationality must be met. All men felt a dread of what many saw to be inevitable, and hoped to pass the bitter draught to another generation. The gifted author had hardly closed his eyes on earthly things, when the momentous problem he had pondered with such anxious solicitude was solved.

So long as there was hope of preserving the Constitution by mildness and forbearance, the people of the United States held back from the fated contest. Once convinced that the union was seriously assailed and the existence of the government endangered, they sprang to their feet and scattered to the winds the whole fabric of sophistries which had muddled the brains of political dreamers at home, and fed the hopes of the enemies of freedom the world over. Where are now the visions of Calhoun? Where the cobweb arguments of pragmatical lawyers, who, blinded by prejudice or slaves of literal construction, could not see the difference between a traitor with arms in his hands and a political partisan in ordinary times? Where is now the godlike institution which formed the cornerstone of Alexander Stephens' new empire? Where the nation which, according to high English authority, Jefferson Davis founded?

.   .   .

We should not have taken the pains, after so great a lapse of time, to recur thus particularly to M. de Tocqueville's great work, had we nothing more in view than to show that he had failed to foresee what was perhaps beyond the reach of mortal sight. We have already hinted our opinion, that the views therein expressed have had a great influence in Europe, and no inconsiderable share in the course taken by England and France, especially the former, in regard to our national affairs at a most delicate juncture. . . .

. . . On the strength of his opinion, our Union was looked upon, without the least question, as a mere partnership of states, which any one of the partners might dissolve at will—a fair-weather government, very well so long as all went smoothly, but which must yield to the slightest strain. Up to the outbreak in 1861, nothing had occurred outwardly to weaken in the least the doctrine of M. de Tocqueville in regard to state rights; on the contrary, Europe was filled with emissaries from the South enforcing the same notion, and quoting M. de Tocqueville in its support.

. . .

All this is harmless now, if we only lay it rightly to heart, and profit by it as we should do. As an argument the more in favor of the Union one and indivisible, it is invaluable.

. . .

ON BRYCE'S
THE AMERICAN COMMONWEALTH

The American Commonwealth (1888), wrote J. D. Cox in *The Nation* of January 10, 1889, is "so wise, so temperate, and so able a discussion of American institutions we . . . wish that it may find its way to the library of every patriotic citizen and be studied with care." As Franco-American relations in the 1830's had been conducive to a French intellectual's writing about America, so the 1880's, a time of great Anglophilia in the United States and of proud centennial celebrations of the American Constitution, was auspicious for James Bryce to publish his book. Bryce, a lawyer and professor of civil law at Oxford, had published his monumental *History of the Holy Roman Empire* in 1888 and had traveled extensively in the United States in preparation for writing *The American Commonwealth*. As a leader of the Liberal Party in England, he knew government and politics from the inside as well as from the university library, and he had extensive friendships with American political, literary, and academic figures. Later, he was to become one of the most successful British ambassadors to the United States (1907–13) and to write other major works such as *Studies in History and Jurisprudence* (1901) and *Modern Democracies* (1921). He died in 1922.

The first review printed here, by Edward Eggleston, a newspaperman, novelist, historian, and Methodist minister, was typical of the great majority of responses—extremely favorable. While it was also appreciative and respectful, the second review, written by a thirty-three year old professor of political science at Wesleyan University named Woodrow Wilson, indicated that Bryce had been superb at description but weak in analysis. Wilson had already won laurels with his *Congressional Government,* published in 1885.

LORD BRYCE'S PROFOUND STUDY
Edward Eggleston

There have been hundreds upon hundreds of books written about the United States by foreigners, but in all this number there have been but two "real books," as Carlyle would say. One of these, De Tocqueville's *Democracy in America,* appeared more than half a century ago; the other is Professor James Bryce's "The American Commonwealth," the pages of which are at this writing yet wet from the press.

. . .

Professor Bryce's book, like De Tocqueville's, is not the ill-digested journal of a traveler. It is a careful and profound study of American institutions by a great constitutional lawyer, as well as a full and admirable account of the practical workings of these institutions by a statesman who has played a conspicuous part in the affairs of England. By his large acquaintance with institutional history in general, by his ample experience of public affairs, by his singular freedom from prejudices of nationality, and by a certain rare intellectual and even moral tolerance toward men of every sort, Professor Bryce is fitted beyond all other foreigners perhaps for forming broad and just judgments of our government in its theory and in its results. I think I need not say foreigner. For no American could ever separate himself from the partisanship of his time, or from predilections in favor of the government of his own land, so far as to describe in a purely scientific spirit the workings of our government, as Professor Bryce has done. The matter is too close to us. An American of the better sort, for example, could not treat of a political "boss" without some prejudice, or at least some show of repulsion. The boss is the familiar enemy, and we detest him. But in Professor Bryce's work he appears as one of a species with a naturalist's pin thrust through him. He is examined, his specific traits are carefully noted; the cause and results of his existence as a boss are calculated—and when Professor Bryce has finished with him we know more of one of the unrecognized powers of our government than we could ever have learned from an observer less disinterested.

FROM "A Full-Length Portrait of the United States," *Century,* Vol. 37 (1888–89) (New Series, Vol. 15, No. 5), pp. 789–92.

The favor which the book has meet in America is certainly not because it is flattering, for while the treatment our institutions get is appreciative, no writer has ever laid bare the defects of our system of government and the abuses of its practical workings so amply and so unflinchingly. . . . Like all foreigners, he sees more danger in the quadrennial convulsion of a presidential election than Americans apprehend, but he points out also the advantage of this periodical agitation of the depths of the political conscience. He sees the evil of the acephalous conduct of business in Congress, but, while evidently preferring the English system, he is not blind to certain compensations in the method of making laws in committee rooms.

In many cases Professor Bryce has seen farther into the problems of our government than native writers. In one or two he is misled by the authorities we have supplied him with, particularly in matters of history, for we hardly deserve the compliment he pays us in saying that Americans know their own history better than Englishmen do that of their country. This may be true respecting the diffusion of historical knowledge in America, and it may be true of the work of students upon certain periods of our history, such as the crisis of the Revolution. But the action of cause and effect and the continuity of institutions and usages have been little understood, because some of our most patient and learned historians have been men tolerably incapable of penetration into that history which underlies history. Professor Bryce does not fall into Mr. Gladstone's error of speaking of the federal Constitution as "struck out at a blow." Our own writers have just now learned to trace many traits of that remarkable instrument to the constitutions previously adopted by the several states, and Professor Bryce recognizes this paternity. . . . This connection between the colonial and the United States system . . . throws into strong light Professor Bryce's admirable proposition that "the American Constitution is no exception to the rule that everything which has power to win the obedience and respect of men must have its roots in the past, and the more slowly every institution has grown, so much the more enduring is it likely to prove."

Like most foreign observers, Professor Bryce has a higher opinion of the relative value of the Senate than is held by most Americans. He probably underestimates the amount of corruption in elections to the Senate, and he is surely wrong in supposing that the choice of a Senate is generally foreseen by the voters in electing a legislature, or even that it can generally be fixed by wire-pullers in advance. Something is done in this way in our Eastern States, but many long and bitter struggles after the legislatures assemble, with the rise and fall of the prospects of the various candidates from day to day, go to prove that the legislatures are still as free in the election of senators as their lower houses are in choosing a speaker. There would probably be less corruption if more demagogism, and in the long run we should possibly have more eminent men in the Senate and fewer "lumber barons," "silver kings," and creatures of railroad corporations if senators were chosen by a popular vote. The House of Representatives makes a bad impression on one familiar with the House of Commons, as the mode of procedure in the Commons in turn seems antiquated and arbitrary to an American. But the amount of ability in the lower House is certainly greater than Professor Bryce thinks. The proportion of eminence is greater in the smaller Senate, but the number of eminent leaders of public opinion in the House today is doubtless greater than in the Senate.

Certainly in the recent debates on the tariff question the notable speeches on both sides have been made in the lower House. The accession of merely rich men to the Senate, by means not always laudable, has lowered its tone.

. . .

I can only mention the striking chapter on the growth and development of the Constitution, the elaborate analysis of state and municipal governments, the account of political parties and their workings, the description of "the machine," and the account of "the war against bossdom." But perhaps the crowning part of Professor Bryce's work is his chapter on "How Public Opinion Rules in America," and the chapters connected with it. His account of American national characteristics is much the most acute and discerning that has ever been made.

What then are the traits which this accomplished observer credits us with? He sets it down at the outset that the Americans are a good-natured people, and adds, "Nowhere is cruelty more abhorred." Of our humor he says felicitously that Americans "are as conspicuously purveyors of humor to the nineteenth century as the French were purveyors of wit to the eighteenth." Professor Bryce is impressed with American hopefulness, and with the unanimity of our faith in a democratic system of government and our notion that the majority must in the long run be right. He ranks us as one of the most educated peoples in the world, but holds that the education of the masses is of necessity superficial. He says that the ordinary American voter is "like a sailor who knows the spars and ropes, but is ignorant of geography and navigation." He pronounces the Americans "a moral and well-conducted people," and also "a religious people." Under the last head he notes our philanthropic and reformatory zeal, which he thinks commendable but often indiscreet. "Religion apart," he says, "they are an unreverential people." Ridicule he finds to be a terrible power in this country. "In the indulgence of it even this humane race can be unfeeling."

He notes that we are a busy people, but he does not find this wholly to our advantage. It results in an aversion to "steady and sustained thinking." We are a commercial people, shrewd, and hard to convince, and yet—he notes the paradox—an impressionable people on the side of imagination and the emotions, and "capable of an ideality surpassing that of Englishmen or Frenchmen." Professor Bryce almost overstates the fact that we are "an unsettled people." In many of our states the bulk of the population seems to him "almost nomadic." Notwithstanding our propensity to move, we are "an associative because a sympathetic people. Although the atoms are in constant motion they have a strong attraction for one another." To this he attributes "the immense strength of party" in America. He pronounces us a changeful people, not in opinions, but in moods. "They are liable to swift and vehement outbursts of feeling." "They seem all to take flame at once." And yet he finds us a conservative people, and he reconciles this apparent contradiction with great clearness and adds: "They are like a tree whose pendulous shoots quiver and rustle with the lightest breeze, while its roots enfold the rock with a grasp which storms cannot loosen."

. . .

Without forgetting many noble essays in this kind—Madame de Staël's Germany, Castelar's Italy, Taine's treatment of Italy and England, Emerson's *English Traits,* and others—I cannot forbear saying that I do not believe that the portrait of any nation was ever drawn at full length with so much fidelity and felicity as in these volumes.

DESCRIPTION BUT NOT EXPLANATION

Woodrow Wilson

. . . Mr. Bryce seeks to put American institutions in their only instructive setting—that, namely, of comparative institutional history and life.

.   .   .

De Tocqueville came to America to observe the operation of a principle of government, to seek a well-founded answer to the question: How does democracy work? Mr. Bryce, on the other hand, came, and came not once but several times, to observe the concrete phenomena of an institutional development, into which, as he early perceived, abstract political theory can scarcely be said to have entered as a formative force. . . .

. . . De Tocqueville saw the crude and impatient democracy of Andrew Jackson's time. Mr. Bryce has seen the almost full grown, the measurably sobered America of today, and has seen, therefore, with a fairer chance of just proportion.

.   .   .

Mr. Bryce's conspicuous merit consists, indeed, in perceiving that democracy is not a cause but an effect, in seeing that our politics are no explanation of our character, but that our character, rather, is the explanation of our politics. Throughout his work you feel that he is generally conscious of the operation of historical causes and always guided by a quick appreciation of the degree to which circumstances enter into our institutions to mold and modify them. . . . But it is one thing for a writer to be conscious of such things himself and quite another thing for him to convey to readers not possessed of his knowledge adequate conceptions of historical development. If our politics are the expression of our character and if that character is the result of the operation of forces permanent in the history of the English race, modified in our case by peculiar influences, subtle or obvious, operative in our separate experience, the influences, namely, of a peculiar legal status and of unexampled physical surroundings, then it is to the explanation of these forces and influences that every means of exposition ought to be bent in order to discover the bases of

FROM "Bryce's *American Commonwealth*," *Political Science Quarterly*, Vol. 4, No. 1 (March, 1889), pp. 153–69.

our law and our constitutions, of our constructive statesmanship and our practical politics. A description of our institutions, even though it be so full and accurate as to call for little either of criticism or addition, like this of Mr. Bryce's, will not suffice unless backed by something that goes deeper than mere legal or phenomenal history. In legal history Mr. Bryce leaves little to be desired: nothing could be more satisfying than his natural history of our courts with their powers of constitutional interpretation. The course of constitutional amendment, too, he traces, and all such concrete phenomena as the growth and operation of nominating conventions, the genesis and expansion of the spoils system, or of municipal rings and "bossdom," etc. . . . But if institutions be the expression of the national life, as Mr. Bryce rightly conceives, that national life must be brought constantly forward, even in its most hidden aspects, to explain them.

. . . He permits himself the old expression that we are "trying an experiment" in government. This is not true except in the same sense that it is true that the English are trying an experiment in their extensions of the franchise and in their extreme development of ministerial responsibility to the Commons. We are in fact but living an old life under new conditions. Where there is conservative continuity there can hardly be said to be experiment. Again, Mr. Bryce's statement—the old statement—that 1789 witnessed the birth of a national government could be made only by one who had not analyzed the growth of the national idea, which is coincident with the conscious development of the national experience and life. . . . Such an analysis is not supplied by his chapter (xxxiv) on "The Development of the Constitution by Usage." That chapter contains a history of measures, of certain concrete practices, but no account of the national sentiment which has so steadily grown into a controlling, disposing, governing force, and which has really become a most tremendous sort of "usage." It is a sketch of the development of the government rather than of the influences which have made the government and altered the conceptions upon which it rests.

.   .   .

There still remains to be accomplished the work of explaining democracy *by* America, in supplement of Mr. Bryce's admirable explanation of democracy *in* America. Comparative politics must yet be made to yield an answer to the broad and all-important question: What is democracy that it should be possible, nay natural, to some nations, impossible as yet to others? Why has it been a cordial and a tonic to little Switzerland and to big America, while it has been as yet only a quick intoxicant or a slow poison to France and Spain, a mere maddening draught to the South American states? Why has England approached democratic institutions by slow and steady stages of deliberate and peaceful development, while so many other states have panted towards democracy through constant revolution? Why has democracy existed in America and in Australia virtually from the first, while other states have utterly failed in every effort to establish it? . . .

Democracy is of course wrongly conceived when treated as merely a body of doctrine, or as simply a form of government. It is a stage of development. It is not created by aspirations or by new faith: it is built up by slow habit. Its process is experience, its basis old wont, its meaning national organic unity and effectual life. It comes, like manhood, as the fruit of youth:

immature peoples cannot have it, and the maturity to which it is vouchsafed is the maturity of freedom and self-control, and no other. It is conduct, and its only stable foundation is character. America has democracy because she is free; she is not free because she has democracy.

.   .   .

ON SIEGFRIED'S
AMERICA COMES OF AGE

By 1927, when André Siegfried, professor of economics and history at the Ecole des Sciences Politiques in Paris, wrote his *America Comes of Age,* the United States had become an industrial society, a continental nation, and a world power. The Republic was almost 140 years old. It was harder now to write a book about the whole United States—everything was bigger and more complex, and for every trend there was a contradiction. But the 1920's seemed to provide a clear moment of truth about American civilization—about "normalcy," business primacy, antilabor and antiforeign movements, Prohibition, the Teapot Dome scandal, isolationism, literary censorship, racial supremacy, and farm depression. These were the sides of America that foreigners saw first, and they obviously struck Siegfried as the essence of American culture.

To H. L. Mencken, the disenchanted and muckraking editor, Siegfried's portrait was marvelously faithful, as this review from *The Nation* shows. But another sharp critic of American business values, Charles A. Beard, professor of history and politics at Columbia University, found Siegfried's account of America shallow and distorted. Writing in *The New Republic,* Beard lashed back at Siegfried with unusual sarcasm and anger.

THE MAN WHO WASN'T FOOLED

H. L. Mencken

This book is so good that it seems almost incredible. From end to end of it I can't find a single misstatement of fact, and in even the most Gallic and unaccustomed of its opinions there is a searching and disconcerting plausi-

FROM "A Frenchman Takes a Look," *The Nation,* Vol. 124, No. 3227 (May 11, 1927), pp. 533–34. Reprinted by permission.

bility. By what process Dr. Siegfried amassed his materials I don't know. He has been in the United States at various times since 1898, and the last time, two years ago, he made a very extensive tour. His eyes must have been open very widely, for they saw not only what was plainly in front of them but also many things that were shadowy and occult, even to the overwhelming majority of Americans. . . . He went home to his stool in the Ecole Libre des Sciences Politiques with the most accurate, penetrating, and comprehensive treatise on the United States ever written, whether by a native or a foreigner. Compared to it the celebrated tome of the lamented Bryce sinks to the level of a text-book, and the works of the Stracheys, Bennetts, and other such soft-soapers become mere trash.

Dr. Siegfried is happily free from the romantic optimism that is so copiously on tap among us. He yields to no man, as the campaign orators say, in his respect for the diligence and ingenuity that have brought the United States to its present high place among the nations, but neither is he blind to the difficulties ahead. Internally, he believes, they revolve mainly around the bitter and apparently irreconcilable conflict between the so-called Anglo-Saxons and the newer varieties of Americans. This conflict, he sees clearly, is at the bottom of most of the political combats that wrack the country, and in the course of time it is bound to have serious industrial consequences. The Anglo-Saxon, clothed in his "self-satisfaction as a member of God's elect," simply refuses to go into his own melting pot. That vessel is reserved for the exclusive use of the Americans of other races. It is their duty to enter it docilely, and to come out as Nordics and Protestants. And having emerged, it is their further duty to take their place at the second table, leaving the original Protestant Nordics in front of the soup bowl.

Dr. Siegfried, as a Frenchman, is unable to grasp the equity of this arrangement, nor does he believe that it will long endure. The non-Anglo-Saxon, non-Protestant, non-Puritan Americans are not actually inferior; on the contrary, many of them are clearly superior. They have certain qualities that the Anglo-Saxons lack, and some of those qualities are immensely valuable. Thus they begin to sweat under the disadvantages that lie upon them, and to resist violently every effort to make those disadvantages greater. The crusade against all the varieties of hyphenism save the English that went on during the late war certainly did not abolish hyphenism: it only made it more resolute, as in the case, for example, of the emerging Negroes. What is the net effect of prohibition? Obviously, its net effect has been to set up a desperate rebellion, not only against prohibition, but also against the whole Puritan *Kultur*. And it is surely no mere accident that the Ku Klux uproar has been followed by the first really serious and determined effort to put a Catholic into the White House.

Dr. Siegfried ventures upon no prophecy as to the ultimate issue of this conflict. What will come of it, indeed, no man can know. The Anglo-Saxons, if the Negroes be counted out as incapable of producing a national hero, have the advantage of numbers and the support of tradition, but they show a decreasing capacity for genuine leadership. Put Coolidge beside Al Smith, and a certain difference begins to be palpable—or, if you choose, put Dr. John Roach Straton beside the Irish archbishops, or Booth Tarkington beside Dreiser, or R. A. Millikan, with his lingering theological sentimentality, beside, say, Jacques Loeb. The new immigration laws will hold down the influx of Loebs and Dreisers, but what of their effect, in the long run, upon the lower orders of Anglo-Saxons? What will happen when the Mexican *Landwehr,* now manning the ditches, is exhausted? The answer, perhaps, is to be found in the South, whence the blacks have begun to flee. The Anglo-Saxon, though Protestant and imperial, already has the hoe in his hands.

Dr. Siegfried is an economist, and is thus greatly interested in our mass production. Its virtues are manifest: it has brought us the greatest prosperity ever recorded in history. But in the long run it may carry us into very serious difficulties. Its excess profits we now invest in loans to Europe, and at the same time we shut our doors to the goods which represent Europe's only capacity to pay us our interest and refund our principal. Obviously, the money must be raised by selling those goods in other markets. But, soon or late, our ever increasing production will force us into those markets ourselves, and then will ensue a gigantic struggle. If Europe wins, we'll lose the markets but get our money. If Europe is beaten, we'll win the markets but lose our money. Dr. Siegfried apparently suspects that we'll be beaten. The machine has conquered in America, but the rest of the world still distrusts its products. In any case, there will be hard problems for the Coolidges and Mellons of the next generation.

America Comes of Age is far too complicated a book to be summarized. The thoughts that I have dredged out of it are not adequately representative of it. Dr. Siegfried must be read at length. He has crowded an enormous mass of facts into his volume and illuminated them with an unfailing sagacity. There is no evident intent in him to argue anything or to prove anything, but nevertheless he argues with great skill and proves a lot. Behind even his lightest obiter dicta there lies a background of sound and extensive knowledge. He has a prejudice, I suspect, against Puritans, but it certainly does not cause him to underestimate them. The American spectacle plainly exhilarates him. He is sensitive to its novelty, to its romantic charm, and to its overwhelming dramatic intensity. He must have enjoyed himself superbly when he was in our palpitating midst. But he was not fooled.

A STANDARD LECTURE
FROM THE "MAGNIFICENT" FRENCH

Charles A. Beard

This is a survey of America by a distinguished French publicist, who visited America in 1898 on a trip around the world, and again during the World War on one of the numerous commissions of observation sent abroad to spread the holy evangel. According to the translators, he is "an unprejudiced econo-

FROM "A Frenchman in America," *The New Republic,* Vol. 51, No. 653 (June 8, 1927), pp. 75–76.

mist and sociologist." The volume falls into three parts. The first covers the ethnic situation: racial origins, religions, color problems, immigration, the melting pot, and race conflicts. The second deals with the economic scene: labor, industrial methods, economic independence, foreign loans, world trade, and monetary policy. The third surveys the political complex: the several parties, relations with England and France, and Asiatic questions. Then there is a concluding chapter on the antithesis between European and American.

In the preparation of this volume, it is evident from every page, M. Siegfried has traveled widely, observed closely, recorded faithfully, and discerned cleverly. Though not so loaded with learning as the works of De Tocqueville and Bryce, the book has neither the flatulent philosophy of the former nor the arid banality of the latter, representing in this respect a distinct advance in realism. Naturally, the chapters and sections vary in depth and excellence, but on the whole it is a book of significance which ought to be read by all Americans who have left the ABC class.

If, at one's peril, one should attempt to grasp the animus and summarize the conclusions of this work, the scheme would run somewhat as follows. With reference to racial issues, there is a mortal collision between the Nordic Protestants, who are hard, money-loving, and crass, and the non-Nordic elements—Catholic, Jewish, and what not, the latter all heirs of "a magnificent civilization" in Europe, somewhat given to liberalism but showing a tendency to conform to mass production. The herd sentiment tends to engulf America, throwing her into violent contrast with the liberty-loving Latin (including presumably the Fascisti). Prohibition is a product of smug Puritanism and efficiency, is good for business (to use the American style), and is likely to remain, in some form, a long time. Liberty of opinion and person is disappearing, especially in the West and South, where anything but straight-laced fundamentalism is challenged on all sides. The American press is well tied to capitalist support, and editors are circumspect. America is swollen with wealth, obsessed by mass production, and the destiny of the country is at stake in the dispute over the candidacy of Al Smith. There is a real Japanese peril on the Pacific Coast. There is a fair working basis for a limited cooperation between American and British imperialisms, but America never, never, can understand the soul of France. Such a summary, of course, does an injustice to M. Siegfried's work, for his volume is packed with facts and made to sparkle with shrewd, often penetrating, and sometimes misleading judgments.

On the point of Franco-American relations, which, presumably, this book was written to illuminate, M. Siegfried writes with dignified reserve, but with a certain air of pained surprise. He tells his readers that "after the armistice the French made the mistake of thinking they could bring into practical discussion the comradeship which the American had felt for a while. . . . From the moment that the Americans refused to admit that they benefited from the military efforts of the Allies, and especially of the French, they denied the moral equality between the brothers-in-arms." Although some American readers will wonder why M. Siegfried expected any "morality" from a nation so given to material things and so wanting in spiritual qualities, they may be moved to remind him that President Wilson proposed taking the United States into the World War early in 1916 on the basis of "a clean peace"—without offering any spoils to the Entente participants; that, since the late adventure in comradeship, the American people have been voraciously reading huge tomes on the war origins, and have been suffering from some resentment over the way in which they were unmercifully gulled by the Entente prophets of the higher morality; and that many Americans think that England and France owe this country an apology for the continuous and mendacious propaganda carried on during the early years of the World War. Hence, if this view is correct, a discharge of the French debt at par would not be violating any moral principles known on this side of the water. Any ill-will between the United States and France is to be deeply regretted, but if the American people are to be regarded as "materialist" and the French as "moral," then an adjustment of the planes of negotiation must be difficult.

The real gravamen of M. Siegfried's case is that America, more than any of the "magnificent" European civilizations, has an obsession with "tangible and material accomplishments." This is the ancient song. It has been repeated so many times that any sophomore in historical studies can sing it to a saxophone. As a matter of fact, is it true? Where are the data, what are the criteria by which to test such a declaration? When a writer tells us that America has produced no great art and very few first-rate thinkers to measure against Europe's best, we can understand and consent; but is there any way of proving that the soil tillers, laborers, merchants, capitalists, landlords, priests, journalists, and warriors of Europe do not chase the material good things of this life to the limit of their abilities and the limit of their environmental opportunities? There is certainly abundant proof that they do not surrender to religion, education, and missionary effort anything like the amount of hard cash which the materialistic Americans do. After all, what is "materialism"? It is a definite term in the history of thought, but, in journalistic usage, utterly meaningless. The present reviewer flatly denies that America is more materialist than any European country, in the sense that, considering the opportunities, no larger proportion of the total human energy in this country is devoted to acquiring material goods than in any European country. The burden of proof rests upon those who make the charge, and pepper shots from M. Siegfried's journalistic gun are simply pepper shots.

Moreover, when a sophisticate from a "magnificent" civilization asks us to roar with laughter at a quotation from Bryan's testimony at Dayton, Tennessee, declaring a belief in miracles (no matter how ridiculous) and then, almost in the same breath, invites us to contemplate the superior wisdom of the Holy Roman Catholic Church, with its miracles, saints' bones, blood of martyrs, and index of forbidden books, we may be permitted a gentle dissent. If there is any creed proclaimed and professed in the hinterland of America that does not derive straight from the literature delivered by the Mother Church, then the present reviewer would like to know what it is. No doubt a forty-gallon Baptist of New York City is quite a different animal from a learned and skeptical priest of Paris who thinks the Church "is good for the people"—a phrase which the present writer has heard a hundred times from ghostly lips under a doubting skull—but, with respect to their essential creeds for publication and popular consumption, it must be said that the hard-shell Baptist makes no bigger demand on the imagination than the Roman Catholic. If anything, it is the two-seeds-in-the-pod believer who is to be forgiven for taking seriously a thousand things which the Catholic Church has been proclaiming for centuries. Likewise, when it is intimated that there is more liberty (except on the liquor question) in the Catholic Church than in the Congregational,

Methodist, or Baptist Church, dissent may also be allowed—with a reference to the Catholic doctrine that the Roman Church is The One True Church, accepting toleration only as a necessity—with a reference to bulls, syllabuses, indexes, and all the other paraphernalia for the suppression of opinion. This is not intended to be a criticism of the Catholic Church or any other claim on a monopoly of the roads to heaven, but a counter-citation in the interest of fairness and balance.

M. Siegfried is not unaware of the excellencies of his own culture, and, with that delicacy which characterizes the French mind, he occasionally refers to it. On page 20 he adverts to "the individualism of the Gaul and the intellectual realism of our Latin culture." The immigrants who come to America lose "the rich heritage of magnificent civilizations.". . .

Indeed, it seems that the contrast between Europe and America is "the contrast between industrial mass production which absorbs the individual for its material conquests, as against the individual considered not merely as a means of production and progress but as an independent ego." Not content with this large and sweeping assertion, M. Siegfried goes on: "From this unusual aspect we perceive certain traits that are common to the psychology of both Europe and the Orient. So the discussion broadens until it becomes a dialogue, as it were, between Ford and Gandhi." If it would not be showing a crass materialistic spirit, the present reviewer, with due reverence for France, the mother of civilization, might point out that in such a dispute M. Gandhi would probably have some difficulty in discovering profound spiritual differences between M. Poincaré and Mr. Coolidge, between the use of Annamese troops to preserve French loot in China and the use of American Marines in the interest of "law and order" in Haiti, between the conduct of French authorities in Asia Minor and American authorities in Santo Domingo, between the Paris banker and the New York stockbroker, between the editor of *Le Temps* and the editor of the *Times,* and so on. Perhaps. Still, since the soul of America is easily discovered by an elevated economist like M. Siegfried, and the soul of France can only be disclosed to the possessor of a peculiar cultural clairvoyance, it would be improper for anyone in the United States to traverse his verdict.

ON LASKI'S
THE AMERICAN DEMOCRACY

HAROLD LASKI'S DE TOCQUEVILLE: AMERICA FROM A SOCIALIST PERSPECTIVE

Arthur M. Schlesinger, Jr.

Harold Laski, one of the foremost British intellectuals and liberals of the early twentieth century (he died in 1950), might almost have qualified for dual citizenship, given the time he spent in the United States and the closeness of his contacts with Americans. Between 1916 and 1920, he taught history at Harvard, Amherst, and Yale. During the next three decades, while he was a professor at the University of London and a leader of the British Labour Party, he visited the United States often as a lecturer and kept up an astoundingly large and constant correspondence with American intellectuals and public figures. After publishing half a dozen distinguished and probing books on political theory between 1917 and 1940, Laski wrote *The American Presidency* (1940), a well-received study of the political and administrative roles of the American chief executive. When *The American Democracy* appeared in 1948, many American intellectuals expected a masterwork. Perhaps this made the reactions of American liberals—Henry Steele Commager, Perry Miller, Oscar Handlin, George Dangerfield, Hamilton Basso, and the other reviewers—to Laski's "misjudgment" of the United States and his fear of its reactionary future all the more pained and sharp. The comment printed here was written by Arthur M. Schlesinger, Jr., a leading member of the American anti-Communist left, professor of history at Harvard, and a Pulitzer Prize winner for *The Age of Jackson*.

The name of Harold Laski, member of the executive committee of the British Labour party and professor of political science at the University of London, on the title page will probably arouse a multitude of reactions in the American reading public, ranging from cold anger to indiscriminate admiration. . . .

The American Democracy can be briefly described as Tocqueville redone for 1948 from the viewpoint prevailing in British socialist circles about 1924 —the period at which Laski became a member of the Fabian Society executive committee. . . .

. . . Theirs was a clear and placid faith that you could bring about democratic socialism simply by changing the system of ownership—a kindly dogmatism strangely reminiscent of the uncomplicated faith in science prevalent in the last decades of the nineteenth century. . . .

FROM "Laski and the Democratic Ways," New York *Times Book Review* (June 6, 1948), pp. 1, 32–33. © 1948 by The New York Times Company. Reprinted by permission.

Laski, in short, is committed to the straightforward doctrine that nations based on private ownership are bad things and nations based on state ownership are good things. Apparently the experience of collectivism has disclosed to him no moral complexities in this rule. The Soviet record, it is true, occasionally irritates and even repulses him; but it does not shake his abstract faith in the theory of the Soviet system. Indeed, if one is to judge by the references in *The American Democracy,* the Soviet experience strikes his imagination a good deal more than the current British experiment in democratic socialism. Soviet totalitarianism figures in his writing as an uncouth and erratic but basically inspiring exercise in human planning, a kind of large-scale Brook Farm. The right changes in the economic institutions, he seems always to imply, will solve most other problems of international relations, of economics, and of morals. The moral and political urgencies which have given rise in the last decade to the enormously revivifying conception of the non-Communist left are altogether absent from Laski.

The American Democracy is consequently colored throughout by the implication that there exists this simple and easy alternative to democratic capitalism, and that all problems will be solved when the American people wake up to this obvious fact. But Laski is not sufficiently ruthless a pamphleteer to write a book to document his thesis. A commitment to the facts still exists for him, and it conflicts with—even if it does not modify—his commitment to ideology. As a result, the pamphleteer and the political scientist hack away at each other through the 761 pages of text. But neither seems aware that he has an opponent.

The image of the United States which obsesses Laski the pamphleteer is of a monstrous capitalist colossus, monolithic in its structure, irrevocable in its purpose, dedicated to the triumph of finance capital through the world. The image of the United States which emerges from the concrete passages of *The American Democracy* is of a great, rich and various nation, multifarious in its possibilities, vigorous in its democratic traditions, almost protected by its history and its native diversities from any descent into a closed society. His concrete observations evidently persuade him that in almost every respect (he excepts social mobility) the United States gives its citizens a more free and democratic life than does the U.S.S.R. But he never lets these observations affect his basic thesis.

Take, for example, the question of what a politically victorious conservatism would do in the United States. Laski's pamphleteering commits him to the Marxist glorification of the businessman, who in *The American Democracy* dwarfs the other characters much as Milton's Satan overshadowed the angels in "Paradise Lost." "The feeling is widespread," Laski claims, that "the great hour of the business man has arrived"; and this demonic figure, clear in his intelligence, settled in his purpose, is about to begin his concerted attack upon democracy at home and abroad. Yet at other times Laski seems perfectly aware that the characteristic American businessman is frightened, confused and politically inadequate; and in a shrewder passage he can write: "But whether the next era . . . be Democratic or Republican . . . no federal government will attempt to repeal the legislation dealing with social security. No federal government will attempt to alter more than the details of the machinery of the Securities and Exchange Commission. No federal government . . ." etc., etc.

This schizophrenia runs through the work. Laski the pamphleteer regards political bosses as "simply the affiliates of Big Business"; but thirty pages later the political scientist points out that bosses, since they want above all else to stay in power, will back progressives against big business. The pamphleteer regards the Supreme Court as the ultimate instrument of capitalist domination; the friend of Holmes and Frankfurter, however, is constrained to note the role in public education which the Court has played through our history. American universities are, in general, terrorized by reactionary trustees and, in particular, staffed by a whole army of bold minds whose work Laski reviews and praises. American foreign policy is dictated by the interests of finance capital; but "the record of the United States as an international power is better than that of most other great nations." The economic system makes "liberty a function of one's place in the market's hierarchy of power" on page 406; but on page 716 "the American system reveals a capacity for the discovery of new men, an anxiety to test new things, an interest in absorbing new experience, which remains notable even when all allowance is made for a visible loss, here and there, of important fluidities."

When he is writing seriously about the American democracy, Laski makes illuminating comments, as in his argument for a single seven-year Presidential term. But ideology keeps breaking in. We are told that one of Hollywood's main efforts is to put across the idea "that a labor leader is naturally a racketeer with whom no responsible man will have any connection"—theory that has no basis in any movies I can think of, even if it has some in Laski's political theology (or in the performance of certain Hollywood labor leaders).

Or, again, we learn that the United States might as well resign from the United Nations so long as it keeps its present economic system. American capitalism, Laski says flatly, cannot be made "the basis of an international political policy which looks to peace through collective security." This, he goes on, is because the American business man is "suspicious of all state intervention in economic life"—a philosophy, Laski strangely asserts, that "differs in degree only, and not in principle, from the central ideas of the Nazi economy and of the quasi-feudal capitalism of Japan." The economic system drives the United States to imperialism, and therein lies the fundamental threat to peace. Russia, as a socialist country, is by definition non-imperialist—and, I suppose, not a threat to peace.

This practice of attributing all values to the economic system reached its British apogee with the Webbs' dreamlike *Soviet Russia: A New Civilization?* Laski's work is an application of the same principles to the United States. But this economic fetishism seems sterile today next to the moral and political insights of socialists like Silone, Koestler, and Orwell. Some old socialists, like Léon Blum, understand the new problems; and Laski himself is no Communist dupe of the Wallace type. He has written, for example, a devastating attack on the British Communist Party in "The Secret Battalion." Yet, as he moves from the concrete to the abstract, he falls under the old spell and seems to regard democratic socialism and totalitarian Communism as (in Stassen's phrase) "two peas from the same pod."

This comes out with startling clarity in his argument for a third party in the United States. Laski holds up the British Labor Party and the Canadian Commonwealth Federation as examples to American liberals and trade unionists. Yet his advice is that an American third party should accept Communist support, since it will be accused of Moscow affiliations anyway, and "it seems rational to be hung for a sheep not less than for a lamb." Both the Labour Party and the Canadian Commonwealth Federation, of course, have bitterly fought Communist infiltration. It is hard to see why Laski should condemn liberals in the United States to the very alliance he has so savagely attacked in his own country.

One can imagine powerful works written about the United States from the viewpoint of the Communists or from the viewpoint of the non-Communist left. *The American Democracy,* which makes no serious distinction between these two positions, ends up as almost an epitome of left-wing confusion. The saving grace is partly that at least it is not in this case a new confusion: it is rather a desperate and doomed attempt by one of the most eminent of the last generation of socialists to adapt the socialist aspirations of 1924 to the actualities of 1948.

.   .   .

3
Contemporary Responses to Foreign Views

REACTIONS TO FOREIGN CRITIQUES

ON WILLIAMS' *THE AMERICAN INVASION*
Drew Middleton

Francis Williams' protest against the "Americanization" of England in *The American Invasion* (a selection from which appears in Part I, pp. 36-39) drew a range of reviews from mildly amused to angry. For example, Benjamin DeMott, professor of English literature at Amherst College, used "Williams' shabby little treatise" as the basis for an ironic essay in *The New Republic* on the value of being anti-American as a weapon in the internal intellectual and political debates of European nations. Part of the reason for American regret at Williams' book was the feeling that a former Ministry of Information official and newspaper editor who had been a visiting professor at the University of California at Berkeley in 1962 should have had a more profound understanding that the cultural force sweeping across England was not so much "Americanism" as full-scale political democracy, a high consumption economy, and the expanded influence of the mass media. The following review was written by Drew Middleton, chief correspondent of the New York *Times* at the United Nations and author of *These Are the British*.

As a people, we Americans find it difficult to believe that anyone, except, of course, Moscow's hirelings, can view us and our civilization with a critical and hostile eye. Our credo holds that the sooner the rest of the world starts collecting green stamps and following "The Untouchables," the better it will be for the rest of the world.

FROM "Our Most Controversial Export Is Our Civilization," New York *Times Book Review* (Oct. 28, 1962), p. 3. © 1962 by The New York Times Company. Reprinted by permission.

This process is proceeding pretty rapidly. Too rapidly according to Francis Williams, whose *The American Invasion* is a well-documented report on the extent of that industrial, commercial, and communications invasion in Britain plus a sharp attack on some aspects of the civilization that sponsored it. His words are of importance to Americans at this stage in our development. For they represent a negative reaction from the closest of our allies and the one in which the process is furthest advanced. But, as the author reminds us in his foreword, the process is going on in Latin America, Africa, Asia, and on the Continent. And not all its critics will be as basically friendly to the United States, or as fair, as Mr. Williams, a British editor and former BBC official.

After reporting the invasion's extent in industry, commerce, advertising, publicity, communications, and social customs, Lord Francis Williams describes the, to him, adulteration of British life that has been the result. Like many other thoughtful Britons he believes that the United Kingdom is ill-suited to some aspects of American life. And he notes a contradiction between the American image of our society and its true position.

"So far from being a tough, individualistic people glorying in the competitive fight," he writes,

The American people are now building for themselves a society increasingly stratified in its social structure. They have stopped being pioneers and become bureaucrats. Instead of dreaming of fighting their way from the wrong side of the tracks to wealth and power, they grab a safe job with a pension the first chance they get.

The author dislikes the conformism he sees in American life and the lingering effects of McCarthyism: "Dear hospitable, warmhearted, nervous people, how much I like you; how much I wish so many of you did not seem to think all thought is dangerous."

When the author is describing the extent of the American invasion, he is on safe ground. Yet he seems to the writer to pay too little attention to the fact that great industrial societies, the United States, Britain, Germany, and even Russia, tend to develop along similar lines. The United States is being blamed for the less attractive consequences of these developments. Even without the United States, however, much that he deplores in his own country—conformism, the disappearance of the rugged independence of the past, the shoddy substitutes that replace the old amusements—would have developed in any case.

Like many of the left abroad, he tends to exaggerate the influence of the right in America. The right is there, just as it has been since the birth of the Republic, but to ignore the depth and strength of the liberal tradition in American life is silly although very popular in left-wing circles abroad.

This reviewer is troubled, too, by the author's manifest suspicion, bordering on distaste, for the greatly improved material conditions of many of his countrymen. Of course, standards of living rose rapidly under successive Tory administrations and Mr. Williams is one of British socialism's most effective spokesmen. Yet when he takes this line, deploring the new factories, new homes, new hotels that are arising in the once depressed cotton towns of the North, the author sounds more like the most rabid Tory of the twenties than a socialist peer of the sixties.

It seems to me that the enterprise and vigor that now animate much of Britain's industrial society is the best assurance for the future. Here is a lively, intelligent people exploring exciting new ways of working and living. What if some of the impetus does come from America? Britain today is a different and a better place than the dull, poverty-stricken land of thirty years ago.

ON ARÉVALO'S *THE SHARK AND THE SARDINES*

Lawrence T. King

Juan José Arévalo was President of Guatemala from 1945 to 1951. He was a leader in the social movement that the United States considered swinging so far toward Soviet influence that the Eisenhower Administration used its weight to topple Arévalo's successor, President Jacobo Arbenz, in 1954, and install an anti-Communist regime in its place. In exile in Argentina, Arévalo began writing a polemic against the United States that first appeared in 1957 as an earlier version of *The Shark and the Sardines,* reviewed here by Lawrence T. King in *Commonwealth* (and excerpted in Part III, pp. 217–19 and 258–60). King is a California newspaperman who writes frequently on political and foreign-policy questions.

Juan José Arévalo was elected President of Guatemala in 1944, after a revolt ended the thirteen-year rule of the dictatorial Jorge Ubico. He served to 1951, when he was succeeded by Jacobo Arbenz, who established the first Communist government in the Western Hemisphere. Before entering political life, Sr. Arévalo had achieved some measure of fame throughout Latin America as an educator, principally for his production of a Spanish equivalent of the *McGuffey Reader.*

In *The Shark and the Sardines* he has written a tirade against what he terms "U.S. imperialism" in Latin America. The shark, of course, is the United States and the sardines are the twenty republics to the south. Since it is the natural function of the shark to devour the sardine, Sr. Arévalo maintains that treaties between the two are a farce and that the Pan-American system, set up to foster hemispheric cooperation, is merely a ruse to keep other sharks away.

The record of U.S. dollar diplomacy gives the author a strong talking point, and it is fully exploited to support the thesis that the State Department is the captive of Wall Street capitalists determined to keep Latin America in a perpetual state of vassalage. This may have been true at one time—and few North-Americans would argue with Sr. Arévalo about it—but to assess our recent diplomacy strictly in economic terms, which the author does, is to ignore the continuing development of American political and economic policy

FROM "Uncle Sam in the Eyes of Latin Americans," *Commonweal,* Vol. 75, No. 24 (March 9, 1962), p. 622. Reprinted by permission.

and, more grievously, the worldwide ideological struggle being waged between representative political democracy and totalitarianism.

In his introduction to the American edition, Sr. Arévalo writes: "In our resistance to the businessman mentality, we are still Spanish, stubbornly Spanish. Also, we have not left off being Catholic nor have we left off being romantic and we cannot conceive of private life without love nor of public life without chivalry nor of our children's education without enlightening ideals. . . . If you want to be our friends, you will have to accept us as we are. Do not attempt to remodel us after your image."

Our policy-makers would do well to ponder these words. At the same time, Latin Americans might just as profitably ask themselves whether the tradition which Sr. Arévalo defends in his introduction—although not in the original edition—can survive at all under the kind of government imposed by an Arbenz or a Castro. Sr. Arévalo's allegory would have been much more effective had he introduced a third character: a red-starred octopus. In this version, the sardines, fearful of being swallowed by the shark, swim for protection into the friendly tentacles of the octopus from the East. Oh yes, they are devoured —one by one.

ON VON BORCH'S *THE UNFINISHED SOCIETY*

George E. Probst

The characteristics of the particular political administration in power in this country have obviously had an impact on the mood and judgment of recent foreign commentary. During the last four or five years of the Eisenhower Administration, the United States was often regarded by foreign observers as tired, unimaginative, fearful, and conformist; during the three years of the Kennedy Administration, adjectives such as youthful, vigorous, dynamic, and flexible became the staples of European and developing-nation commentary. Herbert von Borch, a German journalist working in this country, wrote *The Unfinished Society* (see Part I, pp. 11–17 and 24–31) in 1959, and it appeared in Germany in 1960; the American edition appeared in 1962 and contained only a few additional notes. After reading the review below by George E. Probst, executive director of the Edison Foundation and editor of *The Happy America: A Reader in Tocqueville's America,* one wonders how Von Borch's argument would have been modified had he written the book in 1963. Or how might he have written of the "American dream" and its status during the first term of the Johnson Administration?

[In *The Unfinished Society,* Herbert von Borch] sets forth his thesis that "the best minds in the country know that the American dream has spent itself and

FROM "After Visions, Values," *Saturday Review,* Vol. 46, No. 1 (January 5, 1963), pp. 83–84. Reprinted by permission.

that the nation must live without it." The dream, he says, has passed because the traditional isolationism of the United States has passed.

Not even the status of a major world power, which America has reached, can prevent peace from resting on a balance of terror, when an opposing power in the East of Europe permitted America only a few short years of supremacy. A fermenting mass of two billion underprivileged people, in Asia, Africa, and Latin America threatens to upset the world's equilibrium altogether. Individual freedom has become ensnared in a vast maze of organization.

Von Borch promises, however, that "the following chapters will show that there exists so much capacity for self-redress, so many sources of strength in this as yet unfinished American society, that one surely need not despair about the future of this nation or of the West." Since much of the scant evidence for his optimism is credited to the Kennedy Administration, one wonders whether the original German edition in 1960 had this positive note. The author is both pessimistic ("the dream is dead") and optimistic ("there is no need to despair"), and thus he can accommodate any point of view.

Von Borch's argument that the American dream is dead and the idea and ideals that gave it birth have collapsed would be credible if the U.S. had lost a war, given up the grand scale of its international policies, or suffered an economic and spiritual crash. Instead, the author summons as evidence the organization man, suburban conformity, the Beatniks, American introspection about sex and morals, life-adjustment education, recent calls for a statement of national purpose and goals, the television wasteland, the freedom riders, the 1959 TV quiz scandals, the registered social class of the Social Register, and the dawning age of excess time and automation.

Since Von Borch is stationed in Washington, his discussion of the federal government comes closest to a sure grasp of the facts. He sketches well how our government is administered by a small group of men and how their continuance through different administrations means relative stability of policy under changing Presidents. Also good is his brief account of the prestige system that overlays our social equality:

To the foreign observer, American life appears at first sight as egalitarian. . . . ⟨But⟩* under the surface, there unfolds a fascinating patchwork of consciously cultivated group distinctions, involving not only a bewildering variety of snobberies, but also deeper forces of separation ⟨such as⟩ descent, religion, color, and length of settlement.

When Von Borch writes of intellectuals, education, race relations, love and sex, leisure, society, and so on, he does not depend so much on his own observations as on our recent popular sociologists, from whom he quotes one or two paragraphs each: David Riesman, Cleveland Amory, Russell Lynes, William H. Whyte, Vance Packard, et al. The technique demonstrates how poorly these works survive export. Typically, they represent a dissent from some common view, and when an American reads them, he knows what majority belief is being attacked and why the author suggests a corrective. Von Borch uses them as if they represented the entire story.

A journalist describing another society probably must be allowed a certain freedom with the facts. Von Borch says that our system of checks and bal-

---

* Angular brackets indicate insertions by the author.—Editor.

ances came into being as a result of the Declaration of Independence, that every American child today reads *Uncle Tom's Cabin,* that the Civil War was inevitable, that abundance is the basic problem of the American economy, and that love in conservative Boston is not the same as love in Los Angeles. One suspects that he is being too kind when he writes that "the affluent society is no longer anti-intellectual, and the intellectual is no longer anti-American."

Perry Miller has proved that American self-attack is an old Puritan habit. We have always been convinced that we were not living up to our ideals. The original settlement of New England, "an errand into the wilderness," judged itself a failure in the last part of the seventeenth century because Europe did not copy this new society. The failure of the American dream, then, is not such a recent event as Von Borch considers. It is a constant concern of the American mind, one that commits us to giving our wealth and talent to the service of our ideals.

ANALYSES OF THE ROOTS OF FOREIGN COMMENTARY

STEREOTYPES AND THE IMAGE OF AMERICA

William Buchanan

In recent decades, social scientists have begun to analyze how national images are formed; whether there are really behavioral "national characters" for Americans, Italians, Russians or Nigerians; and what—if anything—can be done to diminish the false images that nations have of one another. This quest for more scientific understanding has brought psychologists, sociologists, psychiatrists, political scientists, and anthropologists into an interdisciplinary venture that many see as a possible step toward reducing intercultural tensions at a time when revolutions in travel and communication make it possible to test this new open-mindedness.

In the selection that follows, William Buchanan, a former newspaper reporter, political scientist, "political psychologist," and member of the Office of Public Opinion Research at Princeton University surveys the principal literature as of the 1950's on national-image formation and its effect on foreign views of America. Buchanan was co-author, with Hadley Cantril of Princeton, of *How Nations See Each Other* (1953), a report on the UNESCO project dealing with "the conceptions which the people of one nation entertain of their own and of other nations."

. . .

Thinking in terms of types, classifying, and abstracting are inevitable economies of time and thought. The danger is that when "we assume that the world is codified according to a code which we possess, we are likely to make our reports of what is going on describe a world run by our code." Thus when the fixed stereotype governs perception, rather than being governed, corrected, and adjusted by it, our behavior becomes disoriented from the real world around us.

. . .

The psychologists have generally considered a stereotype as a special case under the more general classification of attitudes or frames of reference. It has been called an "intense and rigid attitude"; an "ethnic attitude" which is "relatively stable" and modifiable only through "traumatic personal experience, intensive re-education, or major social change"; a "highly standardized perception of all members of a class of objects or, especially, a class of people"; and a widespread "image or representation" of a national or racial group "usually oversimplified in content and relatively unresponsive to objective facts."

. . .

A question repeatedly raised is whether stereotypes correspond in whole or in any part with the "facts"—whether they contain what has been generally called a "kernel of truth."

In one sense, as [Walter] Lippmann suggested, stereotypes *must* be incorrect, since they impose a typology upon a group of people which contains (as reason would tell us even if the anthropologists did not) a wide variety of individuals with diverse characteristics. Any stereotype is incorrect in the sense that "all generalizations are false."

It is also agreed that stereotypes are erroneous to the extent that nonphysical attributes assigned to any race or nation are considered hereditary, fixed, or immutable.

The question remains, however: Are there national norms of conduct, even though culturally transmitted and hence alterable in the long run, which distinguish one nation from another? The answer is not yet definitive: "The existence of different personality norms for modern nations as wholes has not been established, and the development of objective techniques which might be used for the study of national character has barely begun."

. . .

American researchers have generally leaned in the direction of considering stereotypes as both false and dangerous. In the interests of alleviating international tensions or diminishing minority-group prejudice, they may be excused for considering hostile stereotypes to be unsupported by fact until they are proved otherwise. Our present purpose is somewhat different. A leap to the conclusion that all images of Americans held abroad are foolish, fanciful, and unjustified by our own behavior might do us a real disservice.

FROM "As Others See Us," *The Annals of the American Academy of Political and Social Science,* Vol. 295 (September, 1954), pp. 1–11. Reprinted by permission.

"A pattern of stereotypes," Lippmann said, "is not neutral." It is rather "highly charged with . . . feelings." The earliest experiments with students showed that peoples who were described in favorable terms (that is, in adjectives deemed by a panel of judges to represent desirable qualities) were those who were ranked highest in terms of preference for association. This relationship between friendliness and stereotypes was demonstrated to exist for nations as well as individuals in the UNESCO survey. Where a large percentage of the sample in one country picked a particular nation as the one toward which they were "most friendly," this nation tended to be stereotyped in favorable terms.

· · ·

. . . Experiments tell us something about how stereotypes appear and when they appear, but little of where the content of national stereotypes originally came from.

. . . Content analyses have documented the recurrence of stereotype items in the mass media, especially in fiction. From Shylock to Stepin Fetchit, from Sam Weller to Hercule Poirot, stereotyped national, racial, and class types have drawn such ready applause that we must conclude that stereotyping meets a psychological need, probably that of ego inflation.

In 1950 [M. D.] Graham [in "An Experiment in International Attitudes Research," *International Social Science Bulletin*] culled a list of phrases used in British literature and the press to describe Americans, and asked English respondents to check the most applicable. Phrases current *before 1860* were, on the whole, more popular than more recent ones, suggesting that "frequency of response depends chiefly on continued and consistent usage over a long period of time."

· · ·

It may be suggested that the absence of [a] "predictability from introspection"—the failure to really *understand* the motivations of foreigners—is what makes stereotypes so attractive. Lacking the opportunity to communicate frequently over a wide range of subjects, we cannot "put ourselves in their place." We may do one of two things: dismiss them as "unpredictable" or find a satisfactory explanation for their behavior in the attribution to them of certain characteristics. "They behave in this unexpected fashion," we might say, "because they *are* a sly, treacherous people."

Stereotypes or images of another people, then, appear to have two components. The first of these may be called the "preconception," since it is based on second-hand material lying about in the literature and folk culture and would exist even if the individual never saw one of these people in the flesh and never had to reach any conclusions about them on his own. The holder begins to form this image in childhood as he learns what his own nationality means and why his kind of people are superior to others. For they always are superior—no studies have recorded a more flattering picture of the out- than the in-group.

The second component of the image we may call "perception." This is what gives it purpose. "To bridge the gap between his inability to make accurate predictions of the behavior of others and the necessity for his doing so, the modern individual commonly resorts to stereotyping." This component is introduced as the individual tries to organize the incomprehensible, unpredictable behavior of foreigners—particularly those actions which he thinks may affect him personally—into a comprehensible, predictable whole. Under conditions of great stress—in wartime, for example—this process can lead to great alteration in national stereotypes. This perceptual part of the operation may be just as biased as the preconceptual if the observations embodied in the stereotype happen to be irrelevant to the use that is made of it, as, for example, when a Frenchman assumes that the Congress of the United States will act like a group of GI's or tourists in the Louvre.

Some psychologists have concluded that unfavorable stereotypes may predispose a people toward hostility and thus become a contributing cause toward strained diplomatic relations. The evidence collected here suggests instead that unfavorable stereotypes are symptomatic rather than causal. Confronted with inexplicable and hence presumably malevolent behavior on the part of another nation, observers then organize the latent elements in their cultural surroundings into a lifelike, believable picture of an inherently "bad" people—the sort of people who could behave just this way.

Stereotypes are probably more dangerous, both to holder and to object, because they may lead to irrational action, to measures which might never be taken if the actors thought through their implications rather than acting on a plausible oversimplification.

. . .

The image of America revealed in the UNESCO survey of 1948 is generally favorable. We were considered "practical" and "progressive" by most Europeans. "Generous," "hard-working," and "intelligent" were midway down the list. Favorable adjectives which were *not* applied to Americans were "brave," "self-controlled," and, significantly, "peace-loving." Unfavorable adjectives selected were "conceited," applied by Australians and British, and "domineering" by the French. "Cruel" and "backward" were seldom selected. By contrast, the Russians were generally considered "domineering," "cruel," "hard-working," and "backward." Other important components of the stereotype which were not represented on this list of twelve adjectives, of course, could not be elicited. Graham, for example, found in England that "friendly," "informal," "enterprising," and "gregarious" were among the favorable adjectives most frequently chosen, and "cocksure" and "noisy" among the unfavorable. A study of European leaders at the same period by a somewhat different method also disclosed a generally favorable climate of opinion, accompanied by a few widespread views which complicated relations: Americans were "too materialistic," they were "guilty of persecuting the Negroes," and United States policy was "too changeable" and "dominated by Wall Street."

These findings do not differ in substance from the more specific and detailed reports of correspondents and observers, visiting students and travelers. What such mass surveys lack in completeness they make up in perspective. They evaluate the strength of different viewpoints. They indicate which of two conflicting content items is numerically stronger. They reach the inarticulate and inaccessible people and give numerically proportionate weight to their ideas, however sketchy or uninformed. Most important, they permit comparisons of countries, as in the UNESCO survey, and accurate evaluations of change over a period of time.

. . .

Recent surveys made by other Gallup affiliates show that the stereotype of Americans in France and Italy is also about the same is it was in 1948. We are less likely to be called "generous" in France. On the other hand, "domineering," which had pulled an unusually high percentage in France in 1948, had dropped to the level of other countries. The French were more likely to consider Americans "peace-loving" in 1954 than in 1948. If, as seems reasonable, this change has occurred because the French are now themselves directly involved in the East-West conflict, it would be an interesting instance of the *American* stereotype altering because of *French* behavior. The Italian survey showed an image of the American people that was considerably more favorable than the public estimate of United States diplomacy.

WHY VISITORS DON'T ALWAYS "SEE" AMERICA

Bryant Wedge

It has become a tenet of American national policy and of social science literature on cross-cultural images that the greater the flow of visitors between nations (and the flow of information and personal contacts that are expected to follow visitor exchanges), the greater the likelihood of accurate, nonstereotyped perceptions of each other's country. Such perceptions usually include mutual recognition of the controls of ideology, national interest, and government-dictated propaganda.

"On almost any day of the year," writes Bryant Wedge, author of *Visitors to the United States and How They See Us,* "thousands of foreign visitors to the United States sit down to dinner with American families. Hundreds of thousands of others are studying in American colleges, negotiating with American businessmen, or traveling as tourists. Many of these visitors are among the most influential men and women of their own countries." Wedge, a psychiatrist and director of the Institute for the Study of National Behavior, collected the experiences of about one hundred American escort-interpreters assigned by the United States Department of State to accompany foreign leaders on their visits to this country. The following selection from Wedge's book focuses on the sources of the major misconceptions of the United States on the part of African, Latin-American, and Soviet visitors.

AFRICAN VISITORS

This report is based principally on the experiences of visiting leaders from French-speaking African countries, . . . [from] the sovereign states which formerly comprised French West Africa and French Equatorial Africa. Edu-

---

FROM *Visitors to the United States and How They See Us* (Princeton: Van Nostrand, 1965), pp. 6–27 ("Visitors from Africa"), pp. 28–41 ("Visitors from the Soviet Union"), and pp. 54–71 ("Visitors from Latin America"). Reprinted by permission.

cation in the former French colonies was always a *French* education, and the patterns of thinking of the best educated French-speaking Africans are difficult to distinguish from those of continental Frenchmen. To the degree that an African is educated, he is educated in the French system and almost without exception his only European language is French. . . .

Having had no previous contact with America, leaders of recently formed African nations have inherited their concepts of the United States, its people, and their habits in large part from concepts held by the former colonizer. Their notions of the United States have been shaped by the French press which harbored some resentment of American support for independence movements. A hypercritical attitude toward the United States led French journals of every persuasion to emphasize that aspect of American life in which the African had the most profound interest—the racial issue. The press, in general, spotlighted the violence in the South, minimized the progress being made, and sought to show the African that the United States segregates his kind and deems him innately inferior and fit only for menial labor.

. . .

Few African visitors are prepared for the degree of economic prosperity of northern Negroes and have appeared somewhat disappointed to find that Harlem does not approach their image of what a slum should be; there are no pigs or chickens or open plumbing. Their first reaction to seeing the worst Negro slums is surprise at the comparative luxury that surrounds even the poorest residents of urban America. Then, projecting their own situations, the visitors fail to grasp why the American Negro has not done more to better his own social and educational level: "The African who owns a fine car and elegant clothes will also have the house, servants, and the education to match such purchases. Why is the American Negro lacking in these things?" Their answers reflect extreme attitudes: "The American Negro is, after all, an inferior human being, incapable of raising himself from the ghetto, and to this extent segregation may be feasible"; or "That the American Negro has sunk to these depths is proof of the strong restrictions imposed upon him. With this wealth and our freedom, we could have conquered all of Africa."

The visitors, of course, lack the economic framework in which to view these material possessions. Mass-market consumption is unknown in French Africa, and they fail to realize that television sets and cars are cheap here by comparison and can be bought on credit. But after the initial jolt of seeing "luxurious slums," visitors gradually come to recognize the disparity between Negro and white facilities.

. . .

The great majority among Africa's vast population is barely cognizant of the existence of the United States. "America is very rich and very far away." And although we are here concerned with visitors who have had better-than-average educations, not all enjoyed more than a few years of elementary school. Disparities in knowledge range from the African parliamentarian who mistook the red light on the wing tip of his jet plane for an active volcano to persons as worldly and educated as their counterparts in any European city.

The educated African élite which has grown up in French colonial systems shares characteristic French thought patterns and concepts of government.

These leave little room for understanding federalism and states' rights—concepts so highly valued on the American scene. Nor do former French Africans understand the pragmatism with which Americans approach social problems, calling us "unphilosophical." They tend to think in extremes: If the federal government does not impose its will on the states, it is because it does not wish to resolve the issue. And if the philosophic ideal of racial equality is qualified in terms of practical possibilities, it must not be believed in at all.

These viewpoints lead the French-educated African with typical "logic" to profound misestimation of the American racial situation. If equality is not enforced, then the opposite—suppressive domination—must prevail. French rule left the African with a great respect for the law, and it is inconceivable to him that the *law* could *still* be unjust when the government claims to oppose segregation. Many visitors have voiced feelings that our government is not sincere in its avowed stand on segregation and that the President has not done more because he does not want to. Here the broad powers of African leaders are projected onto the office of the American President without comprehending the political and social problems caused by such action. By contrast, the former British African, because of his background in common law, more easily understands the moderate approach which sees attitude-change as the basis for legal revision.

The French African's reaction [to segregation] stems directly from his French outlook and inability to understand how local legislation can pre-empt the authority of the national order. For them, segregation in the schools ended the day of the Supreme Court decision on the matter. That citizens could be imprisoned for attempting to integrate the schools *after* the decision had been made by the highest court in the land seems incomprehensible. It can be understood only in one of two ways. Either the Supreme Court is lacking in strength and cannot carry out its decisions (in which case it should arm itself with the National Guard and see to it that it *is* obeyed), or else the commandments of the Supreme Court are merely words to pacify certain elements of the society and the entire system is based on sham and hypocrisy.

There is no parallel in the French or African experience for the phenomenon of federalism. To the French-educated mind, it exemplifies American pragmatism (a word per se with negative connotations) to the extreme. Even when the system is understood, it is considered as cumbersome at best and illogical at worst.

Under the French colonial governments, a greater degree of contact on the social level existed between Africans and Europeans than was common in the British colonies, so the French-speaking African is apt to say: "No matter what they did, the French never isolated us. They never looked at us as a people completely apart." The once-French African will almost invariably be appalled by the *concept* of segregation and be keenly upset to find that in our highly developed country, the Negro might be judged in terms of his color.

Few French-speaking Africans appear to understand how the racial situation developed in American history or to comprehend the political ramifications of the situation, for their French philosophic and legal training underlying their approach to all problems does not provide a background for such an understanding. The French colonials, unlike the British, did not discriminate against Negroes as such. Discrimination was based on education and "culture" rather than on skin color, and the French-speaking African has had little experience with explicitly sanctioned segregation such as "White Only" or "Europeans Only" signs. Segregation was based on tacit understanding, quietly enforced, rather than on legalized governmental policy. The former French African is amazed to find that our advanced and powerful nation still harbors some "codifications of stupidity," as one Senegalese visitor characterized them.

.   .   .

At the root of these anxieties about United States power and influence in Africa lie fears of economic exploitation and of being brought into the cold war. The reluctance of Africans to align themselves with either power bloc stems in part from their desire to remain aloof from world problems while concentrating on internal development and in part from a desire to maintain smooth relations with both the Soviets and Americans to receive aid from both. Independence is the foremost issue in Africa, and the former colonials want to avoid all involvements that might jeopardize it.

.   .   .

Time and again in their discussions with American officials, African ambassadors or ministers have used the following image: "You are like an older brother to us," or "We address ourselves to you as we would to our eldest." These repeated statements lead to a possible formulation: from the father image supplied by colonial powers, the African is making the transition to a brother image. He is trying to establish an identity in more concrete terms, and the United States is the logical choice for the living embodiment of his elder-brother image.

It has been suggested that communication at precisely this level of emotion corresponds to a very deep need in the African personality. A satisfying foundation for a long-term relationship between the United States and the newly emerged African countries may be the image of our country standing as a helpful elder brother to the younger, less experienced countries of that continent.

.   .   .

LATIN-AMERICAN VISITORS

The sensitive nationalism of Latin-American peoples is expressed in many ways: in a desire for recognition and a fear of "interference," in a pride of country and an awareness of national problems, in a feeling of deserving special attention and aid from the giant to the north combined with a fierce determination to assert independence from United States policies. These attitudes contribute to the distinctive Latin-America images of the United States, including the image of the good neighbor and the neocolonial power, of the rich uncle and the capitalist exploiter, of the bastion of freedom and a threat to Latin-American freedoms. Thus ambivalence, ambiguity, and sensitivity appear to characterize the attitudes of visiting Latin Americans toward the United States. These are generally concealed beneath an air of dignity and punctiliousness, it is true, but they are there nevertheless.

Latin-American leaders who visit the United States usually bring with them two preconceptions that are particularly fertile sources of misunderstanding. The first is the idea that the United States is "exploitive," especially toward their countries; and the second is extensive doubt concerning the morality of North American society and its people.

These two stereotypes appear to be well-nigh universal in Latin America. They are shared by representatives of parties of the left and right and by businessmen and labor leaders. While revolutionary-minded students have often expressed them in the form of raw accusations, visiting statesmen have indicated more subtly that their conceptions were substantially the same.

. . .

The idea that the North American economy is based on class exploitation is nourished by a basic misunderstanding of our mass-market economy, heightened by superficial contacts with American tourists, diplomats, businessmen, and technical advisors. Electrical appliances and gadgets, television sets, cars, and expensive clothes displayed by American personnel and tourists have the same status value they would have in a Latin society. For example, Latins tend to assume that a North American car owner must be as wealthy as his Latin counterpart. That automobile ownership is normal to workers as well as employers and that its actual cost in terms of working hours may be quite low are possibilities either unknown or hard to comprehend. Accustomed to a polarization of classes and to the resulting luxury market that supplies a few expensive goods for the rich, Latins are prepared to find the same sharp cleavages in North America's social and economic structure.

. . .

This pattern of expectation appears to spring in part from the very understandable assumption that our society must work in somewhat the same way that theirs does. In Latin America, the privileged class is allowed to enjoy its great wealth with little restraint from taxation or social legislation, while the average annual income per capita is about $225. Indeed, in most of the twenty republics the income for the vast majority falls well below the average. More than half the total population lives at the subsistence level, and only a small fraction enjoys a high level of wealth. Private capital, while it has many public functions in the United States, travels a closed circuit in Latin America. The huge network of philanthropic and voluntary organizations spreading over North America is unknown to the south.

The private capital that the visitor knows at home is thus exploitive by its very nature, and the accumulation of capital depends on such devices as tax evasion, bribery, and removal of profits from the country. These practices are not denied, even by the wealthy themselves; they seem so "normal" as to be expected. They are the natural outgrowth of a two-class economic system in which privilege accompanies wealth.

Reasoning by analogy, the United States is a wealthy country and therefore must act as do wealthy persons in Latin America. It will exploit poor nations and reap the profits. Similarly, just as moneyed interests have been able to influence governments in some Latin countries, it is easy to believe that North-American business may control United States policies.

This view is also supported by Latin experience with the United States dating from the days of "dollar and gunboat diplomacy," when our government was frankly zealous in protecting the interests of capital investment in Latin America. Since the inception of the Good Neighbor Policy in the thirties, however, the United States government has officially foresworn intervention in Latin-American political affairs, and there is every evidence that it has tried to adhere strictly to this policy. American business, too, including the much-maligned United Fruit Company, has made strenuous efforts to "improve its image" by pursuing enlightened management policies. It has brought Latin Americans onto directing boards and into management positions, provided education for workers and their children, promoted nationals to positions of responsibility as their training merited, contributed to local causes, and tried seriously to demonstrate a responsible and knowledgeable interest in the countries and their people. But the myth persists. It still influences the actions of Latin-American governments and is used as the "explanation" of United States policies.

The persistence of the exploitive myth, even though North-American policies have changed, is due not only to the experience of Latin visitors with capital behavior in their own countries, but also to a lack of understanding of legal, social, and political life in the United States. It is only when Latin visitors actually see our systems in operation that these become meaningful to them. . . .

The difference in legal systems provides a good case in point. In Latin-American legal systems, the law is the embodiment of the ideals of society and is deeply respected as such. It is regarded as an instrument for the shaping of behavior; its passage precedes the practices that it is supposed to determine. Thus, the laws express the hopes and the values of a people in universal and often absolute terms. Ideally, reasons the Latin, if we could only devise the perfect set of laws, we would be well on the way toward attaining the perfect society. . . .

When Latin Americans view the laws of the United States, they naturally apply their own terms to interpreting their significance. Without federal legislation, they ask, how can there be universal education? Don't we believe in universal education? If so, why don't we express this belief in legislation? The same sort of criticism is leveled against the failure of the Congress to pass absolute antidiscrimination laws. If we do not do so, it is reasoned, we must believe in discrimination. Similarly, the discussion of legislation for medical care for the aged has been criticized as representing resistance to such care, not as a debate on how this goal might be achieved.

Along with this attitude toward law is the view that the federal government should exercise ultimate and final control in all legal matters. Among Latin countries, only Brazil has a decentralized federal system like our own, and even in Brazil the states are subject to federal veto. A central, authoritative structure of government seems absolutely logical and necessary to the maintenance of an orderly society.

This attitude compounds the Latin's difficulty in appreciating the relegation of legislative powers to the states.

Similarly, the behavior of our political leaders is confusing to our visitors from the south. Latins are extremely responsive to individual personalities, and tend to be attracted to the firm, audacious leader who can define issues clearly and logically, even though they know the price of tyranny. If the leader believes he is right, says the Latin, he should proceed rapidly, forcefully, violently if necessary, without questions or doubts. If he delays or if he uses complicated legal and extralegal machinery while testing the winds of public opinion, as North American politicians have done in seeking solutions to our racial problem, the Latin begins to question whether his desire for change is sincere. . . .

In the Latin view, then, the failure of our laws to express our ideal aspirations, the autonomy of the individual states in exercising the powers not delegated to the federal government by the Constitution, and the cautious behavior of our politicians appear as weaknesses in our political system. This makes it appear all the more likely that powerful interests, especially capital interests, are able to work their will with the government. Since the will of capital is expected to be exploitive, it is believed that this power is used to grind down labor domestically and smaller countries internationally. This perfect logic, in terms of Latin assumptions, contributes substantially to the myth of exploitation.

The conception of North American society as immoral likewise stems in large part from prevailing Latin assumptions about law and economics. The notion that immorality is the inevitable companion of wealth and materialism is strongly held. Since the United States is wealthy, it must therefore also be immoral. Furthermore, in Latin eyes, morality should be authoritatively sanctioned and expressed in a clear-cut moral code, and the code should be reinforced by social restraints designed to protect individuals from temptation. The systems of chaperonage in Spanish-speaking countries are thought to be necessary to prevent promiscuity, and the dating system of North America is shocking to most Latins. Since they have no concept of the kind of self-restraint and self-control implicit in the dating system, they look on this custom as tantamount to an open invitation to misbehavior. South Americans are especially confounded by the fact that parents sanction young men and women's being alone together.

.   .   .

SOVIET VISITORS

Visiting Soviet leaders envision the United States in terms of a distinctly Soviet point of view. This authoritative point of view certainly influences their ability to perceive this country as it is, and more importantly, largely determines the visitor's interpretation of what he does observe. Furthermore, the concepts with which Soviet visitors come equipped, the patterns of argument familiar to them, and the connotative implications of the words they use are sufficiently different from American forms to complicate the process of communicating an accurate understanding of the United States.

.   .   .

The preconceptions of Soviet visitors about the United States are naturally conditioned by government-controlled information, but in general their preconceptions are remarkably accurate in regard to the material and technical conditions of life. Visitors are prepared for the American standard of living, they expect to find a high level of technological development, and they are prepared for the friendliness of the American people—although, like most visitors, they find the actual encounter with American openness and familiarity almost overwhelming.

In the sphere of social and political life, however, Soviet visitors arrive with deeply embedded stereotyped misconceptions. They anticipate that the United States government exercises complete control over local affairs and the lives of its citizens, down to the smallest detail. This view stems from long experience with the role that the Soviet government plays in all aspects of life, from the Marxist image that capitalism dominates the society, and from a typically Soviet pattern of thinking that requires social organization to be conceived in terms of central control. Thus, in Soviet eyes, nothing happens by accident; an anti-Soviet demonstration or discussion *must* have been sanctioned by Washington, difficulties in train schedules or hotel reservations *must* reflect deliberate policies, and so on. This is one reason why visitors believe that they are under constant surveillance and that they are permitted to observe only what our government wishes. If they are introduced to "workers," it must be that the truly exploited workers are being hidden. If a host offers to show the visitor anything he wishes to see, he still assumes that he is being guided.

It is a Marxist article of faith that the industrial economy of "capitalist" countries is based on the exploitation of the working class, and Soviets expect that this fact will be hidden from visitors. The image of the exploited workers and the starving unemployed may gain little support from actually meeting employed or unemployed workers; but this preconception is maintained in the face of evidence to the contrary by their clinging to the assumption that these circumstances are being concealed. In fact, this preconception may gain support from Americans "admitting" their desire to make money. To many Soviets, the word "profit" elicits an almost Pavlovian reflex; for, by definition, profit *is* exploitation.

Another ideologically based conviction holds that the American government is dominated by capitalistic "ruling circles" (lately the military has been included in these mysterious circles). Lacking any real experience with a free, democratic political system in the American sense, it becomes almost a necessity for well-indoctrinated Soviet citizens to posit some kind of ruling interests. In Marxist terms it follows that "capitalist" circles are hidden behind the government. It may even be believed that the American people, allegedly victimized by these circles, do not agree with their government and that even the nation's President may be helpless against such hidden forces. The fact that evidence to support this state of affairs is lacking does not, to this type of Soviet mind, affect the dogma.

The most difficult aspect of American life for the Soviet visitor to understand is the role of local or even personal initiative in the American political process. This difficulty does not seem to rest on ideological grounds or on positive misconceptions but rather on an almost total unfamiliarity with the theory or practice of grass-roots democracy. Political initiative, in the Soviet experience, springs entirely from the Communist Party which guides the policies of the Soviet government. These policies are expressed as policy "lines." It is unthinkable in the Soviet Union that political action could be initiated locally or independently of a theoretically justified line, and this political approach has profound consequences for the Soviet visitor's interpretation of his observations in the United States.

WESTERN EUROPEAN VIEWS OF AMERICA

André Visson

Sometimes the deepest insights into foreign preconceptions of America come not from Americans but from people who share the cultural frame of reference of the foreign commentator, and yet have come to know the United States well enough to place the commentary in perspective. Foreign-born American citizens provide such a pool of potential middlemen in the cross-cultural exchange process.

The selection that follows was written by André Visson, author of *The Coming Struggle for Peace* (1944), who described himself as "one of the 13 million foreign-born Americans." This excerpt from the book *As Others See Us* interprets one culture for another and in the process catalogues some of the primary European misconceptions of the United States.

. . . European misconceptions of America and the American way of life . . . can, broadly speaking, be divided into two groups—deep-seated and recent. Most European misconceptions and criticisms are almost as old as America. But some are the result of America's new position in the world, which has at the same time given new intensity to many of the old misconceptions and has sharpened many of the old criticisms.

Until World War I, which marked the beginning of Europe's growing dependence on America's wealth and power, Europeans were either interested in America as a great laboratory for a new political and economic experiment, or amused by it as a remote, exotic country inhabited by very queer people with extravagant manners and manias.

Among the old misconceptions and criticisms, the chief ones are that there is "no spiritual, intellectual, or artistic life" in America. That Americans are "money-making and money-adoring materialists." That their "puritanism made them intolerant conformists." That their "passion for equality has produced incredible mediocrity, vulgarity, boastfulness, and brashness." That they are boys who refuse to grow up, because they believe that adults cannot be happy. That their women occupy a more important place in America's society than the women of Europe and have made of the country a matriarchy. That their children are so spoiled that they grow up without manners and without respect for their parents—particularly the father. That Americans are "either naïve or hypocrites"—or both—because they try to conceal from themselves and from the rest of the world their real motives under the grandiloquent cloak of "devotion to moral principles," "high intentions" and "humanitarian feelings!"

Since America's accession to her new position of world power she is believed to be out to "Americanize" the world, to "standardize" it, to "depersonalize" it; to raise the level of international well-being only because it is of vital importance to American industry, which would otherwise be unable to sell the surplus of her increasing mass production. But in the process she would bring the world down to the low "mental age" of her movies and comic strips and would deprive it of the eternal human joy, the real human happiness—all that had been lost in a country which made of the "pursuit of happiness" its credo. Since America emerged as the strongest and richest nation in the world, so many Europeans have been at pains to discover anything that would confirm their belief that Americans—however prosperous—are profoundly unhappy; that their capitalistic system of free enterprise is "inhuman" because it favors the strong, crushes the weak, and exposes the whole world to the dangerous convulsions of boom and bust. American family life, they said, was crumbling; that ten years from now half of the marriages would end in divorce; that Americans had to establish "marriage clinics" in their colleges to teach the American boys and girls how to solve the problems which the Europeans have for generations been taught to solve by their writers and philosophers. Since America began to insist on a minimum of moral decency in international affairs and on respect for international law, many non-Communist Europeans have been anxious to expose and play up all the shortcomings of American democracy—the color line, racial segregation, the double standard of private and public morality. In brief, since America has become the last strong and well-armed watchman of Western civilization, certain Europeans wonder whether America really belongs to this civilization —as it is understood in Europe.

I have tried to indicate what I believe to be the main causes of these misconceptions and criticisms: the fundamental, historic ignorance of America; the difficulty of understanding the real differences between the European and American conceptions of life; the too great emphasis on what was queer, unusual, "exotic" on the surface of American life; the fundamental prejudice of the European intellectual elite toward the American conception of the "common man"; the failure of Hollywood and of the GI's to convey to the Europeans a picture of the real America; the frustration that comes from Europe's growing dependence on America's wealth and power; the envy of America's newly acquired wealth and power; the fear that America, intoxicated with her wealth and power, and with her political and diplomatic inexperience, may precipitate the world into the nightmare of another war.

There is no doubt that the influence of European history—so different from American history—on the European mentality has been much greater than that exerted by American history on what we call American philosophy.

Europeans, even when they ignore their history, have for it a kind of deep family affection and an almost religious respect. Many of them live with a feeling that their history continues to determine their life. They are prisoners of their history and they can rarely escape it. Not only their statesmen, but even the common people of Europe, have been taught to think in "historical perspective." They were greatly shocked to hear Henry Ford declare: "History is bunk," particularly because they looked on Henry Ford as a historic character. The British novelist, Aldous Huxley, in his satirical novel on the neo-industrial age, *Brave New World,* even imagined a new era "in the year of our Ford."

Most Europeans know very little about American history; a few lines on George Washington and Abraham Lincoln are all they found in their schoolbooks. But they are puzzled by American history. It does not fit into the common European historical pattern—no feudal princes; no peasant classes; no religious wars; no conflicts between the State and the Church; no social revolutions. Could this be the clue to the American success story? They do not think so, because many Americans, even leading Americans, appear to be uninterested in their own history. Americans turn their backs on it. Therefore, think the Europeans, something must be wrong with it. Americans perhaps have reason to be ashamed of it. And some European intellectuals jump to the wrong conclusion that Americans are ashamed of their history because there was no Napoleon in California, no Charlemagne in Kansas, no Joan of Arc in Kentucky.

The national structure of the United States is fundamentally different from that of the European nations. The American conception of a nation is all inclusive—the embodiment of a great idea. The European conception is exclusive—on the order of a family. Many Americans think of Europeans as either "miscarried" or "potential" Americans. Europeans know that Americans, who are descendants of former Europeans—or themselves former Europeans—would never again become Europeans. This is rather a frustrating feeling, which many Europeans try to counterbalance by telling themselves that even if Americans should want to become Europeans, they could never achieve it.

The political structure of western European parliamentary democracies is substantially different from that of the American presidential democracy, with its system of checks and balances. Europeans, who find it natural to have innumerable political parties, each expressing a certain political and social shade of the right and of the left, are at a complete loss to understand the functioning of the two American parties, neither of which has a definite political or social program. To most Europeans American parties are not political parties at all, but just national associations of various local interests banded together to win the electoral battle and to pay off its associates according to their importance. "Nothing would be easier to demonstrate than the intellectual vacuum of the programs of the American parties," remarks the talented British historian of American democracy, D. W. Brogan, who, being one of the most penetrating analysts of American institutions, hastens to add that this "intellectual vacuum" was the price for a "more perfect union."

The different political structure as well as the different political terminology makes it very hard for Europeans to understand Americans—and this, incidentally, is also true in reverse. The word "radical" in the name of a political party has an absolutely different meaning in the United States than it has in Europe. In Europe—many right-of-center, strongly nationalistic, and even conservative parties stick to their obsolete "radical" label, which they took in the nineteenth century. They long ago ceased to favor any "radical" changes and are most anxious to conserve their privileged political and economic positions, but they are proud to describe themselves as "radicals." It is a well-introduced political brand which has the confidence of many conservative-minded voters. In France, for instance, the members of the famous Radical-Socialist Party, which has been the backbone of the Third Republic, are no more radical or even socialist than the Daughters of the American Revolution are revolutionary. Many Europeans, therefore, are puzzled and shocked to find that the word "radical" is used in America to describe the near-to-subversive elements. This leads them to think that Americans who use the word "radical" in that sense are the blackest of reactionaries, at least as bad as the Fascists. The word "conservative" also has a different meaning in the United States than it has in continental Europe. While we frequently employ it as a synonym for "sound," "careful," "cautious"—"my conservative judgment," or "to estimate conservatively"—continental Europeans use it mostly in political terminology. And even there it is used very rarely, as it is not a vote-getting label. Conservative parties on the continent of Europe prefer to call themselves by any name but conservative.

The word "capitalism" also acquires a different meaning when it crosses the Atlantic. The Europeans who are familiar with the trust brand of capitalism usually speak of the American economic system of free enterprise as "monopoly capitalism," advocating absolute economic freedom, which degenerates into economic anarchy—a kind of jungle in which the strong can with impunity strangle the weak and take the spoils. Nine out of ten Europeans have either never heard of American antitrust legislation or believe that it is just a "screen of high economic intention and moral principles" behind which American big business dismembers the carcass of small business.

Many European writers and journalists who visited the United States are in great part responsible for the European misconceptions of America. . . . Many of these foreign interpreters and painters of America have been honest, intelligent, and sometimes penetrating observers, who made some excellent, very personal, but at the same time very valuable, portraits of America, its institutions, and its people. The list, from Crèvecoeur, Cobbett, Tocqueville, and Bryce to Guglielmo Ferrero, André Siegfried, W. L. George, and D. W. Brogan, is very long. Unfortunately, the honest and penetrating observers are read much less than those who, in a superficial or malicious approach, have ridiculed rather than criticized America.

Europeans who criticize Hollywood for giving a fictitious picture of America by showing everything excessive should realize that many of their writers and journalists have given an equally fictitious picture by their emphasis of everything that is excessive in America. Instead of trying to find what the Americans and the Europeans had in common, they concentrated on all that was different—and overplayed it. In search of easy success, they chose to entertain their readers rather than to inform them. And they also chose the easiest form of entertainment: they amazed and amused their readers by over-emphasizing everything that was different, queer, and excessive in America, until it became even more different, more queer, and more excessive. They treated America as if it were an exotic country—like Japan or Tibet. They described those American phenomena that were rare or did not exist in Europe: millionaires, gangsters, Hollywood stars. They described the American machine civilization as a kind of super-Frankenstein which gradually turned its masters into its slaves. They missed nothing that might amaze their readers and make them laugh at people with such strange manners and habits. Those who were more intelligent and more astute finessed, with half-truths and even quarter-truths, to present a colorful balderdash which they knew would both entertain and flatter their readers. The more sophisticated did their best to convince their readers that behind the glitter of prosperity Americans were fundamentally insecure and unhappy. But some didn't even take the trouble to look for half-truths or paint surrealistic portraits of America or even to caricature it. They were perfectly satisfied with presenting the queer, coarse, and laughable features with which they had been struck. One of the most typical examples of this kind of literature is a series of articles on America which appeared in a very conservative political and literary French periodical in 1947, under the title "Brutal and Secret America." When I read these articles I could hardly believe my eyes. They might just as well have been written in 1927, or even earlier. At a time when the eyes of mankind with all its hopes and fears were directed toward America, the French reporter—a well-known and gifted novelist who came to the United States apparently for the first time—devoted his first article to the funeral parlors in San Francisco; the second to the spirituals in the Third Baptist Church of the Golden Gate City; the third to a Bowery show with three-hundred-pound chorus girls and to a Harlem night club; and the fourth to the domesticated bear and geysers in Yellowstone Park! I am afraid that the "mental age" of such reporting is no higher than that of those successful Hollywood movies or the comic strips, which so many of his compatriots delight in taunting us with.

On the other hand, European writers on America are not alone to blame for the many European misconceptions of American life and character. Many American writers must take their share of responsibility. Some of them, such as Henry Miller, in the typically American violence of their soul-searching, do more to discredit America than most of her foreign detractors. All American writers who refused to accept American life as it stands and who in their passionate crusade for improvement of American social conditions created what is known as the "literature of refusal," have been the most widely read in Europe, and frequently the most misinterpreted. In order to catch the attention of their American readers and to impress them properly authors such as Henry Mencken, Ernest Hemingway, Sinclair Lewis, Erskine Caldwell, John Steinbeck, Philip Wylie, Richard Wright, and Lillian Hellman presented everything in the darkest shades and raised their voices to the highest possible pitch. The American readers could adjust their mental attitudes and view American evils in proper perspective. But the European readers, who were even more impressed by these writings than Americans, were unable to make the necessary mental adjustments. Instead of accepting these violent denuciations of American evils as artistic expressions of human indignation in the extravagant style to which Americans are inclined by temperament and by their religious background, Europeans accepted them as artistic representations of general life in America.

. . .

When a European hears Americans . . . denounce American foreign policy for its hypocrisy and for being loaded with the danger of war, or when he meets in Europe a most heterogeneous group of Americans who, for one reason or another, feel ill-adjusted at home and tell him that Europe is the "only place" where they can lead a "cultured life" and "breathe the spirit of intellectual freedom and tolerance," he is inclined to believe that these Americans represents the élite of America, and he wants to reject the moral leadership of a country that is renounced and deserted by its own élite.

When a European, accustomed for generations to having his poltical writers use extremely polite and generally circumscribed language in commenting on international affairs so as not to irritate the unpleasant neighbors who live just across the street, opens an American newspaper with its snappy headlines and its dramatic presentation of the news; or when he reads that a former governor of a state and former American envoy recommend the immediate dropping of atomic bombs on Soviet Russia, he not only feels uneasy but is frightened. He has lately been told again and again that most of the crucial decisions on American foreign policy will be approved by the Congress and public opinion only if the Administration succeeds in presenting the need in a sufficiently dramatic atmosphere. He would like to believe this, but he sometimes cannot help the cold shiver that such presentations send down his spine.

THE MIRROR IMAGE
IN SOVIET-AMERICAN VIEWS OF EACH OTHER

Urie Bronfenbrenner

Probing the sources of Soviet attitudes toward America produces a rich variety of theories to choose among. During the summer of 1960, Urie Bronfenbrenner, professor of social psychology at Cornell University, visited the Soviet Union to study Soviet work in his discipline. He spoke Russian well, he was able to travel freely without a guide, and because of the thaw in U.S.-Soviet relations at that time, he could talk with Soviet citizens from all walks of life. "At first," Bronfenbrenner said, "I was troubled only by the strange irrationality of the Soviet view of the world—especially their gross distortion of American society and American foreign policy as I knew them to be. But then, gradually, there came an even more disquieting awareness . . . that *the Russian's distorted picture of us was curiously similar to our view of them—a mirror image.*" What follows is Bronfenbrenner's presentation of the "mirror-image theory" of U.S.-Soviet perceptions of each other.

.   .   .

Let us . . . briefly examine the common features in the American and Soviet view of each other's societies. For the Russian's image I drew mainly not on official government pronouncements but on what was said to me by Soviet citizens in the course of our conversations. Five major themes stand out.

1. *They* are the aggressors.

The American view: Russia is the warmonger bent on imposing its system on the rest of the world. Witness Czechoslovakia, Berlin, Hungary, and now Cuba and the Congo. The Soviet Union consistently blocks Western proposals for disarmament by refusing necessary inspection controls.

FROM "The Mirror Image in Soviet-American Relations: A Social Psychologist's Report," *Journal of Social Issues,* Vol. 17, No. 3 (1961), pp. 45–46. Reprinted by permission.

The Soviet view: America is the warmonger bent on imposing its power on the rest of the world and on the Soviet Union itself. Witness American intervention in 1918, Western encirclement after World War II with American troops and bases on every border of the U.S.S.R. (West Germany, Norway, Turkey, Korea, Japan), intransigence over proposals to make Berlin a free city, intervention in Korea, Taiwan, Lebanon, Guatemala, Cuba. America has repeatedly rejected Soviet disarmament proposals while demanding the right to inspect within Soviet territory—finally attempting to take the right by force through deep penetration of Soviet air space.

2. *Their* government exploits and deludes the people.

The American view: Convinced Communists, who form but a small proportion of Russia's population, control the government and exploit the society and its resources in their own interest. To justify their power and expansionist policies they have to perpetuate a war atmosphere and a fear of Western aggression. Russian elections are a travesty since only one party appears on the ballot. The Russian people are kept from knowing the truth through a controlled radio and press and conformity is insured through stringent economic and political sanctions against deviant individuals or groups.

The Soviet view: A capitalistic-militaristic clique controls the American government, the nation's economic resources, and its media of communication. This group exploits the society and its resources. It is in their economic and political interest to maintain a war atmosphere and engage in militaristic expansion. Voting in America is a farce since candidates for both parties are selected by the same powerful interests leaving nothing to chose between. The American people are kept from knowing the truth through a controlled radio and press and through economic and political sanctions against liberal elements.

3. The mass of *their* people are not really sympathetic to the regime.

The American view: In spite of the propaganda, the Soviet people are not really behind their government. Their praise of the government and the party is largely perfunctory, a necessary concession for getting along. They do not trust their own sources of information and have learned to read between the lines. Most of them would prefer to live under our system of government if they only could.

The Soviet view: Unlike their government, the bulk of the American people want peace. Thus, the majority disapproved of American aggression in Korea, the support of Chiang Kai-shek, and, above all, of the sending of U-2. But of course they could do nothing since their welfare is completely under the control of the ruling financier-militaristic clique. If the American people were allowed to become acquainted with Communism as it exists in the U.S.S.R., they would unquestionably choose it as their form of government. ("You Americans are such a nice people; it is a pity you have such a terrible government.")

4. *They* cannot be trusted.

The American view: The Soviets do not keep promises and they do not mean what they say. Thus while they claim to have discontinued all nuclear testing, they are probably carrying out secret underground explosions in order to gain an advantage over us. Their talk of peace is but a propaganda maneuver. Everything they do is to be viewed with suspicion since it is all part of a single coordinated scheme to further aggressive Communist aims.

The Soviet view: The Americans do not keep promises and they do not mean what they say. Thus they insist on inspection only so that they can look at Soviet defenses; they have no real intention of disarming. Everything the Americans do is to be viewed with suspicion (e.g., they take advantage of Soviet hospitality by sending in spies as tourists).

5. *Their* policy verges on madness.

The American view: Soviet demands on such crucial problems as disarmament, Berlin, and unification are completely unrealistic. Disarmament without adequate inspection is meaningless, a "free Berlin" would be equivalent to a Soviet Berlin, and a united Germany without free elections is an impossibility. In pursuit of their irresponsible policies the Soviets do not hesitate to run the risk of war itself. Thus it is only due to the restraint and coordinated action of the Western alliance that Soviet provocations over Berlin did not precipitate World War III.

The Soviet view: The American position on such crucial problems as disarmament, East Germany, and China is completely unrealistic. They demand to know our secrets before they disarm; in Germany they insist on a policy which risks the resurgence of a Fascist Reich; and as for China, they try to act as if it did not exist while at the same time supporting an aggressive puppet regime just off the Chinese mainland. And in pursuit of their irresponsible policies, the Americans do not hesitate to run the risk of war itself. Were it not for Soviet prudence and restraint, the sending of U-2 deep into Russian territory could easily have precipitated World War III.

.   .   .

I am . . . calling attention to the operation, in a specific and critical context, of a phenomenon well known to psychologists—the tendency to assimilate new perceptions to old, and unconsciously to distort what one sees in such a way as to minimize a clash with previous expectations. In recent years, a number of leading social psychologists, notably Heider (1958), Festinger (1957), and Osgood (1960), have emphasized that this "strain toward consistency" is especially powerful in the sphere of social relations—that is, in our perceptions of the motives, attitudes, and actions of other persons or groups. Specifically, we strive to keep our views of other human beings compatible with each other. In the face of complex social reality, such consistency is typically accomplished by obliterating distinctions and organizing the world in terms of artificially simplified frames of reference. One of the simplest of these, and hence one of the most inviting, is the dichotomy of good and bad. Hence we often perceive others, be they individuals, groups, or even whole societies, as simply "good" or "bad." Once this fateful decision is made, the rest is easy, for the "good" person or group can have only desirable social characteristics and the "bad" can have only reprehensible traits. And once such evaluative stability of social perception is established, it is extremely difficult to alter. Contradictory stimuli arouse only anxiety and resistance. When confronted with a desirable characteristic of something already known to be "bad," the observer will either just not "see" it, or will reorganize his perception of it so that it can be perceived as "bad." Finally, this tendency to regress to simple categories of perception is especially strong under conditions of emotional stress and external threat. Witness our readiness in times of war to exalt the virtues of our own side and to see the enemy as thoroughly evil.

Still one other social psychological phenomenon has direct relevance for the present discussion. I refer to a process demonstrated most dramatically and comprehensively in the experiments of Solomon Asch (1956), and known thereby as the "Asch phenomenon." In these experiments, the subject finds himself in a group of six or eight of his peers, all of whom are asked to make comparative judgments of certain stimuli presented to them, for example, identifying the longer of two lines. At first the task seems simple enough; the subject hears others make their judgments and then makes his own. In the beginning he is usually in agreement, but then gradually he notices that more and more often his judgments differ from those of the rest of the group. Actually, the experiment is rigged. All the other group members have been instructed to give false responses on a predetermined schedule. In any event, the effect on our subject is dramatic. At first he is puzzled, then upset. Soon he begins to have serious doubts about his own judgment, and in an appreciable number of cases, he begins to "see" the stimuli as they are described by his fellows.

What I am suggesting, of course, is that the Asch phenomenon operates even more forcefully outside the laboratory where the game of social perception is being played for keeps. *Specifically, I am proposing that the mechanisms here described contribute substantially to producing and maintaining serious distortions in the reciprocal images of the Soviet Union and the United States.*

. . .

BEHIND THE SOVIET IMAGE OF AMERICA

Frederick Barghoorn

Urie Bronfenbrenner's theory of the mirror image would not be accepted by all historians or political scientists who specialize in Soviet affairs. Some would say that this theory is superbly rational but irrelevant to the way the Soviet citizen gets his views of America, and how and why the Soviet regime manipulates these attitudes.

A leading American expert on Soviet attitudes toward the United States is Frederick Barghoorn, professor of political science at Yale University. In 1950 Barghoorn published a widely praised scholarly study, *The Soviet Image of the United States*. Between then and 1964, he traveled extensively in the Soviet Union. On October 31, 1963, during one such trip, he was arrested by the Soviet State Security Police and held for two weeks as a "spy". He was released only after President John F. Kennedy publicly assured the Soviet government that Barghoorn was a scholar and was not on an intelligence mission. The article that follows is from the book Barghoorn published in 1964, *Soviet Foreign Propaganda*, dedicated to the late President Kennedy.

Soviet propaganda, even in the post-Stalin era, continues to present a . . . simplistic "two-world" imagery. . . . Marxist theory, in the name of which Soviet propaganda operates, could, if interpreted with understanding and sophistication, be a subtle tool of analysis. However, most Soviet propaganda is couched in terms of crude contrasts between the stereotypes applied by Soviet communicators to "socialism" and "capitalism." Theodore Kruglak, for example, found in a survey of communications transmitted to Moscow from the United States in October and November, 1959, by the Soviet news agency TASS, a picture of East-West and especially of Soviet-American relations which features a struggle of the "good guys against the bad guys." Regarding "images of East and West in TASS," Kruglak [in *The Two Faces of TASS*] writes that

The impression to be gained from an examination of the TASS World Service reports and the Moscow press is that there is unanimity among the countries of the Soviet bloc, discord and strife in the Western bloc, and friendship toward the U.S.S.R. among the neutral nations. An examination of the New York *Times* for the same period gives no clear-cut impression of anything remotely resembling a world behavior pattern based on political loyalties.

.   .   .

Immediately after the death of Stalin the Kremlin began a propaganda campaign designed to force the United States to settle major international problems, such as the German question, on Soviet terms. However, instead of being depicted, as it had been since 1947, as a nation led by militant warmongers, the United States was now cast in the role of a somewhat fumbling but still dangerous obstructor of progress toward the solution of the great problems of our time. Because it was less shrill in tone than the Stalinist line, the new presentation was probably more acceptable to a conflict-weary world propaganda audience. Neatly turning the propaganda tables, Moscow, with the odious figure of Stalin out of the way, posed as the champion of "normalization" of international relations.

For example, the May Day slogans for 1954, published in *Pravda* on April 21, contained an assertion that there was no question that could not be settled by negotiation. Soviet spokesmen, particularly when talking to foreign businessmen, now attempted to create the impression that ideological differences were not important. Simple good will, they averred, could solve the most difficult international problems. At the same time, epithets, such as "cannibal," or "bloodsucker," which abounded prominently in the vocabulary of Soviet foreign propaganda in the late Stalin period, virtually disappeared from 1953 on. . . .

Soviet efforts to pin the onus on the United States for refusal to cooperate in relaxing international tensions were facilitated by the difficulties confronting Washington in its efforts to achieve consensus, both at home and throughout the free world, regarding which policies to adopt to counter Soviet expansionism. American wares and ways became all too visibly involved in the daily life of the peoples of many nations. . . .

Stalin's successors, taking shrewd note of growing American involvement throughout the world, and the frictions which often resulted therefrom,

FROM "The Image of the Adversary," *Soviet Foreign Propaganda*, pp. 47–79. © 1964 by Princeton University Press. Reprinted by permission.

worked to render more plausible the traditional Communist propaganda charge that United States policy sought the economic exploitation, for the benefit of "Wall Street," of all countries where American business operated or American capital was invested. Particularly but not exclusively in the developing areas the Soviet image of American exploitation and "neocolonialism" reinforced local demands for the curtailment or elimination of American business and the substitution for American and other Western commercial ties of links with the Soviet bloc. One interesting concurrent aspect of Soviet propaganda on the subject of American foreign economic policy was the charge that United States business enterprises intended to displace the European powers in their colonial empires. This theme can be traced at least as far back as the San Francisco Conference in 1945, at which Soviet representatives energetically reasserted their traditional interest in the "colonial problem." Insinuations and charges of this nature were calculated to play on the fears of the developing countries as well as to sow dissension among the Western allies.

. . .

Especially after the beginning of the Korean War in June, 1950, Soviet propaganda frequently attacked American foreign economic aid, and particularly the Point Four Program inaugurated in 1949. American aid programs were pictured as devices for penetrating into colonial and semicolonial countries and seizing control of them. When Secretary of State John Foster Dulles made his tour of the Near East in the spring of 1953, Soviet propaganda expressed the opinion that one of the purposes of his trip was to push American plans for "liquidating" the economic interests of Great Britain in that part of the world. Even the modest American-supported village community development program in India was attacked in 1952 as an effort to enslave the Indian people. As early as 1954 Staley observed that Soviet propaganda to discredit America in the less industrialized lands was reverberating around the world in publications, in local Communist agitation, and, to a disquieting extent, in non-Communist media. Among the latter he mentioned the Peronista press of Argentina and various nationalist periodicals in Asia and the Middle East. Wrote Staley, "Sometimes Communists have picked up popular prejudices useful to their propaganda and given them further circulation. In other cases ideas originally of Communist manufacture have caught on and spread." The significance and impact of this aspect of Soviet propaganda grew steadily during the post-Stalin period, especially with the launching in 1954 and 1955 of a Soviet bloc program of foreign economic aid and technical assistance that was intended in part to counter American efforts in these fields.

It was Nikita Khrushchev, beginning on the trip that he made with Nikolai Bulganin, then Chairman of the Council of Ministers of the U.S.S.R., to India, Burma, and Afghanistan in 1955, who most effectively disseminated the twin themes of the American threat to the economic development of other lands and Soviet promises of economic assistance. The persuasiveness of Khrushchev's propaganda in this context was enhanced by the fact that he had by this time modified Stalin's tactless thesis that the governments of such countries as India, Egypt, and others were merely "lackeys" of British and American capitalism. This modification of tactics in turn reflected Khrushchev's shrewd appraisal of the upsurge of anti-imperialist movements throughout Asia and Africa, vividly reflected in such events as the Asian-African Conference held at Bandung, Indonesia, in April, 1955. For a time, following Bandung and the Suez crisis of 1956, the Soviet Union seemed to be riding the crest of a wave of nationalism.

.   .   .

The Soviet attack on United States "colonialism," and in particular Khrushchev's personal role in it, rose to a crescendo in 1960. Among the climactic events involved were Khrushchev's trip to Southeast Asia, already mentioned, the visit of First Minister Djuanda of Indonesia to the Soviet Union in July, the political explosion in the Congo, and Khrushchev's agitational activity at the Fourteenth General Assembly of the United Nations, particularly his introduction of a Soviet declaration demanding speedy independence for colonial countries.

The spring and summer of 1960, in fact, witnessed one of the sharpest switches in the kaleidoscopic history of Soviet propaganda and apparently ushered in a new and somber phase of tension. Having met with resistance from the Western political leaders he had been sedulously wooing, Khrushchev jettisoned the "spirit of Camp David" which had reigned for a few months following his 1959 visit to the United States. He took a course in favor of exploiting what must have seemed irresistibly tempting opportunities to harass the West in Asia, Africa, and Latin America.

In 1959, Khrushchev had offered the shadow of universal and complete disarmament without the substance of effective inspection and controls. In 1960, he focused his attention mainly on Western "colonialism." In addition to attacking colonialism, Khrushchev at the 1960 session of the UN General Assembly launched an assault on the institution of the General Secretariat of the UN. This was part of a continuing effort to eliminate obstacles to the political exploitation by the Soviet Union, aided by local Communists, of the situation created by the establishment of independent, but often poor and unstable, new governments in Asia and Africa. Khrushchev in 1960 proposed that the headquarters of the United Nations be removed from New York. In this connection, he charged that the representatives of the young African and Asian states were subjected in the United States not only to racial discrimination but also to "bandit attacks."

Our attention thus far has been directed mainly to the official Soviet image of American and general Western imperialism and colonialism, and especially its alleged economic effects. This is probably the most important single theme of current Soviet foreign propaganda, with the exception of that which is concerned with the war danger. However, the attack on American foreign policy is not confined, of course, to allegations of economic imperialism and neocolonialism. The United States has, in fact, been accused of responsibility for virtually every one of the social and political ills of each and every nation of the world. In Europe . . . for example, American leadership of NATO, which after all developed as a defensive alliance against Communist expansion, furnished a pretext for Moscow to associate the United States with the specter of a revival of German Fascism and aggression. It is a fact, however, that the Soviet Union armed Communist East Germany long before a military force was established in the German Federal Republic. In North Africa, particularly of course in Algeria, Soviet propaganda for years sought to blacken the image of the United States by linking American policy with that of France. In India, the attempt was made to turn Indian resentment regarding the Kashmir dispute with Pakistan, or differences with Portugal over Goa, against America. In Indonesia, Moscow has pictured the United States as the heir of Dutch imperialism. In the Congo, the Kremlin's attack was directed against "the Belgian and American colonizers." In Japan, particularly concerned about the effects of radiation and other consequences of the testing or even the carrying—on Polaris submarines, for example—of nuclear weapons, Soviet propaganda has sought to create the impression that the United States is irresponsible and callous in its attitude toward the handling of such weapons.

.   .   .

This image of a reactionary, greedy, and aggressive American foreign policy has continued since the death of Stalin to be accompanied in worldwide Soviet propaganda by the traditional Soviet picture of American morality, daily life, and culture. The United States is accused not only of seeking to frustrate the legitimate political and economic aspirations of the workers, farmers, small businessmen, and progressive intellectuals of the world, but also of wishing to corrupt them by imposing upon them a decadent civilization. The Soviet image of the American domestic scene presumably serves a number of purposes. One is to hearten the enemies and to discourage the friends of American democracy by demonstrating its weaknesses, or in Leninist jargon, its irreconcilable "contradictions." Another is to destroy the attractiveness of the political, ideological, and cultural freedom of choice offered to the individual by the American system, with the argument that this freedom is only a sham. Still another motive is to establish bonds of sympathy with those foreign intellectuals who are repelled by what they regard as the "materialism" of American culture. Another very important purpose, to which constant attention is directed, is to arouse indignation against the United States for practicing racial discrimination. Finally, Soviet propaganda continues to present an ideologically determined image of the situation of the American workingman as the slave of capital.

The post-Stalin image of the American domestic scene was not as lurid as the one broadcast to the world in the late Stalin era. For one thing, in its effort to woo at least some sections of American public opinion, Soviet propaganda acknowledged that there were some sober and sensible elements even in the ranks of American business. Also, cultural exchanges partially cracked the Iron Curtain and permitted a trickle of uncensored Soviet-American communication. Perhaps the biggest breach in Soviet communications control took place in 1959 when some three million Soviet citizens visited the American National Exhibition in Moscow. Such events presented problems. At home, they posed the danger that the official image of America might be shaken as far as Soviet citizens were concerned. Abroad, they may perhaps have tended to blur somewhat the image traditionally disseminated by Moscow of a world struggle between two bitterly hostile and irreconcilable forces.

To deal with these problems Soviet propaganda emphasized that coexistence among governments did not in any way diminish the intensity of the ideological struggle between socialism and capitalism. It also resorted to a wide variety of other devices. For example, it persistently accused the United

States of seeking to turn cultural exchanges into a political instrument. It denied the representativeness or the authenticity of American cultural exports. A textbook for the teaching of English published in the Soviet Union in 1959, for example, published a purported "Message from American Cultural Workers," which illustrates this point. The "message" stated that "the poetry and music our State Department broadcasts to Europe, to impress everybody with the riches of imperialist culture, are the work of men neglected and scorned throughout their lives by hypocrites who now pretend to honor them."

A central thesis of Marxist-Leninist doctrine on international relations asserts that the foreign policy of "imperialism" flows inevitably from forces generated by the international anarchy of competing economic interests battling fiercely for markets and sources of raw materials. There has been no significant deviation from this Stalinist image of international relations in the post-Stalin period comparable to that which was contained in Eugene Varga's notable book, *Changes in the Economy of Capitalism as a Result of the Second World War*. This book was, of course, repudiated in the course of the Stalinist ideological reconversion following World War II. Varga had suggested that the capitalist countries could, on a modest scale, utilize economic planning measures to partially solve some of the social and economic problems of capitalism. The post-Stalin interpretation of Western capitalism is even less sophisticated than that achieved by Varga in 1945. However, perhaps one element of realism in Soviet propaganda about the American economy was the partial acknowledgment after Stalin's death of the high degree of prosperity enjoyed by the American people as a whole.

An important Soviet reference book entitled *The United States of America,* released for publication by the Soviet censors in November, 1960, presented one of several frequently used Soviet explanations for American prosperity— to the limited degree that the Soviets are willing to acknowledge its existence. This work, edited by a committee of influential Soviet officials, including M. A. Kharlamov, then chief of the Press Department of the Soviet Ministry of Foreign Affairs, attributed the rapid economic development of the United States to such factors as the slave labor of negroes, the abundance of immigrants from Europe, the expropriation of the Indians, the plundering of neighboring states and islands, the availability of European capital, and the wealth of natural resources available in North America. The article in this handbook on "American Capitalism" presented this remarkable view of American economic development and went on to criticize "American bourgeois economists and reformers" for allegedly seeking to explain the rapidity of American economic development by reference to the exceptional nature of American capitalism. The handbook, of course, denied that American capitalism differed from capitalism elsewhere. Capitalism in the United States, it insisted, was founded, like capitalism everywhere, on exploitation and was characterized by class conflict and crisis. Just as world capitalism as a whole, the American form had entered its period of incurable "general crisis" as a result of the First World War and the October Revolution in Russia. Linking its analysis of the internal structure of the American economy with United States foreign policy, the article attributed to the "ruling circles of the U.S.A." a policy of struggling for a redivision of the world in their favor. It further asserted that the United States was "the greatest colonial power" and that it had developed new forms of colonial oppression in the form of military alliances.

As might be expected, the article laid great stress on alleged economic exploitation of American workers, and asserted that under the pressure of a falling standard of living, and of unemployment, the workers were turning increasingly to strikes and other forms of resistance to economic oppression. It added that social conflicts in the United States not only pitted the *bourgeoisie* against the working class but also involved a struggle between the "monopolistic *bourgeoisie*" and all other strata of the people, including the proletariat, the masses of the farmers, the intellectuals, the tradespeople, and other groups. The foregoing brief summary of one representative article in this six-hundred-page book suggests the massive barriers to international understanding interposed by Leninist demonology between the Soviet world and the constitutional democracies.

．　　．　　．

Even the most skeptical of American political scientists would presumably agree that political competition for public office through free elections is close to the heart of Western constitutional democracy. However, the Soviet press has continued to present the traditional Leninist view according to which the American system of elections "is intended to assure the political domination of monopolistic capital in the United States." It may be interesting to examine briefly how this formula was applied to the United States Presidential elections of 1952, 1956, and 1960. (We include 1952 in order to furnish a basis of comparison with the Stalin era.) From the point of view of a non-Communist American political scientist, the Soviet presentation of all three of these elections was shaped by a combination of ideological prejudice and deliberate falsification. The element of falsification was greater in publications such as *Trud, Pravda,* or *Izvestia,* than in the magazine *New Times,* which is intended for foreign distribution and is published in many languages.

This fact perhaps reflected Soviet appreciation of the relative difficulty of falsifying the nature of the American election system to foreign audiences not subject to Soviet controls on communication. Somewhat encouraging was the fact that the reporting of the American Presidential elections in Soviet publications was more accurate in 1956 and 1960 than in 1952. For example, the charges made in 1952 that the American elections took place in an atmosphere of violence and "police terror" were absent in 1956 and 1960. Even *New Times* in its 1952 reporting of the Philadelphia mayoralty election had reported that it was conducted in an atmosphere of "bribery and corruption, blackmail and violence." From this account, it would have been impossible to draw the conclusion, in fact correct, that the election was marked by the victory of a reform ticket.

In their reporting of the 1956 and 1960 elections, Soviet publications contained interesting indications of awareness that there were differences not only between the Democratic and Republican parties, but also within them. However, the main line which they followed was the traditional one that the policy and the purposes of the two parties were identical. Khrushchev himself stated the Soviet position at an industrial exhibition in Hungary in August, 1960, when he said that both Kennedy and Nixon were "servants of monopoly capital, so there is no choice for us here." Interestingly enough, Stevenson, who had been treated in 1952 and 1956 as a typical representative of monopoly capitalism, was presented in 1960 as a relatively desirable possibility for the Democratic nomination, apparently because of his expressed attitudes toward international issues.

Thus the Soviet interpretation of this central aspect of the American political system continued to be shaped by traditional Leninist orthodoxy. At the same time, however, it also reflected some increase of knowledge of the facts of American political life and, at the same time, an irresistible desire to fit these facts into whatever was the Kremlin's propaganda preoccupation of the moment.

Perhaps something should be said here about the Soviet propaganda treatment of the first few months of the Kennedy Administration. A systematic study of Soviet short-wave radio broadcasts in English from Moscow to eastern North America, the United Kingdom, and Europe from the period November 8, 1960, to May 3, 1961, revealed an interesting pattern. The Soviet radio interpreted the victory of Mr. Kennedy as an expression of the dissatisfaction of the American people with the Eisenhower Administration. The keynote of the early attitude toward President Kennedy was struck by Khrushchev in his telegram to Mr. Kennedy on November 9, 1960, expressing the hope that relations between the U.S.S.R. and the U.S.A. would return to the line along which they were developing in the days of Franklin D. Roosevelt. This gambit, combined with a "wait and see" attitude toward Kennedy, was apparently designed to project to the peoples of the world the Soviet desire for a fresh start in international affairs and, at the same time, to throw the onus of failure to achieve this, if need be, on the United States and the American President. Significant was a broadcast on November 17, which stated that cooperation was necessary for progress in negotiations with the Soviet Union, but warned that there were individuals in the leadership of the Democratic Party who did not stick to the "realistic course" which Roosevelt followed toward the Soviet Union.

. . .

While attacking the American "ruling circles" and, less frequently, Presidents Truman, Eisenhower, and Kennedy, Soviet propaganda has continued its effort to persuade both the Soviet people and the other peoples of the world that the "simple people" of America, and also some of the more sensible elements of the American élite, would like to respond favorably to Soviet overtures for a relaxation of international tensions. In fact, many of Khrushchev's most important speeches have contained sections suggesting, in effect, a "deal" between Russia and America. For example, in his speech to the Twentieth Congress of the CPSU in 1956 Khrushchev devoted several paragraphs to the attractive prospects which would be opened up by the "establishment of firm, friendly relations between the two greatest powers of the world, the Soviet Union and the United States of America." One way of lending credence to this professed objective, especially in contacts with businessmen, is to suggest that better political relations will lead to profitable trade. Another is to attempt to cultivate cordial personal relations with individual businessmen, labor leaders, and professionals. Soviet diplomacy and propaganda devoted considerable attention to these objectives in the post-Stalin period, although the results were probably modest.

The generally negative image of the United States that we have been briefly sketching here is extended into the past by Soviet historians. An interesting and widely circulated example of the rewriting of American history to suit the purposes of post-Stalin foreign policy is contained in the section on American history of *The Great Soviet Encyclopedia,* which was published in an annotated translation in 1960 by the State Historical Society of Wisconsin. Unlike the relatively objective 1945 Soviet encyclopedia article on the same subject, this one stressed American "imperialistic expansionism" and racial, social, and economic unrest. Rather interesting, in view of Khrushchev's attempt to manipulate the Roosevelt symbol in world affairs, was the unfavorable characterization of Roosevelt's policies—not quite as unfavorable, however, as that accorded the policies of other American presidents.

. . .

Of course the Kremlin regards Soviet-American relations not only as a power struggle but also as a competition between two cultures, or two civilizations, with Moscow representing the socialist camp and Washington representing capitalism. . . . While working for and waiting for the world cultural revolution the Kremlin continued its campaign against Western culture, and in particular against those aspects of modern culture most attractive to adventurous minds in the Soviet Union itself, such as abstract art or "progressive" jazz. Typical was the statement that "the New York Museum of Modern Art, founded in 1929 by the magnates of capital, has become the avenue for disseminating formalistic, abstract art as the official art of the United States." The long and critical article on American motion pictures in the already cited official Soviet Handbook on the United States concludes with the following statement: "The situation which developed in the postwar years in American film art serves as a clear reflection of the general crisis of bourgeois culture, of the capitalist society, and social system."

As Melville J. Ruggles found, after surveying a vast array of Russian translations of American literature [in "American Books in Soviet Publishing," *Slavic Review*], "The America that the Russian knows from the American literature available to him is a land of Simon Legree, the coonskin cap, the heroic sled dog, the sharecropper, the sweatshop, the dispirited, defeated, and depraved, the frivolous, the bloated billionaire, the regimented traveler in space."

While depreciating the dominant "bourgeois" American culture and its exponents, the Soviet and international Communist press extols as examples of "progressive" American culture a handful of almost unknown Communist or pro-Communist writers, scholars, cinema directors, and artists such as Albert Maltz, Michael Gold, Herbert Aptheker, Rockwell Kent, and a few others. It should be noted, however, that at least in the handbook to which we have several times referred, the attitude taken toward American music was relatively friendly and objective, perhaps partly because so many leading American composers or performers are of Russian origin. Prominence is given in Soviet sources, as we might expect, to evidence of the popularity of Soviet music in the United States.

In view of the generally hostile and fearful Soviet attitude toward modern American culture described above, it is easy to understand why the Kremlin unleashed a press campaign against the American Exhibition in Moscow in

1959. The Soviet leadership was apparently particularly annoyed because the exhibition featured, not heavy machinery, but consumer goods and cultural achievements. The official criticism was that failure to show more heavy machinery was in effect an insult to the Soviet people. For weeks before the exhibition opened, and during the five weeks while it was on display, Soviet newspapers and magazines instructed their readers in the attitude that the authorities expected viewers to take. Measures were also taken to restrict the viewers, insofar as possible, to party members and other well-indoctrinated persons.

Along the same lines, Khrushchev returned from the United States in 1959 with criticisms of American cultural decadence. And, whatever their private opinions may have been, Soviet visitors to America, including the very few among the Soviet participants in American-Soviet academic exchanges who published statements about their experience in the citadel of capitalism, echoed the official line. In spite of this, there was reason to believe that even the relatively limited contact between Russians and Americans after 1953 constituted one of the most hopeful aspects of the total world situation. In considerable part, the official Soviet negative image of America was a defensive measure designed to shield impressionable Russians from what the Kremlin regarded as harmful influences.

Still, Soviet anti-Americanism continues to give much cause for concern. It aggravates international tensions and renders very difficult the achievement of stability and tranquility in a troubled world. It is, ultimately, an instrument of the Communist program for world conquest. It goes hand in hand with the statements of Khrushchev and other Communist leaders and propagandists to the effect that the United States is destined to be defeated, first in the battle of production and then in the world political struggle. Since 1956 Soviet propaganda has been increasingly bold in suggesting that henceforth not Russia but America would face the prospect of encirclement. The pattern was set in an important article published by A. Sobolev in *Kommunist,* No. 14, 1956, which predicted that eventually the United States would be "surrounded" by a "friendly socialist environment." It would then be easy to elect a "government of a new type." It was clear that however figuratively he may have been speaking, Khrushchev was in deadly earnest in his well-known promise to "bury" capitalism.

VIEWS OF AMERICA
FROM "LOW-STATUS" NATIONS

Richard D. Lambert and Marvin Bressler

The underlying assumption of this book, discussed in the General Introduction, has been that there are distinctive views of America expressed by the European, Communist, and developing nations. Though the developing nations share economic problems, anti-colonial attitudes, nonwhite peoples, etc., there are obviously substantial differences in the general cultural position of countries such as Burma, the Philippines, Ghana, Algeria, Iraq, and Chile. However, despite those differences, some social scientists have identified developing countries as "low-status" societies because of the highly defensive attitudes their citizens have toward their nation's image in American governmental and public opinion. It has been argued that American attitudes on "sensitive issues" concerning low-status nations is the central determinant of the views of the United States that visitors from these countries will adopt. This thesis is advanced in the following selection by Richard D. Lambert, a professor of the sociology of India and Pakistan at the University of Pennsylvania, and a colleague in sociology at the same university, Marvin Bressler.

A visitor's attitudes toward and images of an alien culture are affected by his perception of the host culture's view of the status of his own country. The visitor perceives hostility as an active component of low-status ascription when interaction includes verbal references to certain "sensitive areas." The latter are the subjects of long-standing criticism of his culture by colonial powers, the mere mention of which recalls the historical hostility. These perceived assaults enhance his personal identification with the prestige of his home country, and he reacts by erecting a set of mechanisms in defense and praise of his country.

.   .   .

Attitude formation differs significantly as between nationals from countries of "high status" and of "low status." From the perspective of the American value system and employing ideal-typical criteria, a country with "high status" may be defined as one which (a) is European; (b) which has experienced a long period of national sovereignty; (c) whose status as a world power is well established; (d) whose contributions to world culture are universally acknowledged; (e) whose social structure is stable; and (f) whose population is visibly and unmistakably Caucasian. A country with "low status" is one which (a) is non-European; (b) whose independence is of recent origin; (c) whose status as a world power is low or ambiguous; (d) whose contribution to current world culture is meager or unappreciated; (e) whose social structure is unstable; and (f) whose population is non-Caucasian or dark-skinned.

Visitors with low status form their attitudes toward the United States largely as the end product of a "looking-glass" process based on the visitor's perceptions of American attitudes to his country and by extension to him.

In normal social interaction Americans will inadvertently allude to certain national status-rooted "sensitive areas," the mere mention of which even in a neutral or favorable context will cause the visitor to perceive hostility, a condition which will in turn evoke reactive hostility.

The identification of personal and experiential variables associated with desirable attitude formation but not specific to culture is likely to be of little diagnostic value for visitors of low status. Individual variation will be

REPRINTED FROM "The Sensitive-Area Complex: A Contribution to the Theory of Guided Culture Contact," by Richard D. Lambert and Marvin Bressler, in *The American Journal of Sociology,* Vol. 60, No. 6 (May, 1955), pp. 583–90, by permission of The University of Chicago Press. Copyright 1955 by the University of Chicago.

restricted by a historically and culturally imposed set of perceptions; carefully manipulated circumscribed experiences will nevertheless include some abrasion of sensitive areas. Without denying the influence of nonculture-specific personal and experiential factors, it is suggested that these are more likely to be crucial for visitors with high status while operative only within a very narrow range among those with low status.

.   .   .

SENSITIVE AREAS

Temporary international migration characteristically impels the visitor to reappraise his own culture and to feel a heightened identification with his own country and an increased sensitivity to its status. Very early in his visit the Indian student perceives an American image of India which contains elements which appear to him to imply low status for his home country and, by extension, for him. When he encounters Americans who are admittedly ignorant of Indian affairs, this lack of knowledge with its resultant stereotypical conceptions is in itself an affront. Specific statements made by better-informed Americans are likely to touch on areas of cultural sensitivity and be perceived not only as inaccurate but hostile as well.

The stereotype which Indians perceive among Americans pictures India as an "exotic land," the word "exotic" suggesting "uncivilized." Americans are people who reportedly "think of India as a land of magic and mysticism, where sadhus live in caves, grow big beards, and sleep on iron spikes; a land infested with snake-charmers, lions, monkeys, rajas, and maharajas"; or as a complex of characteristics associated with the term "underdeveloped" or "backward," including poverty, sickness, starvation, overpopulation, prehistoric technological conditions, illiteracy, ignorance, and heathenism. Every Indian student interviewed mentioned this stereotype and described it in almost identical terms.

While it is apparent that the Indian students resent the stereotype of their country, it is also true that many of them recognize that ignorance does not necessarily involve hostility. Though ignorant of India, individual Americans often treat individual Indians with special consideration and with the deference sometimes reserved for those thought to be mildly and pleasantly exotic. To most of the Indian students, Americans who have some pretense to knowledge about India are a greater source of irritation. The greater the knowledge, the greater the demand for overt expression of amity. However, it is precisely those Americans who are slightly familiar with India who touch on certain specific subjects which, being associated with colonial status and reactive nationalism, have become "sensitive." The subjects of these statements about India which Indians take as evidence of hostility we are calling "sensitive areas."

.   .   .

During the course of our study we recorded statements or implications appearing in the American press or made by Americans against which Indian students reacted strongly. The areas of sensitivity have been classified inductively into seven major headings. The list is certainly not exhaustive.

1. Indians are basically inferior. Westernization is superficial. India will never be the equal of the Western countries.

. . .

2. India is an undesirable place in which to live.

. . .

3. Indians have objectionable personal traits.

. . .

4. India is too divided to form a nation.

. . .

5. India's social structure is undemocratic, inhumane, unenlightened.

. . .

6. The bases on which India expects acclaim from the West are hypocritical and not in accord with Indian practice.

. . .

7. Indian population increase is a threat to the world; soon they will embark upon an exploitative imperialism of their own.

. . .

DEFENSE MECHANISMS

While the student is reacting to an American image of India which he considers hostile, he constantly compares his perceptions of the United States and his image of the home country. The description of each country usually has a referent to the other. In this connection there are several prominent defense mechanisms the function of which is to raise the status of India above that of the United States.

1. *Skepticism concerning the representativeness of his impressions is confined to those which are favorable.*

When the impression is unfavorable, the individual states the view with assurance; if it is favorable, he adds that his experience is limited and that he may well change his mind when he has had an opportunity to expand his knowledge.

2. *American practice is compared to home-country creed.*

America is condemned because Christians are intolerant; India is praised because Hinduism is tolerant. America is condemned for its politics; India is praised for its constitution. America is condemned for the machinations of the "Wall Street capitalists," "monopolists," and "big business"; India is praised for Gandhi's ideal of trusteeship in economic affairs.

3. *"Favorable" American practice is selectively interpreted.*

For instance, one student came upon a notice on a factory bulletin board which outlined FEPC regulations. These regulations might serve as an indication of America's increasing enlightenment, at least on the official level;

instead, correctly but selectively, the student concluded that, if legislation of this type was needed, then anti-Negro bias must be very widespread indeed.

4. *Experience is sometimes structured so that the Indian student can contrive to become a victim of American malpractice.*

In a wry, somewhat self-deprecatory account, one student after making a trip through the South reported:

I went into a restaurant. All white people there. The servers were white, and those who were drinking coffee or having breakfast were white. So I went there and had my coffee too. There was no discrimination or anything that I came across. So you might say I was disappointed.

5. *American practices are judged in a contemporary value context, while Indian practices are judged in their historical setting.*

For instance Negro-white relations in the United States are discussed in terms of how they refute the American claim to democracy and equality; mistreatment of "untouchables" in India is discussed in terms of the historical circumstances which produced the condition and the inevitable slowness of remedial social change.

6. *American foreign policy is judged as though the United States were free to choose among unlimited options; India's alternatives are thought to be severely restricted.*

America is strong; India is weak. The powerful can elect to be perfect, while the weak can be no more than human. As a self-appointed leader and world power, the United States should behave more righteously than India, which must make compromises in order to survive. An associated thesis is that a rich and powerful benefactor deserves no gratitude but should give to the deserving needy as a matter of simple duty. This attitude enters into personal relations as well as political ones and overlies much of the student's attitude toward his stay here. It is deeply rooted in the Indian culture and is incorporated in religion and in widespread institutional and behavioral contexts. It, of course, runs counter to what the student perceives to be a continual request for expressions of gratitude from the American who asks, "Well, how do you like America?"

.   .   .

WHAT TO DO ABOUT OUR IMAGE

"WORLD OPINION"
ON AMERICAN FOREIGN POLICY

Correspondents of Newsweek

So far, we have been concerned in this part with American reactions to relatively thoughtful books and essays on the United States, and to the formation of attitudes by visitors to this country. The focus has been on the psychological and cultural roots of foreign commentary and on "long-term" patterns of opinion.

There is also the matter of "short-term" opinion on the United States—the type of reaction to American foreign and domestic policies that appears in the daily press of the world, prompts statements by government and civic group spokesmen in foreign capitals, and sometimes erupts into riots and demonstrations. Every student of international relations knows that this is highly volatile, usually manipulated by small élites in the countries, and does not necessarily represent opinions by "the people" in those countries; indeed the "people's" opinions may never enter into the political and diplomatic equation in many nations. The following survey by *Newsweek* correspondents in twenty world capitals during June of 1965, shows the shape of "world opinion" at one moment in the recent past.

.   .   .

The impression that the U.S. image has been badly tarnished abroad [by the Vietnamese war and the Dominican police action] stems, above all, from the recent rash of demonstrations against U.S. policies that have occurred all around the world. . . . Anti-U.S. demonstrations have been staged in Tokyo, New Delhi, The Hague, Paris, Toronto, Santiago de Chile, Mexico City, Bogotá and Buenos Aires. And last week brought still more such outbursts. In Britain three Cambridge University students made a hair-raising climb up the spires of King's College Chapel to hang out a sign protesting the Vietnamese war, and at the first British teach-in on Vietnam, eight hundred London University students cheered lustily when a professor of political science proclaimed: "The guerrillas on the banks of the Mekong—these are my people." In Argentina anti-Americanism took a particularly nasty turn with the wanton shooting of a U.S. consul.

Upon close scrutiny, however, these highly publicized expressions of protest prove to be essentially deceptive; virtually all of them have been the work of relatively small groups of left-wingers who can be counted upon to oppose almost anything the U.S. does. And an examination of the attitude of the general public in most countries reveals a vastly different picture of U.S. prestige overseas.

In some parts of the world, it is true, the picture the man in the street has of the U.S. has indeed changed considerably for the worse. The U.S. image has markedly deteriorated in France, thanks in part to the endless propaganda warfare waged by Charles de Gaulle (who last week referred to U.S. involvement in Vietnam as "a dirty affair"). It has also suffered in the countries of Eastern Europe whose citizens see good relations between Moscow and Washington as an indispensable element in their own struggle to win greater freedom from Soviet domination. A typical Eastern European reaction is that of the Pole who commented: "We thought that with Khrushchev's departure the era of off-the-cuff diplomacy was over. But we were wrong. Johnson is as compulsive a gambler as Khrushchev was."

Against this, however, there are also countries in which U.S. prestige among ordinary citizens stands as high or higher than ever before. West Germans, for instance, mostly applaud Mr. Johnson's tough line in Vietnam; they regard it as proof that the U.S. will stand firm in Berlin. And whatever Prime Minister Shastri's government may say, the average, educated Indian tends to believe that by checking Chinese Communist aggression in Southeast Asia now, the U.S. is acting in India's long-range interest.

But the nations in which there has been a markedly hostile or markedly approving public reaction to U.S. behavior in Vietnam and Santo Domingo are relatively few. In most countries, the attitude of the general public toward the U.S. has not changed significantly. A recent public opinion poll in Canada showed that 62 percent of those surveyed favored the U.S. military presence in South Vietnam and 53.2 percent supported the bombing strikes against North Vietnam. And even in Latin America, the initial wave of public indignation over U.S. intervention in Santo Domingo has given way to relative indifference in all but a handful of countries.

The cold fact is, however, that there are few countries in which the general public has any direct impact on foreign policy. And where real damage has been done to the U.S. image abroad is among intellectuals and those people who are professionally concerned with foreign affairs—diplomats, politicians, and journalists. This group, with its natural affinity for the graceful style and cultivated intellect of John F. Kennedy, is fond of drawing comparisons between J.F.K. and L.B.J.—invariably at the expense of Mr. Johnson. "Even when our two countries were colliding," says one Soviet journalist, "we Russians felt that Kennedy was basically a reasonable man and that a reasonable solution would be found. With Johnson, we're simply not so sure."

But the doubts of foreign opinion-makers about the person and politics of President Johnson go much deeper than mere regrets that he is not another Jack Kennedy. In increasing numbers, responsible foreign officials who are normally well disposed toward the U.S. express the belief that Mr. Johnson has proved himself basically an impulsive Texan who seeks simple solutions to complex problems. One staunchly pro-American journalist in West Germany has taken to referring to the President as "the fastest gun east of the Pecos."

．　．　．

Even among influential Britons who traditionally overlook a lot they don't like in American leadership, criticism of Mr. Johnson is rife. Some members of Prime Minister Harold Wilson's Cabinet are known to be flatly opposed to his support for U.S. policy in Vietnam. And recently Britain's daily *Guardian* demanded: "Why does Mr. Wilson say nothing about the futility and wickedness of what the Americans are doing?"

Such criticism is also found among Asian intellectuals who condemn the U.S. for experimenting with new weapons and tactics on yellow-skinned people and for interfering with a way of life that Americans supposedly can never comprehend. Even Japan's pro-American elder statesman, ex-Premier Shigeru Yoshida, 86, finds fault with U.S. policy in Vietnam. "I have told the Americans many times over," says Yoshida, "that they do not understand the Orient. I believe this applies to Vietnam as well."

Similarly, responsible Africans, who are still rankled over the fact that the United States under Mr. Johnson threw its support behind Congolese Premier Moise Tshombe, now profess concern over what they believe is a developing trend for the U.S. to disregard public opinion on that continent. Hilary N'gweno, editor of Nairobi's respected *Nation,* says: "We have the feeling that African sensitivities are no longer considered. We know that our people do not always understand the intricacies of world power politics, but America's image in Africa is not good."

In private conversations, Washington officials readily concede that the U.S. image has indeed taken something of a beating among élite groups abroad. Recently, in fact, a number of Washingtonians have taken to suggesting that the present situation is merely "Lyndon's Bay of Pigs." As an analogy, this at first seems rather strange, for the current criticism of Lyndon Johnson is milder than that leveled at John Kennedy following the Bay of Pigs fiasco. But in another sense, the comparison may be valid enough. For if President Johnson manages to overcome his present difficulties in a manner impressive to foreign opinion-makers, no lasting damage will have been done to U.S. prestige abroad. But if he fails to do so, the opinion of foreign intellectuals today is apt to trickle down and become the opinion of entire foreign nations tomorrow.

WE MUST CHANGE
THE WORLD'S IMAGE OF AMERICA

C. L. Sulzberger

Many American policy-makers and intellectuals feel that the United States fares dismally in projecting its best points in the arena of world opinion. They believe that our image is tarnished more because we do not explain what we really believe and why we are taking certain actions at home and abroad than because of moral weakness in the substance of our conduct. Sometimes this view leads to childish demands for more "salesmanship" of America, for battalions of Madison Avenue publicists designing snappier advertisements about American values for export. Sometimes the feeling that our image is not well projected leads to advocacy of more informal, people-to-people diplomacy and less formal statecraft, a notion that confuses contact at the margins of national relations with contact at the points of national conflict and tension.

In the essay that follows, C. L. Sulzberger, roving foreign correspondent and columnist for the New York *Times,* adopts a more sophisticated and balanced view of what we can—and must—do to change the world's image of the United States. It is helpful to note that this was written in the early period of the Kennedy Administration when changing the image of America was a frankly admitted aim of the White House.

. . .

One must sadly admit that, in recent years, the image of the United States has become both tarnished and obscured by platitudes. The idealism we assume everyone acknowledges as the foundation of our policy has been diminished by time.

Our wavering attitude during the Spanish Civil War; our isolationism and refusal to see the menace implicit in the rise of Mussolini and Hitler; our timorous neutrality during the late 1930's; all helped to erase respect overseas for the purity of American aims. And, in the wake of Hiroshima and Yalta, fewer and fewer foreigners remained convinced we were truly dedicated to making the world safe for democracy—as we so insistently announced.

The tarnish became even more perceptible as we began to talk pompously of acting in our "enlightened self-interest," and started to lecture fledgling neutrals from a pedestal of fake morality. Furthermore, as world communications improved and as the great anticolonial movement we helped to launch in Wilson's day exploded in success, our own unsettled national problems dirtied that picture of democracy we sought to imprint in foreign minds.

We embarrassed ourselves and infuriated our friends by ridiculous incidents involving delegates to the UN whose skins were dark. Ugly ruckuses between white Americans and black Americans, from Little Rock to the University of Georgia, spread a nasty impression of American racism. And these flaws were widely advertised just as the anticolonialism which has always been a fundament of our policy helped free millions of subjected peoples.

Furthermore, munificent as we have been in helping other lands to save themselves and recover from disaster, the gratitude which should be normal in others—alas—is not. It is a cruel truth that thankfulness is often vitiated by a feeling (wholly unreasonable) that, after all, America is in some way unjustly dripping with prosperous fat and the world's poor have somehow earned the right to aid by the mere fact of poverty. We have been seen as a nation, a great power, whose generosity was tinged with self-interest. This is unfair, but it is the portrait.

Analytically, one might say, our image abroad is essentially compounded of three factors. The first is that American dream reflected in the desire of so

FROM "To Change Their Image of Us," New York *Times Magazine* (March 5, 1961), pp. 30, 96–97. © 1961 by The New York Times Company. Reprinted by permission.

many foreigners to come to our shores and start a new life. The second is the sheer military and economic power of the United States, expressed on every continent; this has brought both our soldiers and our prosperous tourists into direct contact with strange and distant lands. The final element is our policy, above all as advertised in our propaganda and in statements by our high officials, and as interpreted by the comments of our friends and foes.

To all of this one might add the often warped picture given by Hollywood. Millions of people know nothing of us save through its looking glass. And how warped this, on occasion, can be.

While cutting scenes out of the film *From Here to Eternity*, a British censor remarked: "This shows your Army in much too unfavorable a light for our audiences. Our alliance with you is too important to permit this."

Thus we find many images superimposed upon each other like the skins of an onion covering its heart. The heart is the pristine dream; often the skins comprise distortions or obscurations.

Among these obscurations are those we fabricate ourselves. We continually bill the struggle for power as one between West and East or between democracy and Communism. But in reality it is a contest between independent and serf nations, between those favoring real peace and those seeking violent change. And when we loosely refer to "East-West differences" we permit Moscow to appear by inference as the champion of the oriental world.

The confusion concerning us abroad depends in some degree on the number of onion skins peeled off by those who would observe us. The *patronne* of a French bistro once scoffed at me: "Ah, you Americans were *chics* in 1917—but not now." Yet Father Bruckberger, a discerning French priest who knows us well, finds a strange and hopeful ideology developing on our shores. André Fontaine, a distinguished Paris journalist, points out that relatively few Europeans know the U.S.A. from personal experience. They therefore resent our unintended exclusiveness abroad, the tendency of our travelers to "drink Coca-Cola among the most magnificent vineyards."

General de Gaulle has said to me: "There is no hate for the United States in France. France remains friendly to the United States. But the French people don't like the American people."

In England there exists a submerged form of anti-Americanism described by Randolph Churchill: "Many socialists cannot forgive the Americans for making such a triumphant success of the capitalist system; many Tories find it hard to forgive America for becoming the 'top nation.' "

And yet, the Englishman who visits us at home is often enchanted by what he finds. Thus, Lord Kinrose, for example, found "the first difference from Europe: there's perpetual motion, perpetual change."

He also found: "This America is a somewhat Victorian country. . . . It is a polite society, with stern social conventions and moral aspirations and romantic learning, now caught up in a kind of wave of nineteenth-century prosperity which God is assumed to have had a good deal to do with."

The Russians, which is to say the people, not the government, have an odd but genuine attachment for America. Sir William Hayter, former British Ambassador to Moscow, comments:

Russian sympathy for America often takes bizarre forms. When I was in Moscow the smart set there, I was told, used to refer to the Kremlin as the White House and to Gorky Street as Broadway, and they conspicuously affected American clothes, American hair styles, and American popular music.

But more seriously, the American position as the most admired foreign country has been consecrated, perhaps unintentionally, by the Soviet government itself. "Catching up with and overtaking America" is its proclaimed target; how more emphatically could it be admitted that America is the ideal to aim at?

These are somewhat endearing thoughts. But that amorphous public view has no importance. Yesterday Soviet policy told press and radio that we were warmongers. Today it assures them that we are opposed to war. In either case, the sentiment is brushed aside by autocratic decisions imposed for policy reasons.

In India our popularity is perhaps gaining, although it suffers because we are allied to Pakistan, something no Hindu politician permits voters to forget. And there is a feeling that we are well-intended but misguided.

C. D. Deshmukh, one of Nehru's ablest lieutenants, once said to me: "We don't misunderstand your motives. But you are helping colonialism—just as you say we are helping Communism by our actions. You feel we are walking into the spider's parlor. We feel you are wrong in the assumption that military power is needed to negotiate with Communism."

This is a weird, jumbled kaleidoscope. No single pattern of America can be seen through foreign eyes. Still we need not worry about false surface portraits if we are but true to ourselves, our way of life, our initial revolutionary purpose.

The men who lead our Administration are sensitive to these facts. They are intent not on changing the true image of the U.S. but on erasing the false image. They seek a return to the pristine idea which lies at the heart of our political credo.

This is not an easy thing to do. There exists no simple American statement of purpose similar to that marvelously concise, but inaccurate and outdated, piece of propaganda produced by Marx and Engels in their 1848 *Communist Manifesto*. We have a huge body of literature and oratory which Americans absorb from birth, sometimes almost by osmosis; this manages to explain to us the meaning of our political system and the intentions of our global role. But there is nothing which manages to explain these things naturally and simply to foreigners, above all to those naive and newly educated foreigners who have just won their liberty.

Efforts have been made from time to time both by government officials and private writers to produce statements on what America is and what it means. Most of these have been failures and those which have not failed have generally been far too long.

What, in fact, is America, as a concept, as a political entity, as a melting-pot land of immigrants?

In an odd sense America remains as much a poetic ideal as anything else. Its novel concept, when it began to think for itself in the eighteenth century, was as a haven, a refuge for the oppressed, a modest heaven on earth.

That remarkable generation we know as the Founding Fathers seemed to perceive the international implications of the tiny military revolution that broke out on the Atlantic's western shore. In 1765, when we were still an English colony, John Adams said: "I always consider the settlement of

America as the opening of a grand scheme or design in Providence for the 'illumination and emancipation of the slavish part of mankind all over the earth.' "

This resembles the statements of Woodrow Wilson when he finally led our nation into the First World War. The commitment to be true to ourselves has from the beginning implied a commitment to be true to freedom everywhere.

From the start America has felt itself to be a land of the future, and for years of our life as a united country we have managed to convince others of this fact. As long as we ourselves have been fully aware of the meaning of what we call the American dream, we have been able to make foreigners aware of it also.

This is a political fact. The dream is as important as the sinews of our power. When we forget this dream, not even the most skillful propaganda apparatus can revive it overseas.

The so-called American image, as seen abroad, has been compounded not only of the essential philosophical tenet of freedom, of the equal rights of men in governing themselves, but also in a curious sense of a mixture of frontier adventure and homespun experience. The turbulent allegories of Melville, the primeval virtues of Cooper's heroes, and the cozy romanticism of Mark Twain have all helped clothe the naked intellectuality of the American idea.

However, whenever that idea itself tended to be forgotten at home, literary clothing was unable to hide the change. A new look at America began to develop with Theodore Roosevelt's frank imperialism and the flourishing of sometimes crass and arrogant millionaires in this century.

The occasional shots of idealism injected into our political thinking by Wilson and Franklin Roosevelt (during the New Deal) were not entirely able to keep alive the purity of our original credo—either in our own minds or in those of other nations. The revolutionary aspect of our image, which we always assume to be so obvious, was dimmed.

With his youth, his energy, his blunt gift for aphorism and his frank awareness of our spiritual heritage, President Kennedy seems to be setting our nation back on the traditional course from which it never has wavered for too long in the past. And he seems immensely conscious of the fact that whenever we did waver from this course, our purpose became confused and our image became obscured.

Foreigners, and here I refer to friendly foreigners, are happy that we are rich since they hope we will be generous and they are glad we carry a stick, militarily and politically, so long as we use that stick with restraint and talk gently about its existence.

But foreigners also want us to speak openly about our philosophical intentions. Their respect for us increases when our President recalls that the citizens of a democracy owe service to their government rather than the reverse. The more these home truths are made plain to us, the more our so-called prestige will be refurbished overseas.

Furthermore, the sooner we perfect the processes of our own democracy the happier will be our diplomatic relations with fledgling lands, aspiring to their own forms of this ancient political formula. The fact that the . . . Administration is naming Negro Americans to important and visibly influential positions should lift our esteem in African and Asian lands. Democracy cannot be exported until it works at home.

We have a greater wealth of nonwhite citizens educated in political responsibility and intellectual balance than any other so-called white nation in the world. It is immensely encouraging that, for the first time, President Kennedy has begun seriously to tap this reservoir.

Not only does this mere act correct a weakness in the democratic patterns we claim to follow; it improves the efficiency of our foreign operations and the regard in which we are held. It removes a blot from our national conscience. At the same time it gives new energy to the purpose of our system. One cannot sufficiently stress the importance of this point.

We should not overly concern ourselves with the constantly shifting, superficial reflection overseas of what we deem our image. Neither France's Henri IV nor our own Benjamin Franklin was wrong in conceiving honesty as the best policy; and this applies to propaganda policy. However, let us make more coordinate and attractive what we have to tell.

In terms of coordination, President Kennedy has already seen the need to prevent misguided public utterances by public officials. He recognizes that a glib jingo phrase by a bellicose admiral or general or hasty quip by a Cabinet member can undo weeks of careful overseas broadcasting.

And there are other points to be remembered. It would be useful were our propaganda to admit that most of this world is politically neither black nor white. Ideological hectoring can be offensive and unrealistic.

Finally, when we issue blanket condemnations of "colonialism"—a word we almost invented—we must recall that it is a varying system which is not always bad—even, for example (let us hope), in Panama or Okinawa. Let us cease thinking merrily in pat and simple terms designed, primarily, to please ourselves.

THE AMERICAN IMAGE
WILL TAKE CARE OF ITSELF

Dean Acheson

While he might not take issue with C. L. Sulzberger's preceding selection, Dean Acheson quarrels vigorously—as he always does in a contest—with those whom he feels take far too seriously, and interpret far too naively, "world opinion" about the American image. One of the most distinguished members of the realist school of American analysis of foreign affairs, Acheson was a lawyer and Undersecretary of the Treasury during the Franklin Roosevelt Administration before he became Assistant Secretary of State in 1941 and Secretary of State under Harry Truman between 1949 and 1952. Since 1952, he has written extensively on foreign policy and domestic political issues and served as an advisor and special envoy under both President Kennedy and President Johnson.

. . . An American is apt to stare like Narcissus at his image in the pool of what he believes to be world opinion, until he pines away; or else, he makes himself over into the image he would like to see, only to have his shrewder self tell him that he looks a fool.

Each would shape his image a little differently, but the main ingredients would include a bit of Thomas Jefferson, Alexander the Great, the Statue of Liberty, Henry Ford, and the Ford Foundation. We catch this Narcissus psychosis from Madison Avenue, but the reason for the mask lies deeper. "Man's crude spontaneous self," Lord David Cecil explains, is "merely a bundle of impulses without value or significance: he should therefore choose and assume a mask that represents his personal ideal, his conceptions of what, taking account of his capacities and limitations, he should aspire to be. Thus he will endue his life with beauty and meaning: if he retains the mask and consistently acts in character with it, he may even ultimately assimilate his nature to it, become substantially the personality he presents to the outer world."

To be susceptible to Narcissus-image worry, a society must value more highly than its own some outside opinion of itself—in other words, feel insecure. Some don't, and some do. For a time our ancestors worried about what was thought about them in heaven and tried to adapt their image accordingly. But we don't worry about that any more. Some of us believe that we are on the side of the angels, or vice versa; others that there aren't any. When we worry, we worry about foreigners—and how we worry!

It has always been this way; and it has always got us down. We started out as colonials, or worse, and being treated as such—George III set the fashion. Old Ben Franklin and John Adams resented it when they got to London. But not even Charles James Fox and Edmund Burke could get the British to lower their eyebrows; and the French let us into their houses by the front door only because they knew it would annoy the British.

Even when we thought, and with justice, that we were getting to be somebody, Mr. Charles Dickens told us just what sort of a somebody it was. For over a century we have paid foreign lecturers millions to cultivate our inferiority complex. We have learned to double our tips when English butlers eyed [us] coldly, and to believe that every glance directed at us, whether from patrons of sidewalk cafes along the Champs Elysées or peasants up to their knees in Asian paddy fields, was double-sighted along a nose as elegant and elevated as General de Gaulle's.

What is more, we are even led to worry not only about the impression we make but about the truth of what we have actually done. For instance, we had believed that last autumn we joined the Belgians for purely humanitarian reasons to save the lives of unfortunate doctors, teachers, priests, and nuns in the Congo, whose only offense had been the simple and admirable desire to minister to its people. But after the debate in the United Nations some of the more advanced cases of reflection-worry began to see the operations as imperialist-capitalist-monopolist interference in the internal affairs of a sensi-

FROM "The American Image Will Take Care of Itself," New York *Times Magazine* (February 28, 1965), pp. 24–25, 95. © 1965 by The New York Times Company. Reprinted by permission.

tive and innocent people engaged only in their normal preparations for Thanksgiving.

At any event, a country half slave—or all slave—to foreign criticism cannot stand, except as a mental institution. We cannot gird ourselves for the war against poverty or in Vietnam until we exorcise image worship. The Greeks have given us the prescription; psychiatry, the method. "Know thyself," said Socrates. Today we say the same thing a little differently. "Be yourself." But how? The symbol of the Greek command was a mirror. But our mirror reflects not ourselves, rather the masks we wear in our pathetic eagerness to please others. So turn from the mirror, like the Lady of Shalott, and look at the world directly. The mirror will not crack from end to end. It exists only in our minds. No curse will come upon us, for we shall have exorcised the curse.

Psychiatry exorcises by exhuming fears, from the darkness in which troubled minds have buried them, for candid examination in the light of consciousness. So, we may ask, what is this world opinion which so deeply impresses us and which we are so eager to impress? How is it formed and on what grounds? Who holds it? Who discovers and reports it? When we answer these questions, we shall be free once again.

No one, I suppose, imagines that world opinion is discovered by pollsters going from door to door in Lancashire, Provence, and Hesse asking, "Do you approve of the mutilateral force?" Or in Indonesia, soliciting views on whether Malaysia is good or bad for Indonesian exports; or in India, inquiring about agreement or disagreement with American policy on settlement of the Kashmir dispute; or in Ghana, about the American demand that our sovereign equals in the United Nations pay up or quit voting. Honest answers to these questions would be unanimous "don't knows."

Of course, protests could be arranged in all these disparate places against any positive American action. People could be induced to march and, perhaps, sit in driveways in Europe, and to march, break windows, and even burn American Information Libraries elsewhere. But these protests would not represent local popular opinion; they would represent instigation and organization.

World opinion simply does not exist on the matters which concern us. Not because people do not know the facts—facts are not necessary to form opinion—but because they do not know that the issues exist. Opinion, like yeast, is produced by fermentation from other opinion. When a man, after reading a pundit's column at breakfast, holds forth himself at lunch, he does not know any more about the subject than he did before, but he has an opinion. A bit of the pundit's yeast has fermented within him; and since often there was little else within him to be fermented, the result is likely to be hot air.

But I am getting ahead of my story. Granted that pundits, by written and spoken word, disseminate a nonexistent world opinion, where do they get it, and what do they give for it? They give the means and often the assurance of dissemination. World opinion they get from one another, from lesser disseminators, demeaningly called "the working press"—and as the result of an annual "fact-finding" tour. On this tour they visit the sources of opinion open to the working press, which in most of the world is the government, or those kept by the government. If they are pundits of prestige, they may have a private interview with (until recently) Mr. Khrushchev or General de Gaulle.

Governments produce local opinion, chiefly for export, on subjects which are deemed suitable for opinion. It may be designed to please or to frighten, to assure loyalty or threaten defection; or the source may spar for time, in which case opinion is said to be "vacillating." The working press meets working press meets working businessmen, who have drunk from the same spring. Over different drinks they confirm one another's impressions; and someone gives the word to the CIA. Occasionally one of our own Ambassadors, and not always a political appointee, takes to excessive consumption of local source material and becomes, himself, a producer of world opinion.

In the more sophisticated countries sources of opinion may be controlled by antigovernment as well as government groups; and there is a possibility, though not a great one, that a fraction may be independent.

The London and Paris opinion factories reward with appreciated attentions those who play the game with them. At small and exquisite luncheons in the Quai d'Orsay leaks, true or speculative, are sprung; a bit of racy gossip dropped about a colleague; a good story told of a fellow countryman's gaucherie at the last meeting of NATO ministers, and so on. In London distribution is aided by political society. It is rather less subtle, but quite as effective. In Rome even the working press is too confused to devise a pattern of opinion from the minuet danced by Christian Democrats of varying shades, Communists, Socialists (Saragat and Nenni), Liberals, Neo-Fascists, and Monarchists.

If one would like to see opinion factories at work, an interesting exhibit centers in the United Nations Building on the East River, at the time of the Assembly's general debate, and spreads out of meeting rooms into lobbies, hotels, restaurants and bars all over New York. These factories vary from chromium-plated noiseless ones, where all is automation and the human hand never appears, to little one-room jobs with two girls, a boy, and a mimeograph. Often, too, the whole process is run off in one day as a sort of classroom demonstration, from the contrived incident abroad to the report, "African Opinion Condemns U.S." in the New York newspapers.

But usually, of course, the span between production and publication of opinion is longer. First, reports as numerous as lumps in a cargo of metal ore are shipped home, then smelted into opinion ingots. Then the ingots must be cast, rolled, bent, twisted, and hammered into world opinion, or area—usually large area—opinion. "Europe Cool to M.L.F.," "Latin America Disillusioned on Alliance," "Africa Rejects Tshombe," and so on.

Out of such stuff is formed the body of folklore which Americans accept as World Opinion—world judgments on what they are, what they do, and why they do it. Not by any stretch of the imagination could the folklore represent the opinions of people. Its very sources, manner of collection and preparation for the market preclude that. It may, and often does, give a good idea of what the government of a country and occasionally the opposition would like to have believed was the opinion of its people. But, as to their actual opinions, if on these subjects more than a few have any, the folklore purveyed gives not a clue.

The effect and use of this artificial folklore is curious, too; and a little unexpected. The immediate result is to convince those who produce it that it is the genuine article, and to furnish ammunition for controversialists whose positions have already been taken for quite different reasons. Upon the customers, the American people, the effect is very gradual and very general. In a way it is not unlike that of the automobile. The automobile kills a lot of people, but doesn't frighten anyone. It has made the whole population mobile, but hasn't led anyone to go to any particular place.

So it is with this matter of world opinion. It plays overtime upon our inferiority complexes. We are setups for the caricatures of the Ugly American, of the stupid diplomat, the contemptuous, grasping, wily foreigner taking our money at the other end of the rat hole down which we fatuously pour it, or our obtuseness in getting into wars we should have stayed out of, and getting out of wars we should have stayed in and enlarged. Sometimes when we worry about a task which is hard, or unrewarding, or complicated, or all three, it is tempting to listen to foreign sirens, even if spurious ones, telling us to rest in the shade and eat the lotus.

The short of the matter is that world opinion, whether thought of as fairy light or hobgoblin, to beguile or to frighten, is, like them, pure fancy—no more substantial a ghost than the banging of a shutter, or the wind in the chimney. It is like that elusive man in the verse:

> As I was going up the stair,
> I met a man who wasn't there.
> He wasn't there again today.
> I wish to God he'd go away!

The American Image, too, will take care of itself if we get on with what we have to do in, as our great-great-grandfathers would have said, the station to which it has pleased God to have called us, or less elegantly, in the spot we're in. Old Mark Twain summed it up pretty well. "Always do right," he said. "This will gratify some people, and astonish the rest."

Index

Imperialism (*Cont.*)
  See also Latin America, Africa, Asia, *and specific countries*
India, 252–53, 345, 346, 354–56, 358, 362
Individual
  bureaucracy and, 131–38
  conformity and, 39–43
  in industrial society, 2, 43–47
Inflation, 54, 157
Intellectuals
  end of alienation of, 2, 11–17
  ineffectiveness of, 17–20
  in power élite, 31
  See also Dissent
Izvestia, "The Assassination of President Kennedy," 117–18

Jefferson, Thomas, 99–101, 103–06, 223, 264
Johnson, Lyndon B., 81, 179, 195, 200, 232, 233, 358–59
Judicial system, 219–22, 329, 332–33

Kazin, Alfred, 17
Kefauver, Estes, 243
Keller, Robert, "The American Economy," 56–64
Kennan, George, 12, 84, 253
Kennedy, John F., 81, 108, 120, 127–28, 153, 241, 243, 350, 358, 363–64
  assassination of, 117–18, 200, 266
  foreign policy of, 65, 70, 71–75, 78, 79–80, 170–71, 174–76, 183, 184, 263, 264
  intellectuals and, 16–17
  power élite and, 29–31
Kennedy, Robert, 35, 149
Khrushchev, Nikita S., 35, 81, 88, 112, 117, 123, 177, 249, 345–46, 349, 350, 352
  on ideological conflict, 85–86, 93
  "The Present International Situation and the Foreign Policy of the Soviet Union," 168–73
King, Lawrence T., "Uncle Sam in the Eyes of Latin Americans," 320–21
Kissinger, Henry, 67, 186
Kohn, Hans, 101, 102
Korea, 80, 156, 187, 249, 251
Krippendorff, Ekkehart, "The Failures of American Conservatism in Southeast Asia," 76–78
Kruglak, Theodore, 344
Kudryavtsev, V., "Deep Reconnaissance of Neocolonialism," 189–91

Kumar Das, Deb, "An Indian in America," 233–36
Kuusinen, Otto, *Fundamentals of Marxism-Leninism,* 155–57

Labor unions, 30–31, 50–51, 160–65
Lambert, Richard D., "The Sensitive-Area Complex," 353–56
Laos, 73, 74, 76–78, 252
Laski, Harold J.
  The American Democracy, 314–17
  "The Parliamentary and Presidential Systems," 21–24
Latin America
  Alliance for Progress and, 79, 261–71
  American economy and, 245–47
  American imperialism in, 79–81, 188–89, 217–19, 258–60, 262–63, 320–21, 331–32
  revolution in, 264–65
  spiritual values of, 201–07
  visitors from, 330–33
Lavergne, Bernard, "America's Imperialist Record," 79–81
Lerner, Max, 131–32, 151
Liberalism, 15–18
Lima, Alceu Amoroso. *See* Amoroso Lima, Alceu
Lincoln, Abraham, 103, 219
Link, Arthur, 166
Lipset, Seymour M., 141
  The First New Nation, 284–88
Lleras, Alberto, "The Alliance for Progress—After Kennedy," 265–71
Lobbying, 23, 115–16
"Low-status" nations, 353–56. *See also* Developing nations

Mailer, Norman, 13, 14
Malcolm X, 232
Malik, Charles, 193
  Man in the Struggle for Peace, 207–10
Mao Tse-tung, 249
  "Racism and the Class War," 152–54
Marshall Plan, 181, 216, 254, 267, 270
Martineau, Harriet, 281, 284–85
Marx, Karl, 19
Marxism, 17–20, 58–59, 61, 87, 315, 348–49. *See also* Class war; Communism
Massive retaliation, 65, 66, 182–83, 250
Mass media, 26, 37–39, 125–26, 277
Materialism, 19–20, 107–09, 194, 201–07, 234, 237–38, 281–82, 312

Vil'khovchenko, E. D., "The Awakening Working Class," 160–65
Visson, André, *As Others See Us,* 335–40
Von Borch, Herbert, *The Unfinished Society,* 11–17, 24–31, 321–23

War. *See* Military policy; Nuclear weapons
Weber, Max, 33, 133, 288, 294–96
Wedge, Bryant, *Visitors to the United States and How They See Us,* 327–34
West Side Story, 142–43
Williams, Francis, *The American Invasion,* 36–39, 318–20
Williams, G. Mennen, 219
Williams, Robert, 152
Williams, Tennesee, 12

Wilson, Edmund, 12–13
Wilson, Harold, 358–59
Wilson, Woodrow, 27, 81, 311, 363
"Bryce's *American Commonwealth,*" 306–08
Wolde-Giorghis, Hailou, "An African Encounters the United States," 228–31
World War II, 180

Yakovlev, A. N., 87
The Intellectual Poverty of the Apologists of the "Cold War," 112–16

Zamoshkin, Y. A., 92
"Bureaucracy and the Individual," 131–38
Zorin, I. N., "The Awakening Working Class," 160–65

A 6
B 7
C 8
D 9
E 0
F 1
G 2
H 3
I 4
J 5